Recalibrating Reform

Some of the most important eras of reform in U.S. history reveal a troubling pattern: often reform is compromised after the initial legislative and judicial victories have been achieved. Thus Jim Crow racial exclusions followed Reconstruction; employer prerogatives resurged after the passage of the Wagner Act in 1935; and after the civil rights reforms of the mid-twentieth century, principles of color-blindness remain dominant in key areas of constitutional law that allow structural racial inequalities to remain hidden or unaddressed. When momentous reforms occur, certain institutions and legal rights will survive the disruption and remain intact, just in different forms. Thus governance in the postreform period reflects a systematic recalibration or reshaping of the earlier reforms as a result of the continuing influence and power of such resilient institutions and rights. *Recalibrating Reform* examines this issue and demonstrates the pivotal role of the United States Supreme Court in postreform recalibration.

Stuart Chinn is an assistant professor at the University of Oregon School of Law. He received his BA, PhD (political science), and JD degrees from Yale University. Previously, he was a visiting assistant professor at the University of Texas School of Law. His research and teaching interests are in constitutional law, constitutional theory, legislation, and legal and political history. He has published in the journals *Law & Social Inquiry*, *The Journal of Law*, and *Polity*, and he has a chapter in the edited volume *Living Legislation* (2012).

Cambridge Historical Studies in American Law and Society

Series Editor

Christopher Tomlins, *University of California, Irvine*

This series publishes leading-edge work in American legal history, broadly construed. Its watchword is breadth no less than depth of analysis. Methodologically, the series seeks work that extends the boundaries of how legal history is defined. Substantively, the series is interdisciplinary, exploring law and legal history through numerous perspectives and techniques – economic, social, cultural, political, and intellectual – rather than concentrate on particular doctrinal areas.

Previously published in the series:
Yvonne Pitts, *Family, Law, and Inheritance in America: A Social and Legal History of Nineteenth-Century Kentucky*
David M. Rabban, *Law's History*
Kunal M. Parker, *Common Law, History, and Democracy in America, 1790–1900*
Steven Wilf, *Law's Imagined Republic*
James D. Schmidt, *Industrial Violence and the Legal Origins of Child Labor*
Rebecca M. McLennan, *The Crisis of Imprisonment: Protest, Politics, and the Making of the American Penal State, 1776–1941*
Tony A. Freyer, *Antitrust and Global Capitalism, 1930–2004*
Davison Douglas, *Jim Crow Moves North*
Andrew Wender Cohen, *The Racketeer's Progress*
Michael Willrich, *City of Courts, Socializing Justice in Progressive Era Chicago*
Barbara Young Welke, *Recasting American Liberty: Gender, Law and the Railroad Revolution, 1865–1920*
Michael Vorenberg, *Final Freedom: The Civil War, the Abolition of Slavery, and the Thirteenth Amendment*
Robert J. Steinfeld, *Coercion, Contract, and Free Labor in Nineteenth Century America*
David M. Rabban, *Free Speech in Its Forgotten Years*
Jenny Wahl, *The Bondsman's Burden: An Economic Analysis of the Common Law of Southern Slavery*
Michael Grossberg, *A Judgment for Solomon: The d'Hauteville Case and Legal Experience in the Antebellum South*

Recalibrating Reform

The Limits of Political Change

STUART CHINN
University of Oregon

CAMBRIDGE
UNIVERSITY PRESS

University Printing House, Cambridge CB2 8BS, United Kingdom

One Liberty Plaza, 20th Floor, New York, NY 10006, USA

477 Williamstown Road, Port Melbourne, VIC 3207, Australia

4843/24, 2nd Floor, Ansari Road, Daryaganj, Delhi - 110002, India

79 Anson Road, #06-04/06, Singapore 079906

Cambridge University Press is part of the University of Cambridge.

It furthers the University's mission by disseminating knowledge in the pursuit of education, learning and research at the highest international levels of excellence.

www.cambridge.org
Information on this title: www.cambridge.org/9781107667389

© Stuart Chinn 2014

This publication is in copyright. Subject to statutory exception and to the provisions of relevant collective licensing agreements, no reproduction of any part may take place without the written permission of Cambridge University Press.

First published 2014
First paperback edition 2017

A catalogue record for this publication is available from the British Library

Library of Congress Cataloging in Publication data
Chinn, Stuart.
Recalibrating reform : the limits of political change / Stuart Chinn.
pages cm. – (Cambridge historical studies in American law and society)
Includes bibliographical references and index.
ISBN 978-1-107-05753-1 (hardback)
1. United States – Politics and government.   2. Political science – United States – History.   3. Political culture – United States – History.   I. Title.
E183.C64   2014
973–dc23   2013039551

ISBN 978-1-107-05753-1 Hardback
ISBN 978-1-107-66738-9 Paperback

Cambridge University Press has no responsibility for the persistence or accuracy of URLs for external or third-party internet websites referred to in this publication, and does not guarantee that any content on such websites is, or will remain, accurate or appropriate.

For my parents Leung and Betty Chinn

Contents

Acknowledgments *page* xi

PART I. INTRODUCTION

Introduction: Reconstructing Governance 3
1 The Theory and Political Processes of Recalibration 16
2 The Supreme Court and Transformative Recalibration 40

PART II. LEGAL REFORM AND ITS DELIMITATION

3 Emancipation, the Reconstruction Era, and Delimitation 65
4 Labor Rights, the New Deal Era, and Delimitation 109
5 Constitutional Equal Protection, the Civil Rights Era, and Delimitation 152
6 Explaining Judicial Delimiting Behavior 178

PART III. THE CONSTRUCTION AND MAINTENANCE OF GOVERNANCE

7 The Entrenchment and Maintenance of the Jim Crow Order 193
8 The Entrenchment and Maintenance of Industrial Pluralism 237
9 The Entrenchment and Maintenance of the Anticlassification Order 270

10	Explaining Order-Affirming and Tension-Managing Judicial Behavior	298
11	Conclusion	312
Bibliography		321
Index		339

Acknowledgments

I am very pleased to be able to acknowledge in print the many individuals who generously offered their time and energy in support of this project over the past several years. First and foremost, I owe a special debt of gratitude to my teachers and advisors in graduate school: Bruce Ackerman, David Mayhew, and Stephen Skowronek. Bruce Ackerman's feedback and encouragement on a seminar paper were the genesis of this book, and he has been generously supportive ever since. David Mayhew read innumerable drafts of this project, and I have benefited from his vast knowledge of American political history and his tireless attention to detail. Stephen Skowronek has devoted more time and energy to this project over the past several years than any student could reasonably expect. He has been a source of continual assistance, and his influence undoubtedly pervades this entire book.

Others who graciously commented on prior drafts of various chapters or who offered encouragement include Rachel Barkow, Jack Beerman, Mitch Berman, Angelica Bernal, Walter Dean Burnham, Ian Farrell, Willy Forbath, Mark Graber, Joel Grossman, Ken Kersch, Sandy Levinson, Eric Patashnik, Danilo Petranovich, Scot Powe, Dan Rodriguez, Steve Teles, and Robert Tsai.

I also owe thanks to colleagues at the University of Oregon for their direct or indirect support on this project, including, among others, Ibrahim Gassama, John Greenman, Michelle McKinley, Michael Moffitt, Jennifer Reynolds, Joan Malmud Rocklin, Suzanne Rowe, and Dan Tichenor. Erick Hoffman provided timely and valuable assistance on the charts and figures in the manuscript. A number of research assistants provided invaluable assistance on this project as well: Lauren Boyd,

Linda Bruce, Gabe Chase, Sally Claycomb, Karianne Conway, Beth Ford, Sarah Garrott, Dustin Littrell, David Mintz, Carrie Murray, Jennifer Nicholls, and Jacqueline Quarré. I owe thanks to Chris Tomlins and Robert Dreesen at Cambridge University Press for their interest in this project, and for shepherding it through the publication process.

I am grateful to Margaret Hallock and the Wayne Morse Center at the University of Oregon for providing me with a timely semester-long research leave during the course of this project. I am also grateful to the Donald Walker–Norman Wiener Research fund for financial assistance.

Some material in this book is drawn from the work previously published in, and used here by permission from: *The Journal of Law* 1, no. 1 (2011): 95–184; *Law & Social Inquiry* 37, no. 3 (Summer 2012): 535–64; Jeffrey A. Jenkins and Eric M. Patashnik, eds., *Living Legislation* (Chicago: University of Chicago Press 2012), 197–220 (© 2012 by The University of Chicago).

PART I

INTRODUCTION

Introduction: Reconstructing Governance

America's history is marked by periods of dramatic reform, during which established political and social hierarchies were undermined. For example, the reforms of Reconstruction in the 1860s dismantled slavery, and a century later the reforms of the civil rights era brought the demise of Jim Crow segregation and voting disfranchisement laws. These kinds of reforms draw the sustained attention of students of American history as crucial break points in the nation's past and as powerful symbols of then-prevailing public moods and sentiments. Further, and even more importantly, these kinds of reforms stand out as testaments to some of the most admirable parts of American political culture. They remind us of the continuing promise of achieving greater equality and inclusiveness in our own time.

And yet, these reforms also present troubling questions once we consider their aftermath. The reforms of Reconstruction may have dismantled slavery and enshrined within the Constitution new principles of legal and political equality across race, but these principles were undermined by the Jim Crow laws that soon followed. While slavery was abolished, legally sanctioned forms of white supremacy in the southern states survived and ultimately enjoyed an extended life in the post-Reconstruction era.

The civil rights era presents striking similarities. One key subset of those reforms was the transformation of judicial and congressional understandings of constitutional equal protection. Beginning with *Brown v. Board of Education*[1] and continuing through the 1960s, a number of

[1] 347 U.S. 483 (1954).

Supreme Court decisions and civil rights statutes dismantled various facets of Jim Crow in the South, including, perhaps most notably, segregated public schooling. Yet commitments to color blindness and neighborhood schools by southern and northern conservatives helped pave the way for continued de facto racial exclusions, including de facto school segregation (in both the North and South) in the post-*Brown* era.[2]

Consider also a third example that takes us some ways from matters of race or the South: the passage of the Wagner Act during the New Deal era capped the dismantling of an intricate system of employer-employee relations governed by master-servant common law doctrines.[3] Yet despite the Wagner Act's blow to employer interests embodied in the Act's promotion of collective bargaining, employer prerogatives were resurgent in judicial rulings in the late 1930s that dealt with, among other things, employee rights in economic strikes and sit-down strikes. The principled reassertion of employer prerogatives during these years was later reflected and entrenched within the post–World War II system of governance over labor relations as well.

Each of these examples thus suggests not only the possibilities for momentous change in American politics but also the limits attendant upon change. If the reforms during the Reconstruction, the New Deal, and the civil rights eras promised fundamental transformations of the American polity, the aftermath of each demonstrates how that promise can be compromised. Certainly none of these reforms were later reversed or nullified. Slavery never returned to the post–Civil War South, master-servant common law labor doctrines were not categorically resurrected in the late 1930s, and widespread, legally-mandated racially segregated public schools will surely never reappear in the American society. But while each set of reforms marked out important and permanent political changes, conditions in their aftermath also demonstrate the stubborn resilience of older ideas, principles, and institutions that carried elements of the old order into the new.

---

[2] Matthew D. Lassiter, *The Silent Majority: Suburban Politics in the Sunbelt South* (Princeton: Princeton University Press, 2006), 132, 244, 249, 304. On de facto school segregation in urban areas of the South, see ibid., 299–300. Although southern public schools have generally been more integrated than others in the nation, trends since the 1990s indicate heightened resegregation. Gary Orfield, "The Southern Dilemma: Losing *Brown*, Fearing *Plessy*," in *School Resegregation: Must the South Turn Back?*, ed. John Charles Boger and Gary Orfield (Chapel Hill: University of North Carolina Press, 2005), 1, 7–11.

[3] Karen Orren, *Belated Feudalism: Labor, the Law, and Liberal Development in the United States* (New York: Cambridge University Press, 1999).

What are we to make of the partial changes wrought by legal and political reforms? On the one hand, the persistence of older principles into the postreform order aligns with some fairly common intuitions. We know that the dispersal of authority within the American political system – between states and the federal government and also among the branches of the federal government – makes major reform difficult to achieve. Perhaps, then, it is not so surprising that once the transient conditions for reform have passed, older ideas, values, and social arrangements lodged within discrete pockets of the political system are able to reassert themselves.

We have heard the claim, too, that as Tocqueville observed, the law and the legal profession have an inherently conservative nature[4] – traits that might prompt us to expect the tempering of radical political changes. Finally, students of the legal process are familiar with the complexities of implementation and judicial interpretation that follow the passage of any major piece of legislation. The incongruities between reform principles and conditions in the aftermath of reform might also be unsurprising in light of the inevitable intervention of other actors in interpreting and implementing reform. Potential tempering of earlier reforms is perhaps especially likely if those actors intervene with distinct motives, and at markedly different moments in time, than the original authors of reform.

Still, even if certain incongruities between reform and its aftereffects may not be totally unexpected, they can hardly be considered obvious. After all, if such pessimistic views on the possibilities of reform were pervasively obvious, why does rhetoric surrounding new legislation and new judicial rulings often connect these events to "new beginnings" or new states of affairs?[5] Indeed, we often do attribute great meaning to such

---

[4] Alexis de Tocqueville, *Democracy in America*, ed. J. P. Mayer, trans. George Lawrence (New York: Harper Perennial, 1988), 264–65, 268–69.

[5] See, for example, Barack Obama on the Affordable Care Act: "In the end, what this day represents is another stone firmly laid in the foundation of the American Dream. Tonight we answered the call of history as so many generations of Americans have before us. When faced with crisis, we did not shrink from our challenge, we overcame it. We did not avoid our responsibility, we embraced it. We did not fear our future, we shaped it." Remarks on House of Representatives Passage of Health Care Reform Act, 2010 Weekly Comp. Pres. Doc. 193 (March 21, 2010), http://www.gpo.gov/fdsys/pkg/DCPD-201000193/pdf/DCPD-201000193.pdf. Likewise, Lyndon Johnson stated the following on the Voting Rights Act of 1965: "Today is a triumph for freedom as huge as any victory that has ever been won on any battlefield.... Today we strike away the last major shackle of those fierce and ancient bonds. Today the Negro story and the American story fuse and blend." Lyndon Johnson, "Remarks on the Signing of the Voting Rights Act," August 6, 1965, http://millercenter.org/president/speeches/detail/4034.

legal and political acts, and at least at an intuitive level, we often associate such acts with significant social and political changes. The example of Jim Crow and the odd place it holds in any broader narrative of American history is instructive in this regard. The rise of Jim Crow in the late-nineteenth-century South stands out as perhaps the most glaring oddity in American political development precisely because we assume the Reconstruction Amendments were monumental political achievements, and because it is not easy to understand segregated social arrangements and black disfranchisement as logical consequences of those Amendments.

Further, even if one was particularly attentive to the aforementioned conservative influences on American political and legal development, those explanations seemingly offer limited analytical value. With New Deal labor rights or the subsequent transformation of constitutional equal protection, the substance and manner of how elements of the old order carried forward into the new can hardly be intuited by simply referring to law's conservatism, or vaguely nodding to the complexities of judicial interpretation. In the case of the New Deal, only certain kinds of employer prerogatives, framed in certain ways, were resurgent after the passage of the Wagner Act. In the case of the post–civil rights era, only certain kinds of racial exclusions, framed in certain ways, persisted in the constitutional law of equal protection.

All of these examples suggest the need to account for the precise mix of factors that compromise reform aspirations. What structural factors are at play, and which are more important than others? What is the exact sequence of events by which less-radical governing arrangements formally emerge after a moment of reform? Uncovering answers to these questions will at least confirm and give substantive weight to some of our intuitions on conservative tendencies in legal and political development. But beyond this, such answers will also shed light on persistent questions surrounding some of the most important eras in American history, and offer a more conceptually rigorous assessment on the limits and possibilities for achieving political change in American politics.

There is hardly a shortage of scholarly work on the topic of political change in American history. One might expect that among those scholarly works centrally concerned with examining the substance of the political changes ushered in by legal reforms in American history – and that proceed from a theoretical and comparative, multi-case-study approach – some systematic attention to this incongruity might be present given its recurrence. We might expect this topic to arise in those studies that encompass major constitutional changes as well, given that postreform incongruities could be even more conspicuous here.

Yet surprisingly, comparative-theoretical studies of political change in American history largely fail to provide any systematic treatment of the incongruities between intended reforms and postreform conditions. Consider four exemplars of scholarly work along these lines by Walter Dean Burnham, Bruce Ackerman, Paul Pierson, and Richard Valelly. Each examines the dynamics of political change from a comparative analysis, drawing on multiple case studies from American history. Furthermore, the theoretical claims of each encompass instances of major constitutional change. However, while important insights emerge from all of these works to provide hints of the complex relationship between legal reform and postreform governing arrangements, none provide a full or convincing account of this relationship. Indeed, the question of how new governing arrangements are constructed after legal reforms are enacted tends to remain lost or obscured by analytical frameworks preoccupied by important, but distinct, concerns.[6]

Burnham and Ackerman approach the topic of political change by focusing on the *initiation* of such changes. For his part, Burnham stands out as one of the most able defenders of the critical realignment perspective, which posits a basic dichotomy in American political history between "normal" elections and "critical" elections.[7] More ambitious versions of critical realignment theory, such as Burnham's, emphasize that critical

---

[6] A noteworthy exception is Eric Patashnik's book, *Reforms at Risk* (Princeton: Princeton University Press, 2008). It offers a discussion of postreform development in a diverse array of policy contexts. Whereas Patashnik's study focuses on more narrowly defined areas of policy, this book focuses on the creation of governance in broad and highly visible areas of constitutional politics. Thus, the variables on which Patashnik focuses in examining policy durability and postreform effects diverge somewhat from the considerations that are at the forefront in this book. See also Sarah Staszak's relevant discussion of "judicial retrenchment"; Sarah Staszak, "Institutions, Rulemaking, and the Politics of Judicial Retrenchment," *Studies in American Political Development* 24 (October 2010): 168–89. Finally, although it is less preoccupied with theoretical concerns than the present discussion is, Morton Keller's rich and expansive historical survey of late-nineteenth-century America details the interplay between reformist ideals (associated with the Civil War) and more traditional ideals, in a number of policy areas. Morton Keller, *Affairs of State: Public Life in Late Nineteenth Century America* (Cambridge MA: Harvard University Press, 1977).

[7] Walter Dean Burnham, *Critical Elections and the Mainsprings of American Politics* (New York: W.W. Norton & Company, Inc., 1970).

elections inaugurate decisive shifts in public policy that help define the subsequent political equilibrium.[8] The critical elections he identifies as such are those of 1800, 1828, 1860, 1896, and 1932.[9]

In Burnham's model, the engine for these disruptions, and the reason for their short duration, lies in the peculiar nature of the interaction between socioeconomic development and the American governmental system. Because the two coexist largely autonomously from one another, periodic disruptions in socioeconomic life generate losers who find their concerns not addressed by governmental institutions that simply lack the capacity or the inclination to be responsive to them.[10] The consequence is a slow buildup of societal pressures that finally results in a dramatic disruption to political equilibrium and the arrival of a critical realignment.[11] However, just as soon as these pressures break through in this manner, Burnham tells us that they are accommodated and dissipated almost immediately. Once these realignments restabilize the polity, political leaders have no further incentive to push for additional change: "successful routines are established or reestablished for winning office," and "there is no motivation among party leaders to disturb the routines of the game."[12]

Similarly, Ackerman has offered an elaborate normative and descriptive theory for a significant subset of constitutional developments, namely, those developments dramatic and sweeping enough to be called constitutional "transformations."[13] The conceptual cornerstone of Ackerman's theory is the idea that the United States is a dualist democracy; he posits that lawmaking can occur along either a "normal political" track[14] or along a "higher lawmaking" track.[15] During periods of higher lawmaking, electoral choices by citizens and political choices by governing officials take on a much greater deliberative quality. Decisions made during these periods thus sometimes amount to constitutional

---

[8] Ibid., 9–10.
[9] Ibid., 1. In subsequent writing, Burnham has also identified 1968 as a critical election. Walter Dean Burnham, "Constitutional Moments and Punctuated Equilibria: A Political Scientist Confronts Bruce Ackerman's *We the People*," *Yale Law Journal* 108, no. 8 (June 1999): 2258.
[10] Burnham, *Critical Elections*, 177–82.
[11] Ibid., 181–82.
[12] Ibid., 183.
[13] Bruce Ackerman, *We the People*, vol. 1, *Foundations* (Cambridge, MA: Harvard University Press, 1991), 59.
[14] Ibid., 230–65.
[15] Ibid., 266–94.

transformations, and when they do, they ultimately have a lasting effect in structuring the substance of subsequent normal politics.[16] Ackerman perhaps goes beyond Burnham, however, to offer a fuller account of the moment of disruption and punctuation. The critical junctures of Ackerman's historical narrative are extended political processes that can take a decade or longer for the relevant institutional bodies to fulfill their various functions.[17] This framework allows him to identify, with greater clarity, the discrete governing principles that define and constitute the change itself.

While Burnham and Ackerman offer keen insight into the dynamics of "higher lawmaking" or transformational moments, what remains unexplored by both is precisely how those moments translate into new systems of governance. For its part, Burnham's account does not address how momentous political reforms are implemented or to what extent they may or may not structure the new equilibrium. Burnham's theory tells us why windows of political change open, but it is bereft of any institutional logic that explains how the window of change is decisively closed and how the new system of governance emerges.

Similarly, Ackerman's model fails to illuminate the link between constitutional reform and subsequent changes in governance because it does not address how the principles of reform are systematically reshaped and redefined as they confront preexisting institutions and rights. As a result, he is unable to explain the nature of the subsequent equilibrium, or era of "normal politics," with much success. For example, one does not easily find hints of the subsequent Jim Crow era in the energetic, egalitarian, reform-minded politics of Reconstruction in the 1860s, the period to which Ackerman pays most attention. Likewise, one does not easily find hints of the subsequent delimitation of labor rights within the more transformative politics of the New Deal era that Ackerman focuses on. By closing his analysis of these historical eras early, Ackerman casts these episodes in an overly transformative light and leaves the descriptive component of his theory with an incongruity: transformative political goals that reformers supposedly achieved during higher lawmaking – according to his model – often find themselves inexplicably subverted or otherwise redirected in the ensuing era of supposed normal politics.[18]

---

[16] Ibid., 58–59, 59n1, 77, 266–94.
[17] Bruce Ackerman, *We the People*, vol. 2, *Transformations* (Cambridge, MA: Harvard University Press, 1998), 123, 126–27, 246–47, 284, 360–61, 373–74.
[18] Others have noted this problem as well. See Michael V. McConnell, The Forgotten Constitutional Moment, *Constitutional Commentary* 11, no. 1 (Winter 1994): 115–44.

Consider next Pierson's theory of positive feedback. Here the question of how postreform governing arrangements are constructed is again obscured, but for a different reason from that seen with the preceding authors: Pierson's preoccupation is with "normal" politics and institutional resilience rather than transformative politics. Pierson tells us that, when operative, positive feedback mechanisms are structures that constrain political actors by narrowing their choices; positive feedback locks in, facilitates, and reinforces certain political choices and developmental paths facing those actors.[19] While some degree of political contestation and contingency usually exists in most contexts, positive feedback reduces the range of possibilities and ensures that certain choices, power dynamics, and institutional arrangements will persist into the future.

There is much in Pierson's analysis that, as with the previous authors, illuminates the dynamics of political change and non-change. However, his focus on the efficacy of positive feedback raises significant, unanswered questions as to how and when exactly potential positive feedback mechanisms begin to bite and become efficacious. And indeed, answers to the latter question are needed for a theory of positive feedback to illuminate how systems of governance are initially constructed after reform.[20]

Consider in this regard a historical case study that both Pierson and I deal with: the story of post-Reconstruction. Pierson discusses black disfranchisement as a case study of positive feedback at work. As he tells it, initial power asymmetries between Southern Democrats and Republicans – with Southern Democrats emerging victorious and redeeming southern state governments in the late 1870s – served as a positive feedback mechanism that led to the further entrenchment of this initial power

---

For Ackerman's reply, at least for the specific case of post-Reconstruction, see Ackerman, *Transformations*, 471n126. There is, however, another component of Ackerman's theory that might be relevant: his theory of interpretative "synthesis," where he conceptualizes judicial interpretation as weaving together and synthesizing "higher lawmaking" precedents. *Foundations*, 96–98, 115–16. While my theory of recalibration may converge with Ackerman's metaphor of "synthesis" in some important respects, I believe we differ in that I see recalibration as a component of transformative politics, whereas Ackerman appears to treat "synthesis" as a more or less continuous judicial exercise of fine-tuning.

[19] Paul Pierson, *Politics in Time: History, Institutions, and Social Analysis* (Princeton: Princeton University Press, 2004), 21, 63–71.

[20] Orren and Skowronek offer a similar critique of path-dependent arguments in general. Karen Orren and Stephen Skowronek, *The Search for American Political Development* (New York: Cambridge University Press, 2004), 102–04.

imbalance, as Democrats were subsequently emboldened to wage a successful, all-out assault on black voting and Southern Republicanism.[21]

One noteworthy problem with this historical narrative is that if Pierson's account began at an earlier point – say, in 1870, with the passage of the Fifteenth Amendment – the post-Reconstruction story might be interpreted as proving the opposite of his assertion. Indeed, the Fifteenth Amendment's prohibition of racial discrimination in voting in 1870 was an institutional change that seemingly should have been conducive to any number of positive feedback mechanisms – given that it reflected and constituted a power asymmetry that *favored* Southern Republicans and African Americans over Southern Democrats. Yet the shelf life of this latter institutional arrangement proved to be short, and it was decisively supplanted in the 1890s by an arrangement supporting black disfranchisement. Contrary to the thrust of Pierson's argument, this historical era might actually demonstrate the *weakness* of positive feedback processes in structuring politics, given the relatively short time frame before the Fifteenth Amendment was gutted. Some set of factors has to account for why, exactly, potential positive feedback mechanisms were relatively more efficacious in the later 1870s, compared to those that were present in the early 1870s, but Pierson's focus on more normal political dynamics – or political developments further downstream – shifts his attention away from this question.

Finally, Valelly differs in a helpful way from the preceding authors by focusing specifically on the immediate aftereffects of reform. Yet even here the question of how governance is constructed remains obscured because of the analytical framework of "success vs. failure" that he imposes on his case studies. Valelly examines Reconstruction and the civil rights movement and argues that reform "failed" in the former case and "succeeded" in the latter. The two key factors he identifies to explain these divergent outcomes are "party-building" and "jurisprudence-building." That is, the efforts of the civil rights movement to secure black enfranchisement were successful because its proponents were able to embed their goals within political party machinery (the Democratic Party in the South) and new federal judicial rulings. By contrast, Reconstruction failed to achieve lasting success in black enfranchisement, he argues, because reformers of that era were unable to institutionalize their goals in the same manner.[22]

---

[21] Pierson, *Time*, 36–37.
[22] Richard M. Valelly, *The Two Reconstructions: The Struggle for Black Enfranchisement* (Chicago: University of Chicago Press, 2004), 15–20.

Thinking about postreform dynamics through the lens of success or failure may very well be valuable in examining the durability of specific policy commitments. Still, even assuming that Valelly is correct with these labels of "success" and "failure" – a contestable point, depending on the baselines used in evaluating political developments – policy success and failure is only one aspect of the broader question on how legal reforms are translated into governance. To focus on this particular issue is to miss broader, and arguably more fundamental, institutional dynamics that are at play in the aftermath of reform. Indeed, while Valelly is correct that Reconstruction proved to be a relative failure compared to the reforms of the 1960s in achieving the policy goal of securing black suffrage in the South, this leaves unaddressed the fact that both historical eras witnessed momentous reforms being passed, and that new systems of governance were indeed constructed in the aftermath of those reforms. The content of the post-Reconstruction order was undoubtedly the less egalitarian one, and Valelly provides tools to understand why that may be, but he fails to be as attentive to the question of how durable governing arrangements nevertheless arose in the aftermath of Reconstruction, flawed as they may have been.

In this book I examine a critical phase of political development that I label *recalibration*, and it does not fit comfortably under either the labels of "transformative politics" or "normal politics." Specifically, I focus on historical periods in the immediate aftermath of major transformative reforms – those periods of time between moments of major disruption and periods of normality. In focusing on periods of recalibration in American political and legal history, my objective is twofold: first, to illuminate the political processes by which the foundations of governance are initially constructed after major political disruption has occurred; and second, to focus particularly on the key political institutions that are central in the legal reconstruction of postreform governance. Acknowledging recalibration processes and their interplay with recently enacted reforms is, I argue, crucial for understanding conspicuous instances of postreform conservative developments.

Still, if the reconstruction of governance during recalibration is the key for illuminating political developments in the Reconstruction, New Deal, and civil rights eras, it is necessary to clarify what I mean by governance. In a constitutional democracy, governance usually invokes a wide range of topics and themes including notions of democratic consent, the nature of governing authority, and the nature of political institutions. More narrowly, the concept of governance might also imply specific, discrete policy outcomes and policy visions, or specific sets of individual rights and entitlements. I would assert, however, that the defining feature of stable systems of governance in a constitutional democracy is regularity or predictability in the state's exercise of governing authority. This, in turn, entails the presence of established, formalized *boundaries* that clarify what particular institutions or persons are able to do.[23] These boundaries create regularity and predictability in the exercise of governing authority, whether across the entire polity through systemic rules and procedures or merely within specific areas of policy.

Coherent governance first encompasses clear, formal boundaries with respect to *institutional authority*. In this vein, consider the very familiar example of how the Constitution allocates authority among the three branches of the federal government, with "all legislative powers" granted in the Constitution "vested in a Congress of the United States" (Article I, Section 1), executive power vested in the president (Article II, Section 1), and judicial power vested in the federal courts (Article III, Section 1). Of comparable significance, consider also the allocation of authority between the federal government and the states embodied within general principles of federalism. These principles underlie the Article V amendment process[24] and are textually embodied within the Tenth Amendment. While these particular allocations of authority have undergone changes over time, the basic categorical divisions remain. Settled institutional boundaries facilitate coherent governance by minimizing the uncertainties surrounding which institutions possess primary authority and oversight within certain contexts, or for certain issues.

Coherent governance also entails at least some clearly codified boundaries with respect to individual rights. Consider another familiar example: the array of various Fourteenth Amendment rights guarantees to any number of economic and social groups against political majorities, whether under the Due Process or Equal Protection Clauses. Established boundary lines between competing and conflicting sets of individual rights, or between individual rights and state authority, similarly reduce ambiguities over who is entitled to what.

Thus, in examining the span of American political history, the moments that stand out are those moments in which the boundaries

---

[23] See Orren and Skowronek, *Search*, 123. A note on terminology: references to "formal" boundaries or "codified" boundaries are to boundaries between competing authorities and rights that have been established as a matter of law, and *not* as a matter of mere informal practices or informal social norms.

[24] See Ackerman, *Foundations*, 45.

of institutional authority and individual rights were fundamentally challenged – when, indeed, some lines of authority and some sets of rights were legally dismantled. Such moments – or more precisely the aftermath of such moments – are my focus. During these moments the reassertion of preexisting boundaries against reform principles is especially conspicuous, and this reassertion drives the legal reconstruction of governance through recalibration processes.[25]

Finally, to understand how these preexisting boundaries reassert themselves after moments of reform, one must examine the institutional actors that influence the reform. A number of different elements of the American constitutional system stand out as plausible choices to help frame the inquiry. One might track postreform developments in the elected branches, or examine strategies and interactions among key interest groups and key voting constituencies, or identify and track certain key legal and political ideas that went on to shape the new system of governance.

All of the preceding elements significantly inform the analysis in this book. Yet at a relatively early stage of the project, what began to emerge as the primary focal point for my analysis was the Supreme Court. In hindsight, the significance of the Court in recalibration is hardly surprising. Once it is recognized that the legal reforms themselves only partially establish the systems of governance that succeed them, the question then immediately arises as to *how* principles of reform may be elaborated on, delimited, or reoriented as the polity moves past the moment of transformative legal enactment.

As an initial matter, my attention was drawn to the judiciary in light of familiar normative and historical analyses of that institution as a sometimes dynamic political actor. Among other things, commentators have identified the judiciary as a historical or normative solution to problems such as statutory commands that are complicated by changed circumstances,[26] policy issues that are complicated by governing

---

[25] While social norms and informal negotiations between competing institutions and individual rights-holders may constitute important elements of governance at particular times and places, my focus is on those norms and negotiations that were actually codified in the law. This focus is apt for those interested in capturing the essential characteristics of broader systems or orders of governance. Further, one also suspects that any informal norms and negotiations that attain sufficient importance will likely ultimately filter through the law in some form or another, by constitutional amendment, statutory law, or judicial interpretation.

[26] William N. Eskridge, Jr., Philip P. Frickey, and Elizabeth Garrett, *Cases and Materials on Legislation*, 4th ed. (St. Paul: Thomson/West, 2007), 729–42.

coalitional-difficulties,[27] incongruous constitutional principles that are separated by time and in need of overarching synthesis,[28] and the democratic problems posed by aged statutes.[29] All of these analyses suggested that if significant postreform adjustments were likely to take place in central areas of constitutional policy, the judiciary – and the Supreme Court in particular – was likely to be an institution that reliably intersected with these adjustments.

Thus, in the chapters that follow, I explore the reconstruction of governance in the aftermath of the enactment of the Reconstruction Amendments, the enactment of the Wagner Act, and the transformation of constitutional equal protection during the civil rights era. In each of my three case studies, the Supreme Court plays a central role. The reconstruction of governance in each case cannot plausibly be characterized as a purely judicial story in any of these cases. Yet the Supreme Court's actions immediately following each set of reforms formalized a new political baseline in a manner that is minimized by characterizing its opinions as mere "interpretations" of original legislative intents.

In its orientation, then, this is a study of both American politics and constitutional doctrine. I set out with this project to pursue a question about the construction of governance, and as such, I hoped to illuminate one underemphasized aspect of American political development that was situated between theories of political change on the one hand and theories of institutional resilience (or normal politics) on the other. In uncovering and highlighting the central role of the Supreme Court in the formal construction of governance following reform, this book ultimately became a study of legal doctrinal development, judicial behavior, and the role of the Supreme Court within the American constitutional system as a designer of governance.

---

[27] Mark A. Graber, "The Nonmajoritarian Difficulty: Legislative Deference to the Judiciary," *Studies in American Political Development* 7 (Spring 1993): 35–73; Keith E. Whittington, "'Interpose Your Friendly Hand': Political Supports for the Exercise of Judicial Review by the United States Supreme Court," *American Political Science Review* 99, no. 4 (November 2005): 583–96.

[28] Ackerman, *Foundations*, 96–98, 115–16.

[29] Guido Calabresi, *A Common Law for the Age of Statutes* (Cambridge, MA: Harvard University Press, 1982).

I

The Theory and Political Processes of Recalibration

When examining certain significant postreform periods, what emerges is a recurrent process of *recalibration* in American political history, where recently enacted reforms are shaped in light of the continuing influence of preexisting institutions and rights. Recalibration is the period during which vague, open-ended, and universalistic principles embodied in new reforms ultimately confront the constraint of preexisting institutional authority and rights. The product of this confrontation and subsequent resolution are new, concrete standards of governance that define the new political order. Recalibration is not a "Thermidorian Reaction,"[1] a "return to moderation," or a "reversal" of reform, nor can it be wholly attributed to political ideology.[2] It cannot be reduced to being

---

[1] Crane Brinton described revolutionary periods as something like a sickness of the polity, and once the idealism of that moment had sufficiently run its destructive course, the Thermidorian Reaction set in as a kind of "convalescence from the fever of revolution." Crane Brinton, *The Anatomy of Revolution*, rev. and exp. ed. (New York: Vintage, 1965), 205. In other words, this late Thermidorian stage of a revolution marked the point when society desired a return to normalcy and regular pleasures, and when it became apparent that the persistence of certain older forms would outlast the revolutionary spirit. Ibid., 203–05, 207–08, 211, 218–23, 258–59. Brinton viewed the ending of reform as due to general societal exhaustion. However, as discussed in the substantive chapters that follow, recalibration is conceptualized as more the result of institutional and political logics driven by the uncertainties and frictions between competing governing authorities and rights.

[2] James Morone's expansive account of American state-building is attentive to the disjointed nature of this history and frames his narrative against ideological and institutional factors that both help drive political change and contain it. James A. Morone, *The Democratic Wish: Popular Participation and the Limits of American Government* (New Haven, CT: Yale University Press, 1990). Yet with respect to the dynamics that limit or contain such changes, Morone's theory focuses on ideological factors. The ideology of the "democratic wish" appears to constrain reform impulses by rendering new institutional designs defective and by ultimately drawing the attention of reformers away from more

the mere "implementation" of prior, definitive, first-order principles or as the undermining of clearly defined original reform intentions. Rather, recalibration is a distinct and constitutive phase of political development in which institutional actors create *operational meaning* out of abstract reform principles. Recalibration processes do nothing less than help determine the substance of the core principles within the initial legal reforms. In this chapter, I set forth two of the four core claims of this book that are later illuminated in my three historical case studies. Here, I set forth a general theory of recalibration and a claim about the political processes of "transformative" recalibrations. In Chapter 2, I set forth two claims about transformative recalibrations and the Supreme Court.

CLAIM 1: A GENERAL THEORY OF RECALIBRATION

Following up on insights from Orren and Skowronek on the "plenary" nature of authority, the first of two primary claims I make in this chapter is a more general claim about recalibration: *recalibration follows many major political changes when the latter encompass fundamental rearrangements of institutional authority and individual rights* (Claim 1). In most cases, major political change simply cannot be foisted on the larger matrix of governance and fit seamlessly with preexisting constraints.

A recalibration usually follows major reform owing to three primary conditions. First, when such reforms are enacted, they often set forth principles in broad, open-ended, and universalistic terms.[3] Second, those same reforms usually disrupt and rearrange preexisting institutions and individual rights – what Orren and Skowronek refer to as their "proposition of plenary authority."[4] Placed together, these two features ensure that uncertainties about the scope of many major reforms will

---

radical objectives toward narrower issues of administrative organizational maintenance. Ibid., 11–13, 28–30. For a systematic examination of how American political traditions or ideologies have manifested themselves during different political eras, see Rogers M. Smith, *Civic Ideals: Conflicting Visions of Citizenship in U.S. History* (New Haven, CT: Yale University Press, 1997).

[3] Here I draw, in part, on Orren and Skowronek's definition of political institutions as inherently "outward reach[ing]." Karen Orren and Stephen Skowronek, *The Search for American Political Development* (New York: Cambridge University Press, 2004), 18–19. This term describes particularly well the *intrusive* nature of universalistic political reforms that, by their very logic, are inclined to press their underlying principles further into the polity. As I discuss in subsequent paragraphs, however, these aggressive, self-aggrandizing tendencies are not necessarily present in all political reforms.

[4] "Plenary authority means that changing any aspect of politics entails bumping against authority already in existence." Ibid., 23. See also ibid., 20–25, 127.

arise almost immediately on their enactment, demanding a subsequent clarification.

More specifically, when reforms are articulated in broad, universalistic language, they will inevitably disrupt, impinge on, and affect more than just those items that are the primary targets of reform. Universalistic reform principles will also intrude on institutions and rights that are going to be implicated – if only indirectly – in the governing arrangements under attack. Thus, again, when universalistic reform principles are articulated against the backdrop of a polity already constituted by a range of preexisting constraints, the uncertain reach of reform is bound to demand a subsequent resolution.[5] The processes of recalibration speak to this task of critical readjustment and accommodation between old and new, as the latter eventually becomes integrated within a resilient, preexisting institutional and legal fabric.

Finally, a third reason for frequent postreform recalibration is that reformers consistently lack either the foresight or the political consensus to resolve all problems of recalibration up front. Because of the shortcomings of reform coalitions, the end result is reform that promotes universalistic principles, even while its effect on restructuring governance is limited.

These three conditions ensure that a postreform recalibration will take place in the aftermath of many reforms. Only in the postreform period does it become clear just *how much* authority and just *how many* legal entitlements have been implicated in open-ended reforms[6] – questions left unanswered at the time of enactment.

Notably, these conditions not only prompt recalibration, they also influence how immediate, expansive, and pronounced the recalibration will be. For example, when reforms are promoted in language that is particularly broad, universalistic, and open-ended, postreform recalibrations are more likely to be pronounced because the limits of reform in such cases will be especially vague and the need to clarify boundaries more pressing. Moreover, because of their aspiration to universality, open-ended reforms will pose a greater threat to a broader array of preexisting authorities and rights – at least relative to more specific and measured reforms – and thus

---

[5] To be sure, no clarification would be needed if the reforms encompassed a *total* transformation (i.e., one without limits) or if reform took place within a polity free from the constraints of preexisting institutional and rights commitments. However, such perfect freedom for reformers is never the case. Orren and Skowronek, *Search*, 22; Bruce A. Ackerman, "Revolution on a Human Scale," *Yale Law Journal* 108, no. 8 (June 1999): 2292–95.

[6] Orren and Skowronek, *Search*, 127–29.

The Theory and Political Processes of Recalibration 19

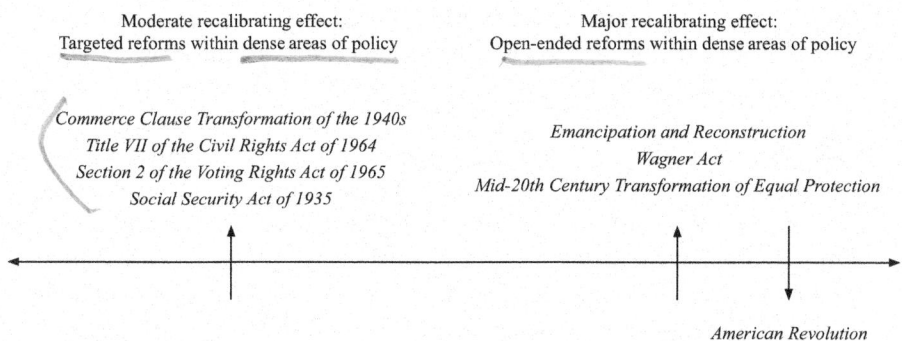

FIGURE 1.1. A continuum of major to moderate recalibrating effects.

the recalibration is likely to be more profound. Similarly, when reformers target "dense" policy contexts – those policy contexts populated by deeply entrenched institutions and rights – the postreform recalibration is likely to be more pronounced. Integrating new reforms into more complex policy areas will be more difficult and will confront a broader and more significant set of uncertainties. Conversely, where political actors craft reform principles that are more detailed, precise, and targeted, or when reform targets policy contexts that are relatively less dense – that is, those contexts in which fewer preexisting authorities and rights are likely to conflict with the principles of reform – recalibration effects are more likely to be weak, insignificant, or perhaps even absent.

By way of illustration, consider this graphic in which I array some historical examples of recalibration on a continuum from "minor" to more "transformative" (Figure 1.1). Three of the examples are familiar, but I include several additional ones to highlight the broader applicability of recalibration and the importance of the preconditions for it, noted earlier.

In providing this graphic, my aim is not to split hairs regarding the overall significance of these various reforms. Rather, the graphic seeks to map the relative importance of recalibration for historical examples drawn entirely from four eras of reform that are commonly recognized as critical junctures in American political history: the American Revolution, Reconstruction, the New Deal, and the 1960s civil rights era.

Let us begin with the American Revolution. The Revolution was a reform movement that assaulted the preexisting social order in the broadest sense. Before the Revolution, Wood asserts that political authority stemmed from connections to royal authority, and social relations were centrally defined by monarchical, hierarchical, and aristocratic elements.⁷ The Revolution, which promoted egalitarian democratic principles (for certain constituencies), constituted a direct attack on some of the most deeply entrenched governing authorities and individual entitlements in all of pre-Revolutionary society. As Wood states, the Revolution "became a full scale assault on dependency."⁸

It should be no surprise, then, that the limits of this transformation were scarcely apparent at the moment of reform. This would hardly have been possible given the depth of the change contemplated. It would take nothing less than another era of transformative change – the founding – before the limits of popular majoritarianism were demarcated within a new system of governance.⁹ Thus, the Constitution itself probably stands out as the most significant instance of recalibration in our history; it was the means by which revolutionary principles were recalibrated and translated into a coherent system of governance.

To the left of the American Revolution in Figure 1.1 are the three historical cases that I mentioned in the Introduction: the dismantling of slavery, the dismantling of master-servant common law labor relations with the Wagner Act, and the dismantling of Jim Crow with respect to constitutional equal protection guarantees. Each set of reforms was characterized by particularly broad, universalistic, and open-ended commitments: a legal guarantee of racial equality, the right to unionize and collectively bargain, and the right to equal protection. These were commitments that defied easy specification at the moment of reform. Furthermore, all three instances implicated areas of policy that were dense in terms of being constituted by deeply entrenched preexisting authorities and rights that were *directly* in conflict with recently enacted reforms. Given these two conditions – a dense policy environment and universalistic reform principles – the postreform recalibration in each case was profound in shaping the new order. The significant uncertainties created by each set of reforms ensured that much of the work of translating these enactments into fully fleshed-out governing arrangements would have to be left to the postreform period, demanding dramatic recalibrations in each case.

Not all instances of recalibration in American political history have been so crucial in shaping governance, however. Consider four examples further to the left in Figure 1.1: Title VII of the Civil Rights Act of

---

[7] Gordon S. Wood, *The Radicalism of the American Revolution* (New York: Vintage Books, 1991), 5–6, 77–92.
[8] Ibid., 179. See also ibid., 175–76.
[9] Ibid., 230; Gordon S. Wood, *The Creation of the American Republic, 1776–1787* (New York: W. W. Norton, 1969), 519–24.

1964, the Voting Rights Act of 1965, the transformation of the Commerce Clause, and the Social Security Act of 1935. In these cases, recalibration effects were present but were more measured. Each of these reforms was of enormous political significance, and each attempted to rearrange governing arrangements and individual rights in areas of policy that were densely constituted by preexisting authorities and rights. Indeed, the transformation in Commerce Clause doctrine in the 1930s and 1940s constituted a direct assault on state authority, judicial authority, and an elaborate body of prior case law, while the Voting Rights Act and Title VII also confronted the authority of federalism and employer prerogatives, respectively, along with very established discriminatory social and political practices. Yet these reforms made no claim to universality. As a result, the recalibration effects were more moderate.

The Voting Rights Act and Title VII both embodied a commitment to racial equality, but the commitment was substantially delimited in terms of enforcement and overall breadth within the reforms themselves – the former was a reform within the policy domain of voting practices[10] and the latter was a reform in employment practices. Unlike the assault on Jim Crow that was carried out under the banner of constitutional equal protection, these two statutory reforms were assaults on older policy regimes that, while still enormously significant, were much more focused in terms of their potential applicability.

Thus, if only because of the density of preexisting authorities and rights within the policy areas of voting and employment, postreform recalibrations were present in both. For example, after the Voting Rights Act, both the Court and Congress had to grapple with uncertainties about what that act demanded with respect to problems of minority vote dilution.[11] Likewise, after the passage of Title VII, both the Court and Congress grappled with, and resolved, the very significant question of whether that provision encompassed a prohibition of hiring practices that had a negative disparate impact on minorities.[12] Both of these postreform developments were recalibrating developments: they clarified the implications of these two statutory provisions for actual governance in the postreform period.

Further, it is worth noting that the postreform recalibrations in both cases pushed in a more *liberal* direction: Congress pressed for – and the

---

[10] Indeed, the absence of a detailed enforcement scheme in the Fifteenth Amendment itself – something analogous to the Voting Rights Act's Section 5 – is why I would classify the former as a more open-ended reform subject to a more dramatic recalibration effect, at least relative to the Voting Rights Act.
[11] See Chapter 9.
[12] See *Griggs v. Duke Power Co.*, 401 U.S. 424 (1971).

Court acquiesced to an "effects" test under Section 2 of the Voting Rights Act in attacking minority vote dilution, and the Court itself was sympathetic to a disparate impact interpretation of Title VII.[13] At the same time, however, these recalibrations were relatively more contained adjustments and did not structure governance and social relations as broadly as the prior four cases of postreform recalibration did. Given the self-conscious focus of these statutes on the specific areas of voting and employment policy, this was hardly surprising.

Likewise, a relatively moderate recalibration followed transformative understandings of the Commerce Clause that occurred in the 1930s and 1940s because this was a transformation in federal authority in which the limits of the reform were ever present and were indeed in the very name of the doctrine itself. New Deal reformers had never claimed unlimited federal authority over American society; the interstate commerce limitation on federal power had, of course, been present and acknowledged in the transformative rulings of the 1940s.[14] Although some sort of recalibration could be expected in the aftermath of such a significant political change – if only because of the depth and resilience of federalism principles during and after the New Deal – it was not a recalibration of the same magnitude seen in post–New Deal labor relations. The absence of any analogous degree of open-endedness in the Commerce Clause transformation – relative to the Wagner Act's transformation of labor relations – precluded the need for this. When a postreform recalibration did eventually occur with respect to the Commerce Clause – one that began to demarcate with greater clarity the limits of federal authority – it came in the form of a Supreme Court ruling more than a half century after the New Deal.[15]

Finally, consider one last example on the left of the continuum: the Social Security Act of 1935 created a new, detailed policy regime for providing economic assistance to various social groups. However, given the aforementioned considerations, the recalibration effects were, not surprisingly, also more moderate. In line with the prior three reforms, there was no claim to universality in the principles of the initial social security legislation; although the act most notably provided aid for retirees, the unemployed, and families with dependent children,[16] it did not include

---

[13] See Chapter 9.
[14] See *United States v. Darby*, 312 U.S. 100 (1941); *Wickard v. Filburn*, 317 U.S. 111 (1942).
[15] *United States v. Lopez*, 514 U.S. 549 (1995).
[16] Social Security Act, Pub. L. No. 271, 49 Stat. at Large 620 (1935).

an abstract, principled guarantee to something like a "basic standard of living for all." Furthermore, whereas the legislation clearly posed a threat to at least one dense policy area, namely the Jim Crow legal and social order[17] – it was not self-consciously designed to uproot or dismantle that system. Indeed, the legislation's possible threat to Jim Crow prompted explicit limits on the act's coverage for old-age insurance, to the disadvantage of racial minorities.[18]

Notwithstanding these initial limitations, political and institutional pressures eventually allowed for original reform commitments – namely, again, old-age insurance – to be renegotiated and revised, allowing those commitments to expand in the 1950s, to the detriment of Jim Crow.[19] Why post-1935 developments in Social Security followed this exact path is beyond my present concern, although worth noting is that the targeted focus of the initial Social Security legislation ensured that subsequent recalibrations of this legislation would remain more moderate in their scope and effect, relative to the previously discussed examples of more major recalibrations. Table 1.1 provides a brief summary of the aforementioned episodes of recalibration.

With these several historical examples in mind, four subsidiary claims emerge. First, whether a significant postreform recalibration occurs is directly related to how difficult it will be for reformers to craft concrete governing arrangements out of the principles embodied in reform. *The more difficult the task of governance construction may be – due either to the strength of the authorities and rights being dislodged or to the vagueness or open-endedness of the reforms themselves – the more likely that a significant postreform recalibration will arise to substantially shape the new order* (Claim 1.1). Table 1.2 elaborates on this claim, with reference to some historical examples.

The historical examples of Reconstruction, the Wagner Act, the 1960s transformation in equal protection, and the American Revolution demonstrate a second subsidiary claim: *when recalibration effects are particularly pronounced, recalibration outcomes delimit rather than complicate*

---

[17] Robert C. Lieberman, *Shifting the Color Line: Race and the American Welfare State* (Cambridge, MA: Harvard University Press, 1998), 23–66.
[18] David M. Kennedy, *Freedom from Fear: The American People in Depression and War, 1929–1945* (New York: Oxford University Press, 1999), 269; Lieberman, *Color Line*, 7–8.
[19] Alice Kessler-Harris, *In Pursuit of Equity: Women, Men, and the Quest for Economic Citizenship in 20th-Century America* (New York: Oxford University Press, 2001), 151–56; Lieberman, *Color Line*, 109–17.

TABLE 1.1 *A Summary of Some Notable Recalibrations*

Reform	Open-Ended Reform Principles?	Dense Area of Policy Targeted by Reform?	Outcome of Recalibration	Significance of the Recalibration Effect
American Revolution	Yes (revolutionary reform principles constituted a dramatic promotion of democratic equality and "a full-scale assault on dependency")	Yes (an intricate web of social and political relations were structured around monarchical authority)	Creation of the Constitution in 1787	Major
Emancipation and the Reconstruction Amendments	Yes (a legal guarantee of racial equality)	Yes (the social and legal institution of slavery)	Jim Crow	Major
Wagner Act	Yes (the right to unionize and collectively bargain)	Yes (master-servant common law system of labor relations)	Industrial Pluralism	Major
Mid-twentieth century transformation in constitutional equal protection	Yes (reform principles potentially encompassed a promotion of "antisubordination" values)	Yes (Jim Crow and de facto racial and class exclusions)	Creation of the anticlassification order	Major
New Deal expansion of congressional Commerce authority	Moderately so (reformers never claimed unlimited federal authority; the limit of an interstate commerce requirement was always acknowledged by reformers)	Yes (reforms cut against state autonomy, judicial authority, and an elaborate body of prior case law)	Articulation of limits of congressional Commerce authority in *United States v. Lopez*	Moderate

Title VII of the Civil Rights Act of 1964	Moderately so (reform principles were self-consciously limited to the policy domain of employment)	Yes (reforms cut against the social order of Jim Crow and employer prerogatives)	Judicial articulation and congressional acquiescence to a disparate impact standard	Moderate
Section 2 of the Voting Rights Act of 1965	Moderately so (reform principles were self-consciously limited to the policy domain of voting)	Yes (reforms cut against the social order of Jim Crow and federalism prerogatives)	Congress pressed for – and the Court acquiesced to – an "effects" test under Section 2 of the Voting Rights Act in attacking minority vote dilution	Moderate
Social Security Act of 1935	No (there was no claim to universality in the act; the act was targeted in its coverage)	Yes, to an extent (reform principles had the significant potential to intrude on the social order of Jim Crow, although the legislation initially precluded such intrusion)	Subsequent expansion of coverage for old-age insurance	Moderate

TABLE 1.2 *The Conditions for Recalibration*

	Open-Ended Legal Reform	More Targeted Legal Reform	
Dense area of policy	E.g., the Reconstruction Amendments	E.g., Title VII of the Civil Rights Act of 1964; Social Security Act of 1935	Recalibration effects are present
Less dense area of policy	Unlikely to occur – open-ended reforms are likely to intrude on established authorities and rights at some juncture	E.g., federal and state highway construction policies in the twentieth century*	Recalibration effects are minimal or largely absent

* Owen D. Gutfreund, *Twentieth-Century Sprawl: Highways and the Reshaping of the American Landscape* (New York: Oxford University Press, 2004). Major highway policies in the twentieth century were subject to a number of key political dynamics that shaped their development, including, as Gutfreund emphasizes, the "undercharging" of motorists for roads and a systematic bias against urban areas. Ibid., 58–59. Further, federalism dynamics intersected with these policies as well. See, e.g., ibid., 20–21. Still, none of these major influences or constraints on highway policy making emanated from deeply entrenched governing authorities or traditional individual rights claims directly oriented against policy change and the basic idea of highway construction. With the possible exception of more principled urban-preservationist and environmental critics of U.S. interstate construction, see Mark H. Rose, *Interstate: Express Highway Politics, 1939–1989*, rev. ed. (Knoxville: University of Tennessee Press, 1990), 105–08, 116–17, the major influences in this area of policy, by and large, merely pressed for alternative visions of highway construction and policy making. Hence, this area of policy might be considered relatively less dense, as I use the term. See also ibid., 12–13, 108–14.

or expand on the original reform ambitions (Claim 1.2). As explained earlier, reforms articulated in broad, open-ended terms threaten not only their primary targets but also elements of the larger political system. In those instances in which newly enacted reform principles spawn uncertainty with respect to their scope, the *only* way that new governing arrangements, with new stable boundaries, might be fashioned out of those principles is by delimiting their scope. Delimitation – and sometimes even apparent curtailment – is the inescapable consequence of integrating system-threatening reforms within a preexisting institutional and legal context.

By contrast, when recalibration effects are more moderate, the recalibration may be either in tension with or supportive of reform ambitions simply because creating new governing arrangements out of more targeted and measured reforms is an easier task. Implicit, then, in the preceding subclaim is a third point: *when the initial reforms are more targeted and specific in their scope and commands, postreform recalibrations may indeed expand on the initial reform principles* (Claim 1.3). Indeed, this was the case with the Voting Rights Act, Title VII, and the Social Security Act. These recalibrations were able to clarify standards for governance, notwithstanding their more expansive orientation, because this latter set of reforms was specific in its scope, right from its inception; no new, *immediate*, system-threatening implications were obviously attendant on more expansive interpretations of any of these pieces of legislation. The more subdued uncertainties in the postenactment period for each statutory provision allowed for *either* delimiting or expansive postreform developments to clarify governing standards.

Fourth, and finally, *the case studies underscore that recalibration and delimitation do not constitute political reversal* (Claim 1.4). Even in instances in which recalibration effects are most pronounced in delimiting the initial reforms, we never see the polity returning to prereform conditions. In each of the three case studies of major recalibration examined in this book in which postreform developments took a conservative turn, only some reform goals were subject to recalibration, whereas other more central reform goals remained stable and durable (as noted in Table 1.3). Recognizing the significance of recalibration does not require one to denigrate or minimize the possibilities for substantive political development. Rather, recalibration illuminates how preexisting authorities and rights that remain entrenched through a period of reform also shape the scope and substance of that reform.

CLAIM 2: THE POLITICAL PROCESSES OF TRANSFORMATIVE RECALIBRATION

My second primary claim, and the primary focus of the substantive chapters that follow, concerns the subset of recalibrations on the right of the continuum on page 19. In these historical cases, reforms may be so open ended, the targeted policy domains so dense, and the ensuing recalibration effect so pronounced that we might attach the label of "transformative recalibration" to them. That is, these are historical cases for which the initial uncertainties created by reform were so great that the recalibration ultimately structured a broad array of institutional and rights relationships. In the same way that the label "transformative reform" is commonly applied to critical junctures in American history where certain reforms left crucial consequences for the polity, these instances of recalibration are aptly labeled "transformative."

TABLE 1.3 *The Scope of Recalibration in the Context of the Post-Reconstruction Era, the Post–New Deal Era, and the Post–Civil Rights Era*

	Issues decisively or largely settled by legally enacted reforms and judicial reform rulings	Some issues that remained contested after legally enacted reforms and judicial reform rulings
Reconstruction	1. The abolition of slavery 2. Black voting in the North	1. The terms of race relations in the South in the context of public accommodations 2. Black voting in the South
Wagner Act	1. The right to unionize 2. Ultimate congressional oversight of labor relations	Various union rights and employer rights that did *not* directly bear on the right to unionize
Civil rights era	1. The dismantling of Jim Crow exclusions in public schooling, public social contexts, and in voting 2. Skepticism of racial classifications in the law in the constitutional context	1. The status of "de facto" racial exclusions in the context of public schooling and constitutional equal protection more generally 2. The status of "benign" color consciousness in the constitutional context 3. The status of "benign" color consciousness in the statutory contexts of voting and employment

My second primary claim is that *when open-ended reforms do prompt such a transformative recalibration, a distinct and recurrent political process emerges, which includes an initial phase of "delimitation," and a subsequent phase of "construction"* (Claim 2). As indicated in Figure 1.2,

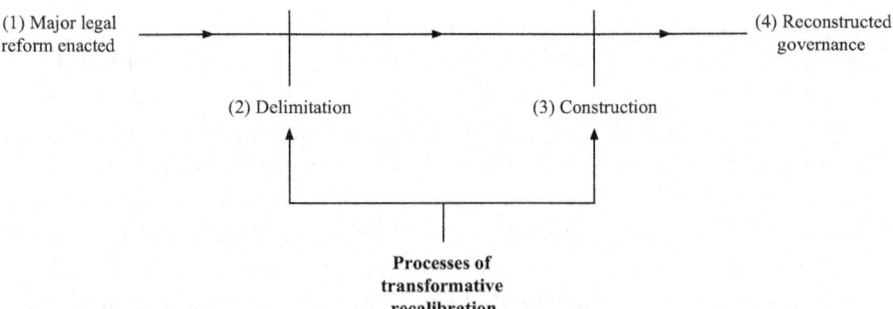

FIGURE 1.2. The political process: Transformative recalibration and the reconstruction of governance.

both phases of political development precede the formal entrenchment of new governing arrangements.

With respect to three of the historical cases identified on the right of the continuum – emancipation, the Wagner Act, and the mid-twentieth century transformation in constitutional equal protection – this same political process recurs in each of these cases.[20]

Let me discuss in turn each component of the political process outlined in Figure 1.2.

The Legal Enactment of Reform

By definition, transformative reforms disrupt some existing institutional and rights relations that defined the prereform order.[21] We might label this an initial *calibration* or measurement of reform. Hence, the process of determining what will constitute the new system of governance in the aftermath of these legal enactments constitutes the *re*calibration of reform.

Delimitation

When open-ended, universalistic reforms intrude on dense areas of policy, the most immediate uncertainty that arises is one of "external boundary drawing." That is, uncertainty arises with regard to *how far* reform principles are going to intrude on authorities and rights that are implicated by the reform. In the immediate aftermath of the Reconstruction Amendments, the uncertainty over external boundary drawing resided in the question of just how far these reforms would displace and disrupt federalism. Likewise, in the aftermath of the passage of the Wagner Act, a

---

[20] The American Revolution stands out as the prominent exception, where a transformative recalibration arose but followed a different path. Yet the Revolution is unique given that the subsequent recalibration encompassed a wholly new federal governmental structure – and did not take place within a stable, continuous federal structure.

[21] In the context of American racial politics, King and Smith have put forth a conception of political order characterized by sustained competition between rival "racial policy alliances" over a prolonged time period. They view these racial alliances as each encompassing (1) some set of foundational governing, economic, and social structures; (2) some set of policy positions; and (3) some set of political coalition alignments. Desmond S. King and Rogers M. Smith, *Still a House Divided: Race and Politics in Obama's America* (Princeton, NJ: Princeton University Press, 2011), 16–26. Whereas there is some overlap in the items we both emphasize as the key markers of order or entrenched governance, we diverge in that King and Smith focus on tracking certain policy "visions" over time, while my interest remains in tracking changes in structures of governance. Hence the key indicators for me are similar to those items in King and Smith's "1" category.

TABLE 1.4 *Recalibration Part I: The Political Process of Delimitation*

(2) Delimitation	Resolves "External" Uncertainties
Political Process	(2a) Legislative stalemate
	(2b) Delimitation by the Supreme Court

similar uncertainty arose over how far the principles of the new collective bargaining regime would intrude on other employer prerogatives that did not directly bear on the right to unionize. And finally, in the mid-twentieth century assault on Jim Crow, uncertainty resided in just how much the judicial transformation of constitutional equal protection would intrude on the traditional prerogatives of nonjudicial institutions – which allowed for de facto racial exclusions. All of these uncertainties concerned the absence of stable boundaries between competing institutional authorities and rights at the outer edges of recently enacted reforms.

The first step in the process of recalibration is *delimitation*, which itself can be separated into two stages: first, a *legislative stalemate* arises over the scope of reform; second, the stalemate then sets the stage and allows for a subsequent *judicial delimitation* of the reform (see Table 1.4).

Political Responses to Reform and Legislative Stalemate

After the enactment of certain momentous reforms, both private and legislative actors are immediately confronted with deep uncertainties over the implications of those reforms. Actors on both sides of the issue must now contemplate how to advance their preferred policies given the existence of new enactments and new transformative judicial rulings. Although ambiguities and gaps in the law may persist indefinitely in some contexts, the same is not true here. The depth of uncertainty in these instances of major reform is so great that both reform sympathizers and reform skeptics seek greater immediate clarification on where reform will lead. And within the undefined space opened by reform's ambiguities, visions, or elaborations on reform will emanate from private actors outside of government and from political actors occupying formal positions of authority. This desire for immediate, definitive clarification is also why we might consistently expect federal political actors, specifically, to possess great interest in addressing and resolving these types of postreform ambiguities.

Some elaborations of reform will ultimately fail to become entrenched as, for example, the southern state legislative attempt to pass Black Codes beginning in 1865 in response to the uncertainties opened up by the

Thirteenth Amendment. However, other tentative elaborations will succeed, become entrenched, and raise new uncertainties themselves as the congressional Republican response to the Thirteenth Amendment and the Black Codes did when it culminated in the enactment of the Fourteenth Amendment.

Most political actors who are more sympathetic to reform goals will largely be preoccupied with the specific question of how to build on, and link, enacted reforms to additional goals – the latter of which might be represented as logical extensions or necessary requirements of the former. For political actors who are reform skeptics – whether they are die-hard opponents of reform or former reformers who have become more conservative over time – the task is different but begins from the same starting presumption: accepting the fact of reform, most are motivated to emphasize the continuing legitimacy of all authorities and rights that have not been explicitly repudiated. Their likely predisposition is to be skeptical that additional incursions on existing rights and authorities can be justified or legitimized as logical extensions of the original enactments.

Yet, despite a reliable interest in and preoccupation with the recalibration question, the prospects for definitive, federal legislative resolution of these issues are quite poor. Stalemate and gridlock is the ironic end result of legislative preoccupation with recalibration; disjointedness and lack of cohesion among both reformers and reform skeptics ensures that neither's vision will carry the day.

For reformers, the fragility of their coalition – and the tenuousness of their hold on federal power – is quickly highlighted by the sorts of problems or governing crises they consistently face in the aftermath of momentous victories. Whether these crises are directly related to reform or not, their effect is to undercut electoral support for further change both by reenergizing die-hard opponents of the initial reforms *and* by creating dissatisfaction and division within the reform coalition itself.

Not surprisingly, then, governing crises directly related to prior reforms – such as the persistence of southern civil disorder in the post-Reconstruction era, the sit-down strikes of 1937, or the urban riots of the 1960s – consistently arise after enactment. These events profoundly intrude on reform politics at the federal level. The repeated appearance of crises in postreform periods suggests that there is a structural dynamic at work in prompting them. These episodes were in great part the result of reform proponents and reform skeptics – both within formal, institutional venues and outside of them – articulating and fighting over distinctive visions of the meaning of recent enactments. That these events ultimately carried negative consequences for reformers in Congress suggests that there is often a steep, deferred price for achieving monumental legislative success.

Unrelated governing crises – such as economic downturns – are also a seemingly unavoidable consequence of reform. The repeated mention of the Panic of 1873, the Recession of 1937, or the Vietnam War in the historical literature as key events that significantly shaped the electoral fortunes of federal reform coalitions underscores the crucial point that outside events can and regularly will intrude on the ambitions of reformers.[22] Given the depth of political disagreement surrounding issues of postreform recalibration, such unrelated crises serve as framing events that provide a standard around which the dissatisfied can rally. Preexisting or emergent dissatisfaction with reform contributed to making these events actual crises of governance. Both types of governing crises highlight the difficulties of maintaining a coalition once attention shifts beyond least-common-denominator issues and indicate that fissures within the reform coalition, at the federal level, will reliably emerge around issues that may have been previously ignored or unanticipated.

Yet governing crises do not give postreform skeptics the upper hand either. Skeptics have their own problems with which to contend. First, they have to deal with the undisputed legitimacy of reforms already in place. Second, they must also confront a reform coalition that, while lacking the cohesiveness to achieve more change, still generally retains sufficient cohesion to head off any legislative repeal of recent enactments – either by virtue of still possessing legislative majorities or by virtue of still possessing sufficient control of federal legislative veto points to prevent any kind of legislative revision. Indeed, when political coalitions come together that are able to accomplish monumental legislative achievements such as the Reconstruction Amendments, the Wagner Act, and the civil rights legislation of the 1960s, they do not disintegrate overnight. Rather, the cohesiveness created within the reform coalition in previous decades, the political momentum of recent victories, the persistence of party loyalties among voters for at least a time, and a staggered electoral calendar all ensure that while the window for change may close relatively quickly, the reform coalition will continue to hang on to at least some of the institutional levers of federal power for some time. As a result, no conservative legislative rollback of reform is likely to occur in the immediate aftermath of enactment.

---

[22] For a notable and broader discussion on the themes of contingency and the efficacy of events in American politics, see David R. Mayhew, "Wars and American Politics," *Perspectives on Politics* 3, no. 3 (September 2005): 473–93.

The outcome or condition of legislative stalemate is caused by two related factors: (1) deep unresolved ambiguities stemming from recently enacted reforms that consistently draw the attention of federal legislators, and (2) the existence of sufficient strengths and weaknesses for both reformers and skeptics such that the two constituencies check each other. This stalemate in turn opens the door for the judicial codification of emergent political trends that could not otherwise be achieved in electoral venues.

Judicial Delimitation

Several institutional and structural considerations conspire to give the Supreme Court the opportunity to issue rulings that will be the *initial statements on delimiting reform* and that will remain *free of subsequent legislative revision*. First, the kinds of reforms that prompt a transformative recalibration present pressing issues of public importance sure to gain the attention of a number of potential litigants. Second, these reforms usually implicate established rights and prerogatives, which make the Court a likely venue for redress.[23] Third, seeking judicial redress will generally require significantly fewer resources – relative to legislative efforts – for those interested in seeking a delimitation of reform. All of these considerations make it likely that the Court will engage in postreform controversies, notwithstanding the generally reactive orientation of the judiciary.

Finally, the judiciary's forays into delimiting the scope of reform ultimately have lasting effect, despite the power and influence of the elected branches, because of perhaps the most important institutional consideration here: the aforementioned condition of legislative stalemate itself. The deadlock between reformers and their opponents creates the opportunity for the Court to step into the void first and offer the earliest, definitive statements on the scope of recent reforms. So long as these judicial rulings stay within the ideological space between the reformers' position and the opposition, the rulings are sustained by the persistence of the stalemate.[24]

Delimiting judicial rulings are thus reflective of a substantive form of judicial independence. Although these rulings are certainly influenced by

---

[23] Orren and Skowronek understand the institutional orientation of the Supreme Court as being predisposed to protect "rights of record" and "existing rules and boundaries." Orren and Skowronek, *Search*, 137.

[24] Others have noted the potential for efficacious judicial actions in the context of legislative stalemate or legislative gridlock in various contexts. For brief observations on this theme, see, e.g., John Ferejohn, "Judicializing Politics, Politicizing Law," *Law & Contemporary Problems* 65, no. 3 (Summer 2002): 55, 57–61; and William N. Eskridge and John Ferejohn, "The Article I, Section 7 Game," *Georgetown Law Journal* 80, no. 3 (February 1992): 548–51 (demonstrating this point in game-theoretical terms).

political circumstances – as is always the case – their substance cannot be wholly reduced to simply judicial appointments dynamics or to the pull of broader political and social forces on judges. In the context of stalemate, it is possible to identify a substantial judicial independence.

To emphasize the primary role of the judiciary in the political processes of delimitation and recalibration is not to deny that the political branches play a role as well. Subsequent pieces of "delimiting legislation" emerged in each of my three historical cases, and indeed getting from the judiciary's delimiting of reform to new governing arrangements required further electoral developments and another round of Supreme Court activity (the construction phase in my schema). The significance of these initial, delimiting rulings nevertheless stems from the fact that they were the earliest, definitive statements of recalibration; they established formal political boundaries that proved resistant to subsequent legislative revision; and they established legal precedents for subsequent antireform legislative efforts.[25]

CONSTRUCTION: THE ARTICULATION OF NEW INSTITUTIONAL ARRANGEMENTS AND JUDICIAL AFFIRMATION

Once the judiciary has marked the boundaries of the reform, certain elements of the emerging system of governance are discernible by political actors. For example, political actors in the mid-1880s could have recognized that slavery was irreversibly dismantled and that a significant state governmental autonomy would survive the threat to federalism embodied in the Reconstruction Amendments; furthermore, they probably could have foreseen at least some degree of widespread subordination of African Americans in the South given the dominance of the Democratic Party in the southern state governments after 1877. Similarly, subsequent to judicial delimitation in the late 1930s, political actors would have recognized that the Wagner Act was firmly entrenched. They could also have easily recognized, however, that the Wagner Act would not challenge a broader array of employer prerogatives, nor would it generally shield militant unionism. Likewise, for political actors in the late 1970s, it would have been apparent that Jim Crow was permanently dismantled and that the

---

[25] I conceptualize this delimiting role of the postreform Court as a consequence of the unresolved problems likely to arise in the immediate aftermath of reform. For a discussion of those instances when Congress exercises "*deliberate* deference" to the courts in drafting vague statutory provisions, see George I. Lovell, *Legislative Deferrals: Statutory Ambiguity, Judicial Power, and American Democracy* (New York: Cambridge University Press, 2003).

constitutional equal protection attack on racial inequality would begin and end with only an assault on *formal* racial classifications in the law. "External" uncertainties had been addressed in each of these eras with delimiting judicial rulings.

Yet an additional and subsequent uncertainty also presented itself in each of these periods of transformative recalibration: even after delimitation, uncertainties still exist with respect to boundary drawing that is "internal" to the reform. Whereas delimiting rulings clarify boundaries between competing authorities and rights at the outer edges of reform, these rulings offer limited clarity on how exactly governing arrangements and competing sets of individual rights will be structured *within* the reformed policy area. Consider one example that I discuss at length in Chapter 7. After Reconstruction, the status of African American voting remained unclear during the latter decades of the nineteenth century; widespread southern electoral fraud aimed at undermining African American voting influence coexisted, for a time, with significant African American voting in some areas of the South. In addition, beyond simply the political context, C. Vann Woodward notably asserted that a degree of flux and uncertainty existed in southern race relations prior to the 1890s.[26] These adjectives are appropriate for describing northern Republican approaches toward African American rights and the South during these years as well. In the decades following Reconstruction, the possibility remained that Republicans might succeed in protecting African American voting either through federal enforcement efforts or through Republican alliances with anti-Democrat southern coalitions. In short, the judicial reassertion of federalism had not definitively established the contours of southern race relations in the post-Reconstruction era.

The scope of such internal uncertainties over authority and rights is never infinite. Given prior delimiting rulings by the Court, the conservative character of the postreform system of governance was already significantly determined before the construction phase began in each of these three periods of recalibration. Still, even if significant elements of the new order were entrenched by delimiting rulings, more subdued – although tremendously significant – uncertainties remained. A lasting recalibration of the competing authorities and competing sets of rights internal to the domain of reform had to occur before a new political order could be established.

During construction, there is, as indicated by Table 1.5, first (a) the gradual emergence of a new, formal system of governance, as other

---

[26] C. Vann Woodward, *The Strange Career of Jim Crow: A Commemorative Edition* (New York: Oxford University Press, 2002).

TABLE 1.5 *Recalibration Part II: The Political Process of Construction*

(3) Construction	Resolves "Internal" Uncertainties
Political Process	(3a) Various institutional entities articulate new governing arrangements. (3b) Conclusive entrenchment provided by the Supreme Court.

institutional entities follow up on the Court's actions and articulate new arrangements, which is then followed by (b) affirmation and conclusive entrenchment of the new governing order with Supreme Court rulings. With respect to part (a), if the processes of delimitation follow a fairly uniform course, it is difficult to discern a uniformity across the case studies in how internal uncertainties are resolved. All of my case studies exhibit a commonality of *result*, as each traces the rise and entrenchment of a new system of political and social relations to govern the interactions of the "newly emancipated" – that is, African Americans in post-Reconstruction, labor in the aftermath of the New Deal, and African Americans again in the aftermath of the civil rights era – with other social groups, and with the state, in the aftermath of reform. With respect to how and where the governing arrangements of the new order first appeared, however, a diverse cast of institutions have played the crucial role of being the first to articulate the new orthodoxy. The laws of Jim Crow were the creation of state legislatures (in the South), the rise of voluntary arbitration and industrial pluralism can be traced to the actions of the National War Labor Board in the early 1940s, and the dominance of the anticlassification principle in constitutional racial equality can be traced to the Supreme Court's energetic opposition to affirmative action.

But this result is not surprising. In each historical era, distinct and sometimes unique political circumstances conspired to allow certain institutional bodies to take the lead in articulating the terms of the new order. The creation of Jim Crow in the southern state legislatures could only have taken place during a time when states possessed a consequential autonomy on racial matters; the creation and existence of a National War Labor Board was tied to the occurrence of World War II; and the Supreme Court's vigorous opposition to affirmative action could only have occurred in a time of judicial assertiveness, with a prominent conservative presence on the Court. The one common procedural thread that ties all three of these historical cases together, however, is with respect

The Theory and Political Processes of Recalibration 37

FIGURE 1.3. A stable political order (prior to reform).

to part (b): the entrenchment of the new order was signaled in each case by *judicial affirmation*. With its blessing of these new orders in *Plessy v. Ferguson*,[27] *Williams v. Mississippi*,[28] the *Steelworkers Trilogy*,[29] *City of Richmond v. J. A. Croson Co.*,[30] and *Adarand Constructors, Inc. v. Pena*,[31] the Court concluded recalibration for each set of prior reforms.

Overview of the Processes of Transformative Recalibration

To take stock of the political processes of recalibration in their entirety, the metaphor that emerges is not one of political-change-as-critical-juncture, or political-change-as-higher-lawmaking nor is it one of political development as positive feedback. Rather, what emerges is a view of political transformation as a form of *contained destruction*.

In line with Orren and Skowronek's claims on the plenary state of authority, think of a mature political order, with its array of authority and rights relationships, as akin to a street grid (Figure 1.3).[32]

---

[27] 163 U.S. 537 (1896).
[28] 170 U.S. 213 (1898).
[29] *United Steelworkers of America v. American Manufacturing Co.*, 363 U.S. 564 (1960); *United Steelworkers of America v. Enterprise Wheel & Car Corp.*, 363 U.S. 593 (1960); *United Steelworkers of America v. Warrior & Gulf Navigation Co.*, 363 U.S. 574 (1960).
[30] 488 U.S. 469 (1989).
[31] 515 U.S. 200 (1995).
[32] See Orren and Skowronek, *Search*, 22–23.

FIGURE 1.4. Open-ended reform with uncertain boundaries both internal and external.

The semiorganized, semichaotic structure of streets in this grid represents the complicated boundaries and accommodations created between various competing authority and rights relationships in any given political order. Figure 1.4 represents what occurs when open-ended reforms unleash instability within this very intricate context.

These open-ended reforms, by their very logic, seem almost viral in their broad applicability and potential disruption to areas of the grid beyond the epicenter of change. Indeed, it is precisely this broad, potential applicability of the reform that feeds the heady aspiration of many reformers earlier on. However, in light of this threat, recalibration

FIGURE 1.5. Delimitation clarifies external uncertainties.

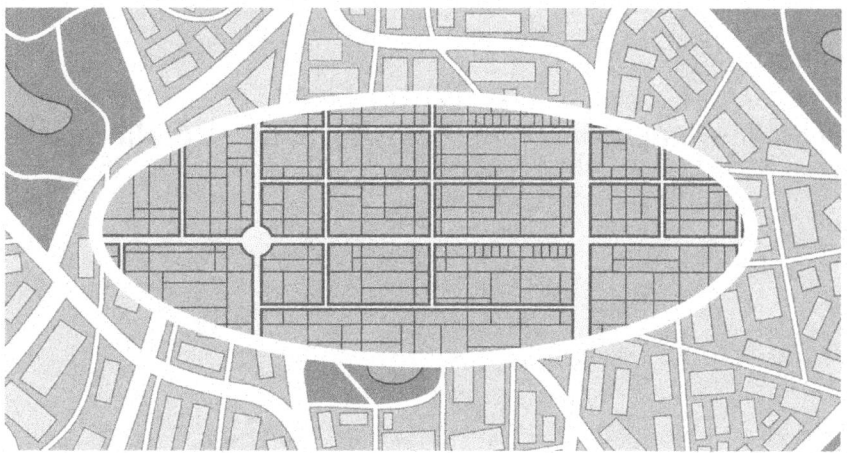

FIGURE 1.6. Construction clarifies internal uncertainties.

processes respond by first containing the instability – during *delimitation* (Figure 1.5).

Finally, during *construction* (Figure 1.6), a new coherent structure emerges and crystallizes within the policy domain that has been transformed.

The new order assumes a different form compared to what previously existed in that space. Furthermore, even while the new order has been reconciled with those portions of the grid that have remained resilient, the organizational logic within the circle – the logic structuring the authority and rights relationships that have emerged after reform – is clearly different from the logic structuring the resilient portions of the grid.

2

The Supreme Court and Transformative Recalibration

The discussion in Chapter 1 of transformative recalibration hints at another noteworthy pattern in American history that merits close examination in its own right. Specifically, the Supreme Court's role as a *delimiter* of reform and its role as an *affirmer* of the new governing order indicate that the Court plays crucial and distinct roles that recur across the case studies. This finding immediately begs two larger questions that are the focus of this chapter. First, what motives account for this pattern in judicial behavior? Even if the Court enjoys opportunities to delimit and affirm, why has it consistently chosen to do so? Second, a question remains as to the nature of the Court's relationship to the broader political system. Do these recurrent judicial rulings reflect the Court "driving" the political development of recalibration, or is the broader political system driving the judiciary's actions?

CLAIM 3: THE SUPREME COURT, MODES OF ADJUDICATION, AND TRANSFORMATIVE RECALIBRATION

My third primary claim is that *in the context of transformative recalibrations, the Supreme Court possesses an institutional interest in promoting stability* (Claim 3). In the aftermath of these types of open-ended reforms, the Court is institutionally and peculiarly inclined to stabilize, clarify, protect, and police the boundaries between distinct institutional authorities – whether between federal, state, and local authority in the 1870s and the 1970s, between judicial and nonjudicial institutions in the 1970s, or between congressional authority and employer prerogatives in the 1930s. Likewise, it is inclined to demarcate and stabilize the boundaries between competing sets of rights directly affected by reform – such as the rights of southern whites versus the newly created rights of the freedmen, employer rights versus union/employee rights, or the rights of segregationists versus those of integrationists. This stabilizing judicial impulse contrasts with the more destabilizing politics of the preceding years, and when subject to the political conditions of postreform periods, it gives rise to two distinct types of judicial action.

First, and most relevant for this book, a judicial interest in stability supplies the necessary motive for the Supreme Court's actions during recalibration in issuing delimiting and order-affirming rulings. These rulings demarcate the outer boundaries of reform, and they structure authority and rights relationships within the area of reform. That said, a theory of judicial-institutional interest in stability is *not* simply a theory of judicial conservatism and antipathy to change. Indeed, the task of promoting stability demands not just that the Court establish the outer limits of reform but also that it police against flagrant attacks on the core principles of recent transformative reforms. In order for the boundaries between reformed and resilient institutions to stabilize, the integrity of portions of both old and new must be maintained. Thus when legal controversies encompass direct challenges to the core principles of recent reforms, the judicial interest in stability presses the Court to engage in a second kind of action during these postreform periods: acting to vigorously *defend* core reform principles. Indeed, we see such actions from the Court during periods of transformative recalibration.[1]

The judiciary's preference for stability is the by-product of its peculiar commitment to basic legality values of notice, settlement, and predictability in the law when placed against the backdrop of transformative recalibration.[2] During certain postreform periods, heightened uncertainties

---

[1] Particularly notable examples of such rulings are *Strauder v. West Virginia*, 100 U.S. 303 (1880) in the post-Reconstruction context, and *Green v. County School Board*, 391 U.S. 430 (1968), *Swann v. Charlotte-Mecklenburg Board of Education*, 402 U.S. 1 (1971), and *Keyes v. School District No. 1*, 413 U.S. 189 (1973) in the post–*Brown v. Board of Education* school desegregation context. Similarly, Dubofsky discusses the Court's vigorous defense of the NLRB in the late 1930s and early 1940s – a period during which the Court was also engaged in delimitation. Melvyn Dubofsky, *The State & Labor in Modern America* (Chapel Hill: University of North Carolina Press, 1994), 164–66. In all of these cases, the problems presented were *not* problems of recalibration, for which the boundaries between distinct governing authorities and distinct sets of rights were problematized by the extensions of open-ended reforms. Rather, the problems presented in these cases concerned attacks on the core principles of recent reforms.

[2] My claim converges to a degree with the familiar Tocquevillian claim about the inherent conservatism of the American legal profession. Alexis de Tocqueville, *Democracy in America*, ed. J. P. Mayer, trans. George Lawrence (New York: Harper Perennial, 1988),

exist over how authority will be allocated and how clashing rights will be reconciled once crucial aspects of the old order have been removed. Furthermore, these postreform uncertainties are presented to the Court in a particularly urgent manner, since they assume the form of adjudication, with discrete, competing parties voicing claims grounded in the new authority of reform, *and* in resilient authorities and rights that predate the reform. Controversies over the scope of clashing authorities and rights are put into stark relief in the judicial arena, as judges are forced to directly confront questions such as "what remains of federalism after Reconstruction?" – questions that, although perhaps pondered in the abstract during the moment of reform, can no longer be avoided in the aftermath.

Against the backdrop of transformative recalibration, the judicial commitment to legality values manifests as a predominant motive to reconcile these clashing authorities and rights. The Court's own institutional orientation demands that it do nothing less than recognize the plausibility of legal claims grounded in older, resilient authorities and rights, even if it may not always find those claims legitimate. At the same time, judicial recognition of the legitimacy of recent reforms requires the Court to concede the legitimacy of new legal claims as well. The judicial impulse to uphold legality values and decisively settle uncertainties, to set clear rules to guide citizen conduct and lower court adjudication, and to try to maintain the integrity and rationality of the relevant laws tends to press the Court to issue stabilizing rulings.[3]

Thus, Supreme Court justices in a moment of transformative recalibration are not led to promote stability simply for stability's sake. Rather,

---

264–65, 268–69. Among other things, Tocqueville attributed the conservative bent of American lawyers to their cultural predisposition to "order" and legality values. Ibid., 266–67. Yet, there are conspicuous instances in American history where the judiciary pressed in destabilizing and transformative directions. These latter examples suggest that, although he offers his own qualifications, ibid., 264, 265, Tocqueville's claim may be an overstatement. These examples also press me to limit my present claims on the judiciary's stability-inclinations to the peculiar context of transformative recalibration. Relatedly, Alexander and Schauer discuss the "settlement function of law" in the context of their normative defense of judicial interpretive supremacy. Larry Alexander and Frederick Schauer, "On Extrajudicial Constitutional Interpretation," *Harvard Law Review* 110, no. 7 (May 1997): 1371–72, 1377.

[3] In periods of *judicial dismantling* and reform, as with the Warren Court and *Brown*, it is possible for these kinds of uncertainties to be obscured or temporarily ignored due to judicial self-confidence in engineering change or to willful judicial ignorance and overconfidence that postreform adjustments might be largely seamless. See Michael J. Klarman, *From Jim Crow to Civil Rights: The Supreme Court and the Struggle for Racial Equality* (New York: Oxford University Press, 2004), 315–16. In the postreform context, however, the necessity for boundary drawing stares justices in the face in the form of concrete disputes; the gritty work of recalibration precludes wishful thinking.

the judiciary promotes stability only indirectly. During these moments, judges are merely applying conventional legality values – as they often do – against the backdrop of a very distinctive political context. This interaction between legality and context produces the distinctive set of judicial rulings that ultimately stabilize authority and rights relations. The judicial concern with stability during these particular moments stems from how judicial adherence to legality values demands particular kinds of judicial actions.

For this reason, no deep judicial self-consciousness of transformative recalibration – and all its deeper implications – emerges in the judicial recalibrating opinions examined in this book. In line with what we might expect of judicial actors living in the moment, pushed by the demands of discrete cases, and lacking the time to discern deeper political dynamics and processes, judges simply respond to issues with the kind of legality-promoting mindset that they might possess in any other context. Some sense of the larger political issues at stake certainly does arise in these recalibrating judicial rulings. Judges may be aware of the political problems of recalibration posed by specific issues. They may be aware of how their rulings might aid in the construction of durable governing arrangements in the aftermath of reform, and they may sense how their failure to demarcate clear, legal boundaries may lead to further uncertainty and conflict between competing authorities and between competing rights-holders. Indeed, a judicial concern with stability and boundary drawing in this basic sense is present in all of the cases that I examine. Yet because the judicial interest in stability is the result of conventional judicial values interacting with an unconventional political context, the judicial concern with stability – and the structural role of this concern in driving the codification and some of the results of transformative recalibration – emerges most powerfully with the benefit of a retrospective examination of multiple historical case studies.

Situating Judicial-Institutional Interests in Relation to Other Influences on Judicial Behavior

In some respects, the image of the Court that emerges from this argument supports some familiar and influential theories of judicial behavior and legal change.[4] One could plausibly view the Court's support for

---

[4] A valuable and more extensive survey of work on judicial behavior is Barry Friedman, "The Politics of Judicial Review," *Texas Law Review* 84, no. 2 (December 2005): 257–337.

core reform principles during episodes of recalibration as evidence of judicial actors behaving consistently with the political forces behind their prior appointment. A theorist of judicial behavior who focused on the appointments mechanism[5] would likely note, for example, that the post-Reconstruction Court was composed of almost all Republican presidential appointees. Further, he or she would accurately note that this Court, during post-Reconstruction recalibration, never challenged the core reform of the Republican political coalition, which was the abolition of slavery.

Similarly, the preceding discussion of transformative recalibration and the Court emphasizes how the desire to solve discrete problems of governance against a backdrop of legislative stalemate drives the Court's behavior. This assertion plausibly resonates with themes and ideas present in the work of judicial behavior scholars from a rational-choice institutionalist perspective, who conceptualize judicial actors as primarily seekers of policy goals but who also emphasize the strategic aspects of judicial behavior and how these preferences may be mediated and altered by constraints either external to a court (e.g., congressional or presidential preferences) or internal to a court (e.g., the distribution of judges' preferences on a given policy issue across a court).[6] My argument also builds on the work of regime scholars, who emphasize how changes in regime politics prompt shifts in judicial behavior,[7] and how the Court's actions may often respond to the interests and needs of the dominant

---

[5] Robert A. Dahl, "Decision-Making in a Democracy: The Supreme Court as a National Policy-Maker," *Journal of Public Law* 6, no. 2 (Fall 1957): 285; Jack M. Balkin and Sanford Levinson, "Understanding the Constitutional Revolution," *Virginia Law Review* 87, no. 6 (October 2001): 1045–1104 (see especially, 1064–66). See also Jack M. Balkin and Sanford Levinson, "The Processes of Constitutional Change: From Partisan Entrenchment to the National Surveillance State," *Fordham Law Review* 75, no. 2 (November 2006): 490–93.

[6] Lee Epstein and Jack Knight, *The Choices Justices Make* (Washington DC: C. Q. Press, 1998); William N. Eskridge and Philip P. Frickey, "Foreword: Law as Equilibrium," *Harvard Law Review* 108, no. 1 (November 1994): 26–108 (asserting a positive theory of "law as equilibrium," in which judicial outcomes tend to track the equilibrium of interests between the three branches of the federal government). See also Keith E. Whittington, "Once More Unto the Breach: PostBehavioralist Approaches to Judicial Politics," *Law & Social Inquiry* 25, no. 2 (Spring 2000): 601–34 (reviewing Cornell W. Clayton and Howard Gillman eds., *Supreme Court Decision-Making: New Institutionalist Approaches* [Chicago: University of Chicago Press, 1999] and Howard Gillman and Cornell W. Clayton eds., *The Supreme Court in American Politics: New Institutionalist Interpretations* [Lawrence: University Press of Kansas, 1999]).

[7] Bruce Ackerman, *We the People*, vol. 1, *Foundations* (Cambridge, MA: Harvard University Press, 1991); Bruce Ackerman, *We the People*, vol. 2, *Transformations* (Cambridge, MA: Harvard University Press, 1998). Some elements of Ackerman's theory align with

governing regime.⁸ Finally, my argument that the Court creates politically significant baselines within the boundaries set by external political forces also resonates, to an extent, with political-cultural theorists of judicial behavior who seek to explain how shifts in judicial values and behavior are prompted by more diffuse social or political-cultural mechanisms – as opposed to more clearly defined institutional mechanisms such as the appointments mechanism or interbranch dialogues.⁹

Although all of these perspectives on judicial behavior are valuable, insofar as one's focus remains with explicating judicial behavior during transformative recalibrations, elements of these theories may often be unhelpful and, at times, irrelevant. Consider that these conventional theories of judicial behavior enjoy their greatest explanatory value when broader political, institutional, and social forces can be clearly delineated, and when the links can be cleanly drawn between those forces and the judicial approval or disapproval of a challenged action. A focus on societal, institutional, and political constraints on judicial behavior could allow one to make convincing claims that those forces allowed for a given practice to be approved or virtually demanded that a given practice be

---

the appointments thesis. See Bruce A. Ackerman, "Transformative Appointments," *Harvard Law Review* 101, no. 6 (April 1988): 1164–84. Yet, as I understand his work, the appointments mechanism is just one component of a larger and more complex higher lawmaking process that is, for him, the more crucial determinant in shifting judicial behavior and legal doctrine.

⁸ Mark A. Graber, "The Nonmajoritarian Difficulty: Legislative Deference to the Judiciary," *Studies in American Political Development* 7 (Spring 1993): 35–73; Keith E. Whittington, "'Interpose Your Friendly Hand': Political Supports for the Exercise of Judicial Review by the United States Supreme Court," *American Political Science Review* 99, no. 4 (November 2005): 583–96.

⁹ Klarman, *Jim Crow*, 4–6, 448–54; Reva B. Siegel, "Constitutional Culture, Social Movement Conflict and Constitutional Change: The Case of the de facto ERA," *California Law Review* 94, no. 5 (October 2006): 1323–31, 1362–66, 1406–09. Klarman qualifies his thesis by asserting that when text, original intent, and precedent are clear, judges will tend to follow them. However, he asserts that political-cultural forces largely drive constitutional interpretation because real legal clarity will usually be absent here. Klarman, *Jim Crow*, 5–6. In the context of heightened political and legal uncertainty during recalibration periods, Klarman's theory would thus clearly suggest the primacy of political-cultural forces in explaining judicial rulings. Other works within this genre include, e.g., Neal Devins, "Explaining *Grutter v. Bollinger*," *University of Pennsylvania Law Review* 152, no. 1 (November 2003): 347–83; Lucas A. Powe, Jr., *The Warren Court and American Politics* (Cambridge, MA: Harvard University Press, 2000), 485–501; Steven M. Teles, *The Rise of the Conservative Legal Movement* (Princeton, NJ: Princeton University Press, 2008); Mark Tushnet, "The Supreme Court and the National Political Order: Collaboration and Confrontation," in *The Supreme Court & American Political Development*, ed. Ronald Kahn and Ken I. Kersch (Lawrence: University Press of Kansas, 2006), 117–37 (Tushnet's theory of a "collaborative Court" might also be categorized as a variant of an appointments theory of judicial behavior).

repudiated by the Supreme Court. Indeed, these sorts of accounts have been put forth about several of the cases I mention in later chapters.

But assume that broader political, institutional, and social forces cannot be so easily delineated; assume, as will commonly be the case in the aftermath of major reforms, that there may be a continuing flux and ambiguity with respect to where the preponderance of public opinion lies on an issue or with respect to how severe certain institutional constraints may be on Supreme Court justices. Furthermore, assume that the links between external forces – that is, political, institutional, and social forces – and the supposed corresponding shift in judicial behavior are *not* so clear; perhaps the length of time between event and changed judicial behavior is somewhat longer, or perhaps the Court's behavior shifts only in certain respects and not in others. Finally, and most importantly, assume that the judicial behavioral question being examined goes beyond whether a Court merely said yes or no in a given dispute. Rather, assume that one is trying to understand or explain the court's use of distinctive modes of adjudication – in other words, *how* it said yes or no in specific cases. In all of these situations, the value of these conventional approaches to explaining shifts in judicial behavior is likely to be qualified. If, for example, one succeeded in demonstrating how appointments, politics, or cultural forces led the Supreme Court to say yes rather than no in a given case, it could remain a separate and difficult task for one to demonstrate that those same forces also dictated the Court's choice of one *form* of judicial approval, or rejection, over another.

Explaining judicial behavior during these periods of transformative recalibration demands, in part, illumination of why judges may pursue one from among several courses of action permitted by the larger political and social context. It is within this analytical gap that a focus on the judicial role and judicial-institutional interests is helpful.[10] Judicial delimiting and order-affirming rulings are, of course, politically conditioned. It is,

---

[10] Others have emphasized how peculiar judicial goals and practices influence and shape the preferences and interests of judicial actors. The key work in this regard is Rogers M. Smith, "Political Jurisprudence, the 'New Institutionalism,' and the Future of Public Law," *American Political Science Review* 82, no. 1 (March 1988): 89–108. See also, Howard Gillman, "The Court as an Idea, Not a Building (or a Game): Interpretative Institutionalism and the Analysis of Supreme Court Decision-Making," in Clayton and Gillman, *Supreme Court Decision-Making*, 65–87; John Brigham, "The Constitution of the Supreme Court," in Gillman and Clayton, *The Supreme Court in American Politics*, 15–27. For valuable surveys of a number of historical-institutionalist approaches to the study of law and courts, beyond the present focus on distinctive judicial-institutional interests, see Clayton and Gillman, *Supreme Court Decision-Making*; Gillman and Clayton, *The Supreme Court in American Politics*; and Kahn and Kersch, *The Supreme Court and American Political Development*.

however, the distinctive judicial-institutional sense of a role or duty to promote legality values during these periods of heightened uncertainty, after reforms are enacted, that gives rise to the stabilizing impulse and to particular modes of adjudication.

The focus on judicial-institutional interests is not meant to minimize the explanatory value of the other theories of judicial behavior. Indeed, as the case studies themselves will demonstrate, it is the juxtaposition of the judicial interest in stability *alongside* other determinants of judicial behavior that ultimately gives rise to delimiting and order-affirming rulings that can be nonunanimous among the justices, or even closely divided and contentious. Further, I make no claim that the judicial-institutional interest in stability, by itself, will lead the Court to ignore clear, decisive, and powerful political and social forces pressing for *destabilizing* legal and political orders.

My assertion is merely that a focus on judicial-institutional interests provides the strongest explanatory thread for recalibrating judicial behavior across the case studies. Further, I would expand on Claim 3 and make this additional subsidiary claim: *the judicial inclination toward stability becomes relatively more significant in explaining judicial actions when external constraints on the Court are weaker* (Claim 3.1).

Consider that in the immediate aftermath of reform, external constraints will consistently be looser. Social and political pressures will be particularly in flux and may not offer any clear indication of where public or elite opinion lies with respect to the primary problems of postreform recalibration. Furthermore, the political pressures exerted through the appointments mechanism may also be weak: the new reform coalition may lack sufficient internal consensus or may simply fail to anticipate the problems of postreform recalibration in their appointments considerations. Additionally, the reform coalition may not have had sufficient time and opportunity to make the necessary appointments to the Court for reshaping the latter's ideological composition. In the immediate postreform context, the weakness of external constraints on the Court may allow for greater judicial independence and, correspondingly, may also allow for the judicial interest in stability to be more efficacious in shaping legal development. The Court's concern with stability may, at these times, dictate both the judicial outcome *and* the mode of adjudication. That is, the judicial-institutional interest in stability has a relatively greater role in dictating the nature of judicial delimiting rulings.

In those circumstances further removed from the moment of reform, however, constraints on the Court may be more efficacious. Social and political fault lines may have hardened. The reform coalition may have had sufficient time to reach preliminary conclusions on the problems of postreform recalibration, and furthermore, it may have had the opportunity to make significant additions to the Court to reflect party sentiment. During these times, the Court may enjoy a more limited range of options, and, as a result, the judicial interest in stability may be of lesser importance in explaining judicial behavior compared to external forces. In these latter instances, the judicial-institutional interest in stability may still be responsible for dictating the mode of adjudication chosen by the Court; it may not, however, necessarily dictate the judicial outcome. That is, the judicial-institutional interest in stability in and of itself has a relatively less significant role in explaining the various facets of order-affirming rulings; external constraints on judicial behavior are more significant in this context.

Modes of Adjudication

As implied by the preceding discussion, political conditions are *not* static during postreform periods. As these conditions change, the Supreme Court's actions will predictably change as well. One of the main tasks of this chapter, then, is to link the claim on judicial behavior (Claim 3) with the claim on the processes of transformative recalibration (Claim 2) toward identifying and explicating distinctive *modes of Supreme Court adjudication*.

Delimiting Judicial Rulings

Constraints on the Court are loosest in the immediate aftermath of reform, with recent political disruptions still fresh in the mind of the polity. In response to the peculiar uncertainties of external boundary drawing, a Court inclined to promote a goal of stability can be expected to engage in rulings that definitively articulate and demarcate the outer limits of the change effectuated by recent reforms. Delimiting rulings serve this function in offering clear, bright-line determinations about when and

TABLE 2.1 *Recalibration Part I: Delimiting Mode of Adjudication*

(2) Delimitation	Resolves "External" Uncertainties
Political Process	(2a) Legislative stalemate
	(2b) Delimitation by the Supreme Court
Mode of Adjudication	Delimiting rulings

where reform principles must give way to separate, preexisting authorities and rights. As a result, when legal controversies probe the outer limits of reform, the judicial impulse toward stability and promoting legality values presses the Court to issue rulings that look stingy and restrictive to reformers with more expansive ambitions for change.

There is also a notable recurring pattern in the *substantive justifications* for delimitation offered by the Court. When judicial delimitation occurs, the Supreme Court has followed a historical pattern of "indirect opposition."[11] It has justified its delimitation of reform *not* by frontally challenging the core achievements of dismantling reforms but rather by emphasizing the continuing legitimacy of separate yet resilient authorities that might be threatened if reform principles are not reined in. Hence a pattern emerges in the Supreme Court's delimiting opinions where it justifies its actions by emphasizing the serious threat of allowing reform principles to spread farther and farther into the polity, potentially resulting in the destruction of other institutional authorities and rights that retain considerable legitimacy. A slippery-slope rationale prominently underlies many of these judicial delimiting rulings, and the Court has often lifted its "indirect" justifications for delimitation straight from the legal briefs of postreform skeptics.

Order-Affirming Rulings

The common dilemma faced by the Supreme Court in periods of construction is an uncertainty regarding boundary drawing between competing sets of governing authorities and competing rights internal to the domain of reform. In response to this form of uncertainty, a Court inclined to promote stability would look with favor upon a mode of adjudication that offered a definitive resolution of these questions. Indeed, this is precisely what order-affirming rulings accomplish: the effect of these rulings, when

---

[11] Reva Siegel has discussed the morphing of reform opposition into new forms, after a reform has occurred, in the context of race and gender hierarchies. Reva B. Siegel, "Why Equal Protection No Longer Protects: The Evolving Forms of Status-Enforcing State Action," *Stanford Law Review* 49, no. 5 (May 1997): 1111–48. Also somewhat relevant to this discussion is Ken Kersch's argument about how the Supreme Court reasserted pre–New Deal Era legal concepts and ideals in the aftermath of the Wagner Act within certain areas of labor law. Ken I. Kersch, "The New Deal Triumph as the End of History? The Judicial Negotiation of Labor Rights and Civil Rights," in Kahn and Kersch, *The Supreme Court and American Political Development*, 169–226. Finally, Vesla Weaver's discussion of "frontlash" in the context of mid-twentieth century crime policy is relevant here. Vesla A. Weaver, "Frontlash: Race and the Development of Punitive Crime Policy," *Studies in American Political Development* 21 (Fall 2007): 230–65.

50   *Recalibrating Reform*

TABLE 2.2 *Recalibration Part II: Order-Affirming Mode of Adjudication*

(3) Construction	Resolves "Internal" Uncertainties
Political Process	(3a) Various institutional entities follow up on the Court's delimiting actions and articulate new governing arrangements
	(3b) Conclusive entrenchment of the new ordering is provided by the Supreme Court
Mode of Adjudication	Order-affirming rulings

they build on delimiting rulings, is to usher in fully formed, definitive, governing principles that will define the new postreform order. Functionally, then, these rulings bring to a close the larger process of clarifying the boundaries between the significant competing authorities and rights that had been implicated and disrupted by reform. For this reason, they are textually distinctive in the definitive, principled nature of their conclusions, which articulate the foundational legal doctrines of the new order.

None of this, however, is to claim that new political orders are ever wholly the product of judicial will. When one considers the case of Jim Crow, for example, this system of governance became entrenched only because there was sufficient convergence of opinion among the federal judiciary, the federal elected branches, and the southern state governments. Especially when compared to its role during *delimitation*, there is a relative modesty to the Court's role or function during this stage of construction. Rather than consistently taking the lead during construction, we find the Court sometimes following up behind other institutions in affirming their actions. This relative modesty of the Court's role, in turn, reflects the reassertion of external constraints on the judiciary during such times, as social, political, and cultural forces became increasingly potent following the moment of reform.

Yet the preceding qualification should not be overstated either. The Court and its order-affirming rulings play one crucial role in this stage of recalibration by offering the benefit of constitutional legitimacy to emerging political orders. Although the permanence of any judicial ruling is always dependent on surrounding political circumstances, a conclusive judicial approval for an emerging set of governing arrangements reduces the scope of future political contestation; if the court is not on board with a proposed resolution of internal boundary disputes, conflicts can be expected to continue in the form of adjudication over

TABLE 2.3 *Tension-Managing Rulings During Periods of Political Order*

(4) Reconstructed Governance	Creation and Maintenance of Political Order
Mode of Adjudication	Tension-managing rulings

fundamental uncertainties – with the attainment of order thereby prolonged. The Court's definitive approval of some set of governing arrangements can, however, bring to an end more fundamental, lingering questions. If any new governing arrangements are to be entrenched in the aftermath of open-ended reforms, the processes of entrenchment and governance construction will run through the Court. Furthermore, in order for those processes to culminate in the codification and entrenchment of a new legal order, the Court must not only legitimize new governing arrangements; more than this, it must legitimize them in a broad, principled manner that puts lingering uncertainties to rest.

Highlighting this distinctive role of the Court in providing the capstone on governance construction similarly puts into focus the crucial role that judicial-institutional interests play during this stage of political transformation. Although external constraints on the Court may largely dictate the outcome of order-affirming judicial rulings, it is the judicial commitment to stability that prompts the decisive and emphatic affirmation of new governing arrangements contained within such rulings.

Order-Maintenance and Tension-Managing Judicial Rulings
Even if external and internal boundary disputes may be resolved with delimiting and order-affirming rulings, new uncertainties may nevertheless arise in subsequent years. Political conditions, values, and judicial commitments may change. When such changes occur, new "boundary tensions" may arise as conflicts and concerns materialize with respect to the integrity and coherence of the newly entrenched boundaries between competing rights and authorities. Indeed, sometimes these boundary tensions will emanate from the judiciary's own inclination to endorse certain values and legal outcomes that sit in tension with either postrecalibration governing principles or with other facets of the broader political status quo.

When this occurs, the Court may find itself pulled in opposite directions. Its legal and political predispositions may push it to disrupt entrenched boundaries established during recalibration. At the same time, it will also evidence a concern for preserving the fundamental integrity of those boundaries, which constitute a broader governing structure that the Court itself previously had been pivotal in constructing. A Supreme Court inclined to maintain stability and to preserve entrenched boundaries, in the face of this more common form of uncertainty, will engage in "tension-managing rulings." In these rulings, as we will see, the Court bends the established foundational doctrines of the postrecalibration governing order in creative and even disingenuous ways in order to accommodate incongruous values *within* that structure. The effect of these rulings is to preserve order and manage tensions, while also sacrificing conceptual purity.

The textual distinctiveness of tension-managing rulings is apparent when contrasted with the characteristics of delimiting and order-affirming rulings. The latter two modes of adjudication are distinctive for their definitive and even principled conclusions. In its tension-managing rulings, however, the Court articulates vague – and sometimes conceptually incoherent – judicial rulings that compromise and cut against the core governing principles of the reigning political order, while emphasizing continuity with that order. Tension-management is thus the best description of notable cases such as *Buchanan v. Warley*,[12] *Vaca v. Sipes*,[13] and *Grutter v. Bollinger*.[14] And although efficacious external constraints undoubtedly influenced the compromise-oriented outcomes reached in these cases, I discuss in Chapter 10 how a focus on judicial-institutional interests in stability may explain the peculiar *form of compromise* chosen by the Court. Indeed, the political significance of these tension-managing rulings stems precisely from the fact that so long as the Court's ruling stays within the constraints imposed by external forces, its choice of the terms of compromise will very likely persist.

Having articulated the broad outlines of this schema of recurrent Supreme Court modes of adjudication, let me conclude this section with the qualification that it should not be taken in an overly rigid or mechanistic way. Although I categorize a number of Supreme Court opinions as delimiting, order-affirming, or tension-managing in subsequent chapters, this is not to implicitly dismiss other plausible points of emphasis in these same opinions or to suggest that Supreme Court justices self-consciously set out to issue opinions in accordance with this schema. Indeed, a number of factors likely preclude such neat simplicity. Among other

---

[12] 245 U.S. 60 (1917).
[13] 386 U.S. 171 (1967).
[14] 539 U.S. 306 (2003).

things, the Court's reactive posture makes its adjudications dependent on the issues presented to it and the issues that happen to be dominant at a given moment in time. Further, the manner in which the Court will decide a given controversy will no doubt be affected by how much precedent may or may not exist on the particular issues presented to the Court. Finally, given the fact that the justices themselves will not be deeply self-conscious about underlying processes of recalibration for reasons noted earlier, we might expect a degree of variability in how delimiting, order-affirming, and tension-managing themes are presented in the Court's rulings. For example, delimiting rulings may also contain powerful elaborations on some elements of reform, or tension-managing rulings may function to expand on the scope of dominant governing principles.

Thus, I do not claim that my schema is the only plausible way to categorize and describe the cases I examine. The significance of a given judicial delimiting statement, for example, may only become apparent with the passage of time and with a heightened focus on specific questions. At a bare minimum, I offer one plausible way of retrospectively evaluating these cases. The analytical thread of continuity running through these expected variations and nuances in the case law encompasses three elements: (1) the recurrent presence, within the background political context, of very particular unresolved questions over boundary drawing; (2) the Court's repeated use of a distinctive set and sequence of adjudicative resolutions (thematically related by the goal of stability promotion) in response to those questions; and (3) a subsequent political reception of those adjudicative-resolutions hospitable enough to ensure that the latter are not subsequently and decisively overturned by nonjudicial actors.

Beyond that, the conceivable applicability of my framework for three distinct historical eras further suggests that the political dynamics and the specific types of judicial resolutions that I focus on do constitute a set of ideas, concerns, and political conflicts that are concomitant with the postreform political context. Notwithstanding any number of other elements or points of emphases that one might plausibly focus on in the cases that I examine, my schema provides one manner to retrospectively evaluate this broad and varied set of judicial opinions.

CLAIM 4: THE SUPREME COURT AND THE POLITICAL SYSTEM DURING TRANSFORMATIVE RECALIBRATION

The question naturally arises as to what these distinctive modes of adjudication imply for the Court's relationship to the broader political system:

What exactly is the nature of the Court's role in shaping recalibration? This leads to the fourth and final claim of this book: *while the rulings produced by the Supreme Court during a period of transformative recalibration codify and crystallize emergent political developments, these rulings are not a but-for cause of the recalibration* (Claim 4). That is, the Court assumes the lead in formally demarcating the limits of postreform governance during these periods; this constitutes a noteworthy role for the Court in shaping political development. But the Court is not the singular driver of events. It is neither the sole causal force of transformative recalibration nor merely the passive instrument of electoral and political forces. The following sections thus seek to flesh out *both* the judiciary's efficacy and those elements that constrain it during periods of transformative recalibration.

Judicial Efficacy

The political significance of the processes of transformative recalibration stems from one simple fact: these processes produce the first, formal markers of postreform governance. These processes produce declarative boundary-drawing statements that are not merely informal or unstated understandings but instead are markers of governance endowed with the force and legitimacy of law. Given this, the political significance of the Court during these historical periods is also apparent: the Court plays a central role in these political processes, and its rulings during a transformative recalibration constitute the first, formal articulation or codification of new postreform boundaries between competing governing authorities and individual rights. For example, scholars would find few formal, definitive markers of recalibration produced by the federal elected branches subsequent to Reconstruction in the 1870s: no constitutional amendment or federal super-statute enshrined, in a principled manner, the dramatic renegotiations of federal and state authority embodied in Southern Democratic Redemption in the southern state governments. Among the three federal branches, this political development found its earliest, definitive expression in Supreme Court rulings. At a minimum, then, even if the Supreme Court may not wholly author any given instance of transformative recalibration, its role in codifying emergent political trends still affords it the opportunity for a different kind of agency: the Court has the opportunity to, within limits, crystallize or distill emergent political developments within the concepts and language of its own choosing. Furthermore, at particular moments when external political constraints on the Court are relatively more relaxed – namely during delimitation – its agency may be even more pronounced than this.

The formal delineations of new boundaries – and the judicial construction of them during episodes of transformative recalibration – are worthy of attention for three reasons. First, by definition, recalibrations that are formalized and endowed with the force of law indicate a particular kind of political settlement that has, at the very least, met a minimum threshold or degree of entrenchment. As is true for many legalized rules or principles, formalized recalibrations will generally be harder for political actors to completely ignore or avoid so long as they remain valid law.[15]

Second, judicial rulings that formally demarcate new boundary lines also introduce certain key concepts and terms that will, at a minimum, have to be contended with by future political actors seeking to change the law. Indeed, the effect may sometimes be even more dramatic: because judicial recalibrating rulings are often *the* guiding standards for individuals and governmental actors on the ground, the concepts and terms that become entrenched in the case law will often help constitute social practices and political-legal argument. For example, one might convincingly trace the prominence of diversity rationales among present-day defenders of affirmative action to the Court's focus on this justification in the *Bakke* ruling – a case that I discuss in Chapter 9.[16]

Third, the political significance of judicial recalibrating opinions also stems from the fact that in the transformative episodes reviewed here, the principles codified in those opinions turned out to be durable markers of postreform governance. A broad convergence among the secondary sources consulted for each historical period confirms that the principles articulated in delimiting and order-affirming judicial rulings accurately reflected formal governing boundaries between authorities and rights – boundaries that persisted in the broader political system for decades after their initial articulation by the Court. While political actors may respond to such legalized boundaries in creative, ambivalent, or even evasive ways, these judicial rulings fleshed out a broader legal framework within which such oppositional responses take place. Thus, these judicial recalibrating

---

[15] Valelly makes a similar point in discussing the political significance of "jurisprudence-building" during Reconstruction and the civil rights era. Richard M. Valelly, *The Two Reconstructions: The Struggle for Black Enfranchisement* (Chicago: University of Chicago Press, 2004), 18–19.

[16] In this sense, one might plausibly conceptualize judicial recalibrating rulings as having positive feedback effects, although of course, these rulings would constitute a particular and very distinctive kind of positive feedback mechanism.

opinions are noteworthy for capturing or crystallizing certain key elements of emergent political orders.

Two general institutional or structural factors allow the Court to play this codifying or crystallizing role. The first stems from the temporal order of lawmaking in the federal governmental system, which essentially thrusts a recalibrating role on the Court. Because its potential for intervening in the lawmaking process generally occurs after legislation has emerged from the elected branches, boundaries newly established in the wake of momentous reforms are inherently tentative until the Court has a chance to confront the legislation. The very possibility of judicial review and the potential for creative constitutional or statutory interpretations of newly enacted legislation provides a legitimate and ready venue for the judicial recalibration – and operationalization – of reform principles.

The second factor stems from the comparative freedom of nonelectoral institutions during times of political gridlock and legislative stalemate. When the mechanisms of elected governance are unable to respond energetically to pressing social and political problems, nonelected institutions of governance such as courts and administrative agencies quite often step to the fore.[17] In the context of postreform recalibration, when the basic contours of a new governing regime are just beginning to emerge, nonelectoral institutions will consistently enjoy relatively greater space for creative actions. And especially in the context of transformative recalibrations, when first-order uncertainties prompt intense conflict and contestation over boundaries that define governance in some area of policy, we might generally expect that the crucial nonelectoral institutions will

---

[17] Robert Kagan has focused on the prevalence of "adversarial legalism" in the American context, which he defines as "policymaking, policy implementation, and dispute resolution by means of lawyer-dominated litigation." Robert A. Kagan, *Adversarial Legalism: The American Way of Law* (Cambridge, MA: Harvard University Press, 2001), 3. He attributes its prevalence in part to the fragmented and nonhierarchical nature of governmental authority in the American governmental system. Ibid., 9, 15–16, 40–50. His theory thus also emphasizes the attractiveness of judicial venues for governance when the electoral alternatives are problematic. However, my focus on judicial recalibration points to a *recurrent* dynamic with respect to the judicial role. Kagan diverges somewhat from this in discussing adversarial legalism as both a *persistent* feature of American politics, and as a *secular development* with heightened importance since the 1960s. Ibid., 35–37, 48–50. Keith Whittington has also discussed a secular growth of judicial authority due to the increasingly fragmented nature of governing regimes in the latter half of the twentieth century. Keith E. Whittington, *Political Foundations of Judicial Supremacy: The Presidency, the Supreme Court, and Constitutional Leadership in U.S. History* (Princeton, NJ: Princeton University Press, 2007), 273–74, 283–84.

be the courts. That is, the courts – and the Supreme Court specifically – are likely to be the first federal institutions to offer formal, definitive statements on transformative recalibrations.[18]

Constraints on the Judiciary

For any kind of successful judicial codification to occur, the judiciary must also navigate certain constraints. Its codifying rulings must garner sufficient support, or adequately muted opposition, in the broader polity to prevent easy legislative revision or an otherwise antagonistic electoral response. Indeed, whether a given decision ultimately becomes a delimiting ruling depends on not only the actions of the Court but also the openings provided by the broader political system for the Court to issue such a ruling, and for the ruling to remain free of legislative revision.

Building on themes raised in the preceding pages, when the Court displays relatively greater initiative during the delimitation stage of this process, institutional and political constraints on the Court are at their weakest. The strategic task of cultivating allies and minimizing dissent is a somewhat less pressing concern given this relative freedom enjoyed by the Court. And this remains true so long as the Court is able to avoid making major political miscalculations such as attempting to nullify recent reforms or attempting to press reform principles far beyond electoral preferences. However, in the later stages of transformative recalibration when institutional and political constraints are more clearly defined and stronger, the Court's actions (and composition) conform to and reflect those constraints in ways that make it align with dominant pressures. Hence, order-affirming rulings are reactive in orientation, with the Court often following the lead of other institutions in the task of entrenching new orders. Likewise, tension-managing rulings elaborate on the issues of recalibration from the standpoint of fine-tuning and making marginal adjustments to political and institutional settlements that already have been successfully entrenched.

---

[18] Administrative agencies may also be crucial institutional players in this context. At least functionally, agencies, too, may offer final, definitive recalibrations on a range of important issues. But for controversial, fundamental matters of governance that attract continuing attention and prompt efforts by disgruntled litigants to appeal to higher authorities, the historical presence and availability of some form of judicial review for a broad range of agency actions suggests, much of the time, looking toward the courts for definitive, formal recalibrations on such matters. Alfred C. Aman, Jr. and William T. Mayton, *Administrative Law*, 2d ed. (St. Paul, MN: West, 2001), 136n5, 137, 352–56, 361–65. The judicial response (or nonresponse) to agency actions would seemingly be more likely to mark a relative sense of finality on such "first-order" recalibration issues.

Not coincidentally, then, more modest judicial actions such as order-affirming and tension-managing rulings tend to reflect and track the increasing solidification and efficacy of political constraints on the Court. The rise of increasingly significant political constraints stems from the fact that, over time, dominant governing coalitions will have the benefit of clarifying and solidifying their positions on the major issues of recalibration. Of equal importance, the passage of more time allows dominant governing coalitions the benefit of being able to make new appointments to the Court – appointments that likely mirror their own views.

In sum, successful judicial codification of recalibration principles stems from the judiciary's adaptability to changing political constraints. In the earlier phases of recalibration, we see a relatively less modest Court operating with the benefit of weaker political constraints during the delimitation phase. Later on, a more modest Court reemerges both during construction and normal politics to operate in the presence of stronger political constraints on it.

Underscoring the Supreme Court's responsiveness to and alignment with broader political constraints fills out the second half of Claim 4. The importance of the Court for transformative recalibrations does not stem from any claim that the Court wholly or even primarily "causes" the rise of conservative policy regimes. It would be hard to claim that the Supreme Court caused the rise of Jim Crow, for example.[19] Although it may not single-handedly drive transformative recalibration, the Court does, possess a more limited significance: but for the Court, there would *not* have been definitive, formal, recalibrating settlements in judicial rulings, at certain dates, after reform. And but for the Court, there certainly would not have been formal, recalibrating settlements in the legal and conceptual terms that the Court ultimately employed in these rulings.

OVERVIEW OF THE CHAPTERS

With my conceptual claims on the table, let me conclude this chapter with a qualification to these claims along with some comments on the

---

[19] To the extent that I offer a qualified theory on the causes of recalibration, it is a theory at the more abstract level of governing principles and governing authority. As described in Claim 1, recalibration processes are driven by incongruities between different governing authorities in the aftermath of open-ended reforms. Even at this more abstract level of inquiry, however, there is no claim that the Court would necessarily have to play a causal role in recalibrations.

research method and an overview of the remaining chapters. With respect to qualifications, one item merits emphasis even though it is addressed in the preceding sections. Although the focus of the book is on episodes of recalibration in which the Court plays a central role in the political processes of recalibration, this will not always be the case. As suggested by the historical references in Table 1.1 on page 24, I do not claim that the Court necessarily plays a delimiting or order-affirming role, or that it necessarily plays a significant role at all, in every episode of recalibration. My primary focus in the following chapters is only on the subset of recalibrations that I label "transformative."

With respect to research method and overview notes, the remainder of the book substantiates the various claims I have made with reference to three historical case studies: first, the dismantling of slavery with emancipation and the post-Reconstruction recalibration; second, the dismantling of master-servant common law labor relations with the Wagner Act and the post–New Deal recalibration of labor rights; and third, the dismantling of Jim Crow by, among other things, transformative understandings of constitutional equal protection and the subsequent recalibration of those changes. The selection of these three case studies reflects my ambition to demonstrate the theory's applicability to three very different historical contexts and to three of the most important eras of reform in American political history. Further, my interest in examining the labor context specifically reflects my goal of demonstrating, in detail, the theory's applicability to a context not centrally defined by issues of race.

Those familiar with these eras of political change will correctly note significant connections between them and how – as with many examples of constitutional change – earlier reforms influenced the enactment of later ones. Still, I treat these three periods as separate case studies precisely because my focus is *not* on what initiates reform but rather on what dynamics come into play once reform has already been initiated and enacted (by whatever means). To that end, for the purpose of examining postreform recalibration, I treat these periods as separate cases for the simple reason that each era of reform – separated by decades – clearly constituted separate clusters of legal reforms.

In addition, those familiar with these historical eras may also find the building blocks of my historical narratives to be familiar. Although the following chapters centrally rely on the examination of primary sources such as judicial opinions and litigants' briefs, I also rely heavily on a subset of well-known secondary historical sources in each of these eras in order to establish the background context for judicial recalibrating rulings. This method of investigation was informed by the belief that if my theory possesses the broad applicability that I claim, then it should be consistent with major eras of political change and with well-known interpretations of certain key events from those eras. Thus, in addition to their primary benefit in providing me with background context, my examination of a range of the secondary sources served a checking purpose in ensuring that my theory was constructed on a foundation of historical interpretations that enjoyed somewhat greater overlapping scholarly agreement. Still, in constructing my historical case studies in part on the basis of well-known facts and interpretations, my aspiration is that the chapters will bring to light a different kind of novelty: the highlighting of patterns and similarities in political development, judicial action, and judicial reasoning across diverse political and social contexts. In demonstrating the existence of some deeper institutional structure, my ultimate aspiration is to uncover a more general theory of political development.

My presentation of this historical material proceeds in line with the analytical framework I have outlined. Chapters 3, 4, and 5 address the *delimitation* phase of recalibration. These chapters highlight recurrent patterns in the substantive justifications for delimitation offered by the Supreme Court in its rulings and also underscore the significance of the Court's actions in being the first among the three federal branches to formally, definitively register postreform adjustments in governance in these three eras. Chapter 6 grapples with these historical case studies as they relate to the theory of judicial behavior presented in this chapter. In Chapter 6, I ask which theory of judicial behavior best explains the Court's behavior in these delimiting periods. Not surprisingly, my answer is that a theory of judicial-institutional inclination toward stability is best able to account for these case studies of judicial delimiting rulings.

Chapters 7, 8, and 9 are devoted to two tasks: illuminating the processes of construction in each historical case and offering some illustration of how postreform systems of governance settled into maturity. Discussion of the former will clarify how new systems of governance become initially entrenched, whereas discussion of the latter aims to demonstrate how these systems remained resilient in the face of newly emergent boundary tensions. Of course, a more comprehensive discussion of postconstruction governing resilience in any one of these three historical eras would require a book of its own. My focus is much more limited: I merely offer some case illustrations of how the judiciary managed tensions within relevant policy areas, and in undertaking this judicially focused task in the decades after Reconstruction, the New Deal, and the civil rights era, a recurrent mode of tension-management judicial rulings emerges across these eras. Finally, in Chapter 10 I address the question of what theory of judicial behavior best accounts for the Court's actions during these latter periods. In that chapter, I again claim that a judicial-institutional interest in stability best accounts for the Supreme Court's various rulings in constructing, and then maintaining, new systems of governance.

PART II

LEGAL REFORM AND ITS DELIMITATION

3

Emancipation, the Reconstruction Era, and Delimitation

The fate of African American rights after Reconstruction presents a significant problem for any theory of American political development. On the one hand, the Thirteenth Amendment permanently dismantled slavery, and two additional constitutional amendments, as well as a cluster of significant federal statutes, enshrined a new national commitment to racial equality in the law. From the early 1870s to the 1880s, however, these commitments were dramatically reshaped. And with the subsequent rise of Jim Crow in the 1890s, a new equilibrium for racial politics emerged that bore only partial resemblance to the aspirational constitutional values embodied in the text of the three Reconstruction Amendments. The arrival of Jim Crow in the post-Reconstruction years thus poses the most striking illustration of the limits of political transformation in American history.

My focus is specifically on formal legal developments surrounding African American rights, even though there are a number of plausible entry points into examining these important decades in the late nineteenth century.[1] And in examining the 1870s to the 1890s with this limited view, the extended process of political development – where the open-ended and ill-defined reforms of Reconstruction gradually crystallized into more concrete and definitive principles of governance – becomes apparent. The ultimate entrenchment of Jim Crow in the 1890s then was

---

[1] Indeed, Keller's survey of this historical period examines a number of important policy developments beyond the issue of African American rights. Morton Keller, *Affairs of State: Public Life in Late Nineteenth Century America* (Cambridge, MA: Harvard University Press, 1977).

TABLE 3.1 *Recalibration and the Post-Reconstruction Era*

(1) **Legal Reform**	Reconstruction amendments legally dismantle slavery
(2) **Delimitation**	(2a) Legislative stalemate after the election of 1874
	(2b) The federal protection of African-American rights is "indirectly" delimited by Supreme Court rulings with reference to the demands of federalism.
(3) **Construction**	(3a) The emergence of Jim Crow as articulated by the southern governments and eventually acceded to by the federal government
	(3b) Supreme Court entrenchment of Jim Crow

not a "reversal" of Reconstruction but rather the result of open-ended reforms being recalibrated in light of still-resilient institutional authorities and rights.

My reexamination of these decades of the late nineteenth century yields three specific insights. First, this historical narrative offers an account of the developmental relationship between Reconstruction and Jim Crow and why legal developments during this period unfolded as they did. Second, and related, this historical narrative offers a distinctive perspective on how formal governing relations are crafted in the aftermath of reform. The dynamic is not simply one of reform creating a new political order; rather, it is a dynamic of reform and recalibration preceding a new political order. Third, the historical narrative demonstrates that although the Supreme Court does not cause recalibration, the judiciary is the venue in which broader recalibrating dynamics are crystallized and codified into new and durable governing principles.

Table 3.1 outlines this historical narrative of post-Reconstruction and recalibration – a narrative that begins here and continues in Chapter 7. In the present chapter, I tell only the first half of the story: the means by which reform principles were recalibrated in light of resilient authorities and rights at the outer edges of reform. Even if the political events of the mid-1860s – particularly the rejection of the Black Codes by the Republican Congress and the Republican victory in the elections of 1866 – had clarified that a return to quasi slavery was impossible,[2] key questions nevertheless remained regarding the scope of this change and its relation to legal and political commitments to federalism. What did this political

---

[2] Eric Foner, *Reconstruction: America's Unfinished Revolution, 1863–1877* (New York: Perennial, 1989), 257, 267–68.

change imply about federal intrusion into the South? Would the abolition of slavery entail some radical restructuring of federalism as well? This period of delimitation in the 1870s and 1880s produced lasting political resolution on these questions of *how far* reform would intrude into the polity.

Two significant crises prompted the eventual resolution of these external uncertainties: persistent civil disorder in the South in the 1870s and the Panic of 1873 that infringed on reform politics by facilitating heavy Republican losses in the 1874 elections. These two events collectively weakened political support for more expansive reform ambitions by reenergizing old opponents of reform and strengthening the doubts of newer skeptics. These events gave rise to a legislative stalemate, thereby opening the door for a consequential judicial delimitation of Reconstruction.

The Supreme Court took up the invitation, beginning a delimitation of African American rights with its ruling in *Blyew v. United States*[3] in 1872, extending up through its ruling in the *Civil Rights Cases*[4] in 1883. Notably, when conservative advocates employed argumentative strategies in front of the Court to directly challenge Reconstruction, they did not enjoy much success. Rather, southern lawyers focused on federalism and the preservation of some degree of state autonomy in the post-Reconstruction world. These arguments – which indirectly opposed Reconstruction by referencing resilient authorities and rights – found substantial agreement in the Court and were often lifted directly from the briefs of southern lawyers into the Court's rulings. Chapter 6 discusses why exactly the Court accepted this invitation to delimit and why it found more conservative arguments to be compelling. But with reformers and postreform skeptics locked in this legislative stalemate for the next two decades, these judicial rulings were free of any subsequent legislative revision. The rulings, aided by a permissible background political context, were crucial in constituting the first steps toward codifying a new status quo for racial politics in the post-Reconstruction era.

Ultimately, the case of Reconstruction suggests that, while legislative enactments such as constitutional amendments and statutes are very relevant to a discussion of political development, there remains a need to look beyond them.[5] The absence of any Redemption constitutional amendment

---

[3] 80 U.S. 581 (1872).
[4] 109 U.S. 3 (1883).
[5] See, e.g., Bruce Ackerman, *We the People*, vol. 1, *Foundations* (Cambridge, MA: Harvard University Press, 1991); Bruce Ackerman, *We the People*, vol. 2, *Transformations* (Cambridge, MA: Harvard University Press, 1998).

or Redemption federal super-statute allows for the story of post-Reconstruction judicial delimitation to be relegated to secondary status.[6] The following developmental account, with its emphasis on key judicial interpretations of transformative legislative enactments, is offered as a helpful correction to this oversight.

THE RISE OF LEGISLATIVE STALEMATE

The Thirteenth Amendment immediately created uncertainties regarding how emancipation would fit alongside legal and political commitments inherited from the antebellum era. Prior to the 1870s, there were two noteworthy and tentative elaborations on earlier reform that surfaced in different parts of the polity. Both, however, failed to provide lasting resolution to these uncertainties.

The first was the passage of the Black Codes in the southern states beginning in the fall and winter of 1865. These state laws blatantly restricted the autonomy of the freedmen and were primarily concerned with tying them to the land to preserve southern agriculture.[7] Congress decisively rejected this very conservative elaboration of the Thirteenth Amendment, and in turn offered its own elaboration: the Fourteenth Amendment.[8] Yet, even though this latter, more expansive elaboration on the meaning of abolition was enshrined in the Constitution, the Fourteenth Amendment's various commitments also prompted similar uncertainties as to how they would fit alongside antebellum legal and political commitments.

---

[6] One could dispute this assertion about the absence of any legislative acts of delimitation by pointing to the near-total legislative repeal of the various sections of the several Enforcement Acts; this effort began in 1894, but major repeals also followed in 1909 and 1911. Xi Wang, *The Trial of Democracy: Black Suffrage and Northern Republicans, 1860–1910* (Athens: University of Georgia Press, 1997), 254–59, 294–99. Perhaps this legislative repeal might be conceptualized as delimitation via legislation. The difficulty with this view, however, is that the legislative repeal of the Enforcement Acts occurred decades after judicial delimitation had started. As I demonstrate later, the political baseline that made it possible for a unified Democratic government to begin repeal of the Enforcement Acts in 1894 had already been set in place. This suggests that the pivotal moment when federalism commitments began to reassert themselves was *not* in 1894; that pivotal moment had arrived much earlier in the 1870s.

[7] Dan T. Carter, *When the War Was Over: The Failure of Self-Reconstruction in the South, 1865–1867* (Baton Rouge: Louisiana State University Press, 1985), 3, 209–20; Theodore Brantner Wilson, *The Black Codes of the South* (Tuscaloosa: University of Alabama Press, 1965), 71, 138–39, 144–46.

[8] Foner, *Reconstruction*, 257.

Emancipation, the Reconstruction Era, and Delimitation 69

This question of how far reform would extend into the broader legal and political fabric of the polity would persist in the southern states and in the federal elected branches through at least the first half of the 1870s. Still, no decisive recalibration of reform emerged from Congress or the president during this time. Governing crises in the form of persistent southern civil disorder and the Panic of 1873 energized reform skeptics and led to a legislative stalemate precluding both further reform and legislative rollbacks of reform. These events nevertheless furthered recalibration because the legislative preoccupation with, and failure to resolve these issues opened the door for the judiciary to articulate how much Reconstruction had transformed the polity and how much it had not.

Governing Crisis: Southern Civil Disorder in the 1870s

Conservative southerners approached the recalibration issue in the 1870s by attempting to reassert traditional principles of federalism and state autonomy on racial matters. These desires were manifested in often-violent campaigns against both black suffrage and the remaining Republican-controlled southern state governments – both of which heavily depended on the federal government for their health and continued existence. With respect to the northern electorate, the two most prominent Redemption campaigns were those in Mississippi and Louisiana.

Political violence in Mississippi began in Vicksburg in the summer of 1874. Conservative whites threatened violence to intimidate black voters in the city's municipal election and to force out Republican incumbents. Subsequent conflict between White League forces and African Americans left 300 African Americans dead and forced President Ulysses S. Grant to send federal troops to Vicksburg to restore order in January 1875.[9] Greater unrest followed, however. In 1875, Mississippi Democrats campaigned to finally put an end to both Republican power and black voting in the state. Republicans and prominent African Americans were repeatedly the targets of violence at various political functions throughout the fall.[10] Disorder was so rampant that Governor Ames asked Grant to send

---

[9] Ibid., 558; Nicholas Lemann, *Redemption: The Last Battle of the Civil War* (New York: Farrar, Straus, and Giroux, 2006), 71–74, 91–92.

[10] Foner, *Reconstruction*, 559–60; William Gillette, *Retreat from Reconstruction, 1869–1879* (Baton Rouge: Louisiana State University Press, 1979), 155; Lemann, *Redemption*, 108–18; George C. Rable, *But There Was No Peace: The Role of Violence in the Politics of Reconstruction* (Athens: University of Georgia Press, 1984), 154–57; Brooks D.

in federal troops in early September. No troops arrived, however. The end result of the cumulative effect of Democratic intimidation, electoral fraud, and the forced removal or resignation of other Republican officeholders (including the governor) was the return of the Democrats to power in the state.[11]

The nature of the federal response – or lack of response – to the civil disorder in 1875 indicated a growing antipathy toward Reconstruction that had seized the North. Grant's intervention in January 1875, after all, was criticized in the North because of the perceived inappropriate use of the federal army in a local dispute (although as the details of this conflict later emerged, many in the North grew more critical of the Southern Democrats as well).[12] Grant learned his lesson when violence broke out the second time around. As he wrote to his attorney general in discussing the Mississippi governor's request for federal troops in the fall of 1875, "The whole public are tired out with these annual, autumnal outbreaks in the South, and there is so much unwholesome lying done by the press and people in regard to the cause and extent of these breaches of the peace that the great majority are ready now to condemn any interference on the part of the Government."[13]

Crucially, then, postreform skepticism was on the rise in the North. John R. Lynch, an African American congressman from Mississippi, claimed that Grant had cited to him an even more specific political motivation in not sending federal troops into Mississippi in late 1875. Grant was apparently concerned that such a move might arouse a negative reaction in Ohio and cost the Republicans the gubernatorial election there.[14] Grant's subsequent policy of nonintervention struck a much better chord in the North.[15]

Yet the most dramatic illustrations of disorder in the South arose from the continuous violence and disorder in Louisiana from 1871–76.

Simpson, *The Reconstruction Presidents* (Lawrence: University Press of Kansas, 1998), 185–86.

[11] Foner, *Reconstruction*, 561–62; Lemann, *Redemption*, 145–47, 154.

[12] Gillette, *Retreat*, 152, 157; Foner, *Reconstruction*, 560–62; Simpson, *Reconstruction Presidents*, 187–88.

[13] Quoted in Gillette, *Retreat*, 157.

[14] Gillette, *Retreat*, 159; Foner, *Reconstruction*, 562–63; Lemann, *Redemption*, 136–37; Simpson, *Reconstruction Presidents*, 186; William C. Harris, "Mississippi: Republican Factionalism and Mismanagement," in *Reconstruction and Redemption in the South*, ed. Otto H. Olsen (Baton Rouge: Louisiana State University Press, 1980), 103–04.

[15] Gillette, *Retreat*, 159–60.

Conflict began in August 1871 when the customhouse wing of the Louisiana Republican Party – affiliated with Grant and his administration – employed federal troops to control admission to the state party convention in order to secure their control of the party. Their intraparty rival at the time was the Warmoth faction of the Republican Party, which occasionally allied itself with the Democrats and was led by the more politically conservative, conciliatory Republican governor Henry Warmoth.[16]

Later, a disputed gubernatorial election in 1872 between William Pitt Kellogg of the customhouse faction and Democrat John McEnery of the conservative coalition – which saw Republicans manipulating vote totals and the Democrats intimidating black voters – resulted in two rival state governments.[17] Spillover from this dispute led to another violent conflict: political differences stemming from the gubernatorial election dispute, plus an additional dispute over a Grant Parish election in 1872, led to the Colfax Massacre in April 1873. African Americans allied with Kellogg were killed, about seventy-one in total.[18]

In September 1874, after some federal troops withdrew in the early summer to avoid the yellow fever season, about 8,000 McEnery men moved on New Orleans. They seized city hall, the arsenals, the statehouse, and police stations, essentially shoving out the Kellogg government entirely. The coup lasted until Grant dispatched 5,000 troops and three gunboats to New Orleans, which ended the insurgency.[19] But only two months later, in November 1874, another dispute grew out of elections for the state legislature. Republicans accused Democrats of intimidating African Americans to prevent them from voting, whereas the Democrats accused the Republican-controlled canvassing board of manipulating the vote totals. Democrats responded with a brief, illegal takeover of the lower state house in January 1875. The Democrats kidnapped three Republican legislators, and with favorable numbers, elected their candidate speaker, and confirmed the election of the five Democratic

---

[16] Ibid., 106–07; Ted Tunnell, *Crucible of Reconstruction: War, Radicalism, and Race in Louisiana, 1862–1877* (Baton Rouge: Louisiana State University Press, 1984), 161, 163–64, 169–70.
[17] Gillette, *Retreat*, 110–13; Rable, *No Peace*, 123–24; Simpson, *Reconstruction Presidents*, 165–66; Tunnell, *Crucible*, 171.
[18] Gillette, *Retreat*, 115; Foner, *Reconstruction*, 437; Lemann, *Redemption*, 3–27; Rable, *No Peace*, 126–28; Tunnell, *Crucible*, 189–92.
[19] Gillette, *Retreat*, 117–20; Foner, *Reconstruction*, 551; Rable, *No Peace*, 138–40; Tunnell, *Crucible*, 198, 202–03.

legislators whose elections had been in dispute. The Republicans returned with federal troops and had the five recently confirmed Democrats ejected. To return the favor, the Republicans seated five of their own legislators and elected their own choice for speaker.[20]

The Louisiana Republicans did not enjoy strong support within the northern electorate. Further underscoring a growing postreform skepticism in the North, Gillette notes that when Grant used the military to intervene in the Louisiana state legislative dispute in early 1875, this intervention "infuriated a majority of people North and South and crystallized public feeling more than any other event of reconstruction."[21] He writes: "It became the most explosive issue of Grant's presidency, and one on which there was a widespread consensus that Washington had gone too far, indicated by the flurry of states' rights resolutions that were adopted in the first fifteen days of January, 1875 – more, one observer noted, than had been issued in the preceding fifteen years."[22] Republican William A. Wheeler's congressional committee eventually worked out a political compromise over the Louisiana situation in April 1875, demonstrating that the Republicans had little desire to ramp up their efforts in Louisiana. The report made no concerted attempt to defend either Reconstruction or the Louisiana customhouse Republicans.[23] Ultimately, the primary lesson for Grant and congressional Republicans after seeing northern reaction to this latest intervention in Louisiana was the same one evident in the Mississippi episode: the North had no stomach for heavy federal intervention in the South.[24]

Criticism toward Reconstruction had been circulating since at least the Liberal Republican Party uprising in the election of 1872,[25] but these

---

[20] Gillette, *Retreat*, 121–23; Rable, *No Peace*, 140–42; Simpson, *Reconstruction Presidents*, 176; Tunnell, *Crucible*, 204–05.
[21] Gillette, *Retreat*, 124. See also Lemann, *Redemption*, 94–95.
[22] Gillette, *Retreat*, 124.
[23] Foner, *Reconstruction*, 555; Gillette, *Retreat*, 132–33.
[24] Foner, *Reconstruction*, 555; William S. McFeely, *Grant: A Biography* (New York: W. W. Norton, 1981), 418–19; Simpson, *Reconstruction Presidents*, 176–77.
[25] Indeed, one can identify the beginnings of Republican postreform skepticism in the early 1870s, which would eventually feed into the rise of the Liberal Republican Party in the 1872 election. Although its electoral influence was minor, the various critiques of Reconstruction articulated by the Liberal Republicans proved to be influential in subsequent years. Foner, *Reconstruction*, 456, 497–99, 500, 503, 509; Heather Cox Richardson, *The Death of Reconstruction: Race, Labor, and Politics in the Post–Civil War North, 1865–1901* (Cambridge, MA: Harvard University Press, 2001), 102, 104, 119, 128.

various crises only heightened the northern inclination to rethink reform ambitions by the mid-1870s.[26] Northern reevaluation of the merits of intervening in the South was pressed on both pragmatic and principled grounds. A much-quoted speech by Joseph Hawley, a Republican congressman from Connecticut, summarized both sentiments well. In discussing a proposed enforcement statute (which did not become enacted) in early 1875, he stated:

There is a social, and educational, and moral reconstruction of the South needed that will never come from any legislative halls, State or national; it must be the growth of time, of education, and of Christianity. We cannot perfect that reconstruction through statutes, if we had all the powers of the State Legislature and of Congress combined. We cannot put justice, liberty, and equality into the hearts of a people by statutes alone.[27]

An editorial in *Harper's Weekly* in early 1875 registered a similar note of resignation, which, while lauding Reconstruction policy as just and humane, evidenced a clear desire to end Republican interference in the Louisiana affair. It stated:

There is a disposition which arises from a humane and generous impulse, but which is not wise, to expect the national power to do by force of arms what can be done only by moral processes and by time. Even when all citizens are made equal before the law, and equally accessible civil remedies are provided for the redress of wrongs, a great deal of injustice, disorder, and outrage will still remain; and the danger, but by no means the necessity, of the Republican policy is that these last will be taken as proofs that still more stringent measures must be provided, which may be pressed from point to point, until the country rises in reaction and overthrows the party whose just and beneficent ends will thus

---

[26] Perman has critiqued some accounts of Reconstruction for ignoring the role of southern agency in bringing reform to an end. Michael Perman, "Counter Reconstruction: The Role of Violence in Southern Redemption," in *The Facts of Reconstruction: Essays in Honor of John Hope Franklin*, eds. Eric Anderson and Alfred A. Moss, Jr. (Baton Rouge: Louisiana State University Press, 1991), 135–40. See also Rable, *No Peace*, 191. In line with his perspective, the preceding argument is that southern Democratic agency had much to do with ending Reconstruction – namely, in making Republicans think twice about what they were willing or not willing to do to achieve their highest reform aspirations. Separately, Heather Cox Richardson has emphasized how changing northern conceptions of political economy – and the concomitant rise of a northern concern about African Americans making class or group demands on the polity through the federal government – fed into a growing northern disinterest and apathy toward African American interests. Richardson, *Death*, 241–45.

[27] Cong. Record, 43rd Cong., 2d Sess., 1853 (1875), mentioned in Gillette, *Retreat*, 287 and in Foner, *Reconstruction*, 556.

have been defeated by a want of that tact which is the highest genius of practical statesmanship.[28]

Although the policy failure of federal intervention in Louisiana motivated these sentiments, a strong commitment to federalism also underlay such negative assessments. As the *Harper's* editorial also stated:

> The new amendments to the Constitution undoubtedly intend that the new citizens shall be protected, just as the whole instrument intends that all citizens shall be. But it means, of course, that that protection shall be in harmony with the character and condition of our whole system of government. It certainly does not mean that the risks of freedom and of local rule shall not be taken. The new amendments do not change the national administration into a "paternal government," and certainly do not intend to destroy that manly self-dependence which is the characteristic of the race to which we belong, and to which we owe our political institutions.[29]

Consider the references to "freedom," "local rule," and "manly self-dependence" that seem to endorse federalism and state autonomy over the threat of encroaching federal authority (or as the editorial referred to it, "paternal government"). Similarly, Hawley grounded his opposition to the new enforcement statute on the basis of maintaining federalism and state sovereignty:

> This [the federal government] is a Government of certain defined and limited powers. It was constituted upon the belief that, taking an enlarged view and running through a long series of years, the personal rights of the citizen would be best protected by this limited local State sovereignty around him; that on the whole these twenty, thirty, forty, or fifty State sovereignties would protect in general the personal rights of the citizen, while this Federal Government, constituted in whatever way you please... would protect a certain wider range of rights [such as national defense, or protection of citizens in the states from domestic insurrections].[30]

As the quotations suggest, what troubled northerners with respect to these federal intrusions into internal state disputes was that federal military rule seemed to be subordinating civil law, and federal autocracy seemed to be displacing local self-government.[31] Furthermore, the easy overthrow of the Kellogg regime in Louisiana in September 1874 only reinforced the view that this governing regime existed at the pleasure of a distant federal

---

[28] "A Doubtful Law," *Harper's Weekly*, February 27, 1875, 171. This editorial is mentioned in Gillette, *Retreat*, 287.
[29] Ibid.
[30] Cong. Record, 43rd Cong., 2d Sess., 1853.
[31] Gillette, *Retreat*, 112.

government instead of at the will of "the people."[32] By the mid-1870s, such sentiments were on the rise among northern Republican elites and the northern electorate.[33]

In sum, although it had been clear since at least the dramatic Republican electoral victory in 1866 that most northerners had no trouble dismantling slavery, no analogous consensus existed for dismantling federalism.[34] Once voluntary southern compliance was off the table, only an uncomfortable choice remained for reformers: either abandon achieving Reconstruction's full promise for African American rights in the South or contemplate further transformation in the domain of federalism. What the latter option entailed was employing the coercive arm of the federal government as a ready and permanent tool – either through extremely vigorous Department of Justice prosecutions or through federal military action – to force the South into line. With northern sentiment as it was in the early to mid-1870s, and with economic concerns moving to the forefront of northern Republican worries in light of the Panic of 1873 (discussed in the following section), it is no surprise that the former option ultimately prevailed.[35]

Governing Crisis: Panic of 1873

Although somewhat separate from the events of Reconstruction, the Panic of 1873 was a governing crisis of major proportions that also affected recalibration dynamics. First, it was a major diversion for the northern electorate. Because of the economic shocks created by the panic, northern voters were even less inclined to deal with the perpetual headache of the South. Second, and more important, the Republicans suffered major losses in the 1874 election as a consequence of this economic shock. Although the electoral loss was partly because of northern disappointment with reforms in the South, it was mostly the result of an electoral desire to punish the party in power for major economic problems. These

---

[32] Ibid., 118, 120, 237; Rable, *No Peace*, 140; Simpson, *Reconstruction Presidents*, 172; Tunnell, *Crucible*, 213–14. This concern could obviously be carried over to other states where southern Republicans were tenuously in control. Gillette, *Retreat*, 181.

[33] Vincent P. DeSantis, *Republicans Face the Southern Question: The New Departure Years, 1877–1897* (Baltimore: Johns Hopkins University Press, 1959), 221; Foner, *Reconstruction*, 554–56; Gillette, *Retreat*, 155, 252–56, 293–95; Simpson, *Reconstruction Presidents*, 177, 181, 184; Rogers M. Smith, *Civic Ideals: Conflicting Visions of Citizenship in U.S. History* (New Haven, CT: Yale University Press, 1997), 289.

[34] Foner, *Reconstruction*, 242–43.

[35] Ibid., 557–58, 563.

Republican losses created an enormous obstacle to any new Reconstruction legislation.[36]

The panic also influenced Reconstruction reforms through its effect on the performance of the southern Republican Party. As a result of the panic, campaign contributions dried up, leaving the southern wing of the party with even less financial help from the North. Furthermore, the panic itself counted as another failure of practical governance for those southern Republican governments still in control in their respective states, damaging the party's quest to gain credibility in the South. And the panic significantly reduced the policy options available for southern Republican governments to pursue; possibilities of cultivating Republican votes among lower-class whites through government spending programs were entirely abandoned by the new necessity of economic retrenchment. Meanwhile, the panic helped along the cause of Southern Democratic Redemption in some states by giving Southern Democrats the upper hand in their electoral contestation with Republicans.[37]

The Inauguration of Legislative Stalemate

The electoral losses stemming from the panic and, to a lesser extent, the increasing civil disorder in the South, resulted in disastrous losses for the Republicans in the 1874 election. Along with significant Democratic victories in a number of northern state elections, a Republican 110-vote majority in the House transformed into a Democratic majority of 60 votes. This shift constituted the greatest partisan reversal in the nineteenth century. However, with Republicans still controlling the White House and the Senate, the election inaugurated an extended era of political stalemate rather than Democratic control.[38] Indeed, this election facilitated a delimitation of Reconstruction – not a reversal of it.

Fallout from the election was felt even during the lame-duck congressional session that started in December of 1874. Republican attempts to pass another enforcement bill and a two-year army appropriations bill (intended to fortify the federal military in the South from likely appropriation cuts by the incoming Democratic House) failed.[39] Lame-duck

---

[36] Ibid., 523–24; Simpson, *Reconstruction Presidents*, 173–74.
[37] Foner, *Reconstruction*, 523–25, 535, 539, 569; Michael Perman, *The Road to Redemption: Southern Politics, 1869–1879* (Chapel Hill: University of North Carolina Press, 1984), 146–48; Simpson, *Reconstruction Presidents*, 165.
[38] Foner, *Reconstruction*, 523; Simpson, *Reconstruction Presidents*, 173.
[39] Foner, *Reconstruction*, 553–56; Gillette, *Retreat*, 291–92.

Republicans did succeed in passing the Civil Rights Act of 1875, which provided for "the full and equal enjoyment" of public accommodations regardless of race, color, or "any previous condition of servitude."[40] However, although on its surface the act appeared to contemplate a profound deepening of Reconstruction reforms by outlawing segregation in public accommodations[41] – and by exerting federal authority even further into the states – it did not have this effect. The public accommodations portion of the act was effectively gutted by the Court in the *Civil Rights Cases*[42] only eight years later (discussed later in this chapter). Even prior to this ruling, however, the act was never fully enforced. Notwithstanding its text, its framers did not expect – and some did not even want – the act to be fully enforced. Its passage was more a symbolic measure to shore up party support among African Americans without offending white voters with vigorous enforcement of it.[43]

The era when Republican electoral dominance could threaten further transformative changes in the South effectively ended with the 1874 electoral result. Even more conspicuously, in 1877, Hayes removed the federal troops protecting the statehouses of South Carolina and Louisiana; Florida, Louisiana, and South Carolina became the last three states of the old Confederacy to be redeemed into Democratic control. Hayes's move was widely recognized at the time as bringing an end to any political role for the military in the southern state governments.[44] After the 1874

---

[40] Civil Rights Act of 1875, ch. 114, § 1, 18 Stat. 335, 336 (1875). Foner, *Reconstruction*, 553, 555.
[41] Foner, *Reconstruction*, 504–05, 532; Gillette, *Retreat*, 197–98; Michael W. McConnell, "Originalism and the Desegregation Decisions," *Virginia Law Review* 81, no. 4 (May 1995): 987–90.
[42] 109 U.S. 3 (1883).
[43] Gillette, *Retreat*, 271, 273; Bertram Wyatt-Brown, "The Civil Rights Act of 1875," *The Western Political Quarterly* 18, no. 4 (December 1965): 774–75; John Hope Franklin, "The Enforcement of the Civil Rights Act of 1875," *Prologue: Journal of the National Archives* 6 (Winter 1974): 226, 229, 235; Foner, *Reconstruction*, 556; James M. McPherson, "Abolitionists and the Civil Rights Act of 1875," *Journal of American History* 52, no. 3 (December 1965): 509–10.
[44] Gillette, *Retreat*, 346. A small number of troops did remain in the South after 1877, and the troops withdrawn from South Carolina and Louisiana were actually just sent to their barracks. Everette Swinney, *Suppressing the Ku Klux Klan: The Enforcement of the Reconstruction Amendments, 1870–1877* (New York: Garland, 1987), 190; Vincent P. DeSantis, "Rutherford B. Hayes and the Removal of the Troops and the End of Reconstruction," in *Region, Race, and Reconstruction: Essays in Honor of C. Vann Woodward*, eds. J. Morgan Kousser and James M. McPherson (New York: Oxford University Press, 1982), 417. But there was very little political support for the troops to play an active role among either northern or southern voters. Furthermore, with all of the

election, Republicans succeeded in gaining a unified government twice before the 1896 election – in 1880 and 1888.

The Democrats, in turn, were never able to mount a successful legislative offensive of their own during these years. Democrats, with their newly acquired control of both houses of Congress in 1878, did attempt to repeal portions of the Reconstruction Enforcement Acts by attaching riders to appropriation bills. Hayes, however, pushed back and vetoed seven of these appropriation bills from 1879 to 1880.[45] Democrats achieved a unified government only once in these decades, in 1892. (And in February of 1894, thanks to their large majorities they were successful in repealing some forty provisions of the various Enforcement Acts. Additional, significant repeals followed in 1909 and 1911.)[46] But at least from the time of the 1874 election to 1892, the most accurate description of electoral politics was that of an extended legislative stalemate between the Republicans and Democrats.

THE JUDICIAL DELIMITATION OF RECONSTRUCTION

Within this context of electoral gridlock, it is not surprising to see the courts, and the Supreme Court in particular, step forward in offering more definitive elaborations of recent reforms. The following discussions of Supreme Court rulings are thus thematically joined in several respects. First, in each ruling we see the Court grappling with the first element of the recalibration problem: determining how far open-ended reform principles will extend into the polity and disrupt still-resilient authorities and rights. Second, there are commonalities across the Court's conclusions in these cases. Taken together, its opinions suggest a judicial inclination to delimit the reach of reform and to clearly demarcate boundary lines between those authorities and rights rooted in reform and those rooted in the old order. Although there is no explicit judicial awareness of the larger questions of

---

southern states readmitted and with Democrats having redeemed all of the southern state governments by this time, the likelihood of any state officials subsequently requesting federal intervention evaporated as well. Gillette, *Retreat*, 346.

[45] Stanley P. Hirshson, *Farewell to the Bloody Shirt: Northern Republicans & the Southern Negro, 1877–1893* (Chicago: Quadrangle Books, 1962, 1968), 56–57; Mark W. Summers, *Rum, Romanism, & Rebellion: The Making of a President, 1884* (Chapel Hill: University of North Carolina Press, 2000), 48–49; Wang, *Trial*, 165–79.

[46] Michael Perman, *Struggle for Mastery: Disfranchisement in the South, 1888–1908* (Chapel Hill: University of North Carolina Press, 2001), 21–22, 43–47; Wang, *Trial*, 254–59. Notably, the repeals of 1909 and 1911 occurred with the 61st Congress, which was part of a unified Republican government.

recalibration found in these opinions, a judicial awareness and concern for smaller-scale, case-specific manifestations of these questions does present itself. These more narrow uncertainties, and the challenge each posed to conventional legality norms such as certainty and settlement in the law, were precisely what pressed the Court to further the broader processes of recalibration.

The Court accomplished the task of delimiting and recalibrating reform across this diverse set of cases in the 1870s and early 1880s by emphasizing a common legal justification for delimitation. Namely, it repeatedly sympathized with the arguments of southern litigators emphasizing the dangers of expansive federal authority. Over and over, Democratic lawyers – and the Court itself – justified conservative interpretations of Reconstruction by raising the specter of a slippery slope, where the horrifying end result was thus the dismantling of state authority. The appeal by southern lawyers and the Court itself to the still-resilient authority of federalism was the primary justification for delimiting Reconstruction reforms.[47] These opinions demonstrate then both a commonality in their respective outcomes and a consistency in the judiciary's inclination to stabilize or clarify legal boundaries implicated in, and rendered uncertain by, recent reforms.

Of course, the judicial motives behind these opinions – and the question of how exactly to categorize them – may have been less than obvious at the time they were written. Indeed, a "delimiting" judicial opinion can ultimately only delimit when that opinion remains free from subsequent legislative or judicial revision. With the benefit of hindsight, however, we know that these rulings took place against a backdrop of persistent legislative stalemate. Because of this stalemate, the Court's delimiting statements remained free of subsequent legislative revision, and these rulings constituted the first definitive statements formally codifying the legal limits of Reconstruction reforms. Indeed, by the time repeal of the Enforcement Acts began in 1894, the reassertion of federalism and the delimitation of

---

[47] Kaczorowski's important work on the judicial rulings of this period notably emphasizes the crucial role that federalism concerns played in influencing these rulings. Robert J. Kaczorowski, *The Politics of Judicial Interpretation: The Federal Courts, Department of Justice, and Civil Rights, 1866–1876* (New York: Fordham University Press, 1985, 2005), 182–83. Orren and Skowronek also focus on the issue of the uncertain reach of the authority of the Reconstruction Amendments, especially as it related to institutional conflict between the Court and Congress. Karen Orren and Stephen Skowronek, *The Search for American Political Development* (New York: Cambridge University Press, 2004), 133–43.

African American rights reflected in this legislative effort had already been pronounced in Supreme Court rulings during the preceding two decades.

Blyew v. United States

In the case of *Blyew v. United States*,[48] two white men had been prosecuted for the murder of an African American woman. The legal complications of this case arose from the presence of a Kentucky state law that did not allow for the testimony of African Americans in civil or criminal cases in which whites were a party. Because of this state law, and because the victim and two of the witnesses to the murder were African American, the case had been removed to federal circuit court where the defendants were convicted. The justification for removing the case rested on both the broad guarantees of civil equality for the freedmen in Section 1 of the Civil Rights Act of 1866, which provided for the right of African Americans to "give evidence,"[49] and more specifically, in Section 3 of the act that provided:

> That the district courts of the United States, within their respective districts, shall have, exclusively of the courts of the several States, cognizance of all crimes and offences committed against the provisions of this act, and also, concurrently with the circuit courts of the United States, of all causes, civil and criminal, affecting persons who are denied or cannot enforce in the courts or judicial tribunals of the State or locality where they may be any of the rights secured to them by the first section of this act.[50]

Given the discrimination against African Americans in testifying under Kentucky law, the key legal question was whether this prosecution "affected" any African Americans. More specifically, could it be said that the African American witnesses or victim were "affected" by the Kentucky law? If so, then removal was justified.[51]

Since *Blyew* dealt with race and the administration of criminal law in the states, the broader legal and political implications of this case were apparent. Hence, the arguments in defense of states' rights posed to the Supreme Court were articulated not by lawyers for the defendants but

---

[48] 80 U.S. 581 (1872).
[49] "Such citizens, of every race and color...shall have the same right, in every State and Territory in the United States, to make and enforce contracts, to sue, be parties, and give evidence." Civil Rights Act of 1866, ch. 31, § 1, 14 Stat. 27, 27 (1866).
[50] § 3, 14 Stat. at 27.
[51] 80 U.S. at 590–91.

rather by lawyers retained by the state of Kentucky.[52] Further underscoring the broader importance of this case was the prominence of counsel retained by the state of Kentucky: Isaac Caldwell, an individual of some local prominence, and, more significantly, Jeremiah S. Black. Black was one of the most distinguished lawyers of the time, having formerly served as attorney general for President James Buchanan, secretary of state, a Supreme Court nominee, Supreme Court reporter, and advisor to President Andrew Johnson after the Civil War. Black had also been involved in the important cases of *Ex parte Milligan* and *Ex parte McCardle*.[53]

Both Caldwell's brief and Black's oral argument offered two distinct kinds of arguments as to why the Civil Rights Act did not confer jurisdiction in this case. The more radical of the two arguments was that the Civil Rights Act was unconstitutional. Indeed, this was the title of Caldwell's brief, and it was the first substantive argument he presented in it. The thrust of the argument was that the civil protections offered to African Americans in the Civil Rights Act lay outside the scope of the Thirteenth Amendment, presumably the sole constitutional warrant for the act.[54] Caldwell additionally noted a related and more structural point: if the Court should find this act a legitimate extension of the Thirteenth Amendment, this would lead to the undesirable consequence that "they [Congress] have the power, to be exercised at will, to cover the entire ground of legislation touching civil and political rights."[55] In other words, should the Court allow the Civil Rights Act of 1866 to stand notwithstanding its tenuous connection to the antislavery principle embodied in the Thirteenth Amendment, this might allow a virtually unlimited congressional power to legislate on anything under the Thirteenth Amendment.[56]

Black likewise directly challenged the constitutionality of the Civil Rights Act in his oral argument before the Court. He asserted that the federal *judicial* power was fundamentally limited by the Constitution and could not be extended by a congressional act, such as the Civil

---

[52] J. S. Black, Argument for the State of Kentucky at 3, *Blyew v. United States*, 80 U.S. 581 (1872); Isaac Caldwell, Brief against the Constitutionality of the Civil Rights Act of April, 1866 at 1, *Blyew v. United States*, 80 U.S. 581 (1872); Robert D. Goldstein, "*Blyew*: Variations on a Jurisdictional Theme," *Stanford Law Review* 41, no. 3 (February 1989): 491; Kaczorowski, *Judicial Interpretation*, 110.

[53] *Ex parte Milligan*, 71 U.S. 2 (1866); *Ex parte McCardle*, 74 U.S. 506 (1869); Goldstein, "*Blyew*," 491–92; Kaczorowski, *Judicial Interpretation*, 110.

[54] Caldwell, Brief against the Constitutionality, 5–10.

[55] Id. at 9.

[56] Id. at 8–9.

Rights Act, to encompass a case like the present one.[57] To be sure, an extension of the federal judicial power would be possible if provided for by constitutional amendment, such as the Thirteenth Amendment.[58] But, Black argued, "not a word is there [in the Thirteenth Amendment] to change the original distribution of the judicial authority."[59]

Alongside these arguments, both lawyers also offered an alternative line of argument: the assertion that even if the constitutionality of the act were conceded, it still could not confer federal jurisdiction in a case such as the present one. As noted earlier, what was crucial in determining the act's applicability to this case was the matter of who was "affected" under Section 3. Caldwell's brief simply denied that either a witness or a victim fell under the "affected" jurisdiction of the Civil Rights Act.

Although part of this argument was based on judicial precedent,[60] of greater interest for our purposes were the more pragmatic and structural grounds for the argument. As Caldwell noted, if federal jurisdiction was conferred by the act whenever a state law such as the present one was at work and an African American witness might be involved, this would seemingly open the doors of the federal courts to almost any type of legal action – including civil suits between white citizens or in instances of white-on-white crime – where some African American witness could always be produced by one side or the other. Surely, Caldwell argued, such an expansion of federal jurisdiction could not have been the intention of Congress in framing the act.[61]

This was an argument motivated by the specter of perverse results. Should the Court start down the road of conferring federal jurisdiction in a case like this – that is, should it open the "floodgates" in federal jurisdiction[62] – this jurisdiction could not subsequently be constrained

---

[57] J. S. Black, Argument for the State of Kentucky, 17–23.

[58] Id. at 23–24.

[59] Id. at 24. Yet perhaps the increase in judicial power provided for in Section 3 of the Civil Rights Act might be justified as a logical extension of the Thirteenth Amendment. On this point, Black rejected the notion of any such relation between the provision for judicial authority in the Civil Rights Act and the Thirteenth Amendment. Furthermore, he argued that even if Section 3 might be inferred from the amendment through some extremely loose method of constitutional interpretation, such an interpretation should still be disfavored for being in tension with a constitutional presumption in favor of a more limited federal jurisdiction. Id. at 23–26. This argument also appears in Caldwell's Brief. Caldwell, Brief against the Constitutionality, 22–24.

[60] The relevant case was *United States v. Ortega*, 24 U.S. 467 (1826). Caldwell, Brief against the Constitutionality, 13–15.

[61] Caldwell, Brief against the Constitutionality, 15–16.

[62] Kaczorowski uses this term. Kaczorowski, *Judicial Interpretation*, 111.

in any principled way.⁶³ This emphasis on how more expansive interpretations of Reconstruction legislation posed the risk of reducing the states to inconsequential political units was also an argumentative strategy repeated by southern lawyers in other cases, to great success.

In contrast to the more confrontational tone of their first line of argument pressing toward repudiation of the Civil Rights Act of 1866, the floodgates argument was distinct in urging recalibration. Indeed, although both Black and Caldwell disputed that the act conferred federal jurisdiction in the present case, they conceded that, if constitutionally valid, the act *did* confer federal jurisdiction whenever a discriminatory state statute might affect an African American defendant or civil litigant.⁶⁴ This latter point in itself constituted a concession by Caldwell and Black to the expansion of federal judicial power under the act. This alternative line of argument thus proceeded not by wholly repudiating the Civil Rights Act but rather by conceding the legitimacy of some parts of it while still vigorously contesting others.

Justice Strong, writing for a 5–2 majority, concluded that the federal circuit court had no jurisdiction in this matter. In doing so, he ignored the more radical repudiation-minded arguments of Black and Caldwell and instead incorporated much of the floodgates argument pressed by the lawyers for Kentucky. As Strong asserted, the only parties affected in a criminal proceeding were the defendants and the state, and obviously, there was no serious concern about the rights of the white defendants not being protected in state court in this case.⁶⁵ The two African American witnesses denied the right to testify under the Kentucky state law could not be said to be affected. Their individual rights were not at stake, and they had no greater interest in the outcome of this case than any other member of the general public. If they were affected by virtue of their interest in testifying, then anyone in the community might also be said to be affected, as any member of the community could potentially be called to testify.⁶⁶ Likewise, it could not be said that the African American victim was affected by the proceeding, both because the result of criminal proceedings generally have no effect on the individual rights of the victim and, more specifically, because the victim in this case was deceased.⁶⁷

---

⁶³ Black, Argument for the State of Kentucky, 10–13.
⁶⁴ Caldwell, Brief against the Constitutionality, 16–17; Black likewise makes the same argument. Black, Argument for the State of Kentucky, 10.
⁶⁵ 80 U.S. 581, 591 (1872).
⁶⁶ Id. at 591–92.
⁶⁷ Id. at 591, 594.

Putting aside the merits of the legal argument itself,[68] the recalibrating concerns that helped drive the Court's conclusion are noteworthy. Strong's opinion evidenced clear concern with the uncertain transformative implications of Section 3 of the Civil Rights Act. Thus, in practically repeating the arguments of Black and Caldwell, Strong noted that if the two African American witnesses in this case were found to be persons affected under Section 3, this would seemingly require that the federal courts open their doors whenever a discriminatory statute such as Kentucky's existed and either party involved claimed to have an African American witness. Encompassed within this wide subset of cases would be any dispute between two white parties in which either claimed an African American witness or any criminal prosecution against a white individual who claimed an African American witness.[69] The expansion of federal judicial authority in such a dramatic way could not have been Congress' intent in the Civil Rights Act of 1866, Strong argued, as its main preoccupation was with protecting African American rights.[70]

---

[68] This legal argument is far from satisfying because, as Justice Bradley quite plausibly pointed out in dissent, the matter of which persons were "affected" in this matter was less about the witnesses and more directly about the victim and "the whole class of persons to which she belonged." The rights of the latter were obviously affected and endangered in a structural sense by the discriminatory nature of the Kentucky law. Id. at 598–600 (Bradley, J., dissenting). Goldstein offers support for this view via a statutory interpretive argument. He notes that in Section 3 of the Civil Rights Act of 1866, there is the provision for "affecting jurisdiction" – which is the focus of the earlier discussion – and a provision that allows for removal to federal court whenever state court defendants "are denied, or cannot enforce" their Section 1 rights in state courts. See § 3, 14 Stat. at 27.

Given these two provisions, and given the statutory interpretative canon to avoid superfluity, Goldstein argues that it must be the case that the "affecting jurisdiction," in the context of criminal cases, refers to something other than the invocation of federal jurisdiction to protect state court defendants. A likely interpretation then is that it refers to the creation of federal jurisdiction for individuals such as victims or witnesses whose rights may be infringed in the state courts. Goldstein, "*Blyew*," 481–83, 501–02, 504–05. More generally, Goldstein offers an insightful discussion on how *Blyew*'s decision on the "affecting jurisdiction" provision significantly constrained the means by which the federal government could address the problem of omissions or non-enforcement of criminal matters (against African American victims) by state actors. Ibid., 507–11.

[69] 80 U.S. at 592–94.

[70] Id. at 592–93. Related to this more structural concern about affecting jurisdiction, the Court also relied on a more textual-doctrinal argument. In the case of *United States v. Ortega*, 24 U.S. 467 (1826), the Court had previously interpreted the use of the word "affecting" in Article III, Section 2's clause, "In all Cases affecting Ambassadors, other public Ministers and Consuls, and those in which a State shall be a Party." As Strong noted in *Blyew*, the Court in *Ortega* had concluded that a witness in a criminal prosecution does not qualify as an individual "affected"; 80 U.S. at 594–95. As noted

Strong's more restrictive reading of Section 3 did not imply a wholesale repudiation of the idea of an expanded judicial power after Reconstruction; he still attributed to it "a far-reaching purpose." Mirroring the arguments pressed by Black and Caldwell, he noted that because the core purpose of Section 3 was one of protecting African Americans, this provision could still be rightfully and importantly employed in removing civil cases in which African American parties were treated unfairly in state courts as well as in removing state criminal cases in which African American defendants were similarly at risk.[71] The Court's opinion in *Blyew* was less about repudiation and more about delimiting the reach of reform.

The *Slaughter-House Cases*

In the *Slaughter-House Cases*,[72] the Court was confronted with white butchers in Louisiana who were contesting the monopoly enjoyed by a state-created corporation. Under this state-granted monopoly, animals could only be butchered at a legislatively designated site for the operations of the Crescent City Stock Landing and Slaughter House Company. In addition, butchers had to pay a fee for making use of the premises. The white butchers claimed that a basic right – their right to freely ply their trade – was protected by the Thirteenth Amendment, the Privileges or Immunities Clause, the Due Process Clause, and the Equal Protection Clauses of the Fourteenth Amendment, and that this right was being infringed on by the Louisiana state legislature.[73]

This very odd case can be historically situated in a number of ways. It might be seen as a peculiarity of Louisiana politics: Since Republicans still controlled the Louisiana state legislature at this point, Louisiana conservatives found themselves in the very odd position of making nationalistic legal arguments with respect to the Fourteenth Amendment in order to oppose the authority of their in-state rivals.[74] The case might also be viewed through the lens of economic rights. Finally, given that this case marked the Court's first interpretation of the Privileges or

---

earlier, this case had also been strongly emphasized in the briefs for the state of Kentucky. Black, Argument for the State of Kentucky, 26–27; Caldwell, Brief against the Constitutionality, 13–15.
[71] 80 U.S. at 593.
[72] 83 U.S. 36 (1873).
[73] Id. at 57–60.
[74] Kaczorowski, *Judicial Interpretation*, 119.

Immunities Clause, one of the key components of Section 1 of the Fourteenth Amendment,[75] the temptation is also strong to view this case as, at least implicitly, about African American rights.[76] Regardless of whether one adopts a more economic or racial perspective on this case, *Slaughter-House*'s result does fit within a broader pattern of judicial delimitation in the 1870s, with subsequent legal consequences for how African American rights might be understood in relation to the Fourteenth Amendment.

The types of legal arguments pressed by the lawyers in this case were largely the opposite of what one might expect, given where their apparent political ideologies lay. The lead attorney for the butchers was John A. Campbell, a former Supreme Court justice whose states-rights credentials stemmed from his previous resignation from the Court in order to take up a position within the Confederate government.[77] Campbell stated in his brief upon re-argument that

> it is apparent by the first clause that the national principle has received an indefinite enlargement. The tie between the United States and every citizen in every part of its own jurisdiction has been made intimate and familiar. To the same extent the confederate features of the government have been obliterated. The States in their closest connection with the members of the State, have been placed under the oversight and restraining and enforcing hand of Congress. The purpose is manifest to establish through the whole jurisdiction of the United States one people, and that every member of the empire shall understand and appreciate the constitutional fact that his privileges and immunities cannot be abridged by State authority.[78]

Furthermore, he stated that the scope of the amendment should be understood to be universal:

> It is not confined to any class or race. It comprehends all within the scope of its provisions. The vast number of laborers in mines, manufactories, commerce, as well as the laborers on the plantations are defended against the unequal legislation of the States. Nor is the amendment confined in its application to the laboring men. The mandate is universal in its application to persons of every class and every condition of persons.[79]

---

[75] Akhil Reed Amar, *Bill of Rights: Creation and Reconstruction* (New Haven, CT: Yale University Press, 1998), 182.

[76] Kaczorowski, *Judicial Interpretation*, 133, 138–39; Smith, *Civic Ideals*, 333.

[77] Ronald M. Labbé and Jonathan Lurie, *The Slaughterhouse Cases: Regulation, Reconstruction, and the Fourteenth Amendment* (Lawrence: University Press of Kansas, 2003), 107–08.

[78] John A. Campbell, Plaintiffs Brief upon the Re-argument at 28, *Slaughter-House Cases*, 83 U.S. 36 (1873).

[79] Id. at 31. For additional statements of a similar nature, see John A. Campbell, Plaintiffs' Brief at 14, 16–17, 36, *Slaughter-House Cases*, 83 U.S. 36 (1873); J. A. Q. Fellows,

In contrast, the case prompted odd statements of state sovereignty from Republican lawyers representing the state-created corporation: "The objects expressed in the title of the act are all of the highest importance to the welfare of the people of the State; they are, beyond all possibility of dispute, matters entirely within State control; such as State legislatures act on every day; such, in short, as are necessary to the very existence of the State."[80]

A principal basis for the above-noted Republican stance, and consequently the focus of much attention in the legal briefs of Thomas Durant and Charles Allen for the state corporation, was the argument that matters falling within the traditional "police power" of the states remained solidly in the hands of the state legislatures. This was true notwithstanding the legal transformation encompassed in the Reconstruction Amendments. And the present act, being an act to regulate the slaughtering of animals through the use of a state-created corporation, clearly fell within this traditional police power.[81]

Past precedent supported this position,[82] and the corporation's lawyers cast strong doubt on the idea that the Fourteenth Amendment had worked to undermine this traditional domain of state authority. Indeed, if municipal matters such as the public health regulation at issue here did fall within the protections afforded by the Fourteenth Amendment, it would place under constitutional scrutiny an unimaginable number of state and local laws that in some way touched on matters of employment, including legally imposed license fees, health and safety regulations, manufacturing regulations, and labor regulations.[83]

Furthermore, going down the path of a more expansive interpretation of the Fourteenth Amendment would open the floodgates on federal jurisdiction: all types of municipal legislation would then become matters appropriate for federal adjudication.[84] This argumentative strategy thus

History, Object, Aim and Intent of the 13th, 14th, and 15th Amendments, and of the Contemporaneous Legislation at 9, 21–23, *Slaughter-House Cases*, 83 U.S. 36 (1873).

[80] Thomas J. Durant, Brief of Counsel of State of Louisiana, and of Crescent City Live Stock Landing and Slaughter House Company, Defendants in Error at 2, *Slaughter-House Cases*, 83 U.S. 36 (1873).

[81] Thomas J. Durant, Brief of Counsel of Defendant in Error at 5–8, *Slaughter-House Cases*, 83 U.S. 36 (1873).

[82] As Charles Allen concluded, past cases "amply show that the power of a State is complete, unqualified, and exclusive in relation to all those powers which relate to merely municipal legislation or internal police." Charles Allen, Brief of Charles Allen, Esq. at 3, *Slaughter-House Cases*, 83 U.S. 36 (1873). See also id. at 5–8; Durant, Brief of Counsel, 12–13.

[83] Allen, Brief, 12; Durant, Brief of Counsel, 14.

[84] Allen, Brief, 13–14; Durant, Brief of Counsel, 8. Even if it were conceded that some matters remained solely within the state's authority as municipal matters, allowing for

mirrored that followed by Kentucky's attorneys in *Blyew*. And as Kaczorowski suggests, this may not have been a coincidence; Jeremiah Black had previously been retained to represent the corporation in this case, and he may have shared his argumentative strategy from *Blyew* with the corporation's counsel.[85]

The similarity between the two cases goes beyond the use of a floodgates argument, however. More generally, by focusing on the status of municipal legislation and the traditional police power, the corporation's lawyers pointed out the risk that this entire domain of state authority could be completely wiped out if the Court were to endorse too expansive an interpretation of the Fourteenth Amendment. To quote Durant,

> To extend the interpretation of the amendment to the length which the plaintiffs in error demand would break down the whole system of confederated State government, centralize the beautiful and harmonious system we enjoy into a consolidated and unlimited government, and render the Constitution of the United States, now the object of our love and veneration, as odious and insupportable as its enemies would wish to make it.[86]

The corporation's lawyers, however, were not engaged in a task of repudiation; they believed that the amendment did encompass certain legal changes. The lawyers went on to articulate a more constructive, recalibration-oriented interpretation of the amendment that attempted to demarcate an outer limit to its scope. The solution for them lay in recognizing the Fourteenth Amendment as primarily directed toward the rights of African Americans:

> The occasion and the necessity, then, for the adoption of the fourteenth amendment was the constitutional status of the people of African descent, and if there had been no such people in the country, no such amendment would have been proposed. It was adopted for them. The contemporaneous discussions and debates at the time of the amendment show that no other object was in view, nor can it be made to embrace any other without sacrificing its spirit.[87]

Writing for the Court, Justice Miller ultimately ruled in favor of the corporation and, in doing so, incorporated many of the defenses of state autonomy offered by the corporation's lawyers. As a presumptive matter,

---

some degree of oversight by the Court in situations like the present would still require the Court to sit in on determining which municipal regulations were reasonable or unreasonable. Allen, Brief, 13–14.
[85] Kaczorowski, *Judicial Interpretation*, 121.
[86] Durant, Brief of Counsel, 15.
[87] Id. at 10. See also id. at 7–11, 15; Allen, Brief, 15.

he noted that states in general possessed the power to undertake this kind of public health regulation under its traditional police powers, even if the regulation involved the grant of exclusive privileges to a state-created corporation.[88] In this, he echoed the sentiments expressed in the briefs of Thomas Durant and Charles Allen. The more complicated legal issue, of course, was whether the recently enacted Thirteenth and Fourteenth Amendments might impose new obstacles on the exercise of this aspect of traditional state police powers.[89]

Miller famously reached a negative conclusion for a closely-divided 5–4 Court. He first asserted that the core meaning of the Reconstruction Amendments was tied to the eradication of slavery and establishing a true, substantive freedom for African Americans after emancipation.[90] Miller relied on this purposive-driven argument to quickly dispose of the claims of the non–African American butchers based on the Thirteenth Amendment[91] and the Equal Protection Clause of the Fourteenth Amendment.[92] In doing so, he thus relied on the aforementioned limiting principle offered by the corporation's lawyers: namely to limit the potential reach of these amendments to the social group that was understood to be their primary beneficiary.

Given this presumptive limiting principle, it effectively left only the butchers' claim based upon the Privileges or Immunities Clause. However, Justice Miller also rejected the argument that this clause protected individual rights that the Louisiana state legislature had violated.[93] According to the conventional reading of this case,[94] Miller rested much of his argument on the mistaken notion that the Privileges or Immunities Clause protected only a relatively stingy set of rights that stemmed exclusively from national citizenship; the more fundamental rights of citizenship that included the butchers' free labor rights stemmed from state citizenship, and as such, were subject to the authority of state legislatures. Hence, no relief could be provided for the white butchers.[95] As Justice Field noted,

---

[88] 83 U.S. 36, 61–66 (1873).
[89] Id. at 66–67.
[90] Id. at 71–72.
[91] Id. at 69.
[92] Id. at 81. Miller also quickly disposed of the Due Process claim on doctrinal grounds. Id. at 80–81.
[93] Id. at 73–80.
[94] Amar, *Bill of Rights*, 175–76, 212–13; Richard L. Aynes, "Constricting the Law of Freedom: Justice Miller, the Fourteenth Amendment, and the *Slaughter-House Cases*," *Chicago-Kent Law Review* 70, no. 2 (1994): 627–28.
[95] 83 U.S. at 73–80.

Miller's sweeping interpretation of the Privileges or Immunities Clause effectively gutted it of any real substantive content.[96]

Viewing *Slaughter-House* through the lens of recalibration and delimitation, what is noteworthy is how the Court definitively reconciled one of the major components of the Fourteenth Amendment with the implicated but resilient authority of federalism. Recall the warning of the corporation's lawyers about the dangerous expansion of federal jurisdiction and threats to state authority. Miller's opinion seized on these points and emphatically nodded to the concern that if the Court were to broadly construe the Privileges or Immunities Clause, it would start the nation down a slippery slope toward federal centralization.[97] Furthermore, congressional oversight over the states would be unchecked by virtue of its authority under Section 5 of the Fourteenth Amendment.[98] Surely, argued Miller, such a radical change could not have been the original intent of the amendment's framers and ratifiers.[99] The following is a well-known passage from this ruling that illustrates the Court's attentiveness to boundary drawing and recalibration concerns:

> The argument we admit is not always the most conclusive which is drawn from the consequences urged against the adoption of a particular construction of an instrument. But when, as in the case before us, these consequences are so serious, so far-reaching and pervading, so great a departure from the structure and spirit of our institutions; when the effect is to fetter and degrade the State governments by subjecting them to the control of Congress, in the exercise of powers heretofore universally conceded to them of the most ordinary and fundamental character; when in fact it radically changes the whole theory of the relations of the State and

---

[96] Id. at 96 (Field, J., dissenting). More recent interpretations of *Slaughter-House* have seemingly cast Miller's opinion in a more sympathetic light due to a more expansive reading of that opinion. See, e.g., Kurt T. Lash, "The Origins of the Privileges or Immunities Clause, Part II: John Bingham and the Second Draft of the Fourteenth Amendment," *Georgetown Law Journal* 99, no. 2 (January 2011): 334; Bryan H. Wildenthal, "The Lost Compromise: Reassessing the Early Understanding in Court and Congress on Incorporation of the Bill of Rights in the Fourteenth Amendment," *Ohio State Law Journal* 61, no. 3 (2000): 1063–64, 1066. Whatever the merit of these alternative interpretations when *Slaughter-House* is viewed on its own, the attractiveness of the conventional interpretation grows when *Slaughter-House* is viewed retrospectively and alongside the Court's other Fourteenth Amendment rulings in the 1870s that encompass strong delimiting themes. Indeed, as is often noted, the federal protection of individual rights against the states had to enter through the Due Process and Equal Protection Clauses after *Slaughter-House*. This legal developmental point suggests, at the least, the plausibility of the conventional interpretation of this case.

[97] 83 U.S. at 78.

[98] Id.

[99] Id.

Federal governments to each other and of both these governments to the people; the argument has a force that is irresistible, in the absence of language which expresses such a purpose too clearly to admit of doubt.[100]

In short, the Court justified delimitation in part not by frontally challenging the validity or goals of the Fourteenth Amendment but rather by emphasizing the massive threat posed by allowing one component of it to further transform the polity. It recognized the threat posed to federalism should the amendment be construed too robustly. As urged by the corporation's attorneys, the Court pulled back from such an interpretation and moved to delimit the Privileges or Immunities Clause instead.

United States v. Cruikshank

Three years after *Slaughter-House*, a similar judicial preoccupation with demarcating the limits of Reconstruction surfaced in *United States v. Cruikshank*,[101] which grew out of federal criminal prosecutions of the white perpetrators of the Colfax Massacre in Louisiana under the Enforcement Act of May 31, 1870.[102] The defendants were charged with various offenses based on the expansively worded Section 6 of the act.[103] In *Cruikshank*, the Court conscientiously backed away from a more expansive interpretation of federal power, the immediate result being the discharge of the defendants due to the legal insufficiency of these various criminal counts on a number of different grounds.

As a clear indication of the broader political significance attributed to the case at the time, the defense team in *Cruikshank* had originally been assembled and funded by a public subscription campaign held by Louisiana Democrats, who recognized this case as a suitable vehicle for

---

[100] Id.
[101] 92 U.S. 542 (1876).
[102] Id. at 548.
[103] "That if two or more persons shall band or conspire together, or go in disguise upon the public highway, or upon the premises of another, with intent to violate any provisions of this act, or to injure, oppress, threaten, or intimidate any citizen with intent to prevent or hinder his free exercise and enjoyment of any right or privilege granted or secured to him by the constitution or laws of the United States, or because of his having exercised the same, such persons shall be held guilty of felony, and, on conviction thereof, shall be fined or imprisoned, or both, at the discretion of the court, – the fine not to exceed $5,000, and the imprisonment not to exceed ten years; and shall, moreover, be thereafter ineligible to, and disabled from holding, any office or place of honor, profit, or trust created by the constitution or laws of the United States." Enforcement Act of May 31, 1870, ch. 114, § 6, 16 Stat. 140, 141 (1870).

challenging the constitutionality of the May 1870 Enforcement Act.[104] By the time this case reached the Supreme Court, the defense team included the previously discussed John A. Campbell, along with David Dudley Field, who was the brother of Supreme Court Justice Stephen J. Field.[105] Equally significant was the involvement of Reverdy Johnson, who was at least as prominent a lawyer as any involved in these cases. Johnson had formerly been a Democratic senator and U.S. attorney general, and he was an outspoken critic of Reconstruction who had previously been hired by South Carolina Democrats as a defense lawyer in the Ku Klux Klan trials.[106]

Although a number of issues in this case implicated the scope of federal authority,[107] the most significant portion of the Court's ruling for

---

[104] Robert M. Goldman, *Reconstruction & Black Suffrage: Losing the Right to Vote in Reese and Cruikshank* (Lawrence: University Press of Kansas, 2001), 53.

[105] Ibid., 76.

[106] Ibid., 37, 76. Lou Falkner Williams, *The Great South Carolina Ku Klux Klan Trials, 1871–1872* (Athens: University of Georgia Press, 1996), 54–55. Johnson and Henry Stanbery, the latter of whom is referenced later, had actually first rehearsed many of the federalism-centered arguments put forth in *Cruikshank* and *Reese* (discussed later) in the course of their representation of South Carolina Klansmen in these earlier lower federal court trials. Ibid., 66–68.

[107] Four of the sixteen counts charged the defendants with violating two specific rights of citizenship. The first and ninth counts charged the defendants with the intent "to hinder and prevent the citizens named in the free exercise and enjoyment of their 'lawful right and privilege to peaceably assemble together with each other and with other citizens of the United States for a peaceful and lawful purpose.'" 92 U.S. at 551. The second and tenth counts similarly charged the defendants with infringing on their victims' right of "bearing arms for a lawful purpose." Id. at 553. The references for the citizenship rights named in these four counts were the First and Second Amendments, respectively.

Following the path set out in *Slaughter-House*, Waite's opinion for the Court did not prove hospitable to an expansive conception of national citizenship rights. Instead, Waite held to a theory of dual citizenship, in which state and national governments were conceptualized to peacefully coexist because of their fully separate jurisdictions – within which each governing body was supreme. Id. at 550. Working within this conceptual framework, the crucial question then became whether the aforementioned criminal counts fell on the federal or state side of the line as a matter of jurisdiction. Taking a cue from *Slaughter-House*, Waite proceeded to paint a picture of state citizenship guarantees as generally much more expansive than national citizenship guarantees, thus finding the offenses falling outside the scope of federal law. Id. at 551–53.

In taking these positions on these specific citizenship rights, Waite was merely following the same line of thought that had been suggested by *Slaughter-House* and that had been urged by the defendants' lawyers in this case – i.e., a line sympathetic to principles of traditional federalism. With respect to the defendants' briefs, see David S. Bryon, Brief for Defendants, *U.S. v. Cruikshank*, 92 U.S. 542 (1876), in *Landmark Briefs and Arguments of the Supreme Court of the United States: Constitutional Law*, eds. Philip B. Kurland and Gerhard Casper (Arlington, VA: University Publications of America, the present argument was its judgment with respect to several other criminal counts that touched on the Fourteenth Amendment. The third and eleventh counts charged the defendants with "the intent to... deprive the citizens named, they being in Louisiana, 'of their respective several lives and liberty of person without due process of law.'"[108] This count was in reference to both the Fifth Amendment and the Fourteenth Amendment. Likewise, the fourth and twelfth counts focused on a different clause of the Fourteenth Amendment and charged the defendants with having the intent to "prevent and hinder the citizens named, who were of African descent and persons of color, in 'the free exercise and enjoyment of their several right and privilege [sic] to the full and equal benefit of all laws and proceedings, then and there, before that time, enacted or ordained by the said State of Louisiana and by the United States.'"[109]

The defense lawyers resorted to arguments that bypassed any attempt to deny the legitimacy of the Fourteenth Amendment or the political changes it had wrought. Rather, they sought to draw sharp outer limits on its reach and to demonstrate how it failed to reach the present case. The defense lawyers did this by pressing on the idea that the guarantees of Section 1 of the Fourteenth Amendment (including the Due Process and Equal Protection Clauses) touched only state actions and not actions by private individuals, thus rendering the crimes in the present case outside the amendment's reach.

To quote from David Bryon's brief for the defense: "The language of that clause of the 14th amendment is, '*Nor shall any* "STATE" deprive any person of life, liberty or property, without due process of law.' This language is addressed to a '*State*' – to the State of Louisiana. What is a 'State?' Is it an individual? Is it one, two, or three persons? Do the accused at the bar constituted [sic] the State of Louisiana?"[110]

Bryon later answered these questions without equivocation:

The fourteenth and fifteenth amendments to the Constitution of the United States, places [sic] certain inhibitions on the several States. The *only way in which these amendments can be violated*, is by the legislative or conventional acts of a "State."

1975), 319, 329–30; John A. Campbell, Brief for Defendants, *U.S. v. Cruikshank*, 92 U.S. 542 (1876), in *Landmark Briefs*, eds. Kurland and Casper, 391–92. On the First Amendment issue, Bryon, Brief for Defendants, 325; Campbell, Brief for Defendants, 386. On the Second Amendment issue, Bryon, Brief for Defendants, 326; Campbell, Brief for Defendants, 386–87.

[108] 92 U.S. at 553.
[109] Id. at 554.
[110] Bryon, Brief for Defendants, 339 (emphasis in original).

All the people of a State in their *personal and individual capacity*, may do what the amendments prohibit a State from doing, and still they are not violated; they may take a man's life, in open combat, or by a secret taking off, they may rob him of his property on the highway, or by stealth; they may restrain him of his liberty, and by violence and intimidation prevent him from voting, and still they have not violated these amendments, because these individuals are not the State, and their acts are not the acts of the "State."[111]

The state action argument was clearly an important element of the defense's legal strategy. Reference to the state action point is present – with varied attention – in all of the defendants' briefs and in the oral argument.[112]

Furthermore, the arguments by the defense lawyers were hardly limited to textual points; more structural and institutional considerations were apparent as well. As Bryon asked, should the Court allow the federal oversight provided for in the Fourteenth Amendment to extend to private actions, "What crime or offense known to the law, committed within [sic] the limits of a State, is there, of which the courts of the United States, may not take jurisdiction?"[113] Ordinary crimes such as murder or robbery, traditionally understood to fall within the province of state government, could all readily be conceptualized in terms of a deprivation of life or property without due process and thus perhaps encompassed by the Fourteenth Amendment. As a result, the more expansive interpretation of the amendment could imply the displacement of local criminal administration entirely.[114] Lawyers for the defendant thus pleaded for the Court to set an outer limit on reform. To quote from R. H. Marr's brief for the defendants: "The time has come when the line of demarcation between State and Federal power must be plainly defined, and maintained

---

[111] Id. at 340–41 (emphasis in original).
[112] Campbell, Brief for Defendants, 406–07; David Dudley Field, Brief for the Defendants *U.S. v. Cruikshank*, 92 U.S. 542 (1876), in *Landmark Briefs*, eds. Kurland and Casper, 415–16; David Dudley Field, Argument of Mr. David Dudley Field on behalf of the Defendants, *U.S. v. Cruikshank*, 92 U.S. 542 (1876), in *Landmark Briefs*, eds. Kurland and Casper, 436; R. H. Marr, Brief for Defendants, *U.S. v. Cruikshank*, 92 U.S. 542 (1876), in *Landmark Briefs*, eds. Kurland and Casper, 364–66. See also Bryon, Brief for Defendants, 334–35. Although our focus is on the state action limitation with respect to the Fourteenth Amendment, the aforementioned citations also illustrate the defense's concern with urging a state action limitation on the Fifteenth Amendment, as four of the criminal counts in this case concerned voting rights. The Court's treatment of these counts, however, is of less interest to us since it essentially reiterated its holding in *Reese* (discussed later). Furthermore, the Court also seemed to implicitly reject a state action limitation with respect to the Fifteenth Amendment in *Cruikshank*. 92 U.S. at 555–57.
[113] Bryon, Brief for Defendants, 340.
[114] Id.

Emancipation, the Reconstruction Era, and Delimitation

with a steady and an even hand, lest it be obliterated and utterly lost, to the ruin of our institutions. This duty now devolves upon this Court, the great conservative department of the government, made independent by the Constitution."[115]

These arguments found a receptive audience on the Court; indeed, Waite's opinion for an essentially unanimous Court[116] helped formulate the state action doctrine. On the third and eleventh counts, which charged the defendants with "the intent to... deprive the citizens named, they being in Louisiana, 'of their respective several lives and liberty of person without due process of law,'" Waite at first merely reasserted points he had made earlier in the opinion on the legitimacy of a robust state sovereignty distinct from federal authority. He noted that the responsibility for rights of "life and personal liberty" – the rights referred to in these counts – "rests alone with the States."[117]

But he also went on to address the state action issues that had been raised by the defense lawyers: "The fourteenth amendment prohibits a State from depriving any person of life, liberty, or property, without due process of law; but this adds nothing to the rights of one citizen as against another. It simply furnishes an additional guaranty against any encroachment by the States upon the fundamental rights which belong to every citizen as a member of society."[118]

With respect to the applicability of the Equal Protection Clause, Waite also articulated a state action limitation:

The fourteenth amendment prohibits a State from denying to any person within its jurisdiction the equal protection of the laws; but this provision does not, any more than the one which precedes it, and which we have just considered [the Due Process Clause], add any thing to the rights which one citizen has under the Constitution against another. The equality of the rights of citizens is a principle of republicanism.... The only obligation resting upon the United States is to see that the States do not deny the right. This the amendment guarantees, but no more. The power of the national government is limited to the enforcement of this guaranty.[119]

Notably, despite his sympathy for the state action arguments urged by the defense, Waite's opinion was relatively light on grand, sweeping statements regarding the threatened demise of the states. In this way, at least,

---

[115] Marr, Brief for Defendants, 378. For similarly sweeping statements, see Bryon, Brief for Defendants, 345; Campbell, Brief for Defendants, 407, 409.
[116] Justice Clifford dissented, but he concurred in the result.
[117] 92 U.S. 542, 553–54 (1876).
[118] Id. at 554.
[119] Id. at 554–55.

he did not mirror the rhetoric of the defense lawyers. Indeed, Waite's opinion failed to even strike down Section 6 of the Enforcement Act as unconstitutional, even though the Court's acceptance of the state action limitation seemed to necessitate such a result.

Benedict and Goldman noted this incongruity and interpreted *Cruikshank* as a somewhat less conservative ruling than has traditionally been assumed.[120] Kaczorowski, on the other hand, read little into the Court's failure to strike down Section 6 as unconstitutional and did not attribute this omission to a more moderate predisposition from the Court.[121] My interpretation is perhaps somewhat distinct: the qualified incoherence of the *Cruikshank* opinion might instead reflect the Court still working itself, in the midst of postreform uncertainties, toward a recalibration settlement that would maintain the institutional changes of Reconstruction while accommodating them to a resilient authority of federalism. Such a settlement would in fact become the state action doctrine, and it would reach maturity with the *Civil Rights Cases*.[122]

United States v. Reese

United States v. Reese[123] came down on the same day as *Cruikshank*, and the Court again declined an invitation to broadly construe federal judicial power in this case. Two municipal elections inspectors in Kentucky had refused the vote of an African American man, and they were prosecuted under Sections 3 and 4 of the May 31, 1870, Enforcement Act.[124] In line with previous cases in which distinguished lawyers represented southern interests, one of the defense lawyers was former U.S. attorney general Henry Stanbery, a member of Andrew Johnson's cabinet and a defense attorney in Johnson's impeachment. Stanbery had been a strong critic of Reconstruction, and along with the previously noted Reverdy Johnson,

---

[120] Michael Les Benedict, "Preserving Federalism: Reconstruction and the Waite Court," *Supreme Court Review* (1979): 74, 77–79; Goldman, *Black Suffrage*, 106.
[121] Kaczorowski, *Judicial Interpretation*, 175–78.
[122] 109 U.S. 3 (1883). Notably, Waite also seemed to entertain the possibility of federal involvement in alleged equal protection violations by private actors where there was state inaction and a racial motivation (the latter of which was not alleged in *Cruikshank*). It is not clear, however, whether Waite saw this as a loophole to the state action requirement of the Fourteenth Amendment's Equal Protection Clause or whether he saw a possible applicability for the Thirteenth Amendment in such cases of private racial discrimination. 92 U.S. at 555.
[123] 92 U.S. 214 (1876).
[124] Id. at 215.

had been hired as a defense attorney for Klansmen in the Ku Klux Klan trials of 1871–72.[125]

The Court, speaking again through Chief Justice Waite for a near-unanimous decision,[126] found these two statutory provisions to be unconstitutional for exceeding the scope of the Fifteenth Amendment. Waite's opinion asserted that the Fifteenth Amendment did not positively "confer the right of suffrage upon any one."[127] Rather, it merely "prevents the States, or the United States... from giving preference... to one citizen of the United States over another on account of race, color, or previous condition of servitude."[128] Given this specific focus of the Fifteenth Amendment, the Court then asserted that the two statutory provisions in question were invalid because they were not similarly confined to racial violations.[129] It was thus disinclined to find an implied racial limitation on these two statutory provisions stemming from Sections 1 and 2 of the same act – which did evidence such a limitation – as Justice Hunt had argued for in his dissent.[130]

One might reasonably ascertain from its actions that the Court was not eager to carve out a role for the federal courts in policing elections. Yet this reluctance did not amount to the judiciary explicitly repudiating Reconstruction either. It bears repeating: the Court struck down the aforementioned statutory provisions because they were not drafted narrowly enough in being limited to voting discriminations based on race. In taking this action, the Court left the door open for Congress to draft a more narrowly drawn statute in the future. There was nothing in the opinion that directly challenged Congress' ability to protect the voting rights of African Americans from racial discrimination. To the contrary, the Court conceded that such a congressional right existed.[131]

Strauder v. West Virginia and Virginia v. Rives

Running counter to the cases discussed so far, *Strauder v. West Virginia*[132] might pose something of a counterexample to the thesis that the Supreme

---

[125] Goldman, *Black Suffrage*, 76–77; Williams, *Trials*, 55.
[126] Hunt and Clifford dissented, although the latter did concur with the result.
[127] 92 U.S. at 217.
[128] Id.
[129] Id. at 218–20.
[130] Id. at 218–22; Id. at 241–46 (Hunt, J., dissenting).
[131] Id. at 219–22.
[132] 100 U.S. 303 (1880).

Court's dominant impulse in the 1870s was to delimit Reconstruction. In *Strauder*, Justice Strong, writing for a 7–2 majority, struck down a West Virginia statute that formally excluded African Americans from jury service as a violation of the Equal Protection Clause. More important, he did so with very strong, sweeping statements on racial equality. In addition, in the opinion for *Ex parte Virginia*[133] – also written by Justice Strong and handed down on the same day as *Strauder* – the Court reaffirmed the authority of a federal district court to indict and hold in custody a Virginia state judge for excluding African Americans from jury service (in violation not of the Equal Protection Clause but rather of the Civil Rights Act of 1875). At first glance, these cases might appear to fit oddly alongside some of the Court's more conservative rulings of the time.

On further consideration, however, both cases fit easily alongside the earlier delimiting rulings. First, both of the jury cases involved particularly blatant legal violations. *Strauder*, for example, involved a very straightforward equal protection violation, given that the law in question encompassed a formal legal discrimination against African Americans. Because the Fourteenth Amendment was motivated by a near-consensual Republican desire to undercut Black Code–like violations, it is quite difficult to see how the West Virginia law could have been made compatible with the amendment, given that it essentially replicated a Black Code regulation.

The same might be said of the state judge's actions in *Ex parte Virginia*. One could dispute whether jury discrimination was a legitimate Fourteenth Amendment concern, as the lawyers for West Virginia had argued in their briefs to the Court.[134] Notwithstanding such arguments,

---

[133] 100 U.S. 339 (1880).

[134] Critiques along these lines might follow one of two argumentative tracks. One track might assert that Section 1 of the Fourteenth Amendment was not intended to reach the domain of racial discrimination with respect to juries. This point was pressed in the brief of Robert White, attorney general for the state of West Virginia. Robert White, Brief at 4–6, 14, 22–26, *Strauder v. West Virginia*, 100 U.S. 303 (1880). A second argumentative track, closely related to the first, might lean on problematic implications flowing from conceptualizing jury discrimination as an equal protection harm to the defendant. If this were a defendant-centered harm, then why would there not also be an equal protection violation to elderly, female, or minor defendants when members of their respective classes were excluded from their juries? The text of the Fourteenth Amendment refers to equal protection for "persons" after all – not just "citizens" or "African Americans." Id. at 3–4, 7–8, 25–26. These critiques were also repeated in Justice Field's dissent in *Ex Parte Virginia*, 100 U.S. 339, 367–69 (1880). In response to these arguments, however, it is the case that class based on race was undoubtedly the primary concern behind the enactment of the Fourteenth Amendment – certainly much

however, *Strauder* and *Ex parte Virginia* could more plausibly be seen as presenting extremely clear-cut legal violations. The Court's desire to address them can be interpreted as perfectly consistent with its statements in *Blyew* and *Slaughter-House*: the core purpose of the Reconstruction Amendments was to protect African American rights. Whereas the latter two cases implicated questions of recalibration and legal uncertainties at the outer margins of Reconstruction's reforms, *Strauder* and *Ex parte Virginia* did not. Additionally, and equally significant, the potential reach of *Strauder*'s ruling was immediately limited by a third important jury case handed down that same day and authored by Justice Strong: *Virginia v. Rives*.[135]

Rives arose out of the indictment of two African Americans for the murder of a white man in Patrick County, Virginia. The defendants petitioned for a removal of their case to federal court, claiming, among other things, that they had been indicted by an all-white jury, that they would be tried before an all-white trial jury, that a strong racial prejudice existed against them in Patrick County, and that they would be unable to obtain an impartial jury without any African Americans present on their trial jury. The defendants further asserted that Patrick County had a consistent history of all-white juries – even in cases where African American interests were affected.[136] After state proceedings had begun, Federal Circuit Court judge Alexander Rives removed the case to his court and took custody of the prisoners.[137] Litigation ensued over whether proper grounds for federal removal were present, with Virginia asserting its right to try the defendants itself.[138]

In *Rives*, the Court gave a clear indication of how the sweeping, principled statements of *Strauder* would be cabined. First, *Strauder* indicated that state-sponsored racial discrimination in juries – in violation of the

---

more so than class based on gender or age. Furthermore, the equal protection harm implicated in jury discrimination may easily be conceptualized as less the harm suffered by a particular African-American defendant facing a particular all-white jury, and more as a systematic harm posed to the subset of African American defendants, who are much more likely as a systematic matter to suffer equal protection harms in facing only all-white juries. Finally, assuming one finds these responses unsatisfying, one might also avoid Field's critiques altogether by conceptualizing jury discrimination as a violation of the Fifteenth Amendment political rights of potential jurors to serve on juries. On this latter point, see Vikram D. Amar, "Jury Service as Political Participation Akin to Voting," *Cornell Law Review* 80, no. 2 (1995): 203–59.

[135] 100 U.S. 313 (1880).
[136] Id. at 315.
[137] Id. at 316.
[138] Id. at 316–17.

Equal Protection Clause – could readily be inferred by a state law mandating such exclusions. But could such a violation be inferred simply by the nature of a trial jury's racial composition itself, as the defendants in *Rives* pressed? Virginia's lawyers argued otherwise: "Hardly will it be maintained that a violator of the criminal law of a State can claim as a civil right to be tried by a jury of a particular race or color. The offender would always demand a jury from that race or color which he thought most favorable to him or least likely to punish the offence. Congress cannot be supposed to have enacted a law tending to this result."[139]

Indeed, if the Court were to allow for a defendant's right to a particular trial jury composition, what would be next along this slippery slope? Perhaps a right to a fair racial composition among judges could also be a requirement under the Equal Protection Clause.[140] On these points, Strong was in agreement with Virginia's lawyers. In his *Rives* opinion, he made explicit what was more implicit in *Strauder*:[141] that no equal protection violation would necessarily be inferred from the prospect of all-white trial juries convicting African American defendants. The Fourteenth Amendment required the *absence* of racial exclusion from jury service, and not the *presence* of mixed trial juries for an African American defendant.[142]

Rives cabined the more expansive equal protection language of *Strauder* in a second, even more significant way: it also imposed consequential limits on the scope of federal oversight of the state courts with respect to equal protection violations. Section 641 of the Revised Statutes, the descendent of Section 3 of the Civil Rights Act of 1866, provided for removal of a case into federal court

> when any civil suit or criminal prosecution is commenced in any State court for any cause whatsoever against any person who is denied, or cannot enforce, in the judicial tribunals of the State, or in the part of the State where such prosecution is pending, any right secured to him by any law providing for the equal civil rights of citizens of the United States, or of all persons within the jurisdiction of the United States.[143]

---

[139] James G. Field and WM. J. Robertson, Brief for the Petitioner at 10, *Virginia v. Rives*, 100 U.S. 313 (1880).

[140] Id. at 10–11.

[141] The scope of the equal protection guarantee in the context of jury composition was touched on in *Strauder*, 100 U.S. at 310.

[142] *Rives*, 100 U.S. at 320, 322–23.

[143] *Strauder*, 100 U.S. at 311. See Benno C. Schmidt, Jr. "Juries, Jurisdiction, and Race Discrimination: The Lost Promise of *Strauder v. West Virginia*," *Texas Law Review* 61, no. 8 (May 1983): 1432.

The Court had found in *Strauder* that this provision should have justified removal of the case to federal court.[144] The *Rives* opinion devoted more attention to this provision and interpreted it to countenance removal of cases only before a trial, and not after a trial had commenced. As a result, it interpreted this removal statute to only touch those equal protection violations that could be apprehended with a degree of certainty before a trial started.

The consequence of these interpretive moves, however, is that they effectively limited the scope of the removal statute to only those equal protection violations that could be discerned in formal legal enactments such as a state law or a state constitutional provision.[145] It was only these types of inequalities – formal legal discriminations such as that in *Strauder* – that

> a defendant can affirm, on oath, before trial, that he is denied the equal protection of the laws or equality of civil rights. But in the absence of constitutional or legislative impediments he cannot swear before his case comes to trial that his enjoyment of all his civil rights is denied to him. When he has only an apprehension that such rights will be withheld from him when his case shall come to trial, he cannot affirm that they are actually denied, or that he cannot enforce them. Yet such an affirmation is essential to his right to remove his case. By the express requirement of the statute his petition must set forth the facts upon which he bases his claim to have his case removed, and not merely his belief that he cannot enforce his rights at a subsequent stage of the proceedings. The statute was not, therefore, intended as a corrective of errors or wrongs committed by judicial tribunals in the administration of the law at the trial.[146]

All other types of equal protection violations would not prompt removal to the federal courts under this statutory provision.

The opinion in *Rives* was indeed candid in admitting that a number of possible equal protection violations in state courts were possible after a trial commenced. These types of violations might be relatively more common, arising in the form of judicial rulings during trial or in the form of sentencing discrimination. Again, however, the latter types of violations could *not* be discerned before a trial had started, and given Section 641's provision for only pretrial removal, these other types of equal protection violations could not come under the remedial scope of Section 641.

---

[144] 100 U.S. at 310–12.
[145] *Rives*, 100 U.S. at 319–20.
[146] Id. at 320.

Congress could theoretically address in-trial equal protection violations with another removal statute. Strong conceded that the scope of the Fourteenth Amendment was broader than that of Section 641. Alternatively, these in-trial violations could also be addressed on review by higher state courts and by the Supreme Court itself on appeal. Such violations alone, however, were simply not sufficient to justify removal under this particular statute.[147]

Strong stated the following in limiting his focus to only formal racial discriminations in state law:

> But when a subordinate officer of the State, in violation of State law, undertakes to deprive an accused party of a right which the statute law accords to him, as in the case at bar, it can hardly be said that he is denied, or cannot enforce, "in the judicial tribunals of the State" the rights which belong to him. In such a case it ought to be presumed the court will redress the wrong.... The court will correct the wrong, will quash the indictment or the panel, or, if not, the error will be corrected in a superior court. We cannot think such cases are within the provisions of sect. 641. Denials of equal rights in the action of the judicial tribunals of the State are left to the revisory powers of this court.[148]

Less formal jury discrimination by prosecutors or other litigators – that is, administrative discrimination – was not touched by Section 641 since it was presumed that the state courts would redress any constitutional violations they came across. Again, moreover, if the state courts failed to act, the error could still reach a higher state court or the Supreme Court on appeal.[149]

To repeat, Strong noted that these were limitations inherent in Section 641 and not the Fourteenth Amendment.[150] In addition, there is an obvious and undeniable tone of good faith in the state judicial machinery as well; that is, a trust in higher state courts to correct errors and violations of the Reconstruction Amendments in its lower courts – in matters such as the illegal discrimination of potential African American jurors by the state officer in charge of such selections. In this respect, Strong echoed the arguments first pressed by Virginia's lawyers.[151]

---

[147] Id. at 319–20.
[148] Id. at 321–22.
[149] Id.
[150] Id. at 319–20.
[151] Field and Robertson, Brief for the Petitioner, 17.

Following the path set by *Rives*, the Court ruled in the subsequent case of *Neal v. Delaware*[152] that removal of a criminal case to federal court was improper despite virtual concession by the state's attorneys that purposeful discrimination against African Americans for jury service was the norm in its state courts. The reason for this was disturbingly simple: the state had not formalized its discriminatory practices with a legal enactment.[153] The Court did find the racial exclusions in this case to be an equal protection violation for the African American defendant, however, and reversed the state court ruling on those grounds.[154]

During the next fifty years, jury-related equal protection violations would thrive in those areas that the Court declined to reach in *Rives*. The common technique of discriminatory southern legal administration was to engage in racially discriminatory jury exclusion without any formal rules and without any subsequent correction of these violations in the state courts. Again, the *Rives* opinion indicated that in-trial violations could still be corrected through the Supreme Court's appellate jurisdiction of state cases, but this hardly constituted an adequate response to the problem.[155]

One can thus glean from the *Rives* opinion that the Court was not anxious to open the doors to federal removal for all possible equal protection violations and therefore assume the role of overseer for all state court matters dealing with African American defendants. *Rives*'s statutory conclusions on the proper institutional balance between the state and federal courts constituted another delimiting conclusion on the reach of Reconstruction. Although it remained consistent with *Strauder*'s protection for African American defendants from formal legal discriminations – a

---

[152] 103 U.S. 370 (1880).
[153] Id. at 393–95.
[154] Id. at 396–98.
[155] Schmidt, "Juries," 1434. Furthermore, it is also not clear that the Court's limitation on federal removal in *Rives* was necessarily based on a good legal argument. First, it is not clear that removal was only appropriate as a pretrial matter. The removal provision in Section 3 of the Civil Rights Act of 1866, the statutory precursor to Section 641, had not indicated when removal could occur. It was only with its codification into the 1875 Revised Statutes, as Section 641, that removal became only a pretrial option. Ibid., 1432. But, as Schmidt notes, even if we assumed that removal was only appropriate pretrial, it would still be possible to apprehend equal protection violations before a trial without the benefit of a formalized statutory or constitutional discriminatory law. For example, mere evidence of systematic discrimination as practiced in certain state courts would be equally informative of likely violations of constitutional rights before a trial began. Ibid., 1434–36.

clear concession to the legitimacy of Reconstruction – *Rives* nevertheless served as a moderating and restraining influence against potentially more expansive interpretations of *Strauder*'s language. In this manner, the post–Reconstruction Court's cases on juries also reflected the recalibrating tenor of the period.

Civil Rights Cases

The Court's delimiting orientation toward Reconstruction, beginning with *Blyew* in 1872, aligns with its 1883 decision in the *Civil Rights Cases*.[156] The statute involved in the *Civil Rights Cases* was the Civil Rights Act of 1875, which provided for equality of rights with respect to public accommodations, without regard to race. Justice Bradley, writing for the Court, struck down Section 1 (the equality in public accommodations provision) and Section 2 (the provision imposing penalties on violators of Section 1) of that act as unconstitutional. Within this case, judicial delimitation found its clearest, principled expression in the form of the state action doctrine.

First, Bradley asserted for an 8–1 Court that the act could not be justified as a valid exercise of congressional power under Section 1 and Section 5 of the Fourteenth Amendment because Section 1 provided guarantees of individual rights – including a guarantee of equal protection – against actions of "the State" only. Such state actions might include state legal enactments or state proceedings. Section 1 did not purport to address private action, however, and given that the Civil Rights Act appeared to be oriented toward dealing with private actions and private violations without any limitation to state actions, the Civil Rights Act could not be justified under the Fourteenth Amendment.[157] This was largely the same argument offered in *Cruikshank*.[158]

---

[156] 109 U.S. 3 (1883).
[157] Id. at 10–15.
[158] The state action requirement was also articulated in the case of *United States v. Harris*, 106 U.S. 629 (1883), decided almost nine months before the *Civil Rights Cases*. In this case, Section 5519 of the Revised Statutes, a statutory descendent of Section 2 of the Ku Klux Klan Act (Wang, *Trial*, 212), was struck down because it purported to punish civil rights violations by private parties. The Court ruled that the act could not be justified under the Fifteenth Amendment, the Fourteenth Amendment's Section 1 and Section 5, the Thirteenth Amendment, or Article IV Section 2. In discussing the Fourteenth Amendment, the Court stated, "It is perfectly clear from the language of the first section that its purpose also was to place a restraint upon the action of the States." 106 U.S. at 638.

Second, the Court also took up the question of whether the act could be justified under the Thirteenth Amendment. Although it acknowledged that the Thirteenth Amendment had no state action limitation, the Court was unable to recognize refusal of service at an inn or theater as amounting to a badge of slavery.[159] With no basis in either the Thirteenth or the Fourteenth Amendments, Bradley concluded that the act was unconstitutional.[160]

Bradley's opinion is particularly interesting for the structural concerns motivating the state action limitation.[161] Similar to several of the opinions already discussed, Bradley also broached the subject of likely perverse consequences arising from a ruling that would uphold the broad exertion of federal authority in the Civil Rights Act. As he stated, "If this legislation is appropriate for enforcing the prohibitions of the amendment, it is difficult to see where it is to stop. Why may not Congress with equal show of authority enact a code of laws for the enforcement and vindication of all rights of life, liberty, and property?"[162] Furthermore, if Congress could do this, "that would be to establish a code of municipal law regulative of all private rights between man and man in society. It would be to make Congress take the place of the State legislatures and to supersede them."[163]

This language was not entirely novel by 1883, and the Court's decision to step away from the terrifying prospect of centralization is telling of the delimiting and recalibrating impulse at work. The significance of

---

[159] 109 U.S. at 24–25.
[160] Id. at 25.
[161] Justice Harlan's dissent offered a powerful set of counterarguments. First, given that public accommodations possess a quasi-public character, it is far from obvious that legislation aimed at regulating them amounted to legislation directed at private actors. Given their quasi-public status, Harlan found racial discrimination by these types of entities in particular to be sufficient to constitute a badge of slavery and to fall under the authority of the Thirteenth Amendment. Id. at 37–43 (Harlan, J., dissenting). Second, given this quasi-public nature, public accommodations might readily be conceptualized as state actors in a sense, making the Civil Rights Act valid legislation *even if* we assume a state action limitation in the Fourteenth Amendment. Id. at 58–59. Finally, the state action requirement is debatable, particularly if one notes that the Citizenship Clause is the first sentence of Section 1 of the Fourteenth Amendment, and that it has no state action limitation. If one conceptualized this act as an exercise of Congress' Section 5 powers to protect the rights of citizenship affirmed in the first sentence of Section 1 of the Fourteenth Amendment, then this would seem to point out yet another plausible constitutional basis for it. Id. at 46–47, 50–56.
[162] Id. at 14.
[163] Id. at 13.

the *Civil Rights Cases* lies in the Court's attempt to offer a clear, principled articulation of how far the scope of national authority – and the authority of Reconstruction – extended. In delimiting this authority, Reconstruction was not directly repudiated; the authority of the federal government to address equal protection violations in state actions was explicitly recognized. That same federal authority did not extend to addressing private acts, however. The scope of Reconstruction principles was thus delimited, in significant part, with reference to the continuing legitimacy of state autonomy.[164]

Seen through the lens of recalibration, the significance of these rulings for the subsequent rise of Jim Crow is apparent. They constituted the first principled, definitive reassertions of federalism by the federal government after Reconstruction because the Supreme Court was able to undertake certain actions that lay beyond the reach of conservative actors in the elected branches. Furthermore, by enshrining these principles in constitutional law, the Supreme Court imposed a heightened burden on those proponents of Reconstruction who were inclined to press their transformative goals further. After 1883, proponents of reform would have to contend with not only a strengthened foe in the elected branches but also with the burden of overcoming the pronouncements of the Court – pronouncements that now constituted the status quo.[165]

Yet Jim Crow itself was not a foregone conclusion after the *Civil Rights Cases*. It remained possible – although highly unlikely – that reformers could have regained the upper hand and aggressively pressed forward with Reconstruction. This would have meant Congress steamrolling over the Court in the late nineteenth century. More plausibly, the potential

---

[164] Pamela Brandwein has forcefully argued that the state action limitation established in the *Civil Rights Cases* was less expansive than conventionally understood. Specifically, she argues that the state action limitation still allowed for federal actions in response to both state actions and instances of state neglect with respect to racially based private violations of core civil rights. The upshot of Brandwein's argument is to suggest a different perspective on the Waite Court as not die-hard opponents of Reconstruction but rather racial moderates. Pamela Brandwein, "The *Civil Rights Cases* and the Lost Language of State Neglect," in *The Supreme Court & American Political Development*, ed. Ronald Kahn and Ken I. Kersch (Lawrence: University Press of Kansas, 2006), 275–325. To an extent, her view of the Waite Court aligns well with the interpretation of the post-Reconstruction cases offered here: although these cases did delimit the scope of Reconstruction, it is quite clear that they did not reverse or undo Reconstruction either.

[165] Valelly makes this point as well. Richard M. Valelly, *The Two Reconstructions: The Struggle for Black Enfranchisement* (Chicago: University of Chicago Press, 2004), 19.

remained even in the 1880s for a system of race relations to emerge in the South that could have been at least marginally more receptive to African American interests than was Jim Crow. After all, the Supreme Court itself offered a surprising defense of African American voting rights in *Ex parte Yarbrough*[166] in 1884. The most consequential political effect of this ruling was, in turn, to encourage the federal government to attempt to pass another enforcement act, which it came close to doing in 1890–91. Indeed, the proposed Lodge Bill would have employed the federal courts and newly created boards of canvassers to punish southern electoral fraud by decertifying questionable congressional elections results.[167] Although neither this enforcement mechanism nor the *Yarbrough* decision itself would have amounted to a return of federal governmental intervention in the South on the order of a military presence, such reforms might still have alleviated some of the abuses of Jim Crow.

In sum, while these delimiting rulings did not conclusively entrench Jim Crow on their own, they helped facilitate that outcome. As the nineteenth century progressed, the scope of viable alternative governing arrangements for southern race relations increasingly narrowed. By taking the path that it did in reasserting the authority of federalism in the 1870s and 1880s, the Court played a significant role in pressing the path of development toward more conservative alternatives.

CONCLUSION

This chapter provides a first look at general processes of delimitation that are repeated in our subsequent case studies. As seen here, these processes encompassed a sequence of legislative and judicial dialogue: legislative action toward reform is stalled by governing crises – such as the southern Redemption efforts and the Panic of 1873 – which then opens the door for the judiciary to delimit the scope of political change by recalibrating reform principles in light of resilient institutions and rights. Persistent legislative stalemate then allows for these judicial rulings to stand without revision.

The processes of delimitation directly implicate and involve those governing authorities and rights at the outer margins of reform. In the case of Reconstruction, the crucial authority at the center of recalibration and delimitation dynamics was federalism – specifically federalism's

---

[166] 110 U.S. 651 (1884).
[167] DeSantis, *Southern Question*, 198–99; Perman, *Struggle*, 39–40; Wang, *Trial*, 236–37.

uncertain status in the aftermath of Reconstruction reforms. The processes of delimitation in the 1870s and 1880s were thus crucial, considering that judicial delimiting settlements reestablished the boundaries between reform principles and preexisting authorities and rights, while also providing much of the content and political meaning of the original reforms. The substance of the Reconstruction transformation in governance was not determined or apparent in the 1860s; it was just beginning to reveal itself by the conclusion of these delimitation processes in the early 1880s.

4

Labor Rights, the New Deal Era, and Delimitation

Like the Reconstruction era, the New Deal is well documented by both historians and political scientists as a clear case of political transformation. Yet, whereas standard historical accounts document a "waning of the New Deal" in the late 1930s, their discussion of judicial delimitation and recalibration in the post–New Deal years oddly remains sparse or nonexistent.[1] This neglect likely stems from the broad array of policy developments during the period. The most conspicuous examples of reform and recalibration from the New Deal era lie in the transformation of labor relations embodied in the Wagner Act and the subsequent judicial attempts in the late 1930s to reconcile this change with resilient authorities and rights. However, because many historical accounts of the New Deal treat the labor story as just one of several important policy developments, the recalibration of labor rights is often ignored or lost in the larger picture.[2]

---

[1] As discussed later, however, noteworthy works in labor and labor-law history have been quite attentive to these issues.

[2] While my treatment of the New Deal focuses on issues surrounding the Wagner Act and unions, this is not to imply that the multitude of other policy and institutional developments of the New Deal are less significant or unimportant. Indeed, the story of the New Deal is clearly much broader than a story about labor rights. My focus on the labor issue, however, stems from its clear parallels to the other historical case studies examined here.

By way of illustrating the point, consider several works focused on New Deal economic policy that have emphasized how a relatively milder, less governmentally intrusive Keynesian alternative for managing the economy eventually triumphed over more radical statist alternatives by the 1940s: Alan Brinkley, *The End of Reform: New Deal Liberalism in Recession and War* (New York: Vintage Books, 1996); Dean L. May, *From New Deal to*

With the legislative enactment and judicial validation of the Wagner Act, a hierarchical system of employer-employee relations – which had previously been embedded in "master-servant common law doctrines"[3]

> *New Economics: The American Liberal Response to the Recession of 1937* (New York: Garland Press, 1981); John W. Jeffries, "The 'New' New Deal: FDR and American Liberalism, 1937–1945," *Political Science Quarterly* 105, no. 3 (Autumn 1990): 397–418; John W. Jeffries, "A 'Third New Deal'? Liberal Policy and the American State, 1937–1945," *Journal of Policy History* 8, no. 4 (October 1996): 387–409; Ira Katznelson and Bruce Pietrykowski, "Rebuilding the American State: Evidence from the 1940s," *Studies in American Political Development* 5 (Fall 1991): 301–39; Michael K. Brown, "State Capacity and Political Choice: Interpreting the Failure of the Third New Deal," *Studies in American Political Development* 9 (Spring 1995): 187–212. As a result, one might be tempted to see within these accounts something analogous to the processes of delimitation seen in the Reconstruction case with respect to African American rights. One might be tempted to claim that during the New Deal a recalibration took place in the realm of political economy instead of, or in addition to, developments in the realm of labor rights. Yet, as significant as these shifts in political economy may have been from more to less radical reformist ideas, the analogy to emancipation and Reconstruction breaks down due to the absence of any preceding dismantling reforms.
>
> As noted in Chapter 3, the Thirteenth Amendment's uprooting of slavery ensured that subsequent defenses of slavery as an ideal and as an institutional alternative were simply beyond the boundaries of legitimate political debate. As a result, proponents of reimposing racial subordination on African Americans were forced to find alternative ideals and authorities to contest reform; that is, they were forced to take the fight to issues of recalibration. If a similar dismantling type of reform had occurred during the New Deal – whether in the context of political economy, or even perhaps in the context of social welfare policy as others might plausibly argue, see, e.g., William F. Forbath, "The New Deal Constitution in Exile," *Duke Law Journal* 51, no. 1 (October 2001): 165–222 (noting a New Deal revolution and a Dixiecrat-driven "counterrevolution" in the context of social welfare policy, although I am not sure he would concur with the appropriateness of the "dismantling" and "recalibration" descriptions in that context) – we should expect to find an analogous, lasting repudiation of a similar institution or ideal after the 1930s. Market capitalism, antistatism, or states' rights could be among the likely candidates in these particular policy contexts.
>
> Yet, even though these latter political ideals and institutions suffered dramatic defeats in the 1930s, all also undeniably retained a significant degree of vitality and legitimacy in the post–New Deal years – more so, I would argue, than the set of employer prerogatives directly repudiated by the Wagner Act. Indeed, for those who follow the political economy theme in the New Deal, this is demonstrated by the fact that, at the end of the day, reformers actually reconciled themselves to capitalism and a less intrusive state by choosing the Keynesian alternative. Market capitalism, antistatism, and states' rights were dramatically reshaped by the New Deal then, and recalibration dynamics intersected with policy changes in at least some of these areas. However, they were political changes that followed a different template from the dismantling-transformative recalibration pattern seen with respect to labor rights in the New Deal era.

[3] To quote Orren: "Common-law tenets of master and servant sanctioned the employer's authority and bound the worker over time to his labor. Common-law writs of trespass, assault and battery, and enticement encircled those relations and protected them from outside intrusion." Karen Orren, *Belated Feudalism: Labor, the Law, and Liberal*

and enforced by the courts – was permanently dismantled. It was replaced by a new regime of government-sponsored collective bargaining, which was established and to be overseen by Congress.⁴ As was the case with the Reconstruction Amendments, the exact nature of the political changes contemplated by the Wagner Act was not apparent from the start. To be sure, as a matter of original intent, substantive review of labor contracts by the federal government – or anything more radical – was likely never in the cards.⁵ Yet, as with the uncertain relationship between the Reconstruction Amendments and federalism, a postreform question, or an "external" uncertainty, was prompted by the passage of the Wagner Act: Where would new lines be drawn between reform principles and still-resilient employer prerogatives that did *not* directly bear on the right to unionize? Regardless of whether one is inclined to more conservative or more radical interpretations of the Wagner Act, it was this uncertainty over how it would be integrated with resilient authorities that demanded resolution. The New Deal, and its postreform period of recalibration, offers a second example of how difficult it is for reformers to achieve broad changes in dense areas of policy. The New Deal case study also demonstrates that the peculiarities of transformative recalibration are hardly limited to policy areas fundamentally linked to either race or to the region of the South.

In line with the case study of post-Reconstruction delimitation, the recalibration and delimitation of reform in the New Deal era also followed a clearly defined process. First, the New Deal coalition was shaken by a number of events or governing crises. In 1937 there were the sit-down strikes, the Court-Packing Plan, Executive Reorganization, and the Recession of 1937. These crises facilitated the delimitation of the Wagner Act by blunting the general electoral impulse for further reform, which led to an eventual stalemate between reformers and postreform skeptics in the elected branches.

Development in the United States (1991; repr., New York: Cambridge University Press, 1999), 29; see especially 68–117.

⁴ Ibid.; Christopher L. Tomlins, *The State and the Unions: Labor Relations, Law, and the Organized Labor Movement in America, 1880–1960* (Cambridge: Cambridge University Press, 1985), 148–49.

⁵ Matthew W. Finkin, "Revisionism in Labor Law," *Maryland Law Review* 43 (Fall 1984): 41–42; Comment, "The Radical Potential of the Wagner Act: The Duty to Bargain Collectively," *University of Pennsylvania Law Review* 129, no. 6 (June 1981): 1399–1409. See also Karl E. Klare, "Judicial Deradicalization of the Wagner Act and the Origins of Modern Legal Consciousness, 1937–1941," *Minnesota Law Review* 62, no. 3 (March 1978): 307.

This stalemate afforded the Court a degree of freedom to set forth and codify the limits of reform. Like the Supreme Court's rulings on race in the 1870s and early 1880s, several of its rulings in the late 1930s are noteworthy for constituting the first formal statements on the reach of the Wagner Act. Specifically, the broader question confronting the Court was how far the protection of the Wagner Act would extend toward supporting the unions. In response, these rulings in the late 1930s displayed an unmistakable judicial antipathy toward more expansive conceptions of labor rights. Thus again, a recurrent process of delimitation and a recurrent mode of delimiting adjudication are evident in the New Deal era. With the prevailing climate of legislative stalemate after the 1938 elections and an increasing hostile public opinion toward labor, reformers simply lacked the political strength to respond to the Court after 1938.

The present case study further demonstrates a recurrent pattern in the substantive justifications for judicial delimitation. After *NLRB v. Jones & Laughlin Steel Corp*[6] upheld the constitutionality of the Wagner Act, the political feasibility of conservatives frontally challenging this new labor regime – and the legitimacy of collective bargaining – would have been almost as daunting as post-Reconstruction conservatives seeking to challenge emancipation. Thus, political success for conservatives in the 1930s and 1940s did not lie in attempting to resurrect judicial oversight of labor relations through master-servant common law doctrines or in making appeals to repudiated principles and ideals such as substantive due process or "Lochnerism."[7] Rather, in line with the legal strategies of postreform skeptics in the 1870s and 1880s, postreform skeptics in the late 1930s latched onto an alternative language, alternative ideals, and alternative institutions in support of their desire to limit the expansion and intrusion of reform principles. The goal for these groups, then, at least in their arguments before the Court, was not to repudiate reform but rather to contain it with reference to other still-credible governing authorities and rights. The resilient authorities that proved to be most helpful to their aims were various still-legitimate employer prerogatives not directly tied to the right of employees to unionize. The legitimacy of these prerogatives was defended in the name of securing "industrial peace." This was a goal, perhaps ironically, of the Wagner Act itself, as declared in its preamble.

---

[6] 301 U.S. 1 (1937).
[7] As Gunther and Sullivan note, "No socioeconomic law has been invalidated on substantive due process grounds since 1937." Kathleen M. Sullivan and Gerald Gunther, *Constitutional Law*, 14th ed. (Westbury, New York: Foundation Press, 2001), 477.

TABLE 4.1 *Recalibration and the New Deal Era Transformation in Labor Rights*

(1) Legal reform	The judicial governance of labor relations via master-servant common law doctrines is dismantled by the Wagner Act.
(2) Delimitation	(2a) Legislative stalemate after the election of 1938
	(2b) The scope of labor rights is "indirectly" delimited by the Court with reference to the validity of employer prerogatives *not* directly tied to the right of employees to unionize and the demands of industrial peace.
(3) Construction	(3a) The emergence of voluntary arbitration as the federal government's preferred method of managing labor conflict
	(3b) Conclusive Supreme Court entrenchment of voluntary arbitration (industrial pluralism)

Although the Court's delimiting rulings from the late 1930s were not as explicit in their reasoning as the post-Reconstruction cases on race, it appears to have found these delimiting arguments of postreform skeptics convincing. As such, the scope of reform principles in the realm of labor relations was again delimited, indirectly, by the judiciary.

As referred to in Table 4.1, once the dust had cleared after judicial delimitation, it became apparent that while unionization was to be a permanent feature of the new status quo, unions would remain constrained by the demands of employer and ownership prerogatives. As with the rise of Jim Crow, the system of labor relations that ultimately took root in the post–World War II era – industrial pluralism – would have its genesis in these twin commitments to unionization and employer prerogatives.[8] The first was firmly rooted in reform principles enshrined in the Wagner Act, whereas the second was firmly rooted in delimitation, articulated in these judicial rulings from the late 1930s.

THE RISE OF LEGISLATIVE STALEMATE

Standard historical accounts of the later New Deal all note the reversal of fortune for Franklin Roosevelt in 1937. Just months after securing a landslide victory in the presidential election of 1936, a series of

---

[8] See Chapter 8.

events occurred that strained the solidarity of the Roosevelt coalition. One of these events – the sit-down strikes – was directly related to recalibration uncertainties in the realm of labor politics. The other two events – FDR's executive and judicial reforms and the Recession of 1937 – impinged on labor politics more indirectly. Taken together, these events sapped energy from the reform coalition, energized postreform skeptics, and paved the way for a legislative stalemate in the late 1930s.

Governing Crisis: The Sit-Down Strikes

In 1935, the Wagner Act was passed by substantial majorities in both the House and Senate, along with the belated endorsement of Roosevelt.[9] Although some have suggested that the act's support in the Senate stemmed in part from expectations that the Court would strike it down,[10] the depth of this political support, and the subsequent durability of the newly enacted collective bargaining regime against later attacks, suggests that reform had deep and sustained support.

Notably, support for the act had been influenced by a year of violent strikes in 1934.[11] However, the economic disorder posed by the sit-down strikes of 1937 would have a very different political effect on the fortunes of labor.[12] The initial event was the sit-down strike by General Motors employees in Fisher Body Plant Number One in Flint, Michigan. The strike ran from December 1936 to February 1937. Other GM plants in Flint were taken over by strikers during the course of these weeks as well.[13] Roosevelt refused to call out troops, and although Governor Frank Murphy called out the National Guard, they were only used

---

[9] Irving Bernstein, *Turbulent Years: A History of the American Worker 1933–1941* (Boston: Houghton Mifflin Company, 1970), 341–45, 348–49; Melvyn Dubofsky, *The State & Labor in Modern America* (Chapel Hill: University of North Carolina Press, 1994), 127–28; William E. Leuchtenburg, *Franklin D. Roosevelt and the New Deal, 1932–1940* (New York: Harper & Row, 1963), 150–52.

[10] Bernstein, *Turbulent Years*, 341.

[11] On these strikes, see ibid., 217–317; David M. Kennedy, *Freedom from Fear: The American People in Depression and War, 1929–1945* (New York: Oxford University Press, 1999), 292–96.

[12] The distinctive aspect of the sit-down strike was that instead of leaving the plant to strike in the conventional way, employees stopped work and retained occupancy of the plant to prevent others from continuing to work.

[13] Bernstein, *Turbulent Years*, 525–26; Dubofsky, *State & Labor*, 138; Kennedy, *Freedom*, 308–11; Leuchtenburg, *Roosevelt*, 239–40.

to maintain the peace between the strikers and the company.[14] Facing a continuing loss of revenue, and without the aid of state coercive means, GM finally caved in on February 11 and gave union recognition to the UAW-CIO.[15] Moreover, the effects of this strike spread beyond Flint, as the tactic was widely emulated afterward.[16] Bernstein notes that there were 477 sit-down strikes (with 398,117 workers involved) in 1937, compared to 48 sit-down strikes in 1936, and 52 in 1938.[17]

For some segments of labor, and for some governing officials sympathetic to labor, the sit-down strikes were plausible and logical extensions of the labor rights afforded by the Constitution and the Wagner Act.[18] However, in stark contrast to the wave of strikes that hit the nation in 1934 and that preceded the Wagner Act, the sit-down strikes had the opposite effect of sparking widespread antipathy to labor. The general public's foremost concern was that the sit-down tactic entailed a gross violation of private property. In its more extreme forms, this property concern flowed into the related fear among some that the sit-down strikes would lead up to all-out socialist revolution. Public antipathy also grew from concerns about traveling labor agitators and labor's persecution of nonunionists.[19] Finally, the potential for violence from these strikes was a public concern as well. This was validated with the Little Steel strikes that occurred over the summer of 1937 – when a total of eighteen workers were killed in clashes between police, company forces, and strikers.[20]

In the case of Reconstruction, the specter of continued white southerner resistance had a sobering effect on the reform ambitions of northern Republicans, convincing them to rethink their southern policy goals. The

---

[14] Dubofsky, *State & Labor*, 139–40; Kennedy, *Freedom*, 312; Leuchtenburg, *Roosevelt*, 242.
[15] Bernstein, *Turbulent Years*, 550–51; Dubofsky, *State & Labor*, 141; Kennedy, *Freedom*, 314.
[16] Kennedy, *Freedom*, 316; Richard Polenberg, "The Decline of the New Deal, 1937–1940," in *The New Deal: The National Level*, eds. John Braeman, Robert H. Bremner, and David Brody, vol. 1 (Columbus: Ohio State University Press, 1975), 257.
[17] Bernstein, *Turbulent Years*, 500.
[18] Jim Pope, "Worker Lawmaking, Sit-Down Strikes, and the Shaping of American Industrial Relations, 1935–1958," *Law and History Review* 24, no. 1 (Spring 2006): 48, 74, 93–94. See also ibid., 61–73.
[19] Dubofsky, *State & Labor*, 146–47; Kennedy, *Freedom*, 316; Leuchtenburg, *Roosevelt*, 242–43; Milton Derber, "The New Deal and Labor," in Braeman, *The New Deal: The National*, 116; Polenberg, "Decline," in Braeman, *The New Deal*, 257; Pope, "Worker Lawmaking," 76.
[20] Kennedy, *Freedom*, 316–19.

sit-down strikes had a similar effect in the late 1930s. Recall that northern Republicans during Reconstruction shied away from the prospect of continued, pervasive federal oversight of the South and the implied encroachment on still-credible commitments to federalism and states' rights. Similarly, portions within the New Deal coalition were troubled by the prospect of giving labor a free pass. Unlike the strikes of 1934, the sit-down strikes implicated legal rights, such as the property rights of employers, which extended beyond those of collective bargaining. These additional rights were at risk of being jeopardized if unions were allowed to press more expansive interpretations of their Wagner Act rights without any legal or political check.[21]

Thus, strong majorities sided against labor after the Flint strike. In a February 1937 Gallup Poll, two-thirds of the poll's respondents "believed that GM was right not to negotiate with the sit-downers."[22] This shift in public sentiment was reflected in governmental responses to the Little Steel strikes in the summer of 1937. In contrast to the state and federal governmental support the Flint sit-down strikers had received, responses to the Little Steel strikers from state governors and FDR ranged from neutral to hostile.[23]

Within the New Deal coalition specifically, members of the middle-class party base were particularly troubled by the antiproperty, anti-law-and-order tone of the sit-down tactic. The urban, working-class members of the coalition (particularly among the Irish and the German) who focused on the socialist overtones of the sit-down strike were likewise troubled.[24] Also, a third component of the New Deal coalition similarly concerned were Southern Democrats, who worried about the possibility of increased federal and union intrusion into their regional labor system should the sit-down tactic remain unchecked.[25] The concern of Southern Democrats was noteworthy, since some Southern Democrats had, of course, been previously friendly to labor. For example, in June 1936, South Carolina's senator James Byrnes introduced the "antiprofessional

---

[21] Ibid., 310.
[22] Ibid., 316. Richard Polenberg also notes that "two out of every three people favored outlawing sit-down strikes and employing force against unions engaged in them." Polenberg, "Decline," in Braeman, *The New Deal*, 257.
[23] Dubofsky, *State & Labor*, 148–49.
[24] Leuchtenburg, *Roosevelt*, 243; Polenberg, "Decline," in Braeman, *The New Deal*, 257.
[25] Dubofsky, *State & Labor*, 146; James T. Patterson, *Congressional Conservatism and the New Deal: The Growth of the Conservative Coalition in Congress, 1933–1939* (Lexington: University of Kentucky Press, 1967), 134–36; Polenberg, "Decline," in Braeman, *The New Deal*, 257; Pope, "Worker Lawmaking," 93.

strikebreaker bill," which made it a felony to transport strikebreakers for the purpose of obstructing peaceful picketing.[26] After the sit-down strikes, however, Byrnes pressed for an amendment to the Guffey Coal Bill that would outlaw sit-down strikes in the coal industry.[27] Although the amendment was defeated by Senate Majority Leader Joseph Robinson of Arkansas, a resolution declaring sit-downs to be "illegal and contrary to public policy" was later passed by the Senate.[28]

Governing Crisis: The Court-Packing Plan and Executive Reorganization

On February 5, 1937, Roosevelt introduced legislation that would have allowed him to dramatically reshape the federal judiciary. Stating (somewhat disingenuously) that his primary concern was the insufficient and aging personnel in the judiciary, he proposed a plan that would allow him to make appointments to the lower federal courts and the Supreme Court whenever a sitting judge with at least ten years of service failed to retire within six months of turning seventy. The legislation, if passed, would have given Roosevelt the authority to make up to six new appointments on the Court, and up to forty-four new appointments on the lower federal courts. Roosevelt's main interest, however, lay more in securing some control over a hostile Court that seemed poised to strike down much of the New Deal.[29] The crucial question posed by the Court-Packing Plan was ultimately whether the broader support in the electorate for reform would carry over to support a broader restructuring of the judiciary.

The answer turned out to be no. Even among Democrats sympathetic to the New Deal, the Court-Packing Plan was viewed as an implied attack on traditions of judicial independence and the "dignity of the bench." For these critics, the immediate policy goals that motivated Roosevelt's plan proved to be less compelling than their preference for a judiciary held beyond the sway of electoral politics.[30] Other constituencies were

---

[26] Dubofsky, *State & Labor*, 133–34.
[27] Ibid., 147; Patterson, *Congressional Conservatism*, 136; Pope, "Worker Lawmaking," 93.
[28] Kennedy, *Freedom*, 316–19; Patterson, *Congressional Conservatism*, 137; Pope, "Worker Lawmaking," 95.
[29] Brinkley, *End of Reform*, 18–19; Kennedy, *Freedom*, 325–31; Leuchtenburg, *Roosevelt*, 232–33; Patterson, *Congressional Conservatism*, 85–86.
[30] Brinkley, *End of Reform*, 20; Kennedy, *Freedom*, 331, 333; Leuchtenburg, *Roosevelt*, 234–35; Patterson, *Congressional Conservatism*, 87–88; Polenberg, "Decline," in Braeman, *The New Deal*, 249.

also opposed to the plan on more pragmatic grounds. Many Southern Democrats, for example, opposed the plan out of the fear that Roosevelt might appoint more liberal justices that could then take up an assault on southern race relations.[31]

At nearly the same time, in January 1937, an executive reorganization bill was submitted to Congress that sought, among other things, to appoint six assistants for the president, expand the merit system, create two new cabinet positions, establish the National Resources Planning Board as a central planning agency under the control of the White House, and grant the president broad discretion to transfer agencies and even some functions of the various independent commissions.[32] Like the Court-Packing Plan, this bill ran into vigorous opposition for a number of reasons. Various interest groups – such as veterans, medical professionals, labor groups, and conservationists – felt threatened by the broad presidential discretion to transfer agencies, thereby potentially disrupting the established relationships these groups enjoyed with their patron agencies.[33]

Legislators found additional reasons to be unhappy with the bill. To some, it posed a disruption to their carefully established relationships with certain federal agencies. To others, the bill constituted yet another step in the subordination of Congress to the executive bureaucracy and an increasingly empowered Roosevelt. Indeed, concerns emerged about a dictatorial president, especially when the bill was viewed alongside the Court-Packing Plan.[34] The end result of executive reorganization was the same as that of court packing – the bill ultimately divided liberals and constituted another defeat for Roosevelt. Although the bill passed in the Senate, it was defeated in the House in April 1938 with, notably, 108 Democrats in opposition.[35]

Both court packing and executive reorganization had unmistakable consequences for political development in labor rights. Although Roosevelt saw some victory on executive reorganization in 1939, and the Court later had its "switch in time" – which secured the immediate goal of securing key New Deal reform goals – these controversies caused much

---

[31] Kennedy, *Freedom*, 333.
[32] Patterson, *Congressional Conservatism*, 215; Polenberg, "Decline," in Braeman, *The New Deal*, 250.
[33] Polenberg, "Decline," in Braeman, *The New Deal*, 250.
[34] Brinkley, *End of Reform*, 22–23; Patterson, *Congressional Conservatism*, 216–18, 229; Polenberg, "Decline," in Braeman, *The New Deal*, 251.
[35] Brinkley, *End of Reform*, 22; Polenberg, "Decline," in Braeman, *The New Deal*, 251.

internal division within the Democrats, left the party badly divided, and left the prospects on further legislative reform – of any type – fairly poor.[36] Because these events had strengthened an emerging bipartisan conservative coalition, reformers would also have to deal with this new political obstacle in their future endeavors.[37] The window for achieving any further movement on labor rights in the electoral arena was quickly closing.

Governing Crisis: The Recession of 1937

In August 1937, the economy suddenly took a violent downturn. As a result, one of the major sources of appeal for the Roosevelt administration – its success on the more pragmatic grounds of securing economic gains on the road toward recovery – was suddenly no longer such a sturdy support.[38] For those who follow the story of economic policy through the New Deal, this recession was the formative event in pushing the New Deal away from more statist and regulatory economic visions and toward the less intrusive Keynesian vision of "compensatory liberalism."[39] For more categorical opponents of the New Deal who favored a balanced budget and a friendlier governmental attitude toward business, the recession provided new ammunition for questioning the government's approach to the economy.[40] Although these New Deal opponents did not necessarily gain the upper hand,[41] the recession did much to cool popular impulses for further reform. This was a downturn that happened on Roosevelt's watch, and it raised serious questions about his administration's competence.[42] Like the Panic of 1873, this was a crisis decidedly separate from labor policy that nevertheless impinged on labor's prospects for further reform. Indeed, Leuchtenberg credits the recession as the key factor in the relatively poor showing of Democrats in the 1938 election.[43]

---

[36] Brinkley, *End of Reform*, 23; Kennedy, *Freedom*, 337–38; Leuchtenberg, *Roosevelt*, 238–39; Patterson, *Congressional Conservatism*, 88–91.
[37] Leuchtenberg, *Roosevelt*, 238–39; Patterson, *Congressional Conservatism*, 85, 128, 229.
[38] Leuchtenberg, *Roosevelt*, 243–44.
[39] See generally, Brinkley, *End of Reform*; May, *From New Deal*.
[40] Leuchtenberg, *Roosevelt*, 254.
[41] Ibid.
[42] Patterson, *Congressional Conservatism*, 335–36; Polenberg, "Decline," in Braeman, *The New Deal*, 255–56.
[43] Leuchtenberg, *Roosevelt*, 271.

The Inauguration of Legislative Stalemate

As historians note, these events, although separate, became joined in the public mind as a series of missteps by the formerly politically invincible Roosevelt. The immediate consequences for further reform were clear. With the exception of the Wagner-Steagall National Housing Act – a measure for public housing weakened by Southern Democrats and passed in the summer of 1937 – there were no other legislative reform achievements in 1937, nor were there any additional successes in a special session Roosevelt called in November 1937.[44] Roosevelt did get the Fair Labor Standards Act passed in June 1938, but with the conservative coalition gaining in strength as a veto threat, the act was weakened by exceptions and faced strong opposition from an assortment of rural Republicans, Southern Democrats, and the American Federation of Labor (AFL).[45]

The fallout from these governing crises was not only a loss of Roosevelt's authority in dealing with Congress.[46] In addition, and as consequential, there were stunning reversals for the Democrats in the 1938 elections. Roosevelt's purge effort against conservative Democrats failed.[47] Furthermore, the election also saw Republicans gain eighty-one seats in the House, eight seats in the Senate, and thirteen governorships. The election did not suddenly put the Republicans in the driver's seat, however, nor did Republicans secure their wins with campaign promises to dismantle the New Deal – Democrats still held majorities in both the House and the Senate. But if the Democrats still nominally held greater numbers, the election had nevertheless put the reformers in retreat. Furthermore, the post-1938 environment was one in which Roosevelt would need the support of some southerners or Republicans to form majorities.[48] The prospect of gaining help from these quarters was not reassuring. Polenberg notes that "every opinion poll in 1938 and 1939 indicated much the same thing: between two-thirds and three-fourths of the American people preferred that the Roosevelt administration follow a more conservative course."[49] Thus, the governing crises of 1937 did not spark

---

[44] Kennedy, *Freedom*, 339–40; Leuchtenburg, *Roosevelt*, 135–36; 250–51; Polenberg, "Decline," in Braeman, *The New Deal*, 252–53.
[45] Leuchtenburg, *Roosevelt*, 261–63; Patterson, *Congressional Conservatism*, 245–46.
[46] Kennedy, *Freedom*, 331–32; Leuchtenburg, *Roosevelt*, 250.
[47] Kennedy, *Freedom*, 348; Leuchtenburg, *Roosevelt*, 266–68; Polenberg, "Decline," in Braeman, *The New Deal*, 258–59.
[48] Leuchtenburg, *Roosevelt*, 271; Patterson, *Congressional Conservatism*, 289; Polenberg, "Decline," in Braeman, *The New Deal*, 259.
[49] Polenberg, "Decline," in Braeman, *The New Deal*, 254.

an environment ripe for a Republican countertransformation; rather, the crises created an environment of political stalemate that helped facilitate a subsequent judicial delimitation of labor reform.

THE JUDICIAL DELIMITATION OF NEW DEAL LABOR RIGHTS

Section 7 of the Wagner Act guaranteed that "employees shall have the right to self-organization."[50] Section 13 of the act stated: "Nothing in this Act shall be construed so as to interfere with or impede or diminish in any way the right to strike."[51] Alongside these strong statements of collective rights for employees, the preamble articulated a goal of reducing "industrial strife or unrest."[52]

The act's framers clearly envisioned these various goals working together. Nonetheless, lawyers for employer interests indirectly opposed the Wagner Act, urging its delimitation by appealing to the goal of industrial peace. By opposing the act in this manner, and by largely bypassing any frontal attacks on labor rights that employed the language of *Lochner* or master-servant common law doctrines, lawyers who represented the interests of employers in the post–New Deal years followed the same pattern of reasoning employed by the southern opponents of Reconstruction. This strategy proved to be as efficacious for the former as it had been for the latter: a majority of the Supreme Court in the late 1930s found that appeals to industrial peace were a compelling rationale for delimiting reform.[53]

The result was several key rulings by the Supreme Court that, due to the opening provided by the inauguration of legislative stalemate, constituted the first codified recalibration of the Wagner Act by the federal government. These rulings – while serving as only tentative resolutions of

[50] National Labor Relations Act of 1935 (Wagner Act), Pub. L. No. 74-198, § 7, 49 Stat. 449, 452 (1935).
[51] Id. at § 13.
[52] Id. at § 1.
[53] Although it is beyond the scope of my present inquiry, Christopher Tomlins has notably identified post–Wagner Act recalibrating effects present in the NLRB's decisions on bargaining unit issues. Tomlins, *The State*, 198–99, 227–37. In addition, Ken Kersch has argued that the Supreme Court, in the aftermath of the Wagner Act, reasserted pre–New Deal era legal concepts and ideals in areas of labor law that are not my focus here. Ken I. Kersch, "The New Deal Triumph as the End of History? The Judicial Negotiation of Labor Rights and Civil Rights," in Kahn and Kersch, *The Supreme Court & American Political Development*, 169–226. Kersch's case studies, however, focus on instances in which the judiciary employed prereform legal concepts with the goal of elaborating or deepening reform principles rather than delimiting them.

key boundary-drawing questions at the times they were issued – displayed the Court's own uneasiness with the more radical, open-ended implications of the act. They thus reflected a judicial inclination to provide clarity in the law by demarcating the outer boundaries of reform and stabilizing the boundaries between competing authorities and rights. Further, these rulings crystallized and reflected the broader political developments that preceded them and would likewise align with developments in labor politics in the federal elected branches that would follow.

Notably, the following three cases that constituted the judicial delimitation of labor rights – *NLRB v. Mackay Radio & Telegraph Co.*,[54] *NLRB v. Sands Manufacturing Co.*,[55] and *NLRB v. Fansteel Metallurgical Corp.*[56] – do not enjoy much attention in conventional historical overviews of the New Deal. Rather, these cases remain well known largely among labor historians and labor-law historical scholars.[57] In part, the reason for this may be that these decisions were nestled in the midst of many more judicial decisions that were actually sympathetic to labor's interests from 1938 to 1941.[58] One cannot examine this historical period and find a rout of labor rights in the Court's rulings in the same way that the judicial rulings of the 1870s exhibited a clear pattern of antipathy toward African American rights. Yet, as labor scholars have noted, this oversight remains unfortunate and unwarranted given the significant consequences for labor that followed from these judicial decisions.[59]

---

[54] 304 U.S. 333 (1938).
[55] 306 U.S. 332 (1939).
[56] 306 U.S. 240 (1939).
[57] *Mackay* and *Fansteel* are not uncommonly mentioned as early antiunion cases before the Court. They – and to a varying extent the topic of early conservative judicial rulings on the Wagner Act – are discussed in Klare, "Deradicalization," 304; James B. Atleson, *Values and Assumptions in American Labor Law* (Amherst: University of Massachusetts Press, 1983), 19–34, 45; Tomlins, *The State*, 239–40, 260–61; Paul Barron, "A Theory of Protected Employer Rights: A Revisionist Analysis of the Supreme Court's Interpretation of the National Labor Relations Act," *Texas Law Review* 59, no. 3 (March 1981): 422–23; Paul Weiler, "Striking a New Balance: Freedom of Contract and the Prospects for Union Representation," *Harvard Law Review* 98, no. 2 (December 1984): 388–89 (discussing *Mackay*).
[58] Dubofsky, *State & Labor*, 164–66, 263n71–72; Klare, "Deradicalization," 318–19.
[59] Much of the analysis in this section should sound a sympathetic note with work by Karl Klare and James Atleson. My work owes much to their scholarship. Both scholars are attentive to conservative shifts in judicial doctrine in the late 1930s with respect to labor rights, and although neither uses the term, both describe legal and political developments that clearly speak to recalibration dynamics.
   However, my analysis diverges in some important respects. Given both scholars' singular focus on the post–New Deal Era, these authors inevitably miss the greater

NLRB v. Mackay Radio & Telegraph Co.

In *NLRB v. Mackay Radio & Telegraph Co.*, the Court confronted the question of how far the Wagner Act's protection would extend to workers engaged in an economic strike – that is, workers striking for higher pay or shorter hours as opposed to striking because of an employer's unfair labor practices.[60]

In this case, after workers had engaged in a short-lived economic strike, it soon became clear to at least some of the strikers that the effort would fail; some then inquired to the company about the possibility of returning to work before their jobs were permanently lost to replacement workers. Mackay Radio informed the strikers that their former positions were in fact open to them, except for eleven positions, which had been promised to eleven of the replacement workers as permanent positions. Eleven of the strikers were told that instead of returning to work, they would have to file applications for reinstatement, subject to the approval of a company executive. Six workers eventually resumed their positions without further difficulty. The remaining five men, who were all members of the union (and four of whom were strongly connected to the local branch of the union and to the strike effort), were directed to fill out job applications and were told that, although there were no available positions, they would be considered in the future if any vacancies opened up. Not being reinstated after three weeks, the secretary of the local branch of the union presented a charge to the NLRB that Mackay Radio had violated Section 8(1) (interference with employee right to self-organize) and Section 8(3) (discrimination in hiring or tenure of employment with respect to union membership) of the Wagner Act. After much legal sparring before the NLRB and the Ninth Circuit Court of Appeals, this case came before the Supreme Court.[61]

---

significance of these judicial decisions when placed in a comparative historical framework. The primary importance of these decisions for the present argument lies in how they illuminate a *general* process of delimitation that is applicable to other instances of political transformation. Further, given my more systematic focus, I believe my theory also offers a more in-depth institutional examination of why recalibration occurred in these particular cases.

[60] 304 U.S. 333 (1938). Notably, Lovell discusses the *Mackay* ruling as an instance of the judiciary following up on a legislative deferral to it. George I. Lovell, *Legislative Deferrals: Statutory Ambiguity, Judicial Power, and American Democracy* (New York: Cambridge University Press, 2003), 223–24, 242–46.

[61] *Mackay*, 304 U.S. at 337–39; Julius G. Getman and Thomas C. Kohler, "The Story of *NLRB v. Mackay Radio & Telegraph Co.*," in *Labor Law Stories*, eds. Laura J. Cooper and Catherine L. Fisk (New York: Foundation Press, 2005), 13, 34, 34n48. Apparently, a total of sixty-eight strikers were involved. Louis W. Myers, Howard L. Kern, and

The primary legal question was whether these five particular workers were entitled to be reinstated to their jobs. In dealing with this question, however, the broader issue of how much protection workers might expect from the Wagner Act while engaged in an economic strike was also implicated. In the briefs of the NLRB and Mackay Radio, four possible responses to this question were articulated. The arguments are presented here in order from most to least conservative, and as they demonstrate, the Court's ruling constituted a clear step back from the most transformative implications of the act.

(1) *The workers were not entitled to be reinstated since they had voluntarily walked off the job*

This position was maintained by Mackay Radio in its brief under two distinct, supporting lines of argument. Mackay Radio's first argument focused on the Fifth Amendment. It insisted that the workers' employee status terminated on their resort to a strike "without provocation" (i.e., a strike not precipitated by an unfair labor practice), and as such, these workers could not resume their status without the consent of the employer. The Wagner Act by itself did not empower the NLRB to order an employer to either reemploy or hire any particular individuals. Furthermore, even if the Wagner Act were employed to such an end, this would amount to a constitutional violation: the effect of the NLRB forcing an employer to reemploy or hire an individual against the former's will would be tantamount to forcing on it a new contractual relationship. Such a result would be beyond the power of Congress to demand through legislation because it would constitute an illegitimate taking and an infringement on liberty of contract under the Fifth Amendment.[62]

This argument sat in obvious tension with the Court's previous ruling in *NLRB v. Jones & Laughlin Steel Corp.*,[63] where the Court had little difficulty in upholding impairments to an employer's freedom of contract by requiring the reinstatement of discharged employees subsequent to an employer unfair labor practice.[64] Despite Mackay Radio's attempt to distinguish its case, the Court cited *Jones & Laughlin Steel* and quickly rejected Mackay Radio's frontal assault on the constitutionality of the Wagner Act.[65]

Homer I. Mitchell, Brief for Respondent at 4, *NLRB v. Mackay Radio & Telegraph Co.*, 304 U.S. 333 (1938).
[62] Myers et al., Brief for Respondent at 40–53, *Mackay*, 304 U.S. 333.
[63] 301 U.S. 1 (1937).
[64] Id. at 47–49.
[65] *Mackay*, 304 U.S. at 347–48.

Mackay Radio's second argument presented a more measured defense focused on the definition of an "employee" under the act. The company argued that even under the expanded definition of an "employee" under Section 2(3) of the Wagner Act, the five workers did not enjoy that status and thus were not entitled to the act's protections. Section 2(3) defined "employee" as including "any individual whose work has ceased as a consequence of, or in connection with, any current labor dispute or because of any unfair labor practice." The company argued that there was no finding that the five men had quit working because of a labor dispute or because of an unfair labor practice.[66] This argument fared no better with the Court, however. While conceding that there was no evidence the company was guilty of an unfair labor practice, the Court thought it clear that the strike was called in relation to a "current labor dispute."[67]

(2) The five workers were entitled to consideration for reemployment free of discrimination due to their union activities; and (3) the five workers were entitled to reinstatement

These two options might be treated together as they are closely related. Both concede the wrongfulness of discriminating against the five workers for their union activities. However, they potentially depart on the issue of remedy.

The position of the NLRB in its brief encompassed both options (2) and (3), and it supported these positions by a straightforward analysis of the facts and the text of the Wagner Act. The two key points it sought to demonstrate were that (a) the employee-litigants fell under the act's definition of an "employee" under Section 2(3),[68] and (b) that the discrimination of the five workers was the direct result of their union activities.[69]

Proving (a) allowed the NLRB to implicate three key provisions of the Wagner Act and to apply them to the five workers in the case. The first provision was Section 8(1), which guaranteed the employee right to self-organize against employer interference; the second was Section 8(3), which prohibited employer discrimination against union members with regard to hiring or tenure of employment; and the third was Section 10(c), which empowered the NLRB, on finding the occurrence of an unfair

---

[66] Myers et al., Brief for Respondent at 17–21, *Mackay*, 304 U.S. 333.
[67] *Mackay*, 304 U.S. at 344.
[68] Robert H. Jackson et al., Brief for the National Labor Relations Board at 20–23, 25–33, *Mackay*, 304 U.S. 333 (1938).
[69] Id. at 19, 54–67.

labor practice, to "take such affirmative action including reinstatement of employees with or without back pay, as will effectuate the policies of this act."[70]

Proving (b), that the employer's discrimination against the workers was indeed because of their union affiliation, would prove the actual violations of Sections 8(1) and 8(3), thus prompting the remedial power of the NLRB under Section 10(c) to reinstate the men. The NLRB's brief attempted to demonstrate the (b) point with an extended review of the evidence brought before it[71] and concluded that there were indeed violations of Sections 8(1) and 8(3) here,[72] stating: "If the employer is permitted to discriminate, either in selection or discharge, against persons who are active members of labor organizations, employees are not free to choose their own representatives. Many employees would be afraid to participate in union activities if in the event of a strike the employer could discriminate against them for that reason alone."[73] The NLRB concluded, under its Section 10(c) authority, that the proper remedy for the employer's unfair labor practice of discriminating against the union workers was reinstatement.[74]

Mackay Radio articulated in its brief a different perspective on these issues. Consistent with its previously noted arguments contesting the right of the workers to be reinstated, the company also strongly contested, at points, the idea that discriminating against the union leaders amounted to an unfair labor practice. As it stated provocatively: "The discouragement of union *leaders* from leading their followers into unprovoked and unnecessary strikes will not tend to discourage *membership* in the union. It will have a negative tendency to encourage collective bargaining, in lieu of the strike, and thus will tend, in the long run, to *encourage* union membership."[75]

---

[70] Id. at 19–20.
[71] Id. at 54–67.
[72] Id. at 13, 19–20, 45–47.
[73] Id. at 45–46.
[74] Id. at 20, 47. Separately, the NLRB also argued that reinstatement would be appropriate even if the Court failed to find that the five men were still "employees" under the act – through more expansive readings of Section 8(1), Section 8(3), and Section 10(c). Id. at 49–54.
[75] Myers et al., Brief for Respondent at 33, *Mackay*, 304 U.S. 333 (emphasis in original). Even more aggressively, it states: "After all it is only common justice that if anyone must suffer because of this uncalled for strike, it should be the leaders who caused it. One of the four leaders who were the last to apply for re-employment, was man enough to take this position." Id.

Yet the company's brief also argued that, even if discrimination against the union activists in rehiring did discourage membership in the union and thus constituted an unfair labor practice, the remedial power of the NLRB was limited to ensuring that the five men were considered for reemployment free from any such discrimination.[76] This, in short, is option (2), noted earlier. Before dealing with the Court's reaction to these arguments, however, a fourth possible response to the question of the Wagner Act's protections of economic strikers should be noted.

(4) *Just as workers in a strike precipitated by an employer's unfair labor practice may be generally reinstated under Section 10(c), economic strikers should likewise enjoy the protection of general reinstatement*
Not surprisingly, this was an option that the company refused to entertain seriously in its brief. For Mackay Radio's lawyers, it would have the effect of giving workers an unacceptable degree of economic bargaining power. It would handcuff the employer in its ability to manage business during an economic strike.[77] More generally, and more significantly, it would push the bargaining terrain between an employer and a union too far in favor of the union. To quote the company's brief: "By guaranteeing a striker his job, where the strike was neither provoked nor prolonged by the refusal of the employer to negotiate or by any other unfair labor practice, peaceful negotiation would be discouraged and strikes would be encouraged. Such a result is not in accord with the purposes of the Act, nor is it consistent with its philosophy."[78]

More notably, option (4) was also explicitly rejected by the NLRB in its reply brief as follows:

The Board has never contended, in this case or any other, that an employer who has neither caused nor prolonged a strike through unfair labor practices, cannot take full advantage of economic forces working for his victory in a labor dispute. The Act clearly does not forbid him, in the absence of such unfair labor practices, to replace the striking employees with new employees or authorize an order directing that all the strikers be reinstated and the new employees discharged. Admittedly the strikers are not "guaranteed" reinstatement by the Act.[79]

---

[76] Id. at 33–38.
[77] Id. at 27.
[78] Id. at 27–28, 39–40.
[79] Robert H. Jackson et al., Reply Brief for the National Labor Relations Board at 15–16, *Mackay*, 304 U.S. 333.

The NLRB thus made it particularly clear that its order for reinstatement for these five workers was wholly precipitated by Mackay Radio's unfair labor practice in discriminating against the five men for their union activity.[80]

Still, despite the NLRB's lack of support for this position, one can imagine how the Wagner Act could plausibly support general reinstatement for economic strikers. Section 7 guarantees employees rights to self-organization and collective bargaining, and Section 8(1) makes it an unfair labor practice for employers to "interfere with, restrain, or coerce employees in the exercise of the rights guaranteed in section 7." At least as a conceptual matter, one might see the threat of losing one's job because of being on an economic strike as an interference with the right to collective bargaining through self-organization. Such a threat could certainly have a chilling effect on union activity and, more directly, on a union's willingness to bargain aggressively for its members. In the same way collective bargaining under Section 7 was justified as a means to equalize employer-employee bargaining, there is no obvious reason why a guarantee of reinstatement to economic strikers could not be conceptualized in the same way as an aid toward more equal bargaining. Further, if the firing of economic strikers could qualify as an unfair labor practice, Section 10(c) would allow the NLRB the right to reinstate workers if it found an unfair labor practice.[81]

Further support for this position could be drawn from Section 13 of the act, which, at the time, stated: "Nothing in this Act shall be construed so as to interfere with or impede or diminish in any way the right to strike." The NLRB drew attention to this clause in support of its point that the five workers were entitled to the act's protection from discrimination for their union activities.[82] But the provision might also justify the extension of its protection to economic strikers. In short, there is no principled reason why economic strikers had to be denied the benefit of guaranteed reinstatement.[83]

As things turned out, the Court's ruling essentially followed the broad outlines of the NLRB's brief. It ruled that the strikers were employees, that the evidence indicated that they had been discriminated against because of their union activities, that this discrimination was an unfair labor

---

[80] Id. at 16.
[81] See Klare, "Deradicalization," 301n117.
[82] Jackson et al., Brief for the NLRB at 33, *Mackay*, 304 U.S. 333.
[83] The above arguments are likewise reiterated in Atleson, *Values*, 24; Klare, "Deradicalization," 301n117.

practice, and that the NLRB's relief of reinstatement was appropriate.[84] More notably for the present argument, the Court explicitly *rejected* the idea that economic strikers were entitled to reinstatement as a general principle; rather, it concluded that they could lawfully be permanently replaced (in the absence of any antiunion discrimination).[85] For our purposes, this latter point is the most notable aspect of the case because it suggests a delimiting impulse at work in the ruling. The Court was not engaged in the task of repudiation with this ruling – its support of the NLRB's reinstatement of the five workers was wholly grounded in an analysis of the Wagner Act and thus an implicit, unquestioned recognition of the latter's constitutionality. But in stating where the protection of the act did not extend – in this case, toward the general right of reinstatement for economic strikers – the ruling demarcated the act's outer boundaries.

Unfortunately, Justice Owen Roberts, in writing for a 7–0 Court, was not particularly verbose in reaching his conclusions on the nonright of general reinstatement. His most detailed comment on this subject was the following:

> Nor was it an unfair labor practice to replace the striking employes [sic] with others in an effort to carry on the business. Although § 13 provides, "Nothing in this Act shall be construed so as to interfere with or impede or diminish in any way the right to strike," it does not follow that an employer, guilty of no act denounced by the statute, has lost the right to protect and continue his business by supplying places left vacant by strikers. And he is not bound to discharge those hired to fill the places of strikers, upon the election of the latter to resume their employment, in order to create places for them.[86]

Significant in this passage is Roberts's reference to the employer's "effort to carry on the business" and his "right to protect and continue his business" as justifications for bringing in permanent replacement workers. As noted earlier, the NLRB's reply brief was sympathetic to this view as well.[87] Both Roberts and the NLRB brief spoke strongly to a type of "business necessity" rationale behind rejecting a general right of reinstatement for economic strikers – that if this general right were extended to workers under the Wagner Act, it could in some fundamental way imperil the ability of a manager or employer to successfully run his business.

---

[84] *Mackay*, 304 U.S. at 346–48.
[85] Id. at 345–46.
[86] Id.
[87] Jackson et al., Reply Brief for the NLRB at 15–16, *Mackay*, 304 U.S. 333.

Although neither the Court nor the NLRB was particularly rigorous in unpacking the concerns behind this business-necessity rationale, Mackay Radio's brief was, not surprisingly, more detailed on this point. To the company, rejection of reinstatement rights for economic strikers was driven by a belief that to do otherwise would constitute a license to unionized employees to run amok. With such a strong guarantee of employment and with the employer's right to fire workers so impaired, what could possibly function to check the demands and actions of employees?[88] In its brief, Mackay Radio reasoned that "by guaranteeing a striker his job, where the strike was neither provoked nor prolonged by the refusal of the employer to negotiate or by any other unfair labor practice, peaceful negotiation would be discouraged and strikes would be encouraged."[89] Such an interpretation of the act "*guarantees* their jobs to employees, upon whatever terms and conditions they may demand, unless the employer shall elect to give up his business."[90]

The company also noted that a bargaining terrain shaped so decidedly to the advantage of workers would have the effect of not only rendering employers impotent but also perverting the system of economic bargaining that the Wagner Act had, by its own terms, protected and modified with its defense of employee rights to self-organize.[91] In the company's view, an interpretation of the act guaranteeing reinstatement to economic strikers would "paralyze" one of these forces in economic bargaining – namely the threat of employees losing their jobs – and thus would create an obstacle to industry functioning, commerce moving, and collective bargaining itself.[92]

It is notable how the company's arguments diverge from employer-rights arguments based on freedom of contract or property rights under the Fifth Amendment. Although the arguments in the preceding paragraph were no doubt driven by similar concerns to protect employer rights with respect to property and managerial control, they also concede the legitimacy of the Wagner Act's system of collective bargaining.[93] They speak less to the idealistic notion of fundamental impairments to employer prerogatives and more to the pragmatic recognition of threats posed to a well-functioning economy. Accordingly, these arguments aligned well

---

[88] Myers et al., Brief for Respondent at 27–28, *Mackay*, 304 U.S. 333.
[89] Id. at 27.
[90] Id. at 39–40 (emphasis in original).
[91] Id. at 26.
[92] Id. at 27–29.
[93] Id. at 27–28, 32.

with the Wagner Act's self-articulated goals of facilitating an environment of healthy industry and industrial peace. The company's arguments used the language of delimitation and recalibration: the furtherance of still-credible political ideals and values to accomplish not a frontal assault on the Wagner Act but rather a delimitation of the Wagner Act's transformative reach.[94]

One might be cautious in simply attributing the views expressed in Mackay Radio's brief to the Court itself, given how little discussion the latter offered on these questions. Nevertheless, given that the company's brief provided the only extensive defense of employer prerogatives, and given the Court's clear endorsement of the Wagner Act and given its own delimiting conclusions, Mackay Radio's brief is instructive. Reading the earlier quotations from the Court's opinion as informed by the company's brief, references to the employer's right to "carry on his business" take on a meaning that embodies more than Fifth Amendment individual rights

---

[94] Yet should this result be that surprising? After all, the NLRB itself had not even pressed for a general right of reinstatement for economic strikers. Can this case really be seen as a delimitation of the Wagner Act and the delineation of uncertain boundaries of reform when both litigants were in agreement on this issue? To the contrary, it would be a mistake to infer from the litigants' agreement that no real choice existed for the Court to make on the rights of economic strikers. The broader implications of the ruling for economic strikers were easily apparent not only to Mackay Radio's lawyers but also to both the NLRB and the Court. This is reflected by the fact that both of the latter felt the need to address the issue – the NLRB in its reply brief to the Court, and the Court in its opinion.

Furthermore, little can be inferred from the fact that the agent of reform in this case – the NLRB – concluded that the general right of reinstatement was unwarranted by the Wagner Act. Litigants, including those generally sympathetic to reform, may have any number of reasons for presenting more or less radical legal arguments before the Court. Recall that in *Slaughter-House*, Republican litigants made states' rights arguments to the Court while their Democratic opponents pressed for expansive, nationalistic interpretations of the Reconstruction Amendments – all because of the peculiarities of Louisiana state politics at the time. In this case, the NLRB's choice to concede the point on a general right of reinstatement for economic strikers stemmed from the carefully restrained legal strategy set by J. Warren Madden and Charles Fahy, chairman and general counsel of the NLRB, respectively. Their cautious attitude was apparently the result of both personal predisposition and concern that too expansive an interpretation of the act by the NLRB at such an early stage might prompt a hostile reaction from the Court, challenging the act's constitutionality. Julius G. Getman and Thomas C. Kohler, "The Story of *NLRB v. Mackay Radio & Telegraph Co.*," in *Labor Law Stories*, eds. Laura J. Cooper and Catherine L. Fisk (New York: Foundation Press, 2005), 44. If we focus on the effect of the ruling, however, there is no question that *Mackay* constituted an initial, important clarification on the extent of the institutional change contemplated by the Wagner Act, and that this clarification took the form of a delimitation of the act's protections to economic strikers.

protection for employers. In addition, this phrase suggests how the maintenance and preservation of employers' rights was a valuable prerequisite of a well-functioning industrial system.[95]

NLRB v. Sands Manufacturing Co.

This case arose out of a contract dispute between the Sands Manufacturing Company, a business that manufactured water heaters in Cleveland, Ohio, and "Mesa," which was an independent labor organization to which most of the company's employees belonged. The NLRB previously concluded that the company, in actions arising out of a labor contract dispute, had engaged in several unfair labor practices as defined in Sections 8(1), (3), and (5) of the Wagner Act.[96]

Section 8(5) of the Wagner Act stated: "It shall be an unfair labor practice for an employer – To refuse to bargain collectively with the representatives of his employees, subject to the provisions of Section 9(a)."[97] The elements of this case that are most interesting from a recalibration perspective stemmed precisely from the Court's treatment of that provision. The key uncertainty posed in *Sands* was: How expansively would the Court interpret this collective bargaining duty of employers? The answer it provided was consistent with several themes present in *Mackay*. Namely, as in *Mackay*, the Court's opinion in *Sands* defended employer interests and demarcated the outer boundaries of legally protected union activity – both principally justified by a rationale of promoting industrial stability.

The more specific contract dispute between Mesa and the company arose over hiring and seniority clauses in a labor agreement.[98] Faced

---

[95] The Court's ruling did offer a marginal protection, of sorts, to employees: it offered employee protection from discharge but no protection from being "permanently replaced."

[96] *NLRB v. Sands Manufacturing Co.*, 306 U.S. 332, 334–35 (1939).

[97] National Labor Relations Act of 1935, Pub. L. No. 74–198, § 8, 49 Stat. 449, 452–53 (1935).

[98] Two aspects of the organization of the Sands Company have to be noted before understanding the intricacies of the contract dispute. First, the company's plant was divided into different departments, and wages differed across them. Second, among the workers themselves, men were divided into two groups: "new men," who were all employees hired while the company had been filling a government order in 1934, and "old men," who were all those employed by the company prior to this order. This division was most immediately relevant for pay scales, since old men generally received higher wages than new men in the same department. *Sands*, 306 U.S. at 336–37. It was also relevant for job security. During times when business was slow and the company had to make cuts

with a seeming standoff over the proper interpretation of a labor agreement between the two, the company posed a choice to the union's shop committee: accede to the company's interpretation of the contract or have the plant shut down temporarily. The union chose the latter, and the plant closed down on August 21, 1935. Ten days later, the company completed another contract with the International Association of Machinists (a union affiliated with the AFL). On September 3, the company reopened, and a day later, Mesa demanded a meeting. The company refused the meeting and instead informed Mesa that their members had generally been discharged. Litigation followed.[99]

For the NLRB, the company's refusal to meet and bargain with Mesa after the shutdown constituted "a unilateral termination of negotiations" and a violation of its Section 8(5) obligation to bargain.[100] In its brief, it outlined three separate matters for which further bargaining between the two should have taken place. First, according to the NLRB's version of the events, the shutdown was characterized as a temporary solution or

> in certain departments, past company practice had been to transfer the old men working in these particular departments to other departments at their regular wages (instead of laying them off). Id. at 336. This issue of seniority rights, however, came to be a sticking point for the company, which grew increasingly dissatisfied with the inefficiency and added cost of this system of interdepartmental transfers. Thus the issue was supposed to be addressed in three provisions included in a June 15, 1935, agreement between the company and Mesa. These provisions were as follows:
>
> (5) That when employees are laid off, seniority rights shall rule, and by departments.
> (6) That when one department is shut down, men from this department will not be transferred or work in other departments until all old men only within that department, who were laid off, have been called back.
> (7) That all new employees be laid off before any old employees, in order to guarantee if possible at least one week's full time before the working week is reduced to three days. Id. at 337.
>
> These contract provisions became particularly relevant when layoffs of employees began on July 15, 1935, and continued through early August. Both new and old men lost their jobs. In early August, however, the company sought to increase the number of employees in the machine shop department while also closing down other departments. The company wanted to hire new, experienced men for the machine shop department rather than transfer old men from other departments that were shutting down, presumably both because new men could both be paid at a lower wage and because the men hired would have relatively greater experience with the work in the machine shop department. The shop committee for the union, however, interpreted the June 15, 1935, agreement to require the transfer of old men to the machine shop department before any new men could be hired. Id. at 338.

[99] Id. at 338–39.
[100] Robert H. Jackson et al., Brief for the NLRB at 22, *National Labor Relations Board v. Sands Manufacturing Co.*, 306 U.S. 332 (1939).

compromise for the parties' impasse on the contractual issue. Since the buildup of work orders could have made the contractual dispute irrelevant, the shutdown opened the door for future bargaining and even potential agreement on the dispute between the company and Mesa. Second, the company's failure to abide by this alleged compromise by reopening the plant with new workers was itself an issue for further negotiation. And finally, since the company's main issue with the labor agreement was the old seniority system in which higher wages were paid to older employees, an avenue of further negotiation along the lines of a general wage reduction was also available to the parties.[101] There is a general interpretation of Section 8(5) underlying these arguments made by the NLRB. Although it ultimately concluded that the union's interpretation of the contract was correct (while also conceding that the contractual dispute was one in which honest opinions could diverge),[102] it asserted that the obligation of the employer to collectively bargain with the union was present not only for the creation of labor contracts, but for *contract modifications* as well.[103] Thus, according to the NLRB, the employer's obligation to collectively bargain would exist in this case regardless of whose interpretation was correct.[104] It bears emphasizing that the consequences of the NLRB's interpretation of Section 8(5) would have been no small matter. Granting the unions this power to engage in concerted action for midterm contract modifications would make the collective bargaining process not simply a one-shot deal every time a contract needed to be written but also potentially a continuous process. Union power could be brought to bear not only at certain key points in time – that is, only when new contracts had to be negotiated – but at potentially any time.[105]

The Court, however, was not willing to go as far as the NLRB. Writing for a 5–2 Court, Justice Roberts conceded that employers did have a duty to bargain and meet with employee representatives regarding modifications or questions of interpretation of an existing contract. He also found, however, that this duty had been met by the company.[106] A key

---

[101] Id. at 20–27.
[102] Id. at 29n8, 30–31.
[103] Id. at 31.
[104] Id.
[105] Presumably, opening up the possibility of contract negotiations in the middle of the contract's term would also be an entitlement that employers could then claim, although since the focus here is Section 8(5), the obligation to bargain at issue here is the employer's only.
[106] *Sands*, 306 U.S. at 342–43.

element in helping him reach this conclusion was his related conclusion that the company's interpretation of the contract was correct.[107] As he stated:

> The contract provided for departmental seniority, in Section 5 and 6, and Section 7 did not create any ambiguity on the subject. Moreover, the record makes it clear that the committee which negotiated the contract on behalf of the union fully understood its terms in the same sense as did the respondent. In this situation how often and how long was the company bound to continue discussion of the committee's demand that the provisions of the contract should be ignored?[108]

The uncompromising stance of the union made further negotiation pointless, according to the Court. Furthermore, Mesa's threat of a strike, should the company have proceeded with its desired plans, amounted to a breach of the June 15, 1935, agreement. As such, by repudiating their labor contract, the Mesa members were eligible to be discharged and to lose their employee status under the Wagner Act, and the company had no obligation under Section 8(5) to bargain with Mesa after the plant shut down on August 21.[109] To quote the Court:

> Respondent rightly understood that the men were irrevocably committed not to work in accordance with their contract. It was at liberty to treat them as having severed their relations with the company because of their breach and to consummate their separation from the company's employ by hiring others to take their places. The Act does not prohibit an effective discharge for repudiation by the employe [sic] of his agreement.[110]

The *Sands* opinion, like the *Mackay* opinion, was written by Justice Roberts, although it was even briefer in discussing broader considerations. But the key point that pushed the *Sands* Court to diverge so sharply from the NLRB lay in its conclusion that Mesa's actions constituted a breach of contract. Reasons that explain why the Court came to this conclusion, in addition to its interpretation of the textual provisions of the labor agreement, might be deduced through an examination of the company brief's treatment of the issues.

The company argued that its termination of negotiations was justified because an impasse had been reached between the company and Mesa

---

[107] Id.
[108] Id.
[109] Id. at 343–44.
[110] Id. at 344.

on the seniority dispute.[111] Further, it argued that the discharge of the Mesa members was justified by the latter simply refusing to live up to their obligations under the contract.[112] Contrary to the position of the NLRB, the company asserted that the merits of the underlying contractual dispute had everything to do with dictating the extent of the employer's obligation to bargain. If it were the case that the union's interpretation of the contract was clearly wrong and that they were essentially pressing for a modification of the contract (which the company asserted and the Court agreed with), then the extent of the employer's obligation was simply to hear and consider the employees' position.[113] While this was also essentially the position taken by the Court, the company's brief was more explicit as to why the collective bargaining duty could not be any more robust than this in the case of a clear-cut contract modification:

> The Government contends that in collective bargaining between an employer and his employees over a requested change in an existing contract, the merits of the dispute cannot affect the extent of the employer's obligation under Section 8(5).
>
> This statement cannot be the law, else a strike by a group of employees during the term of a contract for the sole purpose of accomplishing a change in the contract between them and their employer, as, for example, an increase in the wage rates specified in the contract, would be lawful on the part of the employees, and filling their places unlawful on the part of the employer.[114]

The broader consequences of this would be obvious: "If the respondent employer did not have the right to stand on its contract and refuse to negotiate further on the MESA refusal to perform, then respondent's contract was worthless. Indeed, the value of every collective bargaining contract would be greatly lessened if the rule stated by the Board and by the Government were held to apply in such situations."[115]

This defense of contractualism did not wholly rest on some abstract notion of the sanctity of contract. A core purpose of the Wagner Act's provisions lay in the promotion of labor contracts to foster industrial stability. These goals would be endangered if the Court interpreted the Section 8(5) duty to bargain to encompass midterm contract modifications as well. For example, if an employer knew it might be obligated to bargain throughout the life of a contract, the employer's motivation to

---

[111] Harry E. Smoyer and Welles K. Stanley, Respondent's Brief at 44–47, *NLRB v. Sands Manufacturing Co.*, 306 U.S. 332 (1939).
[112] Id. at 51–53.
[113] Id. at 43.
[114] Id. at 43–44 (citations omitted).
[115] Id. at 44.

Labor Rights, the New Deal Era, and Delimitation   137

reach agreement in the first place might be reduced. As the company's brief stated:

> The Act does not compel collective bargaining looking toward a contract and at the same time invalidate the contract it has encouraged by permitting an interpretation to the effect that an employer can not use it as the measure of his conduct toward his employees and of their conduct toward him. The Act does not encourage the making of contracts the breach of which is to be considered immaterial. The Act does not permit such a conclusion and such was not the intent of Congress.[116]

The structural consequences of following such a wrong-headed conclusion would be clear: "Stabilization of business conditions by collective agreements between employers and employees would also be a mere delusion if they be not held to impose mutually enforceable obligations. If, before the Board it is immaterial that the Complaining Employees had willfully violated their contract, then is disobedience of and disrespect for law thereby encouraged and constant strife, not peace, prescribed as our daily portion."[117]

Given the company's argument, one might be tempted to agree that the demands of collective bargaining simply required that unions not be allowed to enjoy a right to collectively bargain over contract modifications (or a right to infringe on employer prerogatives to stand on the terms of a labor contract).[118] Yet such a view obscures the plausible developmental alternatives at this moment in time. After all, one might imagine pragmatic, industrial-peace-driven arguments in *support* of the NLRB's position on Section 8(5) as well. For example, the NLRB argued that "the statute does not define the extent of the obligation [of

---

[116] Id. at 56.
[117] Id. at 57.
[118] By Matthew Finkin's interpretation of *Sands*, the Court's ultimate acceptance of the company's arguments was to some extent a foregone conclusion given the relative quality of the legal arguments offered by the NLRB and the company. After reiterating the company's point that the practice of collective bargaining under the Wagner Act would be undercut if the NLRB's interpretation of Section 8(5) carried the day, Finkin concludes that "one comes away from the briefs in the case with the impression that the Board was simply out-lawyered, for it marshalled no argument or authority to rebut the company's argument, which was firmly rooted in the legislative history of the Act." Finkin, "Revisionism," 40. To be sure, Finkin does outline another argumentative route by which the NLRB's position might have been defensible in this case. In the labor agreement between Mesa and the company, there was apparently a provision that reserved to the union the right to strike during the life of the contract. An argument could thus be made that Mesa's threat of a work stoppage was wholly within the terms of the contract. Ibid., 40–41.

Section 8(5)]; indeed, no precise statement is possible. The policy of Congress, however, not only in this but also in other statutes, is to make of collective bargaining an effective 'instrument of peace' in the settlement of labor disputes."[119] Indeed, this goal might be served by employing collective bargaining in a wider domain of employer-employee relations: "The purpose of the Act is to encourage the procedure of collective bargaining for the settlement of *all* differences, without regard to either the merits of the respective positions of the disputants or the fact that one party may believe that the issue is already covered by an agreement."[120]

A genuine developmental choice seems to have presented itself to the Court, and in choosing the interpretation of Section 8(5) that constrained the scope of protected union activity and increased the freedom of action for employers, *Sands* demonstrates a thematic similarity to the result in *Mackay*: a recalibration of the Wagner Act that reconciled the Section 8(5) duty to bargain with pre-Wagner notions of property, employer rights, and contractualism. Equally important to note is how these legal results were achieved, for neither the company's brief nor the Court's opinion evidences a hint of repudiation toward the collective bargaining system. To the contrary, as noted earlier, the company's strongest arguments in support of its narrower interpretation of Section 8(5) rest on a close, supportive link to core Wagner Act goals of promoting collective labor agreements and industrial stability. It would be reasonable to

---

[119] Jackson et al., Brief for the NLRB at 17, *Sands*, 306 U.S. 332.

[120] Id. at 31–32. An interview by Professor Kenneth Casebeer with Leon Keyserling, former legislative aide to Senator Wagner, on the drafting of the Wagner Act actually provides some support for the NLRB's position as a matter of original intent:

> Casebeer: Was the issue of sitdown strikes or the use of strikes during the course of the contract discussed?
> Keyserling: Well, certainly, the explicit guarantee of the right to strike [in Section 13 of the act] didn't delimit it in any way. They [employees] could strike at any time.
> Casebeer: So that if there was an impasse, for example, over the terms of the contract –
> Keyserling: They could strike.
> Casebeer: It would simply be a matter of the collective bargaining that would go on not only in the formation of the agreement but in its interpretations and in any reopening of negotiations?
> Keyserling: They would still have the right to strike....

Kenneth M. Casebeer, "Holder of the Pen: An Interview with Leon Keyserling on Drafting the Wagner Act," *University of Miami Law Review* 42, no. 2 (November 1987): 353–54. Later on in the same interview, after being read some quotations from the aforementioned Finkin, "Revisionism" article, Keyserling seems to suggest that a more robust employer duty to bargain was intended, even for contract modifications. Casebeer, "Holder," 354–55.

speculate that at least some of these considerations seeped into the Court's decision making, as evidenced by the fact that its ruling sided so heavily with the company's legal conclusions. Thus, a pattern of delimiting judicial decision making emerges that ties *Sands* to *Mackay Radio*. In both cases, resilient employer prerogatives are reasserted against more expansive interpretations of the Wagner Act's protections of employee rights. Furthermore, in both cases, this reassertion was supported to a significant extent by an attendant fear that to do otherwise would be to risk industrial disorder.

NLRB v. Fansteel Metallurgical Corp.

Finally, we come to the Court's treatment of sit-down strikes. The employer in this case was Fansteel Metallurgical Corporation. In *Fansteel*, the NLRB had found that subsequent to employee attempts to unionize in the summer of 1936, the corporation had engaged in a number of unfair labor practices.[121] The Supreme Court subsequently concurred with these findings and agreed with the NLRB's conclusion that the corporation and its representatives violated Section 8(1) (prohibiting employer interference with Section 7 employee rights to self-organization) and Section 8(5) (employer refusal to bargain with employee representatives) of the Wagner Act.[122]

The legal complexity of this case, and its significance for the present argument, lies in what happened next. After the corporation's superintendent refused to bargain with the union on February 17, 1937, the union committee decided to engage in a sit-down strike by taking possession of two of the corporation's key buildings on the same day. As a result, work stopped in the two buildings, and work stopped in the rest of the plant. The occupying employees were forcefully driven out on February 26.[123]

This sequence of events implicated the same kinds of uncertainties confronted by the Court in the prior two cases, namely: How far would the protective cover of the Wagner Act extend to aid and support unions? The corporation's engagement in unfair labor practices would, by itself, normally protect the striking employees from discharge. But occurring in between the corporation's unfair labor practices and the discharge of the employees was the intervening sit-down strike by the employees

---

[121] *NLRB v. Fansteel Metallurgical Corp.*, 306 U.S. 240, 247–248 (1939).
[122] Id. at 251–52.
[123] Id. at 248–49.

themselves. Thus, the specific question here was whether engagement in a sit-down strike would nullify the Wagner Act's protections for the employees and leave the NLRB powerless to reinstate them.

The NLRB's brief, not surprisingly, offered an expansive interpretation of the Wagner Act that would require reinstatement of the sit-down strikers. It focused on the fact that the strike was prompted by the corporation's unfair labor practices and flouting of the Wagner Act's requirements.[124] In response to the obvious concern that the act's protections were nullified by the employees' own illegal acts, the NLRB offered two arguments.

First, the NLRB's brief appealed to statutory text. Again, Section 10(c) of the Wagner Act stated, in part, that the NLRB, on finding the occurrence of an unfair labor practice, may "take such affirmative action including reinstatement of employees with or without back pay, as will effectuate the policies of this Act." And the definition of "employee" in Section 2(3) applied to "any individual whose work has ceased as a consequence of, or in connection with, any current labor dispute or because of any unfair labor practice." The NLRB argued that the sit-down strikers retained their employee status given that their strike resulted from a current labor dispute and the corporation's unfair labor practices. Thus, the NLRB argued, the workers were eligible for reinstatement under Section 10(c).[125] To be sure, the act specified one way in which employee status may be terminated: if the individual "obtained any other regular and substantially equivalent employment."[126] But it would be difficult to argue that this limitation applied to the present case.[127] Thus, the NLRB more generally argued that once an employer had committed an unfair labor practice against employees, the expansive scope of the board's remedial power under Section 10(c) was triggered and the employer had, as a result of its Wagner Act violation, made itself *potentially* subject to the NLRB's authority (including its authority to reinstate) regardless of whether alternative grounds might exist for discharging some of these employees for cause.[128]

---

[124] Robert H. Jackson et al., Brief for the National Labor Relations Board at 35–38, *National Labor Relations Board v. Fansteel Metallurgical Corp.*, 306 U.S. 240 (1939).
[125] Id. at 40–41.
[126] National Labor Relations Act of 1935, Pub. L. No. 74-198, § 2 (3), 49 Stat. 449, 450 (1935).
[127] Jackson, Brief for the NLRB at 40–41, *Fansteel*, 306 U.S. 240.
[128] Id. at 43–45. See also, Robert H. Jackson et al., Reply Brief for the National Labor Relations Board at 20–29, *Fansteel*, 306 U.S. 240. Separately, the NLRB also asserted that

Second, more pragmatically, the NLRB argued that reinstatement of the strikers was necessary to achieve the larger aims of the act as called for under Section 10(c) ("as will effectuate the policies of this Act"). As its brief stated: "Under the circumstances of this case, reinstatement was essential to restore the *status quo* and dissipate the effects of respondent's unfair labor practices, especially when it is remembered that none of the things respondent raises as a bar to reinstatement would have occurred but for respondent's violations of the law."[129] Reinstatement would also be in keeping with the larger purpose of the Wagner Act in promoting industrial peace:

So far as the National Labor Relations Act is concerned, the way to prevent and discourage sit-down strikes, as well as all strikes, is through collective bargaining, not by punishing strikers. It flies in the very teeth of the whole policy of the Act and its constitutional basis as a regulation of commerce to contend that, faced with clear violations of the Act, the Board must withhold the only remedy which can encourage collective bargaining in this case by dissipating the effects of respondent's unfair labor practices because, after such practices were committed, some of the strikers engaged in acts illegal under state law, for which they have been punished under that law.[130]

The corporation's brief took issue with both the NLRB's textual and policy-oriented arguments. With respect to the NLRB's textual argument, the corporation's brief departed from the NLRB's position on the point of how expansively to interpret the board's remedial power under Section 10(c). Recall that the NLRB asserted that this provision, coupled with Section 2(3)'s definition of an "employee," gave it the right to potentially reinstate discharged employees "to effectuate the goals of the Act" once an unfair labor practice occurred – even if an employee discharge was for cause. In contrast, the corporation viewed this remedial power more narrowly. The corporation saw this statutory authority as encompassing only the authority for the NLRB to intervene and reinstate employees who had been discharged specifically for going on a (non-sit-down) strike or for activities related to the right to unionize. At the same time, an

---

its reinstatement power would be appropriate even if the strikers were not "employees" under the terms of the Wagner Act, given the possibility of interpreting the Board's remedial power under Section 10(c) more expansively to cover non-employees as well. Jackson et al., Brief for the NLRB at 45–49, *Fansteel*, 306 U.S. 240. The NLRB used this argument in its brief for *Mackay Radio* as well. Jackson et al., Brief for the NLRB at 49–54, *Mackay*, 304 U.S. 333.

[129] Jackson, Brief for the NLRB at 49–50, *Fansteel*, 306 U.S. 240.
[130] Id. at 58–59.

employer's right to discharge an employee for cause remained wholly intact under the Wagner Act.[131] For the present case, this interpretation of Section 2(3) – and its implications for Section 10(c) – would mean that the corporation's discharge of sit-down strikers was legitimate, as it involved a discharge for cause and *not* for protected activities such as employee self-organization and collective bargaining.[132]

The corporation also disputed the NLRB's more pragmatic policy argument. To the corporation, allowing the sit-down strikers to be reinstated would have precisely the opposite effect claimed by the NLRB and would undercut the Wagner Act's core goal of promoting industrial stability by encouraging lawlessness and chaos.[133] The Wagner Act

was designed to promote industrial peace by encouraging collective bargaining and to provide an orderly process for enforcing the employees' right to self-organization. The reinstatement of discharged employees guilty of the property destruction and lawlessness portrayed in this record cannot advance either the immediate objective of peaceful collective bargaining or the ultimate end of industrial peace.[134]

The corporation's brief also emphasized the moral threat posed by the sit-down tactic: "The Board cannot brush aside and wipe out the property destruction, lawlessness and discharge, and treat the situation as if these events had never occurred."[135] Later, it stated, "Self-help, with force, has no place in organized society. Neither high moral purpose nor integrity of objective can condone or justify the substitution of violence for the orderly processes of government."[136] By the corporation's assessment, the sit-down strike itself constituted a fundamental violation of the Wagner Act:

The Board ignores, as did the men who seized the Respondent's plant, the legal, orderly remedies available under the law. The statutory right of collective bargaining may be enforced either by a proceeding before the Board or by a peaceful strike.... Without waiting for the outcome of their legal proceeding, the men took the law into their own hands. They determined to settle the matter by force and violence "according to their own sense of right" without regard to either the federal or the state laws.[137]

---

[131] Benjamin V. Becker et al., Brief for Fansteel Metallurgical Corporation at 24–25, 32–34, *Fansteel*, 306 U.S. 240.
[132] Id. at 25–29.
[133] Id. at 34–45, 52.
[134] Id. at 35.
[135] Id. at 36.
[136] Id. at 39–40.
[137] Id. at 39.

The Court ultimately concurred with the corporation's position. Equally significant was the rationale supporting the Court's conclusions. The tone for Chief Justice Hughes's opinion for the Court was set early with the following assessment of the sit-down strike: "Nor is it questioned that the seizure and retention of respondent's property were unlawful. It was a high-handed proceeding without shadow of legal right."[138] Hughes asserted that "this conduct on the part of the employees manifestly gave good cause for their discharge unless the National Labor Relations Act abrogates the right of the employer to refuse to retain in his employ those who illegally take and hold possession of his property."[139]

Perhaps the corporation's violations of the Wagner Act might provide partial justification for the employees' use of the sit-down tactic? Again, the Court agreed with the NLRB's findings of the corporation's unfair labor practices discussed earlier. Yet the answer was still no. An employer's unfair labor practice simply did not justify an illegal act against its property in response:

For the unfair labor practices of respondent the [Wagner] Act provided a remedy.... Reprehensible as was that conduct of the respondent, there is no ground for saying that it made respondent an outlaw or deprived it of its legal rights to the possession and protection of its property. The employees had the right to strike but they had no license to commit acts of violence or to seize their employer's plant.[140]

The Court was thus well on its way to concurring with the corporation's more restrained and limited interpretation of the NLRB's remedial power under Section 2(3) and Section 10(c) of the Wagner Act. As the Court stated:

We think that the true purpose of Congress is reasonably clear. Congress was intent upon the protection of the right of employees to self-organization and to the selection of representatives of their own choosing for collective bargaining without restraint or coercion. To assure that protection, the employer is not permitted to discharge his employees because of union activity or agitation for collective bargaining. The conduct thus protected is lawful conduct.... There is thus abundant opportunity for the operation of § 2 (3) without construing it as countenancing lawlessness or as intended to support employees in acts of violence against the employer's property by making it impossible for the employer to terminate the relation upon that independent ground.[141]

---

[138] *NLRB v. Fansteel Metallogical Corp.*, 306 U.S. 240, 252 (1939).
[139] Id.
[140] Id. at 253.
[141] Id. at 255–56 (citations omitted).

By engaging in a sit-down strike, however, the employees "took a position outside the protection of the statute and accepted the risk of the termination of their employment upon grounds aside from the exercise of the legal rights which the statute was designed to conserve."[142] Hence, reinstatement of the workers was not demanded by the Wagner Act.

The Court's reference to threats of chaos and lawlessness, as it related to infringement on the corporation's property rights, is noteworthy. The following quotations from the ruling mirrored the tone taken in the corporation's brief in its discussion of the sit-down tactic: "To justify such conduct [as a sit-down strike] because of the existence of a labor dispute or of an unfair labor practice would be to put a premium on resort to force instead of legal remedies and to subvert the principles of law and order which lie at the foundations of society."[143] The sit-down strike

> was not the exercise of 'the right to strike' to which the [Wagner] Act referred. It was not a mere quitting of work and statement of grievances in the exercise of pressure recognized as lawful. It was an illegal seizure of the buildings in order to prevent their use by the employer in a lawful manner and thus by acts of force and violence to compel the employer to submit.[144]

Even more significantly, the Court mirrored the corporation's assessment of the sit-down tactic as it related to industrial peace:

> We repeat that the fundamental policy of the Act is to safeguard the rights of self-organization and collective bargaining, and thus by the promotion of industrial peace to remove obstructions to the free flow of commerce as defined in the Act. There is not a line in the statute to warrant the conclusion that it is any part of the policies of the Act to encourage employees to resort to force and violence in defiance of the law of the land. On the contrary, the purpose of the Act is to promote peaceful settlements of disputes by providing legal remedies for the invasion of the employees' rights.... We are of the opinion that to provide for the reinstatement or reemployment of employees guilty of the acts which the Board finds to have been committed in this instance would not only not effectuate any policy of the Act but would directly tend to make abortive its plan for peaceable procedure.[145]

Once again, the path toward judicial delimitation did not lie through questioning the core ambitions of the Wagner Act; indeed, much of the opinion was concerned with interpreting the act. Rather, defenses of

---

[142] Id. at 256–57.
[143] Id. at 253.
[144] Id. at 256.
[145] Id. at 257–58.

employer prerogatives were aided, in significant part, by an indirect justification that emphasized the threat posed to the related and legitimate goal of industrial peace – a threat that would emerge if the sit-down strikers were protected by the act. The similarity between Hughes's reference to this pervasive threat and Miller's reference to the threat of federal centralization in the *Slaughter-House Cases* is readily apparent.

The Court's ruling against reinstating the sit-down strikers was by no means a self-evident or obvious legal conclusion. Certain political actors found the reinstatement of the sit-down strikers a plausible legal option. The NLRB emphasized how reinstatement of the sit-down strikers could promote the collective bargaining goals of the act.[146] And Justice Reed, dissenting in part from the Court's ruling, stated a view similar to the NLRB's in noting how "friction easily engendered by labor strife may readily give rise to conduct, from nose-thumbing to sabotage, which will give fair occasion for discharge on grounds other than those prohibited by the Labor Act."[147] Because of this, the act could be interpreted as a means by which "Congress sought by clear language to eliminate this prolific source of ill feeling by the provision just quoted [Section 2(3) of the Wagner Act] which should be interpreted in accordance with its language as continuing the eligibility of a striker for reinstatement regardless of conduct by the striker or action by the employer."[148] In a note of deference to the NLRB, Reed concluded that the ultimate decision on whether reinstatement of employees guilty of breaking the law would promote or detract from industrial peace was one appropriately left for the NLRB to determine.[149] In keeping with the results in *Mackay Radio* and *Sands*, however, the Court chose to reject more transformative readings of the act, and it did so with reference to industrial peace and the need to preserve employer prerogatives that did not directly bear on the right to unionize.

CONTINUING LEGISLATIVE STALEMATE ON LABOR LEGISLATION

The judiciary's attention to recalibration questions, and its inclination to delimit, was not unique within the federal government of the late 1930s. Indeed, these questions remained prominent in Congress. On the one

---

[146] Jackson et al., Brief for NLRB at 49–50, 58–59, *Fansteel*, 306 U.S. 240.
[147] *Fansteel*, 306 U.S. at 266–67 (Reed, J., dissenting).
[148] Id. at 266–67 (Reed, J., dissenting).
[149] Id. at 267 (Reed, J., dissenting).

hand, antilabor sentiment was running so strongly that it was all labor defenders could do to keep conservatives at bay in Congress; after the 1938 election, labor's allies in Congress were largely stuck in a defensive position. Nevertheless, they were not overrun. If seen from the opposite perspective – that of postreform skeptics – the political environment in the immediate aftermath of the 1938 election was not hospitable enough to spark a legislatively driven delimitation; as vigorous as their efforts were in opposition to organized labor, they too ultimately failed to achieve a legislative victory in this period. Hence this was truly a period of legislative stalemate; postreform skeptics would not get a legislative victory until the Smith-Connally Act in 1943.[150] The continuation of a legislative stalemate, in turn, ensured that the judicial delimiting rulings previously discussed would stand unrevised by either more or less labor-friendly legislation, at least for several more years.

Resistance to the Wagner Act did not suddenly materialize in 1938. Indeed, soon after the *Jones & Laughlin* decision, the Chamber of Commerce and the National Association of Manufacturers were urging "equalizing" amendments to the Wagner Act that were largely directed toward imposing reciprocal obligations on unions and employees.[151] Standing alone, however, these more categorical opponents of reform were insufficient to stalemate the elected branches on labor rights. Business interests had learned after 1935 that they lacked the political clout to get far on their own; they needed additional constituencies to join their cause. In the late 1930s and early 1940s, the key swing constituency that aided the efforts of conservatives was the AFL.[152]

The AFL had qualms about the Wagner Act from the start, particularly with respect to its Section 9(b) that granted discretion to the NLRB to determine collective bargaining units. This authority collided head-on with the AFL's traditional authority to essentially distribute territorial rights to different craft unions within an industry under the principle of exclusive jurisdiction. Thus, ironically, the dismantling effect of the Wagner Act prompted conflict not only between employer and employee interests but also between different sets of employee interests.[153]

---

[150] Harry A. Millis and Emily Clark Brown, *From the Wagner Act to Taft-Hartley: A Study of National Labor Policy and Labor Relations* (1950; repr., Chicago: University of Chicago Press, 1957), 354.
[151] Bernstein, *Turbulent Years*, 663; Patterson, *Congressional Conservatism*, 245–46.
[152] James A. Gross, *The Reshaping of the National Labor Relations Board: National Labor Policy in Transition, 1937–1947* (Albany: State University of New York Press, 1981), 42.
[153] Bernstein, *Turbulent Years*, 353; Tomlins, *The State*, 140–45, 183–84.

At first, the Wagner Act's Section 9(b) held only the mere potential to hurt the AFL craft unions and benefit the industrial unions; whether this would actually happen depended on how units were determined and how the workers themselves decided to vote. As a result, the AFL did not launch an attack on the act in 1935.[154] By the end of 1937, however, the Congress of Industrial Organizations (CIO) had managed to win more than 75 percent of union elections in which it had gone head-to-head against the AFL, and it had done so with an 83 percent average majority. The initial qualms of the AFL had indeed materialized, and as they did, its initial concerns steadily turned into outright hostility toward the NLRB from 1936 to 1938.[155] The AFL had not been placated by the NLRB decision in *Globe Machine and Stamping Company*[156] in 1937 either, where the board had allowed workers in each of three units claimed by the AFL to vote *within* their respective units for either the CIO or the AFL. Notably, the NLRB had reached this decision because all other relevant factors in determining the bargaining unit were "evenly balanced."[157] And although the decision essentially respected craft boundaries in allowing for separate voting within each unit, the AFL was still annoyed by the decision because of the latter qualification: the fact that the NLRB was led to this outcome because other factors were "evenly balanced" implied that it had ultimate, unchecked authority to determine unit size. In another case, where the factors were not "evenly balanced," the board could just as easily rule for holding the vote within the single industrial unit.[158]

With the shifts of the 1938 election in place, a conservative coalition of reenergized Republicans, Southern Democrats, the AFL, and business interests all had the potential, if they remained allied, to go on the offensive against the Wagner Act and the NLRB. Indeed, by March 1939, eleven major bills had been introduced in both houses of Congress to amend the Wagner Act.[159] Recent history demonstrated that the AFL's involvement was crucial for attaining any legislative success with these bills: in June 1937, Senator Vandenberg had submitted a bill that provided for mutualizing amendments to the Wagner Act, which basically created a set of unfair labor practices for labor. The bill had gotten stuck in the Senate Labor Committee, however, and when AFL president William

---

[154] Bernstein, *Turbulent Years*, 664.
[155] Ibid., 663–66; Dubofsky, *State & Labor*, 152; Gross, *Reshaping*, 42.
[156] 3 N.L.R.B. 294 (1937).
[157] Id. at 300.
[158] Gross, *Reshaping*, 45; Tomlins, *The State*, 165–66.
[159] Gross, *Reshaping*, 79.

Green had made his opposition to the bill known, it was for all intents and purposes killed.[160]

Recognizing these issues at play, FDR's first move was to try to head off the conservative threat by having the Senate Education and Labor Committee and the House Labor Committee hold extended hearings on possible amendments to the act in the spring and summer of 1939. Roosevelt did this in order to keep the opposition at bay and to try to buy more time to implement additional personnel changes on the NLRB that might placate the AFL.[161] With this in mind, in April 1939, FDR appointed William Leiserson to replace Donald Wakefield Smith on the NLRB, since Leiserson was generally seen as more sympathetic to the AFL's notions of maintaining the integrity of institutionalized and entrenched unions. With the AFL peeled off from the ranks of postreform skeptics, the hope was that the energy for revision of the act would dissipate. However, the appointment did not have the desired effect.[162]

The administration's delay strategy was also not effective in stifling further action from others on the labor issue. Faced with the annoying obstacle of sympathetic labor committees in both houses, conservatives pressed ahead when, on June 22, 1939, Representative Howard Smith – a Democrat from Virginia – proposed a resolution in the House Rules Committee calling for a special committee to investigate the NLRB. The Rules Committee, chaired by Smith himself, favorably reported out a resolution on July 6 to the House, thanks to an alliance between Southern Democrats and Republicans on the committee. The resolution passed in the House on July 20 and established an investigatory committee with Smith, again, as its chair. Support for the resolution largely stemmed from a Southern Democrat-Republican alliance but was also supported by the AFL.[163]

This committee's investigations into the NLRB functioned, along with the Dies Committee on Un-American Activities, to promote a continuing stream of negative attention and criticism of the NLRB and the CIO. The AFL also joined in with its criticisms during these hearings.[164] Gross notes

---

[160] Ibid., 48–49.
[161] Bernstein, *Turbulent Years*, 666–67; Dubofsky, *State & Labor*, 154, 157; Millis and Brown, *From the Wagner Act*, 284; Patterson, *Congressional Conservatism*, 316–17.
[162] Dubofsky, *State & Labor*, 156; Gross, *Reshaping*, 89, 91; Tomlins, *The State*, 195–96.
[163] Bernstein, *Turbulent Years*, 668; Dubofsky, *State & Labor*, 157; Gross, *Reshaping*, 104–06; Millis and Brown, *From the Wagner Act*, 350; Patterson, *Congressional Conservatism*, 317–18.
[164] Dubofsky, *State & Labor*, 152, 158; Gross, *Reshaping*, 171; Millis and Brown, *From the Wagner Act*, 50; Patterson, *Congressional Conservatism*, 318.

that in January 1940, 53 percent of respondents surveyed who had an opinion on the matter were in favor of revising the Wagner Act (another 18 percent were in favor of repeal). The comparable number was 37 percent in November 1939, suggesting that the sixteen percentage point increase over the intervening months was significantly influenced by the work of the Smith committee hearings.[165]

Still, Roosevelt tried to be proactive in warding off more serious attacks on the act. Recognizing that the Smith committee would soon be issuing its recommendations for repeal, he attempted to soften the blow by proposing a compromise: increasing the membership of the NLRB from three to five members. With two additional appointments, Roosevelt could then secure a majority for Leiserson and his relatively conservative views on the board. However, Smith and the two conservative Republicans on the investigatory committee – Charles Halleck and Harry Routzohn – did not bite. These three members of the committee (a majority) instead proposed the following revisions to the act: (1) a toning down of the Wagner Act's Preamble, (2) denial of the act's protection to sit-down strikers, (3) exclusion of the act's coverage to agricultural processing workers, (4) a definition of collective bargaining that would not obligate employers to agree, (5) a separation of the NLRB's judicial and administrative functions, (6) abolition of the board's economic research division, (7) a guarantee of free speech rights for employers, (8) guaranteeing the rights of employers to petition for a union election, (9) denial of the NLRB's authority to make unit determinations in a rival union contest until the unions themselves had resolved the issue, and (10) various procedural changes.[166]

Smith managed to get this bill on the House floor, but he recognized that gaining AFL support would be crucial for its passage. He managed to get the AFL on board by emphasizing themes of worker rights promoted by his bill and by making some key concessions on the bill's substance. These concessions included removing amendments that would revise the Wagner Act's Preamble, along with adding some amendments dealing with procedural issues. With the AFL's support, the bill easily passed the House by a vote of 258–129 in June 1940.[167]

---

[165] Gross, *Reshaping*, 187.
[166] I paraphrase this from Bernstein's account. Bernstein, *Turbulent Years*, 670. The two dissenting members of the committee issued their own minority report that urged only two amendments: (1) Roosevelt's earlier proposal to increase board membership from three to five members, and (2) giving employers the right to call an election if caught between competing unions demanding recognition. Ibid.
[167] Ibid., Dubofsky, *State & Labor*, 160.

But a victory in the House was as far as this legislative delimitation effort went. Senator Elbert Thomas, chairman of the Senate Labor Committee, was also Roosevelt's ally. Once the Smith amendments reached his committee, they permanently languished. By November 1940, it was clear that no Senate action would occur on this bill. Roosevelt did not stop there, however. In August 1940, he replaced J. Warren Madden with Harry Millis as chairman of the NLRB. Millis was, like Leiserson, an appointment meant to quiet or soften AFL criticism of the board. Millis's appointment in turn prompted the departure of Nathan Witt, the more radically minded secretary of the NLRB.[168]

This was housecleaning at the NLRB, and the political motivation for it mirrored the motivation behind all of Roosevelt's previous activity in the domain of post-1938 labor relations. Namely, this was proactive defense meant to placate the AFL and peel them off from the anti-NLRB coalition. This time, however, it worked. With the membership changes at the board and the Smith amendment stopped in the Senate, AFL opposition quieted down.[169]

The legislative frustrations for both Roosevelt and his conservative opponents during this time thus account for why judicial delimitation "stuck." Reformers lacked the support and inclination to attack these rulings in the late 1930s and early 1940s. To the contrary, as this short narrative demonstrates, it was all the allies of labor could do to keep their heads above water and avert a significant conservative revision of the Wagner Act. At the end of the day, of course, conservatives did not succeed in achieving much in the legislative arena either. Their greatest success was in getting the Smith bill passed in the House. But with pockets of labor-friendly influence still present – most notably in the White House – they got no further. Clearly then, the electoral context was characterized by a political stalemate. Whereas insufficient for an electoral counterrevolution, this stalemate was sufficient for securing the judiciary's delimitation in the domain of labor relations.

CONCLUSION

The three judicial rulings discussed in this chapter each constitutes a specific delimitation of labor rights under the Wagner Act. Taken together,

---

[168] Bernstein, *Turbulent Years*, 670–71; Dubofsky, *State & Labor*, 160–61; Tomlins, *The State*, 224.
[169] Bernstein, *Turbulent Years*, 670–71.

however, these decisions evidence the judicial codification of an outer boundary to legitimate union activity. The significance of these cases stems in large part from how they crystallized emergent political developments and helped formally demarcate the scope of labor rights in the post–New Deal and post–World War II eras.

Moreover, the manner in which the Court reached these results was also significant. The postreform skeptics employed legal arguments that self-consciously sought to demarcate the outer boundaries of reform indirectly through the defense of certain employer prerogatives and an appeal to "industrial peace" – a goal found within the language of the Wagner Act itself.

As I discuss in Chapter 8, a new system of labor relations – with a central commitment to voluntary arbitration as the primary means to manage labor disputes – later took hold during World War II and subsequently received the Supreme Court's blessing in 1960. This system of "industrial pluralism" was, in turn, truly the successor status quo in labor relations to the pre-Wagner system of master-servant common law doctrines.[170] As a matter of political development, however, there is no straight and direct line that took the Wagner Act's commitment to unionization to industrial pluralism's commitment to voluntary arbitration. Rather, the rise of industrial pluralism only begins to make sense once the developmental significance of this period of judicial delimitation in the late 1930s is taken into account. Industrial pluralism reflected the reform commitment to collective bargaining, in its emphasis on mutually-agreed upon grievance procedures between labor and management. Industrial pluralism also reflected the principle of restraining aggressive unionism embodied in the judicial delimiting rulings of the late 1930s, in its commitment to channeling and managing industrial conflict in an orderly, bureaucratic manner.

---

[170] See Chapter 8.

5

Constitutional Equal Protection, the Civil Rights Era, and Delimitation

Like the New Deal era, the civil rights era was a period in American history when a number of policy reforms were enacted. One portion of these reforms from the mid-twentieth century merits particular attention: the transformation in constitutional equal protection initiated by the judiciary in 1954 with *Brown v. Board of Education*[1] and supported by congressional statutes such as the Civil Rights Act of 1964[2] and the Elementary and Secondary Education Act of 1965.[3] With these legislative and judicial reforms, the federal government dismantled the system of segregation that defined Jim Crow.

One might reasonably think that a discussion of civil rights reform during this period should encompass the treatment of reforms in public accommodations, fair housing, employment discrimination, voting rights, and perhaps some other areas. Although undeniably significant and worthy of discussion in any historical narrative that aspires to comprehensive treatment of the period, the latter are given, at most, an abbreviated treatment in this chapter and in Chapter 9 (with the exception of voting rights, which I discuss in more detail) simply because my focus is on recalibration rather than the historical period itself.

To refer back to the arguments in Chapter 1 and the continuum of recalibration effects mentioned on page 19, among the various reforms of the civil rights era, only the developments in constitutional equal protection fall into the category of transformative recalibrations. Although

---
[1] 347 U.S. 483 (1954).
[2] Civil Rights Act of 1964, Pub. L. No. 88-352, 78 Stat. 241 (1964).
[3] Elementary and Secondary Education Act, Pub. L. No. 89-10, 79 Stat. 27 (1965).

I make no claim that these changes were the most important aspect of civil rights era reforms in some larger sense, the path of reform in constitutional equal protection did follow a distinctive postreform process. As many have noted about the *Brown* ruling, the laws on school segregation that were repudiated had employed racial classifications in order to subordinate African Americans. As a result, it was not immediately clear exactly what was implied by the forthcoming jurisprudential shift heralded by *Brown*: Would reform principles be defined by a principle of anticlassification, or the repudiation of any racial classifications in the law? Or, would reform principles be defined by an even more expansive antisubordination principle, and the repudiation of laws that – regardless of whether they possessed a racial classification or not – functioned in result or impact to perpetuate the subordinate status of African Americans as a group?[4] Developments in constitutional equal protection thus not only intruded into the "dense" governmental structures of Jim Crow; more distinctively, relative to the other reforms mentioned earlier, changes in constitutional equal protection constituted a particularly open-ended reform. Because of this, these changes implicated broader, systemwide uncertainties that demanded a significant postreform recalibration.

More specifically, the postreform uncertainties within equal protection implicated several important policy issues in the 1970s. For example, affirmative action employs racial classifications – but employs them to aid the condition of racial minorities. Likewise, also in question were laws that were facially neutral with respect to any racial classification but that operated with a disparate negative impact on racial minorities.[5] The scope of these changes in constitutional equal protection could only be delineated once classification and impact were disaggregated and the polity had made its choice between these two values. That choice was ultimately codified through the delimitation processes of the late 1960s and early 1970s.

---

[4] These conceptual categories were articulated in Owen M. Fiss, "Groups and the Equal Protection Clause," *Philosophy and Public Affairs* 5, no. 2 (Winter 1976): 107–77. Other articles that focus on these alternative interpretations of *Brown* include Jack M. Balkin and Reva B. Siegel, "The American Civil Rights Tradition: Anticlassification or Antisubordination?" *University of Miami Law Review* 58, no. 1 (October 2003): 11–13; David A. Strauss, "Discriminatory Intent and the Taming of *Brown*," *University of Chicago Law Review* 56, no. 3 (Summer 1989): 947–54. Interestingly, Strauss also nods to the possibility of a systematic process of "taming" in the law that aligns with the theory of recalibration offered here, although he discusses it only briefly. Ibid., 955.

[5] Fiss, "Groups."

In line with the path of development seen in the prior case studies of the post-Reconstruction and the post–New Deal eras, the polity settled on the more conservative option – the anticlassification understanding of equal protection. To be sure, even with this more conservative choice there is no doubt that constitutional equal protection in the postreform period still constituted a dramatic advance toward greater racial egalitarianism relative to the old order of Jim Crow. Yet the new anticlassification order established an outer boundary to the scope of earlier reform, foreclosing more expansive ambitions and understandings of the transformation initiated by *Brown*. For this reason, the judicial delimitation of the 1970s can easily be compared to the judicial delimiting efforts of the 1870s–80s and the late 1930s.

The processes of delimitation in the 1970s follow a familiar path, with reform uncertainties prompting governing crises, followed by legislative stalemate. The latter, in turn, opened the door for the judiciary to be the first among the three federal branches to codify – through its rulings – the outer boundaries of reform. Crises such as the urban riots of the 1960s and the persistence of the Vietnam War put enormous stress on the reform-minded Democratic coalition then in power. It was because of such stresses that reformers faced a setback in the election of 1968 that saw Richard Nixon ascend to the presidency on a campaign emphasizing "law and order" as an antidote to prevailing societal disorder. However, this election – in line with delimiting elections of 1874 and 1938 – was not a conservative counterrevolution that succeeded in reviving Jim Crow. Rather, by energizing postreform skeptics it inaugurated an extended era of legislative stalemate between the two parties on civil rights issues. Reformers lacked the strength to push the civil rights revolution further, and postreform skeptics lacked the strength – and for the most part, the inclination – to fundamentally undo the major achievements of the 1950s and 1960s.

With the elected branches stalemated, the door was wide open for the Court to take the lead in codifying a recalibration and delimitation of reform. It eventually accepted the invitation, decisively settling on the anticlassification view of racial equality – the option that posed the lesser threat to resilient authorities and rights – in its delimiting rulings in *Milliken v. Bradley*[6] and *Washington v. Davis*.[7] In the aftermath of these rulings, two things were clear: first, Jim Crow was permanently

---

[6] 418 U.S. 717 (1974).
[7] 426 U.S. 229 (1976).

TABLE 5.1 *Recalibration and the Transformation in Constitutional Equal Protection*

(1) Legal reform	Jim Crow is dismantled by *Brown v. Board of Education* and the civil rights legislation of the 1960s.
(2) Delimitation	(2a) Legislative stalemate after the election of 1968 (2b) The scope of constitutional equal protection for racial minorities is "indirectly" delimited by the Supreme Court with reference to the demands of preserving traditional nonjudicial prerogatives. Equal Protection challenges by racial minorities against the state would be permitted only with respect to laws containing racial classifications.
(3) Construction	(3a) Continued consolidation of the anticlassification principle with its application to affirmative action (3b) Conclusive entrenchment by the Supreme Court of the anticlassification principle

dismantled, but second, de facto racial exclusions would also persist. The judicial entrenchment of the latter paved the way for the subsequent rise of an anticlassification order within constitutional equal protection. Table 5.1 summarizes this episode of postreform recalibration.

Recurrent patterns in the substantive justifications for judicial delimitation resurface in the present case study as well. The judicial delimitation of equal protection reform was not driven by any frontal assault on *Brown* or the core achievements of the civil rights movement. Rather, delimitation was carried out indirectly in *Milliken* and *Davis*, with reference to a separate resilient authority that was threatened by the reforms of the era: endangered nonjudicial prerogatives. Hence, the Court very notably appealed to the legitimacy of local governmental prerogatives and nonjudicial-institutional prerogatives in justifying its delimitation of the recent changes in constitutional equal protection.

As in the previous historical cases, careful attention to recalibration and delimitation in the 1970s reveals the limits on achieving transformations in governance in American politics. In the realm of public education specifically, even though tremendous pressure for school integration was imposed on southern school districts by the federal courts, and by the combined pressure of Title VI of the 1964 Civil Rights Act and the Elementary and Secondary Education Act,[8] southerners and other postreform skeptics found a way to push back against reform by championing commitments to color blindness in neighborhood schools. These commitments reflected the views of both die-hard opponents to school desegregation as well as those skeptical of expanding reform to include policies such as busing. The promotion of these commitments facilitated the continuation of de facto racial exclusions in the South and North in the post-*Brown* era, allowing for the creation and maintenance of social structures that replicated in some very crucial respects the segregated system that was supposedly dismantled by reform.[9]

Finally, another complexity in the processes of delimitation is worth noting: the Supreme Court issued a series of key rulings on school desegregation in the late 1960s and early 1970s that furthered reform *before* the Court followed a more conservative path with later delimiting rulings in the mid-1970s. Although these earlier rulings may have held out the potential for the judiciary settling on an antisubordination understanding of equal protection, when evaluated retrospectively alongside the Court's later rulings in the mid-1970s, they can be seen in hindsight as the Court holding fast to nothing more expansive than a commitment to uprooting de jure school segregation. In this sense, the early desegregation rulings are analogous to rulings in the prior case studies, including the Court's prolabor rulings in the late 1930s and the Court's ruling in *Strauder v. West Virginia*.[10] These "proreform" judicial rulings from the 1960s and 1970s similarly demonstrate the ability and inclination of the Court to stabilize boundaries by upholding certain principles at the core of recent reforms; none of the earlier rulings were delimiting for the simple reason that no "external" boundary-drawing uncertainties presented themselves to the Court in these cases.

THE RISE OF LEGISLATIVE STALEMATE

Legislative stalemate on civil rights in the latter half of the twentieth century began with two important events with similar systemic consequences. The first was a governing crisis posed by the urban riots of the

---

[8] Gerald N. Rosenberg, *The Hollow Hope* (Chicago: University of Chicago Press, 1991, 1993), 46–49.

[9] Matthew D. Lassiter, *The Silent Majority: Suburban Politics in the Sunbelt South* (Princeton, NJ: Princeton University Press, 2006), 4–5, 132, 244, 249, 304. See also Introduction, note 2.

[10] 100 U.S. 303 (1880).

late 1960s that grew, at least in some measure, out of the transformative changes legally initiated by *Brown*. Within the actions of the rioters and within the broader political response to the riots, one might see the polity grappling over questions fundamentally related to recalibration, namely: What was the meaning of civil rights reforms, and how far would they transform American society? The second event that carried consequences for civil rights reforms, if only indirectly, was the nation's unsuccessful prosecution of the Vietnam War by 1968 and the resulting problems. Within the federal elected branches, the cumulative effect of these events reenergized the opponents of reform and prompted division within the reform coalition itself.

Governing Crisis: The Urban Riots

In August 1965, just days after the White House signing ceremony for the Voting Rights Act, a wave of riots began – first in Watts – that would have severe consequences for the reforms of the civil rights era. After five days of rioting in Watts, thirty-four people were dead and more than a thousand injured, the vast majority of whom were African American. Property damage totaled more than $35 million, and 4,000 people were arrested.[11] The following year, thirty-eight additional urban riots surfaced in, most notably, the cities of Chicago, Cleveland, and San Francisco.[12] They reached a peak in 1967, with 164 riots occurring in September alone. These included the Newark riot – which left twenty-three dead – and the even more dramatic Detroit riot – which resulted in forty-three deaths.[13]

The relationship between rampant disorder and racial and socioeconomic exclusion was apparent. In Watts specifically, unemployment levels among adult African American males had reached 75 percent. Furthermore, the conclusion of the National Advisory Commission on Civil Disorders (the Kerner Commission), among other observers, was that

---

[11] James T. Patterson, *Grand Expectations: The United States, 1945–1974* (New York: Oxford University Press, 1996), 588; Michael Barone, *Our Country: The Shaping of America from Roosevelt to Reagan* (New York: Free Press, 1990), 407; Michael W. Flamm, *Law and Order: Street Crime, Civil Unrest, and the Crisis of Liberalism in the 1960s* (New York: Columbia University Press, 2005), 58; Robert Weisbrot, *Freedom Bound: A History of America's Civil Rights Movement* (New York: Norton, 1990), 160; John David Skrentny, *The Ironies of Affirmative Action: Politics, Culture, and Justice in America* (Chicago: University of Chicago Press, 1996), 72–73.
[12] Patterson, *Grand Expectations*, 662–63.
[13] Ibid., 663.

this series of urban riots was driven by persistent racial discrimination against African Americans in employment and housing.[14]

As with other governing crises, the urban riots reflected social pressures and anxieties tied up in the reform effort. The dismantling of Jim Crow had itself been driven by the growing dissatisfaction of political elites and others with the "separate-but-equal" legal formalism that had masked glaring social and political inequalities thriving underneath the surface. With the riots, however, African American dissatisfaction surfaced with continuing socioeconomic inequalities that were not grounded in Jim Crow laws. A question of governance seemingly lay underneath the disorder: Would the egalitarian principles driving the dismantling of Jim Crow also push toward a racial equality that would directly address economic inequalities and de facto social exclusions?

As noted in the prior case studies, legislative stalemate arises when crises in governance both prompt internal divisions within the reform coalition and reenergize die-hard opponents of the initial reforms. These dynamics also surfaced in the aftermath of the urban riots. Early evidence of a growing impatience with the rioters – and with Great Society reforms that had pressed toward more expansive forms of racial equality – first appeared in 1966. Republicans succeeded in making substantial inroads against the Democratic liberal coalition in Congress, most significantly in the House. Even though the Democrats retained nominal majorities, liberal Democrats subsequently had to find more votes among Republicans and Southern Democrats to attain majorities in this new political environment.[15] The success of Reagan in the 1966 California gubernatorial race also reinforced the perception that public opinion was turning cool to the further pursuit of reform.[16]

More die-hard opponents of reform suddenly found themselves in a newly hospitable electoral environment. These opponents gained electoral mileage out of locating the cause of the riots in the permissiveness of Great Society programs rather than in socioeconomic exclusions. In addition, some within the liberal coalition itself – shaken by the Newark and Detroit riots in particular – began to wonder if their critics were right, and if liberal reforms might indeed be facilitating societal disorder.[17] A

---

[14] Ibid., 588, 664, 666; Flamm, *Law and Order*, 106–07.
[15] Barone, *Our Country*, 414–16; Allen J. Matusow, *The Unraveling of America: A History of Liberalism in the 1960s* (New York: Harper & Row, 1984), 214; Weisbrot, *Freedom Bound*, 220–21.
[16] Barone, *Our Country*, 415–16.
[17] Flamm, *Law and Order*, 96–100.

theme of restoring law and order was the winning theme of the Nixon campaign in 1968, which marked the triumph of conservative backlash and postreform skepticism. The decline in white support for the Great Society and for expanding the civil rights transformation can be directly linked to the occurrence of the urban riots.[18]

Governing Crisis: The Vietnam War and the Tet Offensive

On January 30, 1968, the first day of the Vietnamese holiday of Tet, the National Liberation Front launched a major attack against the United States and the South Vietnamese, including an attack on the U.S. embassy in Saigon. After three weeks of intense fighting, with major costs to civilians and infrastructure, it nevertheless turned into a clear victory for the United States and the South Vietnamese. The significance of this event, however, was that it turned into a pivotal loss for Johnson and the governing Democratic reform coalition in the domestic political realm.[19]

Indeed, despite the positive military outcome after the embassy attack and the Tet Offensive, the growing perception in America was that these attacks represented a major blow to the U.S. effort in Vietnam. These events widened the "credibility gap" between the administration's positive stance on the status of the Vietnam War and what appeared to be

---

[18] Ibid., 101. Skrentny has also emphasized the developmental significance of the urban riots of the 1960s, but for a different reason than the one offered here. For Skrentny, the legacy of the urban riots turned out to be their important role in aiding the acceptability of affirmative action in the context of employment and employment discrimination. That is, the urban riots seemingly facilitated liberal policy results. Although Skrentny's account seems at odds with the delimiting consequences of the riots that I discuss, it need not be. Skrentny's focus is on a specific policy context, and, as he notes, there are convincing reasons why elite concerns about "crisis management" could have led to liberal advances in that particular policy domain. Skrentny, *Ironies*, 78–110. But in the broader context of constitutional equal protection guarantees, achieving liberal advances in this domain posed a different sort of problem. For example, prohibiting disparate impact became a guiding principle of employment discrimination in 1971 with *Griggs v. Duke Power Co.*, 401 U.S. 424. Yet establishing a principle of prohibiting disparate impact for constitutional equal protection as well could potentially touch on any number of policy domains far beyond the context of employment. As such, the latter would have posed a much more difficult and larger task that would require considerably more political unity within the reform coalition than the urban riots generated. Not surprisingly, as discussed in the following judicial cases, no such liberal advancement materialized in the realm of constitutional equal protection in the aftermath of the urban riots.

[19] Patterson, *Grand Expectations*, 679–80; Irwin Unger and Debi Unger, *Turning Point: 1968* (New York: Scribner, 1988), 102–03.

happening on the ground.[20] Public opinion accordingly shifted against Johnson.[21]

Johnson's public approval was already problematic at 40 percent in November 1967. It fell further to 26 percent after the Tet Offensive.[22] As a growing proportion of the electorate began to question Johnson's competence in handling the war, fissures grew within the Democratic Party as it came under strain from those opposed to the war and those who supported it but who had turned increasingly anti-Johnson. These splits were reflected in McCarthy's surprise showing against Johnson in the New Hampshire primary in March 1968. Johnson ultimately declined the chance to pursue a second term as president.[23]

As with prior historical examples, the contingency of these events in Vietnam and the absence of any direct connection between them and the dismantling of Jim Crow did not preclude the former from having a highly consequential effect. Similar to the Panic of 1873 and the Recession of 1937, it was the intrusion of these events into the political agenda of the late 1960s that distracted the attention of the electorate from the question of civil rights while also creating divisions within the reform coalition itself. As events played out, public reaction to the Tet Offensive had the effect of moving the processes of delimitation along.[24]

The Inauguration of Legislative Stalemate

In the face of these events, prior support for liberal reform within the Democratic Party gave way to dramatic dissensus and the growth of party division. In the 1968 election, an aversion to incumbents stemming from the Vietnam War, a growing concern with rising crime, and increasing conservatism on race issues led to Richard Nixon's election.[25] This election did not signal anything like a popular repudiation of the civil rights advances of the past decade and a half; the Democrats retained firm

---

[20] Patterson, *Grand Expectations*, 680; Unger and Unger, *Turning Point*, 103, 106.
[21] Patterson, *Grand Expectations*, 680–81; Unger and Unger, *Turning Point*, 106–07; Matusow, *Unraveling*, 391.
[22] Patterson, *Grand Expectations*, 681.
[23] Ibid., 681, 683, 688; Matusow, *Unraveling*, 391–92; Unger and Unger, *Turning Point*, 109, 125–26, 130.
[24] Patterson, *Grand Expectations*, 682.
[25] Robert Mason, *Richard Nixon and the Quest for a New Majority* (Chapel Hill: University of North Carolina Press, 2004), 35–36; Patterson, *Grand Expectations*, 705–06, 708.

control of both houses of Congress after the election,[26] and Nixon's victory itself was far from resounding given that he barely edged Humphrey in the popular vote.[27]

Yet Nixon and Wallace's share of the popular vote totaled nearly 57 percent, and this did signal that a new state of affairs had arrived. After several years of momentous reforms, a popular majority crystallized among older and newer skeptics of reform; thus, the engine for further reform in the elected branches was decisively shut down after 1968.[28] If it was not a counterrevolutionary electoral result, the election signaled a growing legislative standstill – and this standstill has been persistent: divided government has essentially become the "normal" condition of American politics from 1968 to the present.[29] With the legislative stalemate created by the election of 1968, a space was cleared for the Court to step to the fore in crystallizing and reflecting emergent political developments. Its rulings subsequently codified precise limits on how far reforms in school segregation and constitutional equal protection would intrude on American society.

The Court was certainly not alone in its inclination to reestablish limits. Delimiting inclinations were also apparent in the actions of both Congress and the president at this time, although neither was able to take the definitive actions the Court did with respect to equal protection matters. Congress, for its part, registered its antipathy to busing by prohibiting the use of federal funds for this purpose in the Education Amendments of 1972.[30] Also, Congress purported to restrain judicial authority to order busing by passing the Education Amendments of 1974.[31] Neither of these legislative acts, however, amounted to a consequential legislative delimitation effort, especially in light of the fact that the latter act also explicitly sounded a note of deference to the judiciary in conceding that

---

[26] The count was 248–187 in the House and 58–42 in the Senate, both in favor of the Democrats. Mason, *Majority*, 35.

[27] Nixon won 43.4 percent of the popular vote compared to Humphrey's 42.7 percent. In terms of electoral votes, Nixon's 301 votes to Humphrey's 191 votes looked more impressive. Unger and Unger, *Turning Point*, 527. See also Skrentny, *Ironies*, 182–83.

[28] Mason, *Majority*, 34–36; Patterson, *Grand Expectations*, 705–08; Unger and Unger, *Turning Point*, 527–28.

[29] Examining party control of the presidency, the House, and the Senate across the twenty-three Congresses between the 1968 election to 2013, there was divided government for sixteen, and unified government for six.

[30] Education Amendments of 1972, Pub. L. No. 92–318, § 802(a), 86 Stat. 235, 371–72 (1972).

[31] Education Amendments of 1974, Pub. L. No. 93–380, § 215(b), 88 Stat. 484, 517 (1974).

"the provisions of this title are not intended to modify or diminish the authority of the courts of the United States to enforce fully the fifth and fourteenth amendments to the Constitution."[32] Commentators have thus generally agreed that these statutes added up to little more than congressional posturing, without much substantive effect on the Court.[33] The reason for this is apparent: congressional conservatives were unable to mount a more definitive attack on busing because they lacked the political strength to overcome pockets of Democratic control in the Senate at the time.[34]

With respect to race, this new electoral mood was exemplified in the somewhat schizophrenic policies of Nixon himself. Although Nixon exhibited antipathy toward the civil rights agenda – particularly busing – in the 1968 campaign, he did not cast himself as a defender of the pre-*Brown* constitutional order either.[35] To the contrary, whether motivated by political calculation or a lack of interest, he stepped aside and allowed for a Democratic Congress to pass a significant amount of legislation in his first term.[36] In the domain of civil rights specifically, Nixon helped promote the cause of racial equality in private employment by backing his secretary of labor, George Shultz, in his implementation of the Philadelphia Plan in 1969. The plan required construction unions in Philadelphia that enjoyed federal contracts to set hiring goals, within appropriate numerical ranges, for employing more African Americans.[37] Although Nixon soon lost interest in employment discrimination, his initial approval of the plan allowed his subordinates – who were more sympathetic and interested in these policies – to expand it to almost all

---

[32] § 203 (b), 88 Stat. at 515 (1974).
[33] Geoffrey R. Stone et al., *Constitutional Law*, 5th ed. (New York: Aspen, 2005), 491; Gary Orfield, "Congress, the President, and Anti-Busing Legislation, 1966–1974," *Journal of Law and Education* 4, no. 1 (January 1975): 108–09, 133; see also, *Drummond v. Acree*, 409 U.S. 1228 (1972), where Powell, sitting as a circuit justice, quickly disposed of a statutory provision in the Education Amendments of 1972 that aimed to postpone judicial decisions involving busing until appeals on the initial decision had been exhausted. § 803, 86 Stat. at 372.
[34] Orfield, "Anti-Busing," 138.
[35] Patterson, *Grand Expectations*, 701–02.
[36] Ibid., 719–21.
[37] Hugh D. Graham, *The Civil Rights Era: Origins and Development of National Policy, 1960–1972* (New York: Oxford University Press, 1990), 326–27; Dean J. Kotlowski, *Nixon's Civil Rights: Politics, Principle, and Policy* (Cambridge, MA: Harvard University Press, 2001), 103–04; Mason, *Majority*, 53; Patterson, *Grand Expectations*, 723; Skrentny, *Ironies*, 193–98.

federal contractors the following year.[38] Historians disagree as to Nixon's actual motives in supporting the plan, but whatever they were, they had consequences that aided the cause of reformers.[39]

At the same time, the antisubordination implications of the Philadelphia Plan remained confined to the domain of employment discrimination. With respect to major advancements in the domain of equal protection, Nixon offered little support. Again, this should not have been surprising after the 1968 election. Nixon was not interested in seeing the civil rights revolution continue at full steam. Strong opposition to busing as a means to desegregate public schools was a constant theme of his administration,[40] and his Justice Department had sided with desegregation opponents and supported their request for a delay in desegregation in the case of *Alexander v. Holmes County Board of Education*.[41]

With no real antireform efforts emanating from the elected branches, the earliest codification of the limits of equal protection reform once again emerged from the Court. As in the previous case studies, the rationales underlying these delimiting opinions lacked any kind of frontal assault on the core achievements of prior reforms. Rather, delimitation was justified, in significant part, by appealing to a tangential consideration, namely the goal of preserving the traditional rule-making prerogatives of other institutional bodies.

JUDICIAL REFORM

Before discussing judicial delimitation, however, it is worth noting that even though the 1968 election had given rise to a new legislative stalemate on civil rights reform, judicial delimitation did not immediately follow

[38] Graham, *Civil Rights*, 342–43; Kotlowski, *Nixon's Civil Rights*, 109; Patterson, *Grand Expectations*, 723; Skrentny, *Ironies*, 210.
[39] The more familiar explanation for Nixon's support of the Philadelphia Plan emphasizes political calculations: Nixon supported it as a means by which to attract African American votes to the Republicans, punish labor (a traditional enemy of the Republican Party), and drive a wedge between African Americans and labor within the Democratic coalition. Graham, *Civil Rights*, 325; Kotlowski, *Nixon's Civil Rights*, 109; Patterson, *Grand Expectations*, 724; Skrentny, *Ironies*, 179–82, 209, 217–21. Kotlowski has argued that Nixon's motives were less about political strategy and more about discrete policy considerations – such as opening the construction unions in order to check rising housing costs – and principled considerations – such as aiding the plight of African Americans. Kotlowski, *Nixon's Civil Rights*, 105–07.
[40] Ibid., 28; Patterson, *Grand Expectations*, 730.
[41] 396 U.S. 19 (1969). Mason, *Majority*, 52; Orfield, "Anti-Busing," 94.

on the heels of this election. Instead, the Warren Court handed down a series of significant school desegregation rulings that were markedly sympathetic to reformist principles. How might these decisions fit alongside the Court's later delimiting rulings?

Recall that in Chapter 1, I conceptualize judicial stability-promoting behavior as actions that stabilized the boundaries between competing sets of authorities and rights. When legal controversies probe uncertainties and instabilities at the outer margins of reform, the stability-promoting impulse manifests itself in the form of delimiting judicial rulings. However, when legal controversies arise that impinge on *core* aspects of reform itself, the stability-promoting impulse of the Court prompts it to defend the integrity of reform. These latter actions also promote stability in their own right by clarifying and demarcating which aspects of the reform will remain standing in the face of resilient authorities and rights that threaten to undermine and destabilize recent political changes.

The Court's defense of African American rights in *Strauder v. West Virginia*[42] was precisely this sort of action. Likewise, whereas the meaning and consequence of these early desegregation rulings may have been poorly defined and tentative when they were issued, when they are evaluated retrospectively and in light of other developments, they might be seen as stability promoting in the same manner as *Strauder*. In these school desegregation cases, the Court was confronted with school districts that had clearly engaged in intentional racial discrimination and that were seeking to evade substantive efforts to address the consequences of their prior acts. The Court's lack of sympathy for the school districts was a consequence of not only its obvious support for reform principles – principles the Court itself had helped establish – but also of its inclination to promote a form of stability by preserving the integrity of the reform effort itself.

Thus, in *Green v. County School Board*,[43] the Supreme Court in 1968 addressed the constitutional adequacy of a desegregation plan for a school district that was guilty of prior intentional discrimination. The school district's plan focused on allowing both white and African American students "freedom of choice" in selecting which public school to attend.[44] In a unanimous opinion for the Court, Brennan ruled against the school

---

[42] 100 U.S. 303 (1880).
[43] 391 U.S. 430 (1968).
[44] Id. at 433–34.

district. Although he conceded that freedom-of-choice plans were not inherently unconstitutional and could even have a place in some desegregation plans,[45] Brennan made it clear that they were not necessarily sufficient when the context was one of disestablishing a prior system of segregated public education – as was the case here.[46]

Three years later, the Court remained sympathetic to reformist principles, even with two new Nixon appointees on the bench (Burger and Blackmun). In the 1971 case of *Swann v. Charlotte-Mecklenberg Board of Education*,[47] the Court weighed in on the constitutional legitimacy of a desegregation remedy applied to another southern public school system with a history of de jure racial segregation.[48] Burger's unanimous opinion for the Court registered its approval for the district court's desegregation plan that countenanced remedial altering of attendance zones[49] and very significantly, the busing of students.[50]

Finally, in *Keyes v. School District No. 1*,[51] handed down shortly afterward in 1973, the Court confronted for the first time a school desegregation case outside of the South. In that case, it was abundantly clear that the Denver School District had engaged in acts of de jure racial segregation with respect to its Park Hill schools. This was not de jure segregation via statute or state constitutional amendment but rather the promotion of racial segregation through discretionary actions such as the school board's deliberate manipulation of attendance zones and use of mobile classrooms.[52]

Because this was de jure segregation practiced through discretionary acts rather than through formal legal rules, the case prompted an immediate question regarding the scope of the Denver School District's violation and the appropriate remedy. One possibility was that evidence of de jure segregation acts in one portion of the school district – such as Park Hill – necessarily implied a districtwide violation, and empowered the courts to issue districtwide remedies touching on other city schools that evidenced de facto – although not necessarily de jure – racial segregation. The other

---

[45] Id. at 439–40.
[46] Id. at 432–33, 440.
[47] 402 U.S. 1 (1971).
[48] Id. at 5–6.
[49] Id. at 27–29.
[50] Id. at 29–31.
[51] 413 U.S. 189 (1973).
[52] Id. at 192.

possibility was that evidence of de jure segregation in Park Hill indicated a violation in only that portion of the school district and thus prompted a desegregation remedy only for the Park Hill schools.[53]

Brennan's opinion for a nearly unanimous Court[54] endorsed a districtwide remedy as presumably appropriate in this case (he actually remanded for further hearings by the district court). The key point underlying Brennan's conclusion was the finding of the school board's de jure segregation with respect to the Park Hill schools. With this ruling, desegregation remedies had spread to school districts outside the South; however, at least within Brennan's reasoning in *Keyes*, desegregation remedies remained tightly linked to prior de jure racial segregation practices.[55] Thus, as with the previous cases, by focusing on how the school district had been engaged in de jure segregation, the Court stayed close to the antidiscrimination and anticlassification principles at the core of recent reforms in equal protection.

THE JUDICIAL DELIMITATION OF CIVIL RIGHTS REFORM

In two key cases in the mid-1970s, the Court confronted different questions about reform. The focus became less about blatant, intentional discrimination and more about the subordinating impact of certain laws. These uncertainties thus probed at the outer edges of earlier reform principles. In this context, the judicial inclination to promote legality values by clarifying the law – and stabilizing boundary lines between competing authorities and rights – pressed it in a different direction from its earlier desegregation rulings. And in its rulings in *Milliken v. Bradley*[56] and *Washington v. Davis*,[57] the Court made a clear choice in favor of an anticlassification understanding of equal protection.

In line with the previous instances of judicial delimitation, the manner in which this choice was made is familiar. Specifically, judicial delimitation did not proceed by undermining the core goals of *Brown* and the civil rights revolution. Rather, it proceeded in an indirect manner, with

---

[53] Id. at 192–93.
[54] Rehnquist dissented, breaking the Court's string of unanimous rulings in school desegregation cases.
[55] The Court's actual ruling remanded the case to the district court to hear further evidence, and to allow the Denver School Board the opportunity to offer additional testimony, before the lower court decided on the appropriate desegregation remedy. Id. at 213–14.
[56] 418 U.S. 717 (1974).
[57] 426 U.S. 229 (1976).

reference to how an expansive interpretation of reform principles could potentially threaten resilient authorities and rights. It was with reference to these other resilient authorities – and the need to preserve them – that the judiciary reined in the more radical implications of changes in equal protection. Just as Reconstruction was indirectly delimited in the name of federalism, and the New Deal labor revolution indirectly delimited in the name of industrial peace, more expansive notions of racial equality were similarly delimited in the 1970s in the name of preserving nonjudicial institutional prerogatives.

Milliken v. Bradley

After the string of pro-desegregation decisions in the late 1960s and early 1970s, reform principles finally reached their limits with the Court's ruling in *Milliken v. Bradley*.[58] At issue in this case was whether an interschool district, city-suburban desegregation plan was constitutionally permissible as a means to remedy a de jure segregation problem in *only* the Detroit School District. The need for such a plan lay in the demographics of the Detroit School District itself: there simply were not enough white students within it that could be shifted around to create racial compositions that reflected the larger metropolitan area.[59]

This case did not necessarily prompt a direct conflict between antisubordination values and anticlassification values. Those who were in favor of the expansive desegregation remedy, such as Justice Marshall, could justify the plan by emphasizing that there had been acts of de jure segregation by officials in the Detroit School District that triggered the need for remedy. Thus, busing children in and out of the suburbs did not have to be understood as simply a means to achieve more equitable racial distributions in public schools – a goal that spoke to more purely antisubordination values. Rather, busing could be seen as the necessary constitutional response for a previous act of racial classifying by state actors and thus consistent with anticlassification values.[60]

Nevertheless, a ruling from the Court allowing for city-suburban desegregation remedies – no matter what its precise rationale – would have bolstered the hopes of those favoring antisubordination values. Similar

---

[58] 418 U.S. 717 (1974). For useful coverage of the background context of *Milliken*, see Joyce A. Baugh, *The Detroit School Busing Case:* Milliken v. Bradley *and the Controversy over Desegregation* (Lawrence: University Press of Kansas, 2011).
[59] 418 U.S. at 732–34.
[60] Id. at 789–90 (Marshall, J., dissenting).

to the situation in *Keyes*, such a ruling would mean that students could be bused in or out of predominantly white suburban school districts, even if there was no evidence that these districts themselves had actually participated in de jure segregation. This would offer support for constitutional analyses of school districts that moved beyond a preoccupation with intentional acts of racial discrimination to also consider the "acceptability" of the particular racial compositions in schools themselves. If that door were opened, it would, in turn, open the door for an expansion of judicial authority in structuring and overseeing public education as well – all at the expense of state and local governmental prerogatives.

Burger, writing for a majority that included three other Nixon appointees and Potter Stewart, opened his analysis of the case with a vigorous affirmation of the anticlassification view of equal protection. He stated: "The target of the *Brown* holding was clear and forthright: the elimination of *state-mandated or deliberately maintained dual school systems* with certain schools for Negro pupils and others for white pupils."[61] In contrast, no constitutional requirement could be gleaned from past precedents for an "appropriate" racial balance of some sort in public schools, which – Burger asserted – seemed to be the driving principle behind this desegregation plan.[62] With this conclusion, the Court clearly demarcated the outer limits of reform in constitutional equal protection.

Burger's opinion is noteworthy for supplementing this legal justification for the anticlassification principle with a recalibration-minded concern. The opinion did not ground its defense of anticlassification goals by frontally challenging the racial egalitarian goals of the civil rights revolution. There was no impugning of *Brown* or its jurisprudential progeny in this opinion. Indeed, *Brown* and other school desegregation precedents were relied on as authority for Burger's defense of anticlassification values.[63] In line with previous cases, Burger justified delimitation by appealing to a resilient system of governing authority that was tangential to reform. Specifically, that resilient authority was the power of local school boards to govern public education within their district lines.

Thus, what also pushed against the legitimacy of a city-suburban desegregation plan, in addition to a doctrinal justification of anticlassification principles, were concerns about local control of education. As

---

[61] Id. at 737 (emphasis added).
[62] Id. at 737–41, 745.
[63] Id. at 737–38.

Burger stated, referring to the recent case *San Antonio School District v. Rodriguez*:

> Boundary lines may be bridged where there has been a constitutional violation calling for interdistrict relief, but the notion that school district lines may be casually ignored or treated as a mere administrative convenience is contrary to the history of public education in our country. No single tradition in public education is more deeply rooted than local control over the operation of schools; local autonomy has long been thought essential both to the maintenance of community concern and support for public schools and to quality of the educational process. Thus, in *San Antonio School District* v. *Rodriguez*, we observed that local control over the educational process affords citizens an opportunity to participate in decision making, permits the structuring of school programs to fit local needs, and encourages "experimentation, innovation, and a healthy competition for educational excellence."[64]

With Burger's default assumption of the importance of local authority over public education, the clear implication was that an interdistrict remedy required careful consideration; equal protection violations calling for such a remedy had to be clear enough and serious enough to override the remedy's impingement on local governmental authority. More precisely, as the majority opinion stated, a desegregation plan that crossed district lines could only be justified by a violation of anticlassification values – either by actors within one or more school districts, or by actors with statewide authority – that had an interdistrict effect. In this case, no such effect could be identified; de jure segregation was limited to only the Detroit School District itself.[65]

This judicial deference to local governmental authority did not emerge from thin air. Justice Powell's concurrence in *Keyes* only a year before had offered an extended comment on the value of the neighborhood school system.[66] Further, as alluded to earlier, a preview of this particular argument was also present in the Court's ruling only a year earlier in *San Antonio v. Rodriguez*.[67] This was another 5–4 ruling with voting alignments identical to the *Milliken* decision, where the Court struck down an equal protection challenge to the Texas state financing system of public education. That system had allowed for major disparities

---

[64] Id. at 741–42 (citations omitted).
[65] Id. at 744–52.
[66] 413 U.S. 189, 246 (1973).
[67] 411 U.S. 1 (1973).

between school districts in per-pupil spending because it provided for each district's revenues to be substantially determined by its own local property taxes.[68] A significant portion of the Court's argument in upholding that system focused precisely on the importance of maintaining state and local control in the domain of education. The Court offered arguments based on precedent,[69] prudential concerns about the judiciary supplanting local and state expertise in managing public schools,[70] and a respect for federalism and localism[71] (with a persistent and very conspicuous note of judicial humility throughout).[72] Within this opinion, the Court expressed a fear of too much judicial oversight of the tax scheme in question that aligned well with the spirit of *Milliken*.[73]

The *Milliken* Court heard similar arguments in various briefs filed against the metropolitan desegregation plan. Both the brief of the petitioners (Governor Milliken et al.) and the amicus brief of the United States in *Milliken* were seemingly aware of the possibility of significant disruption to local and state authority over public education with the metropolitan remedy.[74] And in amicus briefs filed by various other local and state governmental entities opposed to the metropolitan remedy, the case for judicial deference and maintaining state and local authority was articulated even more forcefully. As the state of Indiana asserted in its amicus brief, for example:

Plaintiffs in [*Milliken*] will ask for the consolidation and the redistricting of schools, and for the busing of students to and from systems which were not segregated. That will mean disregarding governmental boundary lines, not only for pupil placement but for teacher assignment, for building construction and the taxable base which supports that construction, and for both administrative and voter control also. These cases would instigate a more major political and social upheaval than the progression either from the "separate but equal" doctrine of *Plessy v. Ferguson* to the "separate is inherently unequal" doctrine of *Brown I*, or from "freedom of choice" of the post-*Brown* era to the "affirmative duty"

---

[68] Id. at 6–9.
[69] Id. at 40–41.
[70] Id. at 41–43.
[71] Id. at 44, 49–50.
[72] Id. at 55, 58–59.
[73] Id. at 41 (footnotes omitted).
[74] Frank J. Kelley et al., Reply Brief of Petitioners at 20, *Milliken v. Bradley*, 418 U.S. 717 (1974); Robert H. Bork and J. Stanley Pottinger, Memorandum for the United States as Amicus Curiae at 13, *Milliken v. Bradley*, 418 U.S. 717 (1974).

of *Green v. County School Board of New Kent County, Virginia, Swann,* and *Keyes.*[75]

Notwithstanding such dire warnings, there was nothing legally predetermined about the *Milliken* ruling. Prior to *Milliken*, these appeals to local governmental autonomy were merely strands of argument that had not been conclusively applied by the Court to interdistrict desegregation. Furthermore, the four dissenters in *Milliken* found much to disagree with in both Burger's assertion of the sanctity of local school district lines as well as his interpretation of past desegregation precedents.

On the former, the dissenters pointed out that the various local school boards involved – including the Detroit school board that all of the justices agreed was guilty of de jure segregation – were agents of the *state* government of Michigan.[76] Justices Douglas and Marshall emphasized that public education was even more directly under the control of the state government in Michigan than it was in other states, which made Burger's ode to traditional local authority over public education in this case sound particularly odd.[77] Further, if it was the state of Michigan that was ultimately responsible for the illegal actions of the local school boards, an interdistrict desegregation remedy was appropriate given the culpability of the larger governmental entity.[78] On the issue of past precedent, the dissenting justices not surprisingly interpreted the Court's past desegregation cases differently from the majority. The former saw these precedents as *supporting* the proposition that flexible and aggressive remedies – in

---

[75] Theodore L. Sendak, Donald P. Bogard, and William F. Harvey, Brief on the Merits in Support of Petitioners Submitted Amicus Curiae by the State of Indiana at 21, *Milliken v. Bradley*, 418 U.S. 717 (1974) (citations omitted). For other similar references in defense of maintaining state and local authorities, see also id. at 7–8, 28–29; Lewis C. Bose and William M. Evans, Brief and Appendix Amicus Curiae in Support of Petitioners, Submitted by Amici Curiae, Metropolitan School Districts of Lawrence, Warren and Wayne Townships, Marion County, Indiana at 13–23, *Milliken v. Bradley*, 418 U.S. 717 (1974); Richard L. Brown and Richard D. Wagner, Brief of the School Town of Speedway, Indiana and the School City of Beech Grove, Indiana, Amici Curiae at 2–6, *Milliken v. Bradley*, 418 U.S. 717 (1974). The National Suburban League also submitted an amicus brief emphasizing, not surprisingly, similar types of arguments. Harold H. Fuhrman, Motion for Leave to File Brief Amicus Curiae and Brief for National Suburban League as Amicus Curiae, *Milliken v. Bradley*, 418 U.S. 717 (1974).
[76] 418 U.S. 717, 759 (1974) (Douglas, J., dissenting); id. at 770 (White, J., dissenting); id. at 792–98 (Marshall, J., dissenting).
[77] Id. at 758–59 (Douglas, J., dissenting); id. at 793–94, 797 (Marshall, J., dissenting).
[78] Id. at 758–59 (Douglas, J., dissenting); id. at 770 (White, J., dissenting); id. at 792–98 (Marshall, J., dissenting).

the service of achieving desegregation – were well within constitutional bounds.[79]

However, just as Reconstruction and the New Deal reforms were indirectly delimited by the Court with respect to federalism and industrial peace, respectively, more expansive interpretations of racial equality were indirectly undercut by the Court with reference to the importance of local governmental legislative prerogatives. As Justice Burger stated:

> But it is obvious from the scope of the interdistrict remedy itself that absent a complete restructuring of the laws of Michigan relating to school districts the District Court will become first, a *de facto* "legislative authority" to resolve these complex questions, and then the "school superintendent" for the entire area. This is a task which few, if any, judges are qualified to perform and one which would deprive the people of control of schools through their elected representatives.[80]

As a result, the majority settled on an interpretation of equal protection that minimized disruption to resilient systems of authority.

Washington v. Davis

Two years later, *Washington v. Davis*[81] pitted anticlassification values even more directly against antisubordination values. And in keeping with *Milliken*, the former were emphatically endorsed at the expense of the latter.

At issue in *Davis* was the civil service exam Test 21, an entrance examination for prospective officers in the Washington, D.C., police force. Although there was no evidence of any intentional racial discrimination in the composition of the test or in the police force's administration of the test, it nevertheless had the effect of excluding a disproportionate number of African American recruits from the force.[82] Indeed, four times as many African Americans as whites failed Test 21.[83] Two African American plaintiffs brought suit challenging the test as a violation of equal protection guarantees under the Fifth Amendment because of this disproportionate exclusion. The case directly presented an equal protection claim on antisubordination or results-oriented grounds. The questions for the Court were these: If it were the case that the test bore no relation to

---

[79] Id. at 774–77 (White, J., dissenting); id. at 798–808 (Marshall, J., dissenting).
[80] Id. at 743–44.
[81] 426 U.S. 229 (1976).
[82] Id. at 232–37.
[83] Id. at 237.

job performance,⁸⁴ would disproportionate impact be enough to strike down this test as a violation of equal protection? Could equal protection violations be divorced entirely from matters of racial classification or racial discrimination?

Even though *Milliken* strongly pushed against a disparate impact interpretation of the Fifth Amendment equal protection claims at issue here, there was some very significant doctrinal support for the disparate impact view. Only five years before in *Griggs v. Duke Power Co.*,⁸⁵ the Court itself had established disparate impact standards for prevailing in racial employment discrimination claims under Title VII of the Civil Rights Act of 1964. That is, plaintiffs could prevail in challenging a given employment qualification with a showing of its disparate racial impact, so long as the qualifications at issue were not shown to be "significantly related to successful job performance."⁸⁶ Also, before *Davis* reached the Court, the Court of Appeals had also previously found in favor of the African American litigants in an earlier stage of this litigation, applying the standards for employment discrimination claims under Title VII to the constitutional claims presented here.⁸⁷

A very real potential still existed in 1976 for the Court to push reformist impulses further with its ruling; it needed only to transfer the standards for Title VII employment discrimination claims from that context to the context of constitutional equal protection claims. However, the Court did the opposite and declined to follow the lead of the Court of Appeals. As Justice White stated, writing for the Court in a 7–2 ruling:⁸⁸

As the Court of Appeals understood Title VII, employees or applicants proceeding under it need not concern themselves with the employer's possibly discriminatory purpose but instead may focus solely on the racially differential impact of the challenged hiring or promotion practices. This is not the constitutional rule. We have never held that the constitutional standard for adjudicating claims

---

⁸⁴ Assuming that employment discrimination standards under Title VII of the 1964 Civil Rights Act were applicable here, the relation of a challenged job qualification to job performance would be legally relevant.
⁸⁵ 401 U.S. 424 (1971).
⁸⁶ Id. at 425–26.
⁸⁷ 426 U.S. at 236–37.
⁸⁸ Brennan and Marshall dissented. Brennan's dissent did not address the constitutional issues in the majority opinion but rather focused on showing how Test 21 fell short of the relevant statutory standards, including those of Title VII of the 1964 Civil Rights Act. Id. at 256–70 (Brennan, J., dissenting).

of invidious racial discrimination is identical to the standards applicable under Title VII, and we decline to do so today.[89]

Rather, the appropriate standard for finding a violation of constitutional equal protection was an anticlassification standard that looked to the existence of either explicit racial classifications in state actions or discriminatory purposes behind state actions (constituting "implicit" racial classifications):

The central purpose of the Equal Protection Clause of the Fourteenth Amendment is the prevention of official conduct discriminating on the basis of race. It is also true that the Due Process Clause of the Fifth Amendment contains an equal protection component prohibiting the United States from invidiously discriminating between individuals or groups. But our cases have not embraced the proposition that a law or other official act, without regard to whether it reflects a racially discriminatory purpose, is unconstitutional *solely* because it has a racially disproportionate impact.[90]

White did not think showings of racially disparate impact were entirely irrelevant to equal protection claims; a showing of disparate impact might itself be indicative of an underlying discriminatory purpose. But impact alone was not enough.[91]

The most relevant facets of the opinion for understanding this case as a delimiting ruling lie in the Court's justifications for turning away from a disparate impact interpretation of equal protection guarantees. Again, as in *Milliken*, there was no hint of repudiation or doubt about the core aims of the civil rights revolution. The first half of White's opinion was a defense of anticlassification values firmly grounded in his understanding of the key precedents reflecting the jurisprudential shifts of the era.[92] However, another argument against the disparate impact standard that was grounded in recalibration considerations came later. As White stated in a notable sentence from this ruling:

A rule that a statute designed to serve neutral ends is nevertheless invalid, absent compelling justification, if in practice it benefits or burdens one race more than another would be far reaching and would raise serious questions about, and perhaps invalidate, a whole range of tax, welfare, public service, regulatory, and

---

[89] Id. at 238–39 (footnotes omitted).
[90] Id. at 239 (citations omitted) (emphasis in original).
[91] Id. at 242.
[92] Id. at 239–45.

licensing statutes that may be more burdensome to the poor and to the average black than to the more affluent white.[93]

These comments thus indicate a familiar judicial anxiety surrounding unstable and ambiguous boundaries between competing authorities and rights. More pointedly, they suggest White's fear of how the core principles of reform, if left ill defined or given their most expansive construction, could swallow up other resilient authorities and potentially create additional boundary uncertainties. His language prompts ready comparison with Justice Miller's opinion in the *Slaughter-House Cases*:

> The argument we admit is not always the most conclusive which is drawn from the consequences urged against the adoption of a particular construction of an instrument. But when, as in the case before us, these consequences are so serious, so far-reaching and pervading, so great a departure from the structure and spirit of our institutions; when the effect is to fetter and degrade the State governments by subjecting them to the control of Congress, in the exercise of powers heretofore universally conceded to them of the most ordinary and fundamental character; when in fact it radically changes the whole theory of the relations of the State and Federal governments to each other and of both these governments to the people; the argument has a force that is irresistible, in the absence of language which expresses such a purpose too clearly to admit of doubt.[94]

Promoting stability in these situations demanded that boundaries be clarified and stabilized. Both justices thus issued rulings that delimited the scope of earlier reforms with reference to these boundary-drawing concerns. Further, White noted that if the Court were to allow the disparate impact principle to spread, and to be applicable to all instances of state action that could have differential results for different races, this would contemplate an enormous expansion of judicial authority at the expense of other rule-making or legislative authorities. He stated:

> Test 21, which is administered generally to prospective Government employees, concededly seeks to ascertain whether those who take it have acquired a particular level of verbal skill; and it is untenable that the Constitution prevents the Government from seeking modestly to upgrade the communicative abilities of its employees rather than to be satisfied with some lower level of competence,

---

[93] Id. at 248 (footnotes omitted). In a footnote to this paragraph, White also went on to list other state actions that might be subject to an equal protection challenge as well, such as "'tests and qualifications for voting, draft deferment, public employment, jury service, and other government-conferred benefits and opportunities...sales taxes, bail schedules, utility rates, bridge tolls, license fees, and other state-imposed charges.'" Id. at 248n14 (quoting Frank I. Goodman, "De Facto School Segregation: A Constitutional and Empirical Analysis," *California Law Review* 60, no. 2 (March 1972): 300).

[94] 83 U.S. 36, 78 (1873).

particularly where the job requires special ability to communicate orally and in writing.[95]

And given that African Americans as a group were disproportionately poor, the Court's adoption of an impact standard would have the additional liability of opening the door to allowing the equal protection revolution in race to become an unintended equal protection revolution in class as well.[96]

Taken together, a general principle emerges as the driving force of judicial delimitation in the post-*Brown* era. In the mid-1970s, judicial delimitation was being driven by, perhaps ironically, a judicial reassertion of the legislative prerogatives enjoyed by nonjudicial institutions – first in the local context in *Milliken* and then in the federal context with *Davis*.

CONCLUSION

The Court's ruling in *Davis* cemented the victory of the anticlassification view and ensured that this vision would hold the high ground in equal protection jurisprudence.[97] While *Brown* remains revered in the canon of constitutional law cases, *Davis* remains entrenched in the law as well. Indeed, no subsequent effort ever emerged from any of the branches of the federal government to revise the settlement imposed by *Davis*. Certainly no impulse was forthcoming from the Court: its reformist zeal in the late 1960s and early 1970s to initiate and extend the civil rights revolution was simply no longer there. Similarly, the persistent condition of divided government in the latter decades of the twentieth century also ensured that major revisions or advances on the judicial delimitation of the 1970s would not be forthcoming from the federal elected branches.

The relevance of this period of history for contemporary racial politics is apparent. Contrary to what a majority of the Court argued in *Parents Involved in Community Schools*, there is no clear and direct line between *Brown* and the Supreme Court's current antipathy to affirmative action.[98]

---

[95] 426 U.S. at 245–46.
[96] Daniel R. Ortiz, "The Myth of Intent in Equal Protection," *Stanford Law Review* 41, no. 5 (May 1989): 1138–39.
[97] The discriminatory intent requirement was later clarified in the gender discrimination case of *Personnel Administrator of Massachusetts v. Feeney*, 442 U.S. 256 (1979), which reaffirmed the Court's aforementioned inclination to settle on less transformative interpretations of equal protection.
[98] 551 U.S. 701, 746–48 (2007).

Brown's denunciation of Jim Crow is capable of bearing the weight of either the Court's current anticlassification approach to equal protection or a competing antisubordination interpretation of racial equality upheld by affirmative action supporters. To understand the path of legal development that has led to the present – with *Adarand*'s definitive establishment of strict scrutiny for both state and federal affirmative action programs[99] in 1995 and *Parents Involved*'s antipathy to voluntary school integration programs in 2007 – it is necessary to recognize the constitutive importance of these cases from the 1970s. The developmental origins of the current anticlassification regime lie in *both* the dismantling of Jim Crow and in these judicial delimitating decisions that imposed lasting constraints on more expansive notions of equal protection.

---

[99] Adarand Constructors, Inc. v. Pena, 515 U.S. 200 (1995).

6

Explaining Judicial Delimiting Behavior

The recurrence of a specific political process across historical contexts as diverse as the 1870s, 1930s, and 1970s indicates that the driving mechanisms behind delimitation and recalibration are systemic, institutional, and fundamental. Indeed, a judicially codified delimiting of reform occurs even when historical anomalies arise, such as the judicially led assault on Jim Crow laws in the 1950s. The case studies have thus far touched on some of the key structural considerations behind recalibration, including the resilience of reform coalitions that aid in facilitating the rise of legislative stalemate, the developmental significance of a "crowded" institutional context within which reform occurs, and the systemwide threats that arise when open-ended reforms are unleashed within the polity. Yet one set of institutional considerations yet to be explored is the motive behind the Court's delimiting rulings, summarized in Table 6.1.

One of the main claims of this book is that when legislative stalemate affords it the opportunity, the Court is *institutionally* predisposed to stabilize boundaries between competing sets of governing authorities and competing sets of rights during a transformative recalibration. The goal of the present chapter is to substantiate this claim more directly.

Recall the delimiting rulings discussed in Chapters 3, 4, and 5, and consider how either the appointments theory or the political-cultural theory of judicial behavior might fare in explaining them. Proponents of the appointments theory would posit that change to the Court membership is the primary means by which shifts in political winds are registered in

TABLE 6.1 *A Summary of Judicial Delimiting Rulings*

Delimiting Rulings	
Reconstruction era	Blyew v. United States
	Slaughter-House Cases
	United States v. Cruikshank
	United States v. Reese
	Virginia v. Rives
	The Civil Rights Cases
The New Deal era	NLRB v. Mackay Radio & Telegraph Co.
	NLRB v. Sands Manufacturing Co.
	NLRB v. Fansteel Metallurgical Corp.
The civil rights era	Milliken v. Bradley
	Washington v. Davis

changed legal doctrine.[1] Alternatively, proponents of the political-cultural theory of judicial behavior instead posit that shifting assumptions, views, preferences, and beliefs in the broader world of politics, society, and culture can prompt changes in judicial behavior and legal doctrine, even independent of the appointments mechanism.[2] Although my case studies do not refute either of these theories, neither completely explains or accounts for the phenomenon of judicial delimitation either.

Post-Reconstruction is a historical context in which the appointments thesis performs poorly. Table 6.2 is a summary of the appointments data and vote tallies for the cases discussed in Chapter 3.[3] Of course, given the diversity of opinions in a given ruling, these and subsequent vote tallies in this chapter are subject to a small degree of interpretation.

With the exception of Justice Clifford (who was a holdover from the Buchanan presidency), all of the justices who voted in these delimiting

---

[1] See, e.g., Robert A. Dahl, "Decision-Making in a Democracy: The Supreme Court as a National Policy-Maker," *Journal of Public Law* 6, no. 2 (Fall 1957): 279–95; Jack M. Balkin and Sanford Levinson, "Understanding the Constitutional Revolution," *Virginia Law Review* 87, no. 6 (October 2001): 1045–1104.

[2] See, e.g., Michael J. Klarman, *From Jim Crow to Civil Rights: The Supreme Court and the Struggle for Racial Equality* (New York: Oxford University Press, 2004); , 4–6, 446–54; Reva B. Siegel, "Constitutional Culture, Social Movement Conflict and Constitutional Change: The Case of the de facto ERA," *California Law Review* 94, no. 5 (October 2006): 1321–1419.

[3] The background information on the justices mentioned in Tables 6.2, 6.3, and 6.4 is drawn from Henry J. Abraham, *Justices, Presidents, and Senators: A History of the U.S. Supreme Court Appointments from Washington to Clinton*, rev. ed. (Lanham, MD: Rowman & Littlefield, 1999), Appendix C.

TABLE 6.2 Supreme Court Justices and the Post-Reconstruction Delimiting Rulings

Justice	Party Affiliation/ Year of Appointment	Appointing President	Blyew v. United States (1872)	Slaughter-House Cases (1873)	United States v. Cruikshank (1876)	United States v. Reese (1876)	Virginia v. Rives (1880)	The Civil Rights Cases (1883)
Samuel Nelson	D/ 1845	Tyler	a					
Nathan Clifford	D/ 1858	Buchanan	x	x	o (concurs in result)	o (concurs in result)	x	
Noah H. Swayne	R/ 1862	Lincoln	o	o	x	x	x	x
Samuel F. Miller	R/ 1862	Lincoln	x	x	x	x	x	
David Davis	R/ 1862	Lincoln	x	x	x	x		
Stephen Field	D/ 1863	Lincoln	x	o	x	x	x	x
Salmon P. Chase	R/ 1864	Lincoln	a	o				
William Strong	R/ 1870	Grant	x	x	x	x	x	
Joseph P. Bradley	R/ 1870	Grant	o	o	x	x	x	x
Ward Hunt	R/ 1873	Grant		x	x	o	x	
Morrison R. Waite	R/ 1874	Grant			x	x	x	x
John M. Harlan	R/ 1877	Hayes						o
William B. Woods	R/ 1881	Hayes						x
Stanley Matthews	R/ 1881	Garfield						x
Horace Gray	R/ 1882	Arthur						x
Samuel Blatchford	R/ 1882	Arthur						x

Note: x = majority, o = dissent, a = absent

cases – from *Blyew* to the *Civil Rights Cases* – were appointed by Republican presidents.[4] With the exception of Clifford and Stephen Field – the latter being a pro-Union Democrat appointed by Lincoln[5] – all of the voting justices themselves were Republicans. If the appointments thesis were our guide, the case of post-Reconstruction presents the striking oddity of judicial delimitation being carried out by the appointees of the reform coalition itself. This, on its own, prompts skepticism of the theory's ability to explain these delimiting rulings.

In light of the aforementioned, a proponent of the appointments thesis might explain post-Reconstruction delimitation by proposing that later changes in Republican Party goals prompted the subsequent appointment of justices known to be hostile to African American rights, thus leading to delimiting rulings. Yet Henry Abraham's discussion of the appointments of post-Reconstruction Court members suggests the implausibility of this hypothesis. With the possible exception of Hayes's consideration of sectional reconciliation in his selection of William B. Woods, a potential nominee's stance on African American rights beyond the matter of abolition did not seem to be a positive or a negative factor for Republican presidents making their judicial selections during these years.[6]

The appointments theory could perhaps explain why it was that Reconstruction reformist goals failed to find a strong institutional advocate in the Supreme Court. Without sustained attention given to a judicial nominee's likely interpretations of the Reconstruction Amendments, the door was open to both delimiters and reformers to be appointed to the Court. Yet the appointments thesis also fails to explain why it was that liberal interpretations of the Reconstruction Amendments enjoyed such consistent hostility on the Court. Although *Slaughter-House* was a 5–4 decision, other cases in which the race and Reconstruction issue were more central are telling. *Blyew* was a 5–2 decision, *Cruikshank* was essentially a unanimous decision, *Reese* was a near-unanimous decision, *Rives* was a unanimous decision, and the *Civil Rights Cases* was an 8–1 decision with only Harlan dissenting. The appointments thesis would seemingly support a more mixed bag among Republican justices' approaches to African American rights, given that the latter was a nonfactor for making appointments and given that consequential pockets of support for

---

[4] Samuel Nelson, a Democrat, did not participate in *Blyew*. Robert D. Goldstein, "*Blyew*: Variations on a Jurisdictional Theme," *Stanford Law Review* 41, no. 3 (February 1989): 500n118.
[5] Abraham, *Justices*, 90.
[6] Ibid., 86–105.

Reconstruction very much continued to exist in the Republican Party – at least up until the failed Lodge Bill in 1891.[7] In short, the appointments theory tells us little of interest regarding why the Court issued delimiting rulings in the 1870s and early 1880s.

Similarly, the political-cultural thesis cannot explain the delimiting rulings during Reconstruction. One could claim that the post-Reconstruction Court was acting in accordance with at least a substantial portion of public opinion in reaching conservative legal conclusions in the 1870s and 1880s. At the least, one cannot say that the Court was acting in a clear countermajoritarian fashion with these rulings. Yet it would be difficult to maintain that political-cultural forces were so uniform and so prevalent in favor of curtailing African American rights that they essentially dictated judicial delimitation. Again, the fact that strong Republican Party interest in African American rights remained in the post-Reconstruction decades undercuts the notion that the Court was merely following a consensus of conservative public opinion. Indeed, because there was significant, continuing Republican interest in African Americans in some quarters, had the Court acted in a more liberal manner and upheld African American rights, such a result might also be viewed as *consistent* with a political-cultural perspective. This is especially true given the emphasis some scholars have placed on the disproportionate weight that elite political preferences carry on the Court.[8] Thus, because a political-cultural theory of judicial behavior could explain both a delimiting Court and a nondelimiting Court, it is as unsatisfying as the appointments thesis in explaining judicial delimitation during the post-Reconstruction era.

Consider next the case of the later New Deal rulings. Here again we have a consequential movement in the doctrine, and the appointments thesis seems largely beside the point. The basic sequence of events was that the Court upheld the Wagner Act and acceded to the New Deal in *Jones & Laughlin Steel* in 1937 by a slim majority of five votes. Yet one year later, with an additional Roosevelt appointment on the Court in Hugo Black, the Court voted 7–0 to deny expansive Wagner Act protections to economic strikers in *Mackay Radio*. The following year, with Reed joining Black as a second FDR appointee, the Court voted 5–2 against the union in *Sands* and 5–2 against the sit-down strikers in *Fansteel* – with the two FDR appointees dissenting in both cases. Table 6.3 presents a summary of these rulings.

---

[7] See Chapter 7.
[8] See, e.g., Klarman, *Jim Crow*, 6.

TABLE 6.3 *Supreme Court Justices and the New Deal Era Delimiting Rulings*

Justice	Party Affiliation/ Year of Appointment	Appointing President	NLRB v. Jones & Laughlin Steel Corp. (1937)	NLRB v. Mackay Radio & Telegraph Co. (1938)	NLRB v. Sands Manufacturing Co. (1939)	NLRB v. Fansteel Metallurgical Corp. (1939)
Willis Van Devanter	R/1911	Taft	o			
James C. McReynolds	D/1914	Wilson	o	x	x	x
Louis D. Brandeis	R/1916	Wilson	x	x		
George Sutherland	R/1922	Harding	o			
Pierce Butler	D/1923	Harding	o	x	x	x
Harlan F. Stone	R/1925	Coolidge	x	x	x	x
Charles E. Hughes	R/1930	Hoover	x	x	x	x
Owen J. Roberts	R/1930	Hoover	x	x	x	x
Benjamin N. Cardozo	D/1932	Hoover	x	a		
Hugo L. Black	D/1937	FDR		x	o	o
Stanley F. Reed	D/1938	FDR		a	o	o
Felix Frankfurter	Ind./1939	FDR			a	a

Note: x = majority, o = dissent, a = absent

An appointments theorist might claim that *Mackay Radio*, *Sands*, and *Fansteel* were simply the result of a holdover conservative Court hostile to the New Deal. Thus, these delimiting rulings resulted from FDR's inability to appoint enough judges to the Court by the time these cases arose. One difficulty with this argument is that it overlooks Black's agreement with the majority in *Mackay Radio*. Furthermore, it overlooks the fact that there was a substantial overlap between the justices who endorsed these delimiting rulings and those that had *upheld* the Wagner Act in *Jones & Laughlin Steel*. Thus, focusing on holdovers as the reason for delimiting conservative outcomes might be difficult if some of those holdovers were also responsible for helping to inaugurate reform itself. An appointments theorist might also direct our attention to the valid point that FDR's appointees dissented in *Sands* and *Fansteel*. The more important question, however, lies in examining the votes of Stone, Hughes, and Roberts, the three justices who voted to uphold the Wagner Act in *Jones & Laughlin Steel* but who also voted in favor of delimitation in *Mackay Radio*, *Sands*, and *Fansteel*. The appointments thesis is of little or no use in explaining why these three justices took a less sympathetic view of labor rights in the latter three rulings.

With respect to a political-cultural argument, one could make a plausible case that perhaps the tide of public opinion had shifted in a more anti-labor direction by the time of these rulings in the late 1930s, and that the Court's delimiting rulings merely reflected this changed public mood.[9] However, with a few notable exceptions, the Court's work in the context of labor relations remained strongly supportive of labor's interests during this time. Indeed, Melvin Dubofsky contends that the Supreme Court was a somewhat liberal outlier between 1938 and 1941 – at least compared to congressional majorities and the NLRB.[10] Although the Court's delimiting rulings likely aligned with an increasingly conservative public opinion, a broader look at judicial behavior during these years suggests the limits of a political-cultural explanation for them. Unless a political-cultural theory of judicial behavior could explain why the Court chose to align itself with growing antilabor sentiment in only its delimiting rulings, as opposed to the other cases where it felt comfortable in continuing to defend labor, political-cultural forces do not appear to be the primary factor driving Supreme Court behavior during this time.

---

[9] See Chapter 4.
[10] Melvyn Dubofsky, *The State & Labor in Modern America* (Chapel Hill: University of North Carolina Press, 1994), 164–65.

Finally, consider the Court's rulings in the 1970s. Among all of the cases examined in this chapter, *Milliken* provides the best support for the appointments thesis: this ruling, which marked a conservative shift in the Court's desegregation cases, closely followed four Nixon appointments: Burger (1969), Blackmun (1970), Powell (1972), and Rehnquist (1972). These four, along with Stewart, made up the five-vote majority in *Milliken* in 1974. Table 6.4 presents the appointments data for the earlier decisions on desegregation and the two delimiting rulings.

Although the appointments thesis does tell us something of interest about judicial delimitation in the 1970s, it also leaves a few items underexplained. First, the addition of Nixon appointees and the shift in the Court's orientation do not correspond perfectly. Even with all four Nixon appointees on the Court, a 7–1 majority (with Rehnquist dissenting) still pressed forward with an aggressive desegregation remedy in the 1973 case of *Keyes*, one year prior to *Milliken*. Second, the other delimiting case from the 1970s, *Davis*, enjoyed a 7–2 majority with Stevens, White, and Stewart joining the four Nixon appointees. A convincing analysis would likely have to extend beyond merely discussing appointments to explain this latter ruling – particularly with respect to the votes of White and Stewart. White's and Stewart's votes in *Davis* are especially interesting because both joined Court majorities in reaching liberal outcomes in *Green* and *Swann*. Stewart also joined a liberal majority in *Keyes*. Thus, their support of more conservative outcomes later in the mid-1970s raises questions whose explanations seem to lie outside the scope of the appointments thesis.

A political-cultural explanation might fill in the gap: perhaps these delimiting rulings were the result of appointments dynamics aided by broader social and cultural influences on the justices. Indeed, the Court's delimiting rulings in the 1970s seem to be well within majoritarian public sentiment. Yet, as with the case of the late 1930s, a political-cultural thesis of judicial behavior is less convincing once a broader set of judicial actions is considered: while public sentiment against busing was on the rise years before *Milliken* in 1974,[11] the Court nevertheless continued to *press forward* for a time with aggressive desegregation remedies in the face of growing conservatism. Although it may have been responding to public pressure in *Milliken* and *Davis*, in order for a political-cultural thesis of judicial behavior to explain delimitation, it would have to explain why those social and cultural forces made a greater impression on the Court

---

[11] See Chapter 5.

TABLE 6.4 *Supreme Court Justices,* Brown, *and the Post–Civil Rights Era Rulings*

Justice	Party Affiliation/ Year of Appointment	Appointing President	Brown v. Board of Education (1954)	Green v. County School Board (1968)	Swann v. Charlotte-Mecklenburg Board of Education (1971)
Hugo L. Black	D/ 1937	FDR	x	x	x
Stanley F. Reed	D/ 1938	FDR	x		
Felix Frankfurter	Ind./ 1939	FDR	x		
William O. Douglas	D/ 1939	FDR	x	x	x
Robert H. Jackson	D/ 1941	FDR	x		
Harold H. Burton	R/ 1945	Truman	x		
Tom C. Clark	D/ 1949	Truman	x		
Sherman Minton	D/ 1949	Truman	x		
Earl Warren	R/ 1953	Eisenhower	x	x	
John M. Harlan II	R/ 1955	Eisenhower		x	x
William J. Brennan	D/ 1956	Eisenhower		x	x
Potter Stewart	R/ 1958	Eisenhower		x	x
Byron R. White	D/ 1962	Kennedy		x	x
Abe Fortas	D/ 1965	LBJ		x	
Thurgood Marshall	D/ 1967	LBJ		x	x
Warren E. Burger	R/ 1969	Nixon			x
Harry A. Blackmun	R/ 1970	Nixon			x

Justice	Party Affiliation/ Year of Appointment	Appointing President	Keyes v. School District No. 1 (1973)	Milliken v. Bradley (1974)	Washington v. Davis (1976)
William O. Douglas	D/ 1939	FDR	x	o	
William J. Brennan	D/ 1956	Eisenhower	x	o	o
Potter Stewart	R/ 1958	Eisenhower	x	x	x
Byron R. White	D/ 1962	Kennedy	a	o	x
Thurgood Marshall	D/ 1967	LBJ	x	o	o
Warren E. Burger	R/ 1969	Nixon	x	x	x
Harry A. Blackmun	R/ 1970	Nixon	x	x	x
Lewis F. Powell	D/ 1972	Nixon	x, o	x	x
William H. Rehnquist	R/ 1972	Nixon	o	x	x
John Paul Stevens	R/ 1975	Ford			x

Note: x = majority, o = dissent, a = absent

in the mid-1970s than they did in the late 1960s and early 1970s. Again, during those earlier years the Court pressed against public opinion with a series of strongly pro-integration rulings.

A judicial-institutional theory, however, can explain these postreform rulings for which the appointments and political-cultural theories fall short. In the case of post-Reconstruction, a judicial-institutional theory would direct our attention to the fact that the post-Reconstruction cases all presented urgent issues regarding the uncertain scope of reform principles in light of possible tensions with resilient authorities and rights. Each case confronted the problem of *how much* state governmental authority had been displaced by the Reconstruction Amendments. Implicated in these uncertainties were additional questions regarding the scope and substance of the African American rights that had been set forth in reforms. Given this, the Court's orientation toward more conservative outcomes in these cases is easily traced to an institutional interest in promoting legality values by clarifying and stabilizing the boundaries between federal and state authority and by beginning to create a new social order in the domain of southern race relations. We might expect this institutional interest to emerge from any Court in the aftermath of an open-ended reform. This is precisely why a Court full of Republican appointees might press in more conservative directions, notwithstanding their affiliation with the party of reform, or the fact that some segments of the Republican Party favored more expansive interpretations of reform at the time.

Second, consider the case of the later New Deal, where in *Mackay Radio*, *Sands*, and *Fansteel* similar questions arose regarding the uncertain extent to which the Wagner Act had displaced employer prerogatives. Again, these judicial delimiting decisions can be explained with reference to an institutional interest in stabilizing authority relations between the prerogatives of employers and the authority of the federal government to protect unions and employees. In contrast to some of the difficulties confronted by the appointments and political-cultural theories in the context of the later New Deal, a judicial-institutional theory illuminates why the Court, generally sympathetic to labor at this time, might have nevertheless handed down more conservative rulings in these three cases. The majority of cases confronting the Court during these years, including *Jones & Laughlin Steel*, dealt with flagrant employer violations of the Wagner Act, such as the undue influence of employers in supporting company unions. These were legal disputes that spoke to violations at the core of reform principles and that did *not* implicate the uncertain reach of the Wagner

Act at the outer margins of its authority.[12] Hence the Court's sympathetic posture to labor in these cases is unsurprising; it was merely stabilizing authority relations by protecting the very integrity of the reform itself. However, with *Mackay Radio*, *Sands*, and *Fansteel*, the issues presented did implicate authority issues at the outer margins of the act. The task of stabilizing authorities and rights relations in the latter instances required demarcating the boundary lines at which reform principles had to give way to still-credible employer prerogatives in the interests of industrial peace. Hence with these delimiting cases, the Court's less sympathetic posture to the interests of labor, and the fact that Stone, Hughes, and Roberts in particular departed from their labor-friendly stance in *Jones & Laughlin Steel*, is unsurprising.

Finally, consider the applicability of a judicial-institutional theory to the 1970s race cases. In both *Milliken* and *Davis*, the Court confronted the question of how much the rule-making prerogatives of federal, state, and local institutions would be displaced by the authority of the federal judiciary in the name of guaranteeing constitutional equal protection to racial minorities. Once again, the delimiting result can be explained with reference to a judicial inclination to stabilize the boundaries of authority between these various institutions. Furthermore, emphasizing the judicial interest in stability also helps explain why the inclusion of four Nixon appointees did not preclude an aggressive desegregation remedy in *Keyes*, a year prior to *Milliken*. Further, it explains why the Court may have pressed forward with aggressive desegregation remedies *against* social and political pressures in several cases and why Justices White and Stewart voted in favor of the delimiting result in *Davis*, notwithstanding their earlier collective support of more liberal outcomes in *Green*, *Swann*, and *Keyes*. As discussed in Chapter 5, the issues presented in *Milliken* and *Davis* held the potential to systemically disrupt authority relations in a way that the earlier school desegregation cases did not. Indeed, in *Green*, *Swann*, and *Keyes*, the Court was remedying local governmental actions that had been in flagrant violation of core reform principles: the school districts had unquestionably been engaged in past intentional discrimination. If the *Brown* principle stood for anything, it certainly stood for the idea of redressing such violations. In *Milliken* and *Davis*, however,

---

[12] See, e.g., *NLRB v. Pennsylvania Greyhound Lines, Inc.*, 303 U.S. 261 (1938), in which the Court supported an NLRB effort to dislodge a company-influenced union. For discussion of other cases from 1938 to 1941 that dealt with "core" Wagner Act commitments, and that resulted in proreform rulings, see Dubofsky, *State & Labor*, 164–66, 263nn71–72; Klare, "Deradicalization," 318–19.

no such core violations of reform were present. These latter cases instead touched on issues at the outer reaches of reform in constitutional equal protection. Indeed, by way of suggesting the efficacy of the judicial interest in stability, I would speculate that even if the Court had *not* had four Nixon appointees by 1974, it would not be difficult to imagine that its institutional interest in stability would nevertheless have led it to issue some type of a delimiting ruling along the lines of *Davis*.

Evaluating the judicial-institutional theory in light of the difficulties of the alternative theories adds to its plausibility as the best general explanation for postreform delimiting rulings. Furthermore, there are basic structural reasons related to the peculiar context of postreform periods that suggest why the alternative theories are so unsatisfactory. The inability of the appointments thesis to explain postreform delimitations stems from the existence of a significant lag before politics can influence the appointments process. That is, in the immediate aftermath of reform, issues are likely to arise that will not have significantly intersected with the appointments concerns of any substantial portion of a postreform Court. For example, Abraham notes how the prosecution of the Civil War, pro-Unionism, and antislavery were the most important considerations for Lincoln in making his appointments.[13] It is unlikely that the precise legal issues at the center of post-Reconstruction recalibration – such as the recalibration of federal authority and African American rights in light of state governmental autonomy – would have weighed as heavily on anyone's mind at the time Lincoln appointed his five justices, who made up a substantial presence on the post-Reconstruction Court. With respect to the political-cultural thesis of judicial behavior, the immediate aftermath of a major reform is also often a context in which social, cultural, and political forces are likely to be too amorphous, transient, or ambiguous to impose firmer constraints on judicial behavior.

The relative softness of the constraints imposed by appointments or political-cultural pressures during these periods is precisely why the judicial-institutional interest so effectively establishes the terms of postreform delimitation. However, as we will see in Chapters 7, 8, and 9, this is *not* necessarily a constant of postreform judicial behavior. In these chapters, I continue the historical narrative for all three eras into subsequent periods during which new governing arrangements were constructed and then maintained. As the polity moved further away from

---

[13] Abraham, *Justices*, 87–93.

the initial period of reform, appointments and political-cultural pressures became more efficacious and imposed increasingly narrow constraints on judicial action. The judicial-institutional interest in stability did remain a crucial determinant of judicial behavior throughout, of course, but as time progressed, appointments and political-cultural pressures forced this institutional interest to operate within an increasingly narrow space.

PART III

THE CONSTRUCTION AND MAINTENANCE OF GOVERNANCE

7

The Entrenchment and Maintenance of the Jim Crow Order

The demise of slavery prompted uncertainties in the postreform legal structure. The first concerned how reform principles might be reconciled with still-resilient governing authorities and individual rights that resided at the outer edges of reform. As discussed in Chapter 3, a series of significant judicial rulings in the 1870s and 1880s legally resolved this question and codified the outer limits of reform. In *Blyew v. United States*,[1] the Court limited the reach of the Civil Rights Act of 1866; in the *Slaughter-House Cases*,[2] it offered a stingy interpretation of the Privileges or Immunities Clause of the Fourteenth Amendment; in *United States v. Reese*,[3] the Court proved reluctant to protect African American voting rights; in *Virginia v. Rives*,[4] the Court was hesitant to allow removal of certain state proceedings, involving some types of equal protection violations against African Americans, into federal court; and finally, in *U.S. v. Cruikshank*[5] and the *Civil Rights Cases*,[6] the Court established the "state action doctrine," which limited the federal government's oversight under the Fourteenth Amendment to only those matters emanating from formal state actions, and not from private actions.

Together, these rulings formally delimited the outer reach of Reconstruction legislation by reasserting the authority of federalism. More precisely, the recalibration of reform embodied in these rulings reflected

---

[1] 80 U.S. 581 (1872).
[2] 83 U.S. 36 (1873).
[3] 92 U.S. 214 (1876).
[4] 100 U.S. 313 (1880).
[5] 92 U.S. 542 (1876).
[6] 109 U.S. 3 (1883).

a legal compromise between federal and state authority, with significant implications for African American rights. Slavery had been discarded, and the federal government enjoyed clear constitutional authority to oversee state government treatment of African Americans. However, by the early 1880s, a second facet of the postreform order was clear: federal governmental oversight of private actions would not be legally permitted, and the federal judiciary would likewise be disinclined to use what formal authority it retained to energetically oversee race relations in the southern states.

The Court's reassertion of federalism meant that white southern Democratic preferences would be the dominant political force in the South. And given the views of the latter, the reassertion of federalism also ensured that some degree of systematic subordination of African Americans would take root in the region. Nevertheless, not everything about the postreform legal structure had been settled with these judicial delimiting rulings. A second uncertainty resided in the question of how boundaries were to be redrawn between competing governing authorities and individual rights more internal to the domain of reform. Thus, even if delimiting judicial rulings had legally codified the notion that the southern state governments would retain, in effect, primary authority over the status and welfare of African Americans in the South, the legal principles that would actually structure southern race relations on the ground were *not* equally clear at this time. After all, the dominant legal supports for the Jim Crow order – in the form of segregation statutes and, especially, disfranchisement laws – began to appear in the 1890s. A new, fully formed system of governance emerged only after the Supreme Court had granted its blessing to Jim Crow, with its affirmation of Louisiana's segregated railroad seating statute in *Plessy v. Ferguson*[7] and its approval of Mississippi's disfranchisement scheme in *Williams v. Mississippi*.[8]

The first task of this chapter is to trace the political processes of "construction" alluded to in the preceding paragraph. My narrative begins by emphasizing uncertainties that lingered in the wake of the prior legislative stalemate and delimiting rulings. Notwithstanding the latter, some degree of contingency and openness remained in the final decades of the nineteenth century with respect to the scope and content of African American individual rights. At the margins, possibilities still existed for the greater or lesser projection of federal authority and Republican Party

[7] 163 U.S. 537 (1896).
[8] 170 U.S. 213 (1898).

influence into the South after the late 1870s. And a greater federal or Republican Party presence in the South could have been consequential enough in these later years to have mitigated the depth of racial subordination against African Americans either through a continued, limited federal effort in prosecuting southern offenders under the Enforcement Acts or through some degree of continued Republican Party influence in the southern state governments.

None of the political developments in these latter decades seriously challenged the allocation of governing authority earlier established in judicial delimiting rulings, and again, probably nothing could have prevented the widespread subordination of African Americans in portions of the South after Redemption and the revitalization of the Democratic Party across the region. Consistent with the notion of path dependence, however, one might say that the contingency and openness in these later years were qualified; although alternatives and different possibilities still existed at this time for how the new system of governance would be structured, all of these possibilities were constrained by the earlier delimiting legal settlement.

With the defeat of the Lodge Bill in 1891, however, even this qualified openness eventually closed. Once federal intervention was no longer on the table, the path was clear for the southern state governments to enjoy considerable leeway in entrenching a new system of race relations, which they did. Thus, the second part of the narrative on construction focuses on the rise of Jim Crow laws from the state governments, and the Supreme Court's definitive affirmation of the new Jim Crow system in the mid- to late 1890s. With Supreme Court rulings in *Plessy* and *Williams v. Mississippi*, developmental processes had, in effect, reached the conclusion of recalibration. This was marked by the solidifying of a new governing order. Table 7.1 summarizes these developments in part.

Examination of this period of construction in the 1880s and 1890s offers two primary illustrative benefits: first, it provides an initial look at how the recalibration of those authorities and rights internal to the domain of reform aided in establishing a new system of governance. Second, it offers a first look at "order-affirming" judicial rulings – such as *Plessy* and *Williams v. Mississippi* – as a recurrent and distinctive mode of Supreme Court adjudication. In such rulings, the Supreme Court acted to affirm an emerging system of governance in sweeping, principled terms. Jim Crow was not "created" by the Court as the preceding paragraphs suggest, but Jim Crow's definitive, legal codification was dependent on the Supreme Court's approval.

TABLE 7.1 *Construction and Tension Management after Reconstruction*

	Structure of race relations in the South
Lingering uncertainty	
Emergence of the new system of governance	From the southern state governments in the form of state legislation
Entrenchment of the new system of governance	By the Supreme Court in *Plessy v. Ferguson, Williams v. Mississippi, Giles v. Harris*
Judicial tension management	(1) In residential segregation: *Buchanan v. Warley*
	(2) In higher education segregation: *Missouri ex rel. Gaines v. Canada, Sweatt v. Painter, McLaurin v. Oklahoma State Regents*

Following the story of construction is only one of the two primary tasks of this chapter, however. A second major task encompasses following the judiciary in its role of managing boundary tensions in the subsequent era of normal politics or political equilibrium. The managing function of the Court during this era was a crucial one, because political and institutional pressures within the Jim Crow system arose long before *Brown v. Board of Education*[9] and the civil rights era of the 1960s. It was in response to this imperative that the Court assumed the role of manager in articulating compromise doctrinal adjustments that accommodated these threats to Jim Crow's legal integrity while also preserving the integrity of that governing order.

The case studies of judicial tension management discussed in this chapter, and in Chapters 8 and 9, are thus helpful in illuminating the political and institutional dynamics of the postreform order subsequent to its initial entrenchment. In this instance, one can recognize the resilience of the Jim Crow order after seeing how conflict and tensions were contained by the Court within the larger governing structure. The case studies of tension management underscore the significance and durability of the legal settlements discussed in the first half of this chapter. In addition, these case studies direct our attention to a mode of adjudication that recurs across the historical periods under examination, but that is distinctive to periods of political equilibrium. The second half of this chapter thus examines the Court's tension-managing rulings in dealing with residential

[9] 347 U.S. 483 (1954).

segregation in *Buchanan v. Warley*[10] and in dealing with segregation in higher education in the cases of *Missouri ex rel. Gaines v. Canada*,[11] *Sweatt v. Painter*,[12] and *McLaurin v. Oklahoma State Regents*.[13]

As with the delimiting rulings discussed in Chapters 3, 4, and 5, the order-affirming and tension-managing rulings discussed in Chapters 7, 8, and 9 do not display an explicit judicial self-consciousness with the larger processes of recalibration. Indeed, some of these rulings possess strands of argument that might suggest alternative interpretations. But taken together, and evaluated retrospectively against the backdrop of the earlier delimiting rulings, one might plausibly find a strong, consistent judicial concern with stability and stabilizing boundary lines present within these rulings too. The order-affirming rulings are labeled as such because they plausibly illustrate a judicial desire to legally entrench new boundary lines between competing authorities and rights. Likewise, the labeled tension-managing rulings plausibly illustrate a judicial inclination to maintain these entrenched boundaries. Thus, even if the Court may not have self-consciously operated with an explicit awareness of recalibration processes in its decisions, the conventional judicial concern with legality and seeking greater clarity in the law nevertheless pressed it to significantly contribute to the codification and legal maintenance of these new postreform governing orders.

PART I: THE ENTRENCHMENT OF JIM CROW

Lingering Uncertainties Unresolved by Delimitation: Republican Coalition-Building and Enforcement Efforts

By the late 1870s, it would have been apparent to most that Republican Party dominance of southern state governments as well as massive federal intervention in the South had permanently ended. Yet the exact role of the federal government and the Republican Party in the political life of the South remained undetermined until the final decade of the nineteenth century. Indeed, even after the mid-1870s, Republicans sought to build political alliances with non-Democratic white southerners and to protect

---

[10] 245 U.S. 60 (1917).
[11] 305 U.S. 337 (1938).
[12] 339 U.S. 629 (1950).
[13] 339 U.S. 637 (1950).

black voting rights in the South. Their efforts indicate that opportunities existed, for a time, for the post-Reconstruction system of race relations to become something other than the Jim Crow system that eventually took hold.

Republican Efforts at Coalition Building in the South

Recall that, in *Reese* and *Virginia v. Rives*, the Supreme Court's delimiting results had been reached with more conservative statutory as opposed to constitutional interpretations. Consequently, these rulings had conspicuously left Congress free to push back against the Court to further Reconstruction through new statutes.[14] However, this invitation was not taken up by the Republican presidents and the Congresses of the latter decades of the nineteenth century. One reason lay in the growing northern antipathy toward continued federal military intervention in the South, as discussed in Chapter 3. This attitude was reflected in the post-1874 legislative stalemate and had allowed for judicial delimitation to occur.

A second reason that no congressional response to the Court was forthcoming lay in the Republican Party's continued failure to gain support from white southerners opposed to the Democratic Party, which might have allowed it to break the stalemate. This failure was not from lack of effort. Coalition building in the South drew serious attention from all of the Republican presidents, from Hayes to Harrison. From the 1870s to the 1890s, many Republicans viewed serious efforts to build bridges to white non-Democrat Southerners as one of the most promising means of breaking the Democrats' grip on the South. In addition, such a breakthrough would have carried ancillary benefits for southern African Americans, who were potentially invaluable as either a possible swing-voting constituency or, more likely, a consistent coalition partner for anti-Democrat southern forces. Thus, at least during these years, Republican political elites did not believe that the window for structuring social relations in the South had entirely closed.

Hayes's presidency illustrates the Republican interest in southern coalition building. It was under Hayes that southern home rule was restored by withdrawing federal troops from the Louisiana and South Carolina statehouses after the 1876 election dispute. Conciliation was the preferred strategy of Hayes as part of the larger electoral goal of making

---

[14] Michael Les Benedict, "Preserving Federalism: Reconstruction and the Waite Court," *Supreme Court Review* (1979): 66–79.

inroads into the Democratic South; specifically, he sought to attract former Southern Whigs – those southerners committed to industry and internal improvements – to the Republican Party. Removal of the particularly contentious presence of federal troops was only one prong of his program of outreach; the other prong, equally important, was his decision to distribute patronage to certain southern Democrats susceptible to conversion, at the expense of southern Republicans.[15] However, the electoral payoffs from Hayes's conciliatory southern policy failed to materialize in the congressional elections of 1878, and the Democrats captured both the House and Senate. Hayes realized that splitting off the southern ex-Whig vote would be unlikely. He admitted his strategy to be a failure and assumed a hardened stance toward the South.[16]

After the failure of Hayes's conciliation policy, Republican Party unity was temporarily revived around waving the bloody shirt; the 1880 Republican campaign emphasized sectional themes and the importance of a fair ballot in the South.[17] Garfield's priorities aligned with this sentiment. His concern for southern African Americans led him to focus on federal aid for education – a relatively nonintrusive federal means to enable African Americans to better guard their political and civil rights.[18] Simultaneously, he toyed with the idea of a Republican alliance with the Readjusters in Virginia – an independent party organized around the goal of repudiating part of Virginia's state debt. The prime motivation for such an alliance was likely electoral, as a cross-party coalition in Virginia and possibly other southern states again presented the tantalizing possibility of breaking the solid Democratic South. Furthermore, such an alliance would have also indirectly benefited southern blacks; because the Readjusters needed all the votes – including African American votes – they could muster to topple Democratic control, an alliance with Republicans would only reinforce their existing incentives to protect southern African

---

[15] Vincent P. DeSantis, *Republicans Face the Southern Question: The New Departure Years, 1877–1897* (Baltimore: Johns Hopkins University Press, 1959), 69, 73–85; Stanley P. Hirshson, *Farewell to the Bloody Shirt: Northern Republicans & the Southern Negro, 1877–1893* (Chicago: Quadrangle Books, 1962, 1968), 24–29; William Gillette, *Retreat from Reconstruction, 1869–1879* (Baton Rouge: Louisiana State University Press, 1979), 336, 348–49; Xi Wang, *The Trial of Democracy: Black Suffrage and Northern Republicans, 1860–1910* (Athens: University of Georgia Press, 1997), 145–48.

[16] Hirshson, *Farewell*, 50–51; Wang, *Trial*, 161–62.

[17] Hirshson, *Farewell*, 79–80; DeSantis, *Southern Question*, 133–34; Wang, *Trial*, 187–88.

[18] Hirshson, *Farewell*, 88–94; Wang, *Trial*, 194, 197–98.

American voting rights.[19] However, Garfield was assassinated before he could carry out any of these proposed policies.[20]

Inheriting no firm policy, Arthur chose to follow through on Garfield's strategy to join the Readjusters. The alliance strategy carried costs to southern African Americans: it required the Republican Party to transfer influence and patronage from southern African American Republicans (and white Republicans) to white Readjusters. Furthermore, some prominent Readjusters had particularly poor records with respect to their past treatment of African Americans.[21] Still, African Americans would potentially benefit from such a union, as Republicans insisted on Independent Party recognition of black suffrage rights as a precondition of alliance as well.[22] Arthur and other Republicans in the administration were also motivated to take an interest in federal enforcement of election laws in the run-up to the congressional elections of 1882 because of electoral imperatives (despite the fact that Arthur himself did not seem to exhibit much of a substantive interest in African American rights).[23] With disappointing results in the 1882 elections, and two key losses suffered by southern Readjusters in 1883, it became clear to Arthur that this strategy ultimately failed to advance the Republican goal of cracking the solid South.[24]

Finally, like his predecessors, Harrison focused on breaking the solid South by forging an alliance with white-only, high-tariff movements that remained separate from the southern Republicans. Like Arthur, Harrison was willing to pursue this strategy even if it meant decreasing the patronage and focus allocated to southern Republican blacks.[25]

Yet, like Hayes, Harrison soon abandoned the strategy of alliance after electoral defeats convinced him of its futility. In 1889, the Republicans lost an important Louisiana congressional race despite great emphasis on

---

[19] Hirshson, *Farewell*, 94–98; DeSantis, *Southern Question*, 147–48; Wang, *Trial*, 196–97. Indeed, the Readjusters appeared to exhibit a notable degree of concern and effort on behalf of African American interests. Mark Wahlgren Summers, *Rum, Romanism, & Rebellion: The Making of a President, 1884* (Chapel Hill: University of North Carolina Press, 2000), 52; Richard M. Valelly, *The Two Reconstructions: The Struggle for Black Enfranchisement* (Chicago: University of Chicago Press, 2004), 57–59.

[20] Hirshson, *Farewell*, 98.

[21] DeSantis, *Southern Question*, 152–57, 172–75; Hirshson, *Farewell*, 106–07, 115.

[22] Wang, *Trial*, 201.

[23] Hirshson, *Farewell*, 99–105; Robert M. Goldman, *A Free Ballot and a Fair Count: The Department of Justice and the Enforcement of Voting Rights in the South, 1877–1893* (New York: Garland, 1990, 2001) 96–98; Wang, *Trial*, 200.

[24] Hirshson, *Farewell*, 119–20; Wang, *Trial*, 203.

[25] Hirshson, *Farewell*, 179–82, 187; Wang, *Trial*, 231–32, 244.

the tariff issue. Similarly, despite strong Republican support and emphasis on the tariff issue, William Mahone – leader of the Readjusters in Virginia – lost to a Democratic candidate in a Virginia gubernatorial race in 1889. After these two defeats, in which Republicans invested so much hope, many began to return to the race issue that was previously relegated to the background. This, in turn, prompted the very notable Republican effort to pass the Lodge Bill, which is discussed later.[26]

Therefore, possibilities existed for the Republicans to gain a foothold in the South, at least up to Harrison's presidency. Although the likelihood of success was questionable since these efforts all ended in failure, they undoubtedly presented better opportunities for cracking the solid South than would exist in subsequent decades. The fact that political elites still felt it a worthwhile gamble indicates a continuing, although qualified, uncertainty within the South's emerging social and political landscape during these years.

However, other avenues remained for Republicans to influence and shape the emerging system of governance regarding race relations in the South. These avenues lay less in political coalition building and more in executive, judicial, and legislative efforts to legally secure and protect African American votes in the region.

Republican Efforts at Enforcement
Republican efforts to enforce black suffrage rights in the post-Reconstruction era indicate some continuing uncertainties lingering in the wake of legislative stalemate and delimitation. The option of pursuing federal prosecutions against southern violators was by no means off the table in the post-Reconstruction decades, and accordingly, each of the three branches of the federal government exhibited some interest in upholding black suffrage rights.

Federal Prosecutions. Republican interest in enforcing black suffrage never entirely disappeared, even during Hayes's presidency. Once Hayes's efforts at conciliation failed to translate into electoral success, he turned toward defending black suffrage rights. This began with his annual message on December 2, 1878, when he asked Congress for larger appropriations for federal enforcement of voting rights.[27] Later, when Democrats

---

[26] Hirshson, *Farewell*, 182–89, 205–07; DeSantis, *Southern Question*, 196–97; Wang, *Trial*, 244.
[27] Hirshson, *Farewell*, 50–51; Wang, *Trial*, 161–62.

attempted to repeal portions the Enforcement Acts by attaching riders to appropriation bills between 1879 and 1880, Hayes vetoed seven of these appropriation bills. His opposition arose partly in defense of presidential independence and partly from a commitment to preserve the Reconstruction Amendments.[28] In addition, Arthur – hardly a strong advocate for black rights – also took a brief interest in enforcement prior to the 1882 elections.[29]

Yet, if the presence of sporadic federal enforcement efforts indicates some uncertainties in post-Reconstruction politics, enforcement statistics, provided in Table 7.2, suggest that these were qualified uncertainties.[30]

Both Wang and Valelly refer to this statistical evidence to suggest that proreform inclinations existed in the Republican Party even after Redemption in the mid-1870s; they correctly note that the Enforcement Acts were not dead letters after 1877.[31] Nevertheless, these numbers give little indication of a sustained federal attempt to use the prosecutorial weapon to contest the judicial reassertion of federalism.

In measuring the efficacy of enforcement by both the number of cases initiated and the degree of prosecutorial success, there was only one year after 1873 that exhibited a relatively significant number of total cases initiated and a relatively high conviction rate. That year is 1881 – Hayes's last year in office – during which there were a total of 177 cases and a 53.7 percent conviction rate.[32] Other than this one year, which by itself cannot constitute a sustained enforcement effort, no other year comes close to replicating the vigorous enforcement between 1871 and 1873.

The enforcement statistics demonstrate a marked shift in policy around the early to mid-1870s. From 1873 to 1874, success in convicting defendants dropped from 40.6 percent to 10.9 percent. Even more indicative of a policy change, the number of cases initiated dropped by about 76 percent from 1874 to 1875. The number of cases initiated in 1876 dropped from 1875 totals by another 50 percent. For the next two decades,

[28] Hirshson, *Farewell*, 56–57; Summers, *Rebellion*, 48–49; Wang, *Trial*, 165–79.
[29] Hirshson, *Farewell*, 100–101; Wang, *Trial*, 200.
[30] Wang, *Trial*, 300 (Appendix 7). Southern states include Alabama, Arkansas, Florida, Georgia, Louisiana, Mississippi, North Carolina, South Carolina, Texas, and Virginia. Alternative presentations of this data can be found in Valelly, *Two Reconstructions*, 67; Gillette, *Retreat*, 43–44.
[31] Wang, *Trial*, xxii–xxiii; Valelly, *Two Reconstructions*, 66–68.
[32] The statistics for 1881 cover the period up to June 30, 1880. Valelly, *Two Reconstructions*, 68.

TABLE 7.2 *Federal Prosecutions in the South under the Enforcement Acts*

Year	Number of Cases in the South	Conviction Rate in the South (%)
1870	16	0
1871	206	52.4
1872	603	74.3
1873	1,148	40.6
1874	890	10.9
1875	216	7.4
1876	108	1.9
1877	133	4.5
1878	23	0
1879	93	15.1
1880	53	0
1881	177	53.7
1882	154	14.9
1883	201	6
1884	160	10.6
1885	107	0.9
1886	8	0
1887	2	0
1888	14	7.1
1889	22	50
1890	42	19
1891	19	0
1892	12	8.3
1893	17	0
1894	25	0

cases-initiated numbers never surpassed the total for 1875 (nor came remotely close to the numbers for 1872–74).

The numbers indicate that presidents after Grant pursued enforcement with a significant degree of ambivalence, and the reason is not difficult to identify: given that many in the North and South opposed military intervention in the latter on states-rights grounds, opposition would likely have attached to vigorous enforcement efforts as well. A genuine commitment to enforcement did persist after 1877 within portions of the Republican Party, as others note.[33] However, the relative unintrusiveness of

---

[33] Wang, *Trial*; Goldman, *Free Ballot*.

enforcement after 1875 and the broader electoral skepticism toward southern intervention suggest that the feasibility of enforcement as a reform tool was tightly – and perversely – linked to how unintrusive it would remain. Enforcement could remain a political option for Republican presidents, but only if it did not seriously challenge the federal-state balance in the same manner that the federal military had during Reconstruction. Thus, although the continued existence of federal efforts to prosecute violations of the Enforcement Acts indicates some political uncertainty during these years, this uncertainty was *within* the boundaries established by judicial delimitation.

Ex parte Yarbrough. Possibilities for facilitating federal protection of African American voting also emanated from the judiciary and Congress during this period. With respect to the judiciary, in *Ex parte Yarbrough*[34] the Supreme Court unexpectedly breathed new life into federal efforts to secure black suffrage in 1884. The defendants in this case conspired to, and did, assault an African American man on account of race to hinder him from voting in a congressional election.[35] The defendants were charged under Section 5508[36] and Section 5520[37] of the Revised Statutes.[38] The primary question was whether these statutory provisions were constitutional.

Because the federal statutory provisions in question aimed to regulate private actions, and the Court decided this case in 1884 after *Cruikshank*, *Reese*, and the *Civil Rights Cases*, it seemed reasonable that it would either strike down the provision and/or rule in favor of the defendants. Surprisingly, the Court did neither.

Justice Miller, writing for the Court, cited structural, prudential, and precedent-oriented arguments to support the federal government's authority to regulate and police elections for its own officials.[39] The Court also invoked a textual argument to support congressional authority to enact the laws in question. The Constitution states: "The Times,

---

[34] 110 U.S. 651 (1884).
[35] Id. at 655–57.
[36] Quoted in id. at 654–55. This provision was originally Section 6 of the Enforcement Act of May 31, 1870. Wang, *Trial*, 294.
[37] Quoted in 110 U.S. at 655. This provision was originally part of Section 2 of the Enforcement Act of April 20, 1871. It was eventually repealed in 1894. Wang, *Trial*, 299.
[38] 110 U.S. at 654.
[39] Id. at 657–60.

Places and Manner of holding Elections for Senators and Representatives, shall be prescribed in each State by the Legislature thereof; but the Congress may at any time by Law make or alter such Regulations, except as to the Place of chusing Senators."[40] Relying on this textual provision, Miller asserted:

> Will it be denied that it is in the power of that body to provide laws for the proper conduct of those elections? To provide, if necessary, the officers who shall conduct them and make return of the result? And especially to provide, in an election held under its own authority, for security of life and limb to the voter while in the exercise of this function? Can it be doubted that Congress can by law protect the act of voting, the place where it is done, and the man who votes, from personal violence or intimidation and the election itself from corruption and fraud?[41]

The Court ultimately upheld the laws in question.

Recall that the Court already applied the state action doctrine under the Fourteenth Amendment in the *Civil Rights Cases*, and that doctrine was also seemingly applicable to the Fifteenth Amendment.[42] Might the statute's regulation of private action render them constitutionally infirm, given the state action doctrine?[43] The Court answered in the negative. Miller asserted that Congress possessed authority to regulate private transgressions of rights inherent to the very functioning of the federal government.[44] His support for this point was not a textual provision but rather a structural argument.[45] Miller reasoned that

> if the government of the United States has within its constitutional domain no authority to provide against these evils, if the very sources of power may be poisoned by corruption or controlled by violence and outrage, without legal restraint, then, indeed, is the country in danger, and its best powers, its highest

---

[40] U.S. Constitution, Article I, § 4.
[41] 110 U.S. at 661.
[42] "The right of citizens of the United States to vote shall not be denied or abridged by the United States or by any State on account of race, color, or previous condition of servitude." U.S. Constitution, Fifteenth Amendment, § 1. The Court ultimately came to the conclusion that the state action limitation applied to the Fifteenth Amendment, notwithstanding *Yarbrough*, in *James v. Bowman*, 190 U.S. 127 (1903). See Note, "The Strange Career of 'State Action' under the Fifteenth Amendment," *Yale Law Journal* 74, no. 8 (July 1965): 1455.
[43] 110 U.S. at 666–67.
[44] Id. at 666.
[45] Id. at 666–67.

purposes, the hopes which it inspires, and the love which enshrines it, are at the mercy of the combinations of those who respect no right but brute force on the one hand, and unprincipled corruptionists on the other.[46]

Thus, *Yarbrough* ran counter to the principles of judicial delimitation previously articulated by the Court. Its defense of federal authority to regulate private transgressions cut against the federalism-oriented jurisprudential themes of earlier cases – particularly, the *Civil Rights Cases* decided only the year before.

Still, it is unlikely this ruling signaled a meaningful continuation of Reconstruction's political transformation at the late date of 1884. The Court alone could not ensure a free and unfettered ballot for southern African Americans, especially as federal enforcement of the Enforcement Acts was winding down at the same time. Furthermore, *Yarbrough* posed no direct challenge to any of the Court's delimiting rulings of the preceding ten years. In a qualified sense, however, *Yarbrough* signaled a notable degree of contingency in post-Reconstruction politics bounded by the constraints of delimitation. At least to some extent, it marked a potentially new and consequential judicial sympathy toward protecting African American voting rights. *Yarbrough*'s most significant political effect was to offer constitutional legitimacy for another congressional effort to pass a new Enforcement Act – the Lodge Bill of 1890.[47] Whether *Yarbrough* would flower into a significant jurisprudential development hinged on the fate of this bill.

The Lodge Bill. Previous Republican presidents had attempted to undermine legislative stalemate through coalition-building efforts. The Lodge Bill, by directly protecting African American voting in the South, proposed a different path toward the same goal. The bill provided for (1) a circuit court to appoint a federal chief election supervisor for each judicial district, (2) the chief election supervisor to appoint three supervisors for each voting district to assist him in overseeing elections, and (3) perhaps most radically, it created a U.S. Board of Canvassers: three men appointed by the circuit court to examine the votes as transmitted by the supervisors.

---

[46] Id. at 667. With respect to *Yarbrough*'s defense of federal prerogatives in regulating federal elections, this was in line with the Court's earlier ruling in *Ex parte Siebold*, 100 U.S. 371 (1879) that involved state judges interfering with and resisting federal election supervisors at a congressional election.

[47] Wang, *Trial*, 238; Valelly, *Two Reconstructions*, 246.

If the board's decision of the election's winner matched the judgment of state officials, the winner was confirmed. If they disagreed, however, the board's decision established prima facie evidence of the election winner, which the loser could appeal in a federal circuit court. If the circuit court heard the case, that court's decision of the election winner would be controlling. The Lodge Bill's enforcement scheme would go into operation upon the petition of (1) 100 citizens in an entire congressional district, (2) 100 citizens in a city of 20,000 or more inhabitants, or (3) 50 citizens in only a portion of a congressional district.[48]

Federal control over certifying congressional election winners was a significant policy innovation, and it very importantly did not require burdensome enforcement machinery to punish southern electoral fraud. Accordingly, some scholars critique the conventional end point of Reconstruction in 1876 as premature, since subsequent discussion of the Lodge Bill in 1890 suggests that Reconstruction enjoyed a longer life span.[49]

Despite the Lodge Bill's genuine potential to expand African American rights in the South, however, it was unlikely that even a vigorously enforced Lodge Bill could have wholly turned the tide of racial subordination there. Injecting heavy-handed federal coercive power into the states was a policy option foreclosed by earlier political developments; the Lodge Bill did not purport to challenge that settlement. For example, the bill lacked provisions for the assignment of federal troops or marshals to police the polls.[50] In addition, nothing in the 1890s provides clear evidence of significant political will, within the Republican Party or the larger polity, for a sustained federal effort to contest Democratic control of the polls (illegal or legal) in the South. Further, the Lodge Bill ultimately failed to pass in the Senate in 1891 because of both sustained filibustering by Democrats and a significant defection in the Republican ranks when the Silver Republicans sacrificed a chance to pass the bill to pursue a free-coinage bill.[51] That such a defection occurred suggests that the postenactment vitality of the Lodge Bill would be questionable.

---

[48] I draw on and paraphrase DeSantis's description of the bill. DeSantis, *Southern Question*, 198–99. See also Wang, *Trial*, 236–37; Michael Perman, *Struggle for Mastery: Disfranchisement in the South, 1888–1908* (Chapel Hill: University of North Carolina Press, 2001), 39–40.
[49] Wang, *Trial*, 249–52, 263; Hirshson, *Farewell*, 251–52.
[50] Perman, *Struggle*, 40.
[51] Hirshson, *Farewell*, 226–35; Perman, *Struggle*, 40–41; Wang, *Trial*, 241–49.

Furthermore, Republicans suffered losses in the 1890 election that some attributed to the bill, and Republicans also fared poorly in the 1892 elections in significant part because the Lodge Bill made an inviting target for the Democrats.[52] The Democratic victory in 1892 established the first unified Democratic government in the post–Civil War era, which in 1894 allowed Democrats to move to repeal some forty provisions of the Enforcement Acts.[53] Undoubtedly, an enacted Lodge Bill would have had some real effect in changing these electoral circumstances and perhaps could have prevented the rise of unified Democratic government after the 1892 elections. Yet these events do not suggest that the Lodge Bill embodied any realistic potential to push reform principles beyond the constraints imposed by judicial delimitation. Although an enacted Lodge Bill potentially could have prevented some of the worst abuses of Jim Crow for some length of time,[54] the transformative potential of an enacted bill was likely constrained from the start.

Whatever transformative potential that existed in the Court's defense of federal authority in *Yarbrough* and the proposals of the Lodge Bill (which did manage to pass the House), any opportunity for federal policing of southern elections ended with the bill's defeat in the Senate.[55] With this defeat, the uncertainties of post-Reconstruction politics were reduced. The Republican Party was moving on to other issues, namely economic ones. And after the 1896 election, it had found a way to break the legislative stalemate of the past two decades and win national elections without having to deal with the South.[56] Developmental alternatives had narrowed to the point where the South would now have a largely free path to articulate the terms of the post-Reconstruction racial order without even relatively minor interferences from the federal government, such as prosecutions or federal judicial policing of elections. However, before the era of construction drew to a close, the South would have to articulate this new order, and the Supreme Court would have to bless it.

---

[52] Hirshson, *Farewell*, 231, 244–46; Perman, *Struggle*, 31.
[53] Perman, *Struggle*, 21–22, 43–47; Wang, *Trial*, 254–59.
[54] Richard M. Valelly, "Partisan Entrepreneurship and Policy Windows: George Frisbie Hoar and the 1890 Federal Elections Bill," in *Formative Acts: American Politics in the Making*, eds. Stephen Skowronek and Matthew Glassman (Philadelphia: University of Pennsylvania Press, 2007), 139–43.
[55] In the aftermath of the failed Lodge Bill, *Yarbrough* would prove to be more a historical oddity rather than a direct challenge to the judicial delimitation of the 1870s (or even a toehold for a more limited judicial protection of African American voting rights). Smith, *Civic Ideals*, 384, 617n216.
[56] Perman, *Struggle*, 41; Valelly, *Two Reconstructions*, 134–39.

The Rise of Jim Crow

A number of important developments in southern state politics occurred in tandem with the events occurring at the federal level. And qualified uncertainties were evident in both policy arenas: although some aspects of racial subordination had already become entrenched at the state level prior to the last decades of the nineteenth century, other important areas remained contested until the 1890s. Because of the noninterference of the Republican Party and the federal government, these developments in the South came to dictate the substance of construction. This burst of southern lawmaking in the 1890s and the first decade of the twentieth century came to constitute the enduring recalibration of reform with respect to internal uncertainties.

Disfranchisement

Absent massive federal intervention, it is highly unlikely that fraud against southern African American voters could have been wholly eliminated. Such practices were widespread, and antipathy to African American voting was pervasive in certain areas.[57] Still, a degree of plurality existed with respect to African American voting practices in the South: scholars note that Hayes's withdrawal of federal troops in 1877 did not completely halt black suffrage. To the contrary, black turnout was still somewhat substantial through the 1880s. Kousser estimates that African American turnout for a group of southern gubernatorial contests in the 1880s ranged from 38 percent in an 1881 Mississippi election to 93 percent in an 1880 North Carolina election.[58] Similarly, Redding's and James's estimates for the 1880 presidential election show black voter turnout in the South ranging from 42 percent in Georgia (where a poll tax was in effect) to 84 percent in Florida. Also, Redding and James estimated a mean differential in white-black turnout – with respect to state mean voter turnouts – to be only 5 percent in 1880; the comparable value significantly increased to 32 percent in 1892, 38 percent in 1900, and 38 percent in 1912.[59] This implies that prior to the 1890s and the passage of disfranchisement laws, some possibility remained for preserving a noteworthy amount of

---

[57] Perman, *Struggle*, 38.
[58] J. Morgan Kousser, *The Shaping of Southern Politics: Suffrage Restriction and the Establishment of the One-Party South, 1880–1910* (New Haven, CT: Yale University Press, 1974), 28.
[59] Kent Redding and David R. James, "Estimating Levels and Modeling Determinants of Black and White Voter Turnout in the South, 1880 to 1912," *Historical Methods* 34, no. 4 (Fall 2001): 148. Some of this data is reproduced in Valelly, *Two Reconstructions*, 128.

black voting in the South.⁶⁰ Prior to the 1890s, no decisive recalibration of African American voting rights had been established.

Southern disfranchisement efforts changed this. These efforts began in the mid-1880s with Florida's enactment of a poll tax in 1885 and extended into the first decade of the twentieth century.⁶¹ A combination of racism and a desire for partisan control motivated white Southerners to employ techniques such as the poll tax, literacy tests, and residency requirements in these efforts.⁶² Specifically, the specter of continued African American voting prompted fears among white Democrats of "Negro Rule": if cleavages ever emerged among white constituencies, a voting bloc of African Americans could potentially become a critical swing constituency.⁶³ This particularly frightened white Democrats, as African Americans seemed unlikely to align with Democrats in the foreseeable future.⁶⁴

A progressive-reformist sensibility was an additional motivating factor behind disfranchisement efforts. The prospect of achieving African American disfranchisement, without the unsavory techniques of fraud and corruption (e.g., voter intimidation or ballot box stuffing) used in previous years, appealed to many southern politicians. Achieving the same outcome through state statutory or state constitutional enactments had the virtue of being simpler, easier, and more transparent to the polity.⁶⁵

---

⁶⁰ Kousser's data very strongly indicates that disfranchisement laws had an independent effect on suppressing African American voting, and were *not* merely ratifying a condition achieved prior to their passage. Kousser, *Southern Politics*, 240–46.
⁶¹ Ibid., 238.
⁶² Helpful overview charts of the disfranchisement techniques employed by the different states over time are at ibid., 239; Valelly, *Two Reconstructions*, 126.
⁶³ Perman, *Struggle*, 22–28; Joel Williamson, *The Crucible of Race: Black-White Relations in the American South since Emancipation* (New York: Oxford University Press, 1984), 230; C. Vann Woodward, *The Strange Career of Jim Crow* (New York: Oxford University Press, 1955, 2002), 83. Hence, the two most prominent works on black disfranchisement concur that the principal force behind the disfranchisement campaigns in the South – although it was of varying influence across the individual states – was Black Belt (i.e., wealthier, privileged) Democrats. Kousser, *Southern Politics*, 238, 246–47; Perman, *Struggle*, 324.
⁶⁴ Perman, *Struggle*, 33. Thus, the Populist threat cannot be credited as the proximate cause of the disfranchisement effort. When Populism took off in the 1890s, the threat posed by Populist-Republican fusion to the southern Democrats helped to spur disfranchisement efforts in a couple of southern states but not in all. Ibid., 31–33.
⁶⁵ Edward L. Ayers, *The Promise of the New South: Life after Reconstruction* (New York: Oxford University Press, 1992), 147; Kousser, *Southern Politics*, 260–61; Perman, *Struggle*, 14–16, 326–28; Williamson, *Crucible*, 229–30; Benno C. Schmidt, Jr., "Principle and Prejudice: The Supreme Court and Race in the Progressive Era, Part 3: Black Disfranchisement from the KKK to the Grandfather Clause," *Columbia Law Review* 82, no. 5 (June 1982): 842–43.

The Entrenchment and Maintenance of the Jim Crow Order

Mississippi created one of the more interesting southern disfranchisement schemes, which was notable for the breadth of its techniques, its relatively early enactment, and the fact that it was the subject of the Supreme Court's significant ruling on disfranchisement in *Williams v. Mississippi*. Under the "Mississippi Plan," a number of voting restrictions were enacted in 1890 as part of a new state constitution: (1) voters had to be registered by state officials and not by local or federal officials, where Republican influence might reside; (2) they had to be registered four months before the election; (3) there was a residency requirement of two years for the state and one year for the electoral district of the voter; (4) individuals could be disfranchised for being convicted of stereotypical "African American crimes" such as petty theft or arson; (5) the secret ballot was introduced; (6) potential voters had to have a record of being up-to-date on all taxes for the past two years, including a poll tax of two dollars; and (7) finally, potential voters were required to either read or, if they could not read, to "understand" a provision of the state constitution when read to them. The distinct benefit to disfranchisers of the "understanding test" was that it provided expansive administrative discretion for state officials to ascertain "understanding" and provided an easy means to exclude more educated African Americans while allowing illiterate whites to vote. This was a significant provision, since it was intended as a permanent loophole for all potential voters – specifically white voters – who might be disfranchised by the previous provisions.[66]

The effect of these suffrage restrictions was substantial. Comparing voter turnout between the 1888 and 1892 presidential elections in Mississippi, the percentage of nonvoting adult males increased from 56.7 percent in 1888 to 81.3 percent in 1892.[67] According to Kousser, the proportionate reduction of African American voter turnout in Mississippi between the 1888 and 1892 presidential elections was 69 percent.[68]

Segregation Statutes

As with disfranchisement, a degree of uncertainty existed in segregation practices at the state level. The possibility of an integrated utopia in the

---

[66] This summary is paraphrased and drawn from Ayers, *Promise*, 148–49; Kousser, *Southern Politics*, 143; Perman, *Struggle*, 83; Schmidt, "Black Disfranchisement," 845.
[67] Kousser, *Southern Politics*, 144.
[68] "Proportionate reduction" = (black turnout in 1888 – black turnout in 1892) / (black turnout in 1888). Kousser, *Southern Politics*, 241. Kousser provides a helpful summary chart of the negative effect of disfranchisement on voter turnout and opposition party strength across the southern states at ibid.

South was never a viable option absent a very vigorous federal intervention. After emancipation, segregation had quickly taken hold in many social contexts – including public schools. However, uncertainty persisted into the 1880s regarding segregation in other social contexts – especially railroad seating.[69] Thus, while there is scholarly debate over the amount of flux in southern race relations in the years immediately following emancipation, all agree that there was at least some degree of fluidity – especially with respect to social practices in public accommodations.[70] No comprehensive and regionally pervasive system of racial segregation, akin to the Jim Crow system of later decades, existed by the 1880s.

However, as southern states enacted segregation laws, possibilities for alternative developmental paths diminished. Reasons for this burst of lawmaking remain a matter of debate,[71] but the effect was clear. Between 1887 and 1891, nine southern states enacted segregation statutes for railroad travel, which typically mandated "separate but equal" seating coaches.[72]

Judicial Affirmation of Jim Crow

With the death of the Lodge Bill, federal enforcement efforts to protect African American voting rights winding down, and the Republican Party persistently unable to gain political traction in the South, southern state governments responded energetically. The result was the twin pillars of what we now know as the Jim Crow system: disfranchisement laws and segregation laws.

Yet before a political equilibrium could take hold, southern governments needed the affirmation of the Supreme Court. Without judicial endorsement, emerging political settlements would always remain vulnerable to subsequent challenges in the courts. Indeed in the 1890s,

---

[69] The assertion that a flux in southern race relations persisted into the 1880s is the "Woodward Thesis." Woodward, *Strange Career*. See also Ayers, *Promise*, 136–43.

[70] Howard N. Rabinowitz, "More Than the Woodward Thesis: Assessing the Strange Career of Jim Crow," *Journal of American History* 75, no. 3 (December 1988): 842–56; C. Vann Woodward, "Strange Career Critics: Long May They Persevere," *Journal of American History* 75, no. 3 (December 1988): 857–68; Ayers, *Promise*, 488n11; John W. Cell, *The Highest Stage of White Supremacy: The Origins of Segregation in South Africa and the American South* (New York: Cambridge University Press, 1982), 82–102.

[71] Rabinowitz, "Woodward Thesis," 849–50.

[72] Ayers, *Promise*, 137, 143–44; Perman, *Struggle*, 247–48.

Yarbrough and Strauder v. West Virginia[73] could have served as potent reminders to southern Democrats that the Supreme Court could, without warning, take a critical look at discriminatory southern laws and take action. However, in the 1890s the Supreme Court broadly and conclusively validated Jim Crow – bringing this era of construction and recaliberation to a close.

The Supreme Court partially validated Jim Crow in *Plessy v. Ferguson*.[74] At issue was the Louisiana railway segregation statute, which provided that "all railway companies carrying passengers . . . shall provide equal but separate accommodations for the white, and colored races."[75] The statute was challenged on both Thirteenth and Fourteenth Amendment grounds.[76]

Justice Brown, writing for seven justices – Harlan notably dissented, and Justice Brewer did not participate – quickly dispatched the Thirteenth Amendment challenge, reasoning that the Louisiana statute did not reinstitute slavery or impinge on the "legal equality of the two races."[77] More interesting was Brown's Fourteenth Amendment analysis: "The object of the [Fourteenth] amendment was undoubtedly to enforce the absolute equality of the two races before the law, but, in the nature of things, it could not have been intended to abolish distinctions based upon color, or to enforce social, as distinguished from political, equality, or a commingling of the two races upon terms unsatisfactory to either."[78] By distinguishing between political and social rights, the Court voiced a common legal categorization of rights from that era. If, as Brown argued, the Fourteenth Amendment only demanded political equality, the crucial question was: Where did railroad seating fall within this spectrum of rights? Was it within the purview of that amendment's equality guarantees?

The central holding of *Plessy* was that railroad seating was a matter of social rights.[79] This conclusion, combined with Brown's interpretation of the Fourteenth Amendment, seemingly suggested that *no* Fourteenth Amendment constraints existed with respect to Jim Crow legislation

---

[73] 100 U.S. 303 (1880).
[74] 163 U.S. 537 (1896).
[75] Id. at 540.
[76] Id. at 542.
[77] Id. at 542–43.
[78] Id. at 544.
[79] Id. On the Court's assertion of differential judicial treatment between political rights and social rights, see also id. at 545.

similarly confined to the social rights realm. That is, so long as state legislation steered clear of political or civil rights, there would seem to be no constitutional prohibition on "separate *and* unequal" statutes, or anything else aiming to subordinate African Americans within the "social" domain.[80] The Court, however, did not go that far. Along with its social rights conclusion, it added that segregation laws, even in the social rights context, would be subject to a requirement of "reasonableness" emanating from the Fourteenth Amendment.[81] Applying this constitutional test to the Louisiana statute, the Court concluded that the statute passed, and the Fourteenth Amendment challenge to it was defeated.[82]

As important as *Plessy*'s validation of segregation in railroad seating was, an equally, if not more important case in cementing the new Jim Crow order was *Williams v. Mississippi*, in which the Court validated southern disfranchisement efforts.[83] Judicial validation of excluding African Americans from the polity ensured that the core political supports of Jim Crow would remain firm and that African American political challenges on secondary matters such as segregation statutes could be structurally eliminated.

The *Williams* decision was not foreordained, at least as a matter of legal doctrine. In the case of *Yick Wo v. Hopkins*,[84] decided twelve years before *Williams*, the Court struck down a San Francisco ordinance that granted full discretion to a board of supervisors to determine whether to allow a laundry to operate if the laundry was housed in a wooden building. The Court viewed these ordinances as granting a "naked and arbitrary power" to the board of supervisors.[85] For this reason, the ordinance was held to violate the Fourteenth Amendment on its face.[86] Equally significant, however, was the Court's determination that the ordinance violated the Equal Protection Clause not just because of the mere possibility of discriminatory administration of the statute but also because the actual administration of the ordinance revealed an extremely

---

[80] See Benno C. Schmidt, Jr., "Principle and Prejudice: The Supreme Court and Race in the Progressive Era, Part 1: The Heyday of Jim Crow," *Columbia Law Review* 82, no. 3 (April 1982): 468–70.
[81] 163 U.S. at 550.
[82] Id. at 550–51.
[83] 170 U.S. 213 (1898).
[84] 118 U.S. 356 (1886).
[85] Id. at 366, 374.
[86] Id. at 369–73.

The Entrenchment and Maintenance of the Jim Crow Order 215

clear and systematic racial discrimination against Chinese laundry operators.[87]

Both aspects of the *Yick Wo* ruling potentially had bearing on aspects of the Mississippi disfranchisement plan.[88] Mississippi's "understanding test" did appear to call for arbitrary administrative discretion, and emphasizing actual, systematic discrimination in applying the suffrage restrictions was a plausible avenue of argument. However, when the Court confronted the Mississippi disfranchisement laws in *Williams v. Mississippi*,[89] it unanimously upheld them because they did not discriminate against African Americans on their face: "The operation of the constitution and laws is not limited by their language or effects to one race. They reach weak and vicious white men as well as weak and vicious black men, and whatever is sinister in their intention, if anything, can be prevented by both races by the exertion of that duty which voluntarily pays taxes and refrains from crime."[90] With respect to the relevance of the *Yick Wo* precedent, the Court distinguished the latter from the present case with little discussion; it seemingly skipped over the question of arbitrary administrative discretion provided for in the Mississippi laws. It also concluded that there was no showing that the administration of the disfranchisement laws was systematically racially discriminatory; the Court asserted that it had merely been shown that discriminatory administration was possible under them.[91] Finally, the Court concluded that evidence of a racially discriminatory intent behind the Mississippi suffrage restrictions was unimportant to the constitutional inquiry.[92]

The decisive affirmation of Jim Crow in *Williams* set the tone for future Supreme Court cases. Five years later in *Giles v. Harris*,[93] the Court confronted Fourteenth and Fifteenth Amendment challenges by an African American man to the disfranchisement scheme of Alabama embodied in its state constitution.[94] The Court determined that the suit in equity brought by the African American plaintiff – which sought a judicial ruling to compel his registration and the registration of other African

---

[87] Id. at 373.
[88] Michael J. Klarman, *From Jim Crow to Civil Rights: The Supreme Court and the Struggle for Racial Equality* (New York: Oxford University Press, 2004), 35–36.
[89] 170 U.S. 213 (1898).
[90] Id. at 222.
[91] Id. at 223–225; Klarman, *Jim Crow*, 35–36.
[92] 170 U.S. at 222, 223.
[93] 189 U.S. 475 (1903).
[94] Id. at 482.

Americans to vote in Alabama – could not be maintained in the federal courts.[95] Holmes, writing for the Court, pointed to two considerations that made this case inappropriate for an equitable remedy (and which thus undermined the appropriateness of federal jurisdiction in this case). First, in an extremely perverse kind of logic, Holmes noted that even if the Alabama scheme were unconstitutional, registering the African American plaintiff would still not be appropriate:

> The plaintiff alleges that the whole registration scheme of the Alabama constitution is a fraud upon the Constitution of the United States, and asks us to declare it void. But, of course, he could not maintain a bill for a mere declaration in the air. He does not try to do so, but asks to be registered as a party qualified under the void instrument. If, then, we accept the conclusion which it is the chief purpose of the bill to maintain, how can we make the court a party to the unlawful scheme by accepting it and adding another voter to its fraudulent lists?
>
> ...
>
> If the sections of the Constitution concerning registration were illegal in their inception, it would be a new doctrine in constitutional law that the original invalidity could be cured by an administration which defeated their intent.[96]

Second, in an equally striking comment pleading judicial impotence, Holmes emphasized the inappropriateness of an equitable remedy on pure pragmatic grounds, namely that the Court by itself could not right the legal wrongs of Jim Crow:

> Unless we are prepared to supervise the voting in that State by officers of the court, it seems to us that all that the plaintiff could get from equity would be an empty form. Apart from damages to the individual, relief from a great political wrong, if done, as alleged, by the people of a State and the State itself, must be given by them or by the legislative and political department of the government of the United States.[97]

The political significance of this remarkably candid opinion lay in the fact that it left very little doubt about the Court's orientation toward Jim Crow disfranchisement: the latter was conclusively affirmed by the Court in *Giles*.

---

[95] Id. at 486.
[96] Id. at 486–87.
[97] Id. at 488. The analytical gymnastics of Holmes's first point were replicated in Justice Day's opinion for the Court in *Giles v. Teasley*, 193 U.S. 146 (1904). Here again, the Court stretched to deny judicial relief for Alabama's disfranchisement scheme.

PART II: THE MAINTENANCE OF JIM CROW

Two Tension-Management Principles

Even after construction has concluded, conflict and tensions will inevitably arise with respect to the integrity and coherence of the newly entrenched formal boundaries between competing authorities and rights. The subsequent period of political equilibrium and normal politics is characterized not by the absence of political conflict, but by the *containment* of conflict within those boundaries. "Boundary tensions" can arise in at least two contexts. First, they may appear in those contexts where newly resurgent values unsettle the existing boundaries between competing rights and authorities. Second, they may arise when largely new policy and legal problems emerge.

In the present case, it is not difficult to discern where the most obvious threats to Jim Crow could have arisen after it had been entrenched and validated by the Court in *Plessy*, *Williams*, and *Giles*. The Jim Crow compromise already embodied a concession to the equality demands of Reconstruction reforms by encompassing a requirement of formal legal equality regarding race. If political circumstances were to later arise leading to a resurgence of egalitarian values, which might push beyond mere formal equality, such circumstances could create internal conflict for the Jim Crow system. Alternatively, and perhaps less obviously, if tangential values unrelated to race or federalism ever were to intrude on the Jim Crow compromise – prompting the rise of new policy considerations and controversies – such a development might also destabilize the delicate compromise embodied within Jim Crow between the southern desire for racial subordination and the continuing federal commitment to a formal racial equality.

The Court was indeed confronted by both kinds of tension in subsequent years, and the two doctrinal standards it latched on to in response, as a means of managing these tensions, were both present in the *Plessy* ruling. Even though tension management was very likely not a goal of the original authors of these legal standards, the Court nevertheless utilized them for this purpose. The first tension-management idea was the tripartite categorization of rights. Recall Justice Brown's emphasis on a dichotomy between political and social rights in the *Plessy* case.[98] The second idea was relatively subdued in the opinion, but it is the main principle

---

[98] 163 U.S. 537, 544 (1896).

for which the case is famous, and it is synonymous with the Jim Crow order itself: the separate but equal standard.

Judicial Tension Management, Case 1: Residential Segregation

The first residential segregation ordinance was passed in Baltimore in 1910. It was followed by similar ordinances in a number of southern cities very shortly afterward – particularly in the border states.[99] The impetus for these laws was the migration of African Americans from the rural South to the urban South and urban North. This migration resulted in a heightened demand for housing among African Americans, which in turn often resulted in a push into white neighborhoods.[100] These ordinances came in three varieties. They "(1) prohibited whites from moving to [all-African American] blocks and [African Americans] from moving to all-white blocks; (2) divided the city into segregated districts and designated a district for each race; or (3) restricted new residences in mixed blocks to the racial group which had established most of the residences on the block."[101] Thus, a new societal circumstance had prompted a new type of policy – and a new extension of Jim Crow.

Yet this was not an unproblematic extension of Jim Crow. These laws also implicated and infringed on property rights at a time when such rights enjoyed considerable support on the Court. How the intersection of race, property, and the larger Jim Crow system could be reconciled in a manner that preserved the integrity of the latter was the key question for the Court when these ordinances were challenged. The Court accomplished this task, however, by turning to the tension-management possibilities inherent in the tripartite categorization of rights.

The Tripartite Categorization of Rights

Justice Brown's differentiation of rights in his *Plessy* ruling was rooted in an axiom of Civil War era–thought that conceptualized individual rights as falling within one of three categories: civil rights, political rights, or

---

[99] Klarman, *Jim Crow*, 79; David E. Bernstein, "Philip Sober Controlling Philip Drunk: *Buchanan v. Warley* in Historical Perspective," *Vanderbilt Law Review* 51, no. 4 (May 1998): 835; Schmidt, "Heyday," 499.

[100] Klarman, *Jim Crow*, 79; Michael J. Klarman, "Race and the Court in the Progressive Era," *Vanderbilt Law Review* 51, no. 4 (May 1998): 902–03, 902n107 (1998); Schmidt, "Heyday," 500.

[101] Bernstein, "Philip Sober," 835–36.

social rights.[102] At their core, these rights could be distinguished as follows. Civil rights encompassed those rights at the core of civil society relationships; they encompassed all the fundamental privileges enjoyed by all nonslave individuals. Thus, the paradigmatic civil rights were those articulated in the 1866 Civil Rights Act.[103] They included the right "to make and enforce contracts, to sue, be parties, and give evidence, to inherit, purchase, lease, sell, hold, and convey real and personal property," and, more generally, the right "to the full and equal benefit of all laws and proceedings for the security of person and property."[104] The paradigmatic political right was the right to vote.[105] And finally, social rights were thought to embody those aspects of society that touched on private associations or social interactions.[106]

Up to a point, categorizing individual rights was relatively free of ambiguities. The proper categorization of a given activity within this scheme was clear if the practice lay close to the core of one of the three categories. And in terms of the legal protections afforded each type of right, there was seemingly legal and political consensus that the Fifteenth Amendment protected political rights, the Fourteenth Amendment protected *at least* civil rights, and social rights were not protected by any of the Reconstruction Amendments.[107]

Beyond these matters, however, the tripartite framework was riddled with ambiguity. A degree of uncertainty existed, for example, with respect to the proper dividing line between the Fourteenth and Fifteenth Amendments regarding certain practices such as jury discrimination.[108] More

---

[102] Harold M. Hyman and William M. Wiecek, *Equal Justice Under Law* (New York: Harper & Row, 1982), 396; Michael W. McConnell, "Originalism and the Desegregation Decisions," *Virginia Law Review* 81, no. 4 (May 1995): 1016, 1024; Mark Tushnet, "The Politics of Equality in Constitutional Law: The Equal Protection Clause, Dr. Du Bois, and Charles Hamilton Houston," *Journal of American History* 74, no. 3 (December 1987): 886.
[103] McConnell, "Originalism," 1024, 1027; Tushnet, "Politics of Equality," 886–87.
[104] Civil Rights Act of 1866, ch. 31, § 1, 14 Stat. 27, 27 (1866).
[105] Tushnet, "Politics of Equality," 886.
[106] Hyman and Wiecek, *Justice*, 396; McConnell, "Originalism," 1017; Tushnet, "Politics of Equality," 886.
[107] Alfred Avins, "Social Equality and the Fourteenth Amendment: The Original Understanding," *Houston Law Review* 4, no. 4 (Spring 1967): 640–56; McConnell, "Originalism," 1017.
[108] Tushnet, "Politics of Equality," 887, 888, 890. The question persists in the present day. See Vikram D. Amar, "Jury Service as Political Participation Akin to Voting," *Cornell Law Review* 80, no. 2 (1995): 203–59 (conceptualizing jury discrimination as a violation of Fifteenth Amendment political rights of potential jurors to serve on juries).

generally, there were questions as to whether the protections of a certain category of rights logically implied the protection of other categories. For example, a common mode of attack for opponents of Reconstruction legislation was to claim that the provisions ensuring civil and political equality, such as the Fourteenth and Fifteenth Amendments, would logically lead to the (undesirable) specter of social equality across the races.[109]

Most interesting for the present argument, there was also ambiguity with respect to certain social practices that could conceivably fall on either side of the line between social and civil rights.[110] There was vigorous debate, for example, over whether prohibiting segregation in public accommodations in the Civil Rights Act of 1875 was a matter that fell on the civil or social side of the divide.[111] The Court in *Plessy* had held, as we have seen, that segregated railroad seating implicated social rights only and *not* civil rights. But this point was not uncontested on the Court. In Justice Harlan's dissent, he argued that the Louisiana statute infringed on civil rights instead.[112]

The tripartite framework was clearly not created to serve a tension-management function. Yet the considerable ambiguities that resided within it allowed judicial actors to use the framework to manage boundary tensions. Depending on how certain social practices were categorized, the Court could justify judicial intervention or nonintervention – while staying within the categorical framework and the larger doctrinal framework of Jim Crow – by simply making a judgment call on how to categorize a given practice. For those issues or social practices for which institutional weight and popular support for Jim Crow principles remained considerable and unchallenged, the move would be to label such items as matters of "social rights" less deserving of judicial protection. Conversely, and more importantly, where institutional and popular pressures pushed particularly hard for racially egalitarian outcomes, the Jim Crow order might be maintained by the judiciary bending toward accommodation and categorizing the latter practices as civil or political rights. Doing so would allow for these practices to be judicially protected without having to call into question the fundamental governing and legal principles of Jim Crow. The delicate compromise between national and

---

[109] Avins, "Social Equality," 642–45.
[110] McConnell, "Originalism," 1017; Reva B. Siegel, "Why Equal Protection No Longer Protects: The Evolving Forms of Status-Enforcing State Action," *Stanford Law Review* 49, no. 5 (May 1997): 1123; Tushnet, "Politics of Equality," 888.
[111] Avins, "Social Equality," 645–55.
[112] 163 U.S. 537, 560–62 (1896) (Harlan, J., dissenting).

state authority – upon which the Jim Crow system had been built – could be preserved and maintained even when new circumstances and new policy problems arose to put pressure on that compromise.[113]

Buchanan v. Warley. At issue in *Buchanan* was a Louisville, Kentucky, city ordinance, approved in 1914, that made it illegal for African Americans to move into majority-white-occupied city blocks and made it illegal for whites to move into majority-black-occupied city blocks (although the ordinance did not purport to affect preexisting residential arrangements).[114] Thus, the ordinance exhibited the formal symmetry and equality of Jim Crow laws. It was subsequently challenged on Fourteenth Amendment grounds "in that it abridges the privileges and immunities of citizens of the United States to acquire and enjoy property, takes property without due process of law, and denies equal protection of the laws."[115]

---

[113] Conceptualizing the tripartite framework of rights in this manner aligns in some respects with an important argument put forth by Reva Siegel; she has also emphasized the political developmental importance of the tripartite framework in the post-Reconstruction era – although in a somewhat different manner than I do. For her, the framework's historical significance stemmed from the analytical tools it provided conservatives in their quest to perpetuate the subordination of African Americans. As Siegel notes, an important recurring justification used by judicial actors to reach results that were both unfriendly to African American interests and aligned with Jim Crow principles was the move of categorizing a contested practice or context as a matter of social rights, and thus beyond the reach of the Fourteenth Amendment. Siegel, "Equal Protection," 1121–29.

Siegel is correct to emphasize the possibilities for reinforcing racial subordination that were inherent in the tripartite framework, and indeed, my argument clearly builds upon her work. But I would claim that she is only half right. A tension-management standard is also defined as such by its capacity to accommodate and reflect the pull of institutional authorities that stand in *opposition* to the reigning order. Indeed, it is this dual orientation, and its facilitation of accommodation, that distinguishes a tension-management standard from other modes of adjudication. The interpretation of the tripartite framework that I offer assumes that racially egalitarian results can emanate from the framework. And indeed, the case of *Buchanan v. Warley* itself would be evidence on this point. 245 U.S. 60 (1917).

Siegel also discusses *Buchanan* briefly. She seems to view this case as merely implicating a practice that resisted easy categorization as a social right, as a legal-conceptual matter. Siegel, "Equal Protection," 1127. As I note later, Siegel seems to fall among the group of scholars who view *Buchanan* as an "easy case." However, such an interpretation of *Buchanan* seems incorrect to me. Furthermore, this interpretation would also seem to cut against Siegel's own arguments and evidence that point to the politically contested nature of the tripartite framework itself – where, for her, the primary forces responsible for categorizing a given social practice within a given category of rights are political and not conceptual.

[114] 245 U.S. at 70–72.
[115] Id. at 72.

This was a fortuitous moment in history for proponents of racial egalitarianism to challenge such a law in the courts; the judicial commitment to property rights was substantial at this time. To be sure, the *Lochner*[116] vision of judicial activism in defense of economic rights had suffered some defeats prior to, and at the same time as, *Buchanan*. *Muller v. Oregon*[117] had upheld a maximum-hours law for female workers nine years earlier, and *Bunting v. Oregon*[118] had upheld a maximum-hours law for females and males the same year as *Buchanan*. Lochnerism was coming under an increasingly strong intellectual attack as well.[119] But the judicial commitment to economic rights – and property rights specifically – was still quite alive after its growth in the earliest years of the twentieth century, and it would later ratchet upward in the 1920s.[120]

The intersection of race and property rights in the residential segregation ordinances posed a particularly interesting problem for judicial order maintenance once these statutes were challenged. Jim Crow commitments to racial subordination, which enjoyed near-unquestioned dominance at this time, would have pushed toward upholding the ordinance. Pushing against this, however, was the pull of the judicial commitment to property rights rooted in *Lochner* era principles.

Ultimately, Justice Day's opinion for a unanimous Court[121] held the statute to be unconstitutional – an unusual result, to be sure, in the middle of the Jim Crow Era. Beyond just the result of the ruling, *how* the ruling was achieved is notable. Although Day did not exhaustively discuss the tripartite framework of rights, it was nevertheless clear that the Court's holding relied on that framework. It was the Court's implicit assumption of a distinction between civil and social rights – and the differential protection each category of rights was accordingly entitled to – that allowed it to strike down this ordinance without directly challenging Jim Crow itself.

The Court's reliance on the tripartite framework can be gleaned in the extended discourse it offered on the fundamental status of property rights. If the *Plessy* Court had dismissed the matter of railroad seating

---

[116] *Lochner v. New York*, 198 U.S. 45 (1905).
[117] 208 U.S. 412 (1908).
[118] 243 U.S. 426 (1917).
[119] Bernstein, "Philip Sober," 841–42; Schmidt, "Heyday," 521.
[120] Klarman, *Jim Crow*, 80–82; James W. Ely, Jr., "Reflections on *Buchanan v. Warley*, Property Rights, and Race," *Vanderbilt Law Review* 51, no. 4 (May 1998): 954; Schmidt, "Heyday," 456.
[121] Schmidt does note, however, that Justice Holmes did come close to dissenting. Schmidt, "Heyday," 511–17.

The Entrenchment and Maintenance of the Jim Crow Order 223

as a mere matter of social rights, the *Buchanan* Court viewed property as implicating rights of a whole different sort. Day's opinion began by conceding that the state possessed broad authority under its police power to protect the public welfare.[122] Presumably, in the present case, the Louisville ordinance would serve this purpose by tending "to promote the public peace by preventing racial conflicts; that it tends to maintain racial purity; that it prevents the deterioration of property owned and occupied by white people, which deterioration, it is contended, is sure to follow the occupancy of adjacent premises by persons of color."[123] But municipal legislation could not run afoul of constitutional guarantees, and the right of property was a particularly prominent constitutional guarantee:

The Fourteenth Amendment protects life, liberty, and property from invasion by the States without due process of law. Property is more than the mere thing which a person owns. It is elementary that it includes the right to acquire, use, and dispose of it. The Constitution protects these essential attributes of property.[124]

Between state police power and property rights, Day gave a strong indication from the start that the property rights of African Americans would prevail. He did so by locating support for that right in the paradigmatic sources of constitutional protection for the *civil* rights of African Americans: the Fourteenth Amendment and the Civil Rights Act of 1866. Thus, among other things, Day quoted the following key clause from the 1866 Civil Rights Act: "All citizens of the United States shall have the same right in every State and Territory, as is enjoyed by white citizens thereof to inherit, purchase, lease, sell, hold, and convey real and personal property."[125]

Although employing other quotations as well, the thrust of the argument is apparent. Even if Jim Crow laws could regulate matters in the realm of social rights, property was clearly more than a matter of social rights:

The statute of 1866, originally passed under sanction of the Thirteenth Amendment and practically re-enacted after the adoption of the Fourteenth Amendment expressly provided that all citizens of the United States in any State shall have the same right to purchase property as is enjoyed by white citizens. Colored persons are citizens of the United States and have the right to purchase property and enjoy and use the same without laws discriminating against them solely on account of

---

[122] 245 U.S. 60, 74 (1917).
[123] Id. at 73–74.
[124] Id. at 74.
[125] Id. at 78.

color. *These enactments did not deal with the social rights of men, but with those fundamental rights in property which it was intended to secure upon the same terms to citizens of every race and color.* The Fourteenth Amendment and these statutes enacted in furtherance of its purpose operate to qualify and entitle a colored man to acquire property without state legislation discriminating against him solely because of color.[126]

The Court reinforced the point in its subsequent discussion of *Plessy* and *Berea College v. Kentucky*[127] – the latter of which upheld, in a narrow manner, a Kentucky segregation statute in education against a challenge by an integrated private college. These cases were distinguished from the present case because, for the Court, the segregation ordinances in *Plessy* and *Berea College* did not encompass a racial exclusion in the same sense as the Louisville residential ordinance.[128] The former two cases were also judged to be distinct because the Louisville ordinance involved a racial exclusion with respect to property.[129] Thus, the Court approvingly quoted the following passage from *Carey v. City of Atlanta*,[130] a ruling by the Supreme Court of Georgia that dealt with the comparison between a residential segregation ordinance and the *Plessy* and *Berea College* rulings:

In each instance the complaining person was afforded the opportunity to ride, or to attend institutions of learning, or afforded the thing of whatever nature to which in the particular case he was entitled. The most that was done was to require him as a member of a class to conform with reasonable rules in regard to the separation of the races. *In none of them was he denied the right to use, control, or dispose of his property, as in this case. Property of a person, whether as a member of a class or as an individual, cannot be taken without due process of law.*

...

The effect of the ordinance under consideration was not merely to regulate a business or the like, *but was to destroy the right of the individual to acquire, enjoy, and dispose of his property.* Being of this character, it was void as being opposed to the due-process clause of the constitution.[131]

Summing up, the Court again noted in conclusion that "the case presented does not deal with an attempt to prohibit the amalgamation of the

---

[126] Id. at 78–79 (citations omitted) (emphasis added).
[127] 211 U.S. 45 (1908).
[128] 245 U.S. at 79.
[129] Id. at 79–80.
[130] 84 S.E. 456 (Ga. 1915).
[131] 245 U.S. at 80 (citations omitted) (emphasis added).

races."¹³² Rather, "the right which the ordinance annulled was the civil right of a white man to dispose of his property if he saw fit to do so to a person of color and of a colored person to make such disposition to a white person."¹³³ The Court thus struck the ordinance down.

Buchanan *as Tension Management*

There are at least two ways to understand the Court's actions in *Buchanan*. One interpretation is that the residential segregation ordinances represented a core violation of the Fourteenth Amendment, and as a result, *Buchanan* was an "easy" case that allowed the Court to give voice to the continuing validity of Reconstruction. Indeed, as suggested in Day's opinion itself, the ordinance quite clearly touched on property rights, which was a core civil right, and the ordinance was thus unambiguously within the ambit of the Civil Rights Act of 1866 and the Fourteenth Amendment. Even if the right to own property for African Americans was not wholly undermined by the Louisville ordinance, the fact did remain that, as Klarman argues, property rights were implicated in this statute – and property lay at the core of Fourteenth Amendment guarantees.¹³⁴ This is a reasonable distinction to draw between *Buchanan* on the one hand – where segregation was struck down by the Court – and cases such as *Plessy* and *Berea College* on the other – which implicated rights in public transportation and education, respectively, and where segregation was upheld.

However, one difficulty with this interpretation is that it minimizes the conceptual flexibility and fuzziness surrounding the Court's determination that a given social practice implicated civil or social rights. One can easily imagine different categorizations of the various social practices discussed here. In an alternative universe, for example, both *Plessy* and *Berea College* could plausibly have been characterized as fundamentally about economic relationships and thus within the core ambit of the Fourteenth Amendment's protection of civil rights. At least as a conceptual matter, one can imagine an argument that African American passengers' economic relationship with the railroad company was being infringed on with a segregated seating statute in *Plessy*, and that students' economic

---

¹³² Id. at 81.
¹³³ Id.
¹³⁴ Klarman, "Progressive Era," 937. See also Klarman, *Jim Crow*, 79–80. *Buchanan*-as-an-easy-case is also how I interpret Siegel's comments on this case. Siegel, "Equal Protection," 1127.

relationship with their private college was being infringed on with a segregation statute in education in *Berea College*.[135] The 1866 Civil Rights Act did, after all, specifically encompass "the right to make and enforce contracts" and the right to "convey real and personal property."[136]

Similarly, although state laws prohibiting interracial marriage were upheld because they were judged to implicate only social rights of association, both Siegel and Tushnet note that it would not have been conceptually difficult for judicial actors – if they were so inclined – to conclude that these laws instead implicated the civil right of contract, and were thus subject to the Fourteenth Amendment's protections.[137] If judicial actors could so easily conclude that transportation, education, and marriage were all contexts comfortably within the realm of social rights – despite plausible arguments to the contrary – it is not difficult to imagine that a Supreme Court could have similarly moved in a more conservative direction in *Buchanan* and could have found laws regulating residence a matter of social rather than civil rights. Again, the fact that the Louisville ordinance did not wholly deprive African Americans of property rights, combined with the apparent flexibility involved in the judicial categorization of rights, suggests that *Buchanan*'s result was not logically or legally compelled by the Fourteenth Amendment. Tushnet correctly notes that "the animating purpose of the Reconstruction Amendments, at its bare minimum, was to eliminate disabilities imposed solely on African-Americans. Once again, then, the ordinance in *Buchanan* was not 'so obviously unconstitutional' that anyone with the most minimal commitment to the Constitution would have to find it unconstitutional."[138]

If we resist the notion that *Buchanan* was a conceptually "easy" case, there is a second interpretation: that the outcome and mode of reasoning displayed in the *Buchanan* opinion stemmed from both the Court's commitment to the protection of economic rights in the *Lochner* era and its concern with stabilizing and maintaining the boundaries that constituted

---

[135] Tushnet, "Politics of Equality," 888. Berea College had argued in its defense that a private school "stands upon exactly the same footing as any other private business." Schmidt, "Heyday," 447–48. With respect to railroad segregation, Ayers notes that at least some southern railroads were quite ambivalent about enforcing segregation due to the threat of being sued and the expense of having to run additional cars. Ayers, *Promise*, 143.

[136] § 1, 14 Stat. at 27.

[137] Siegel, "Equal Protection," 1121–23; Mark V. Tushnet, "Progressive Era Race Relations Cases in Their 'Traditional' Context," *Vanderbilt Law Review* 51, no. 4 (May 1998): 998.

[138] Ibid.

Jim Crow governance. With respect to the influence of economic rights considerations on the Court, there is seemingly near-uniform academic agreement that the influence of *Lochner* was, at the least, a major factor in dictating the liberal outcome of this case. This is not surprising given the heavy textual emphasis on the property theme in *Buchanan*.[139]

With respect to the influence of stability and tension-managing concerns, this is best evidenced by the fact that the Court supported property rights while also emphasizing continuity between its ruling and the legal standards of Jim Crow.[140] This continuity, and the Court's accommodation of property rights, was provided by the tripartite categorization of rights – and more specifically, by the conceptual fuzziness and flexibility of the categorical distinctions between civil and social rights. Since the Court wished to merely "bend" the Jim Crow system to accommodate the judiciary's skepticism toward residential segregation ordinances – without challenging Jim Crow directly – some means had to be devised by which segregation would be prohibited in this particular case without being similarly challenged in other social contexts. The categorical distinction of rights within the tripartite framework precisely allowed the Jim Crow order to bend in this case; the Court accommodated a pro-integration ruling in the property rights context by concluding that residential segregation ordinances implicated a "civil right" worthy of judicial intervention. At the same time, the Court left untouched the remainder of the prosegregation governing structure of Jim Crow by implying that other segregated social practices fell within the domain of mere "social rights."

It is this seamless integration of the ruling within Jim Crow legal principles that is the strongest evidence of the Court's concern with stability. Notwithstanding its liberal outcome, the *Buchanan* ruling was, in its orientation, concerned with preserving Jim Crow governing principles. Indeed, this point is underscored in terms of social effects as well: after *Buchanan*, residential segregation persisted through, among other things, individual racially restrictive covenants – which survived an NAACP challenge in 1926.[141] Both *Brown v. Board of Education*[142] and the civil rights movement were still very much in the future.

---

[139] Klarman, *Jim Crow*, 80–82; Bernstein, "Philip Sober," 872–73; Schmidt, "Heyday," 456, 518–19.

[140] Schmidt, "Heyday," 521. See also Schmidt, "Black Disfranchisement," 904.

[141] Klarman, *Jim Crow*, 90–93; Bernstein, "Philip Sober," 864; Schmidt, "Heyday," 521, 522–24. The case was *Corrigan v. Buckley*, 271 U.S. 323 (1926).

[142] 347 U.S. 483 (1954).

Judicial Tension Management, Case 2: Separate but Equal in Higher Education

By its own terms, the separate but equal standard was a compromise standard and was thus an ideal doctrinal tool for judicial actors to employ in managing tensions. On the one hand, the standard's concession to separation reflected the pull of racial subordination. On the other, the standard's concessions to both a guarantee of access for African Americans, and racial equality in a formal sense, reflected the pull of Reconstruction reforms.[143]

Whether this separate but equal standard was actually going to be employed in a manner similar to the tripartite framework of rights – to mediate between conflicting authorities and rights – remained unsettled for a time. Separate but equal accommodations did not live up to the "equality" requirement in practice, of course,[144] which would suggest skepticism that this doctrinal rule could further racially egalitarian goals.

Further, the question of whether the "equality" component of the separate but equal standard would even serve as a durable legal requirement at all was not immediately apparent after the *Plessy* ruling. As noted earlier, the separate but equal standard had found its way into the *Plessy* ruling only because the Louisiana state legislature had written it into the segregation law at issue in that case; all that the Court had seemingly announced for matters of social rights was a "rule of reasonableness" requirement. Thus, at least up through *Plessy*, the separate but equal standard did not have the clear markings of a viable tension-managing tool. This changed, however, in 1914 with the *McCabe* ruling.

McCabe v. Atchison

In *McCabe v. Atchison, Topeka, & Santa Fe Railway Company*,[145] the equality component of the separate but equal standard was finally judicially validated as a constitutional requirement. At issue was Oklahoma's Separate Coach Law that provided for separate and equal railway coaches for whites and African Americans.[146] Section 7 of the law was noteworthy, which the Court described as follows: "It was further provided that nothing contained in the act should be construed to prevent railway

---

[143] Ayers, *Promise*, 144 ("Laws demanding separate cars seemed a compromise between white sensibilities and black rights."). See also ibid., 144–46.
[144] Ibid., 145–46; Schmidt, "Heyday," 472–77.
[145] 235 U.S. 151 (1914).
[146] Id. at 158.

companies 'from hauling sleeping cars, dining or chair cars attached to their trains to be used exclusively by either white or negro passengers, separately but not jointly' (Section 7)."[147] This provision departed from the separate but equal standard: it would have allowed for railway companies to provide only white sleeping or dining cars and no African American cars. There were reasons why railway companies might favor such a law beyond mere racism. The lower court in this case, the attorney general of the state of Oklahoma, and the defendant railway companies all noted that the demand for these "luxury" sleeping and dining cars could very well be limited among African American consumers; providing equal facilities for both races could be an inefficient business practice.[148]

Hughes wrote for the Court in ultimately ruling against the complaining parties and denying relief on procedural grounds because of the absence of a ripe controversy.[149] More important, however, he concluded that Section 7 was unconstitutional. Hughes asserted that concerns about demand and efficiency were constitutionally irrelevant. Speaking in a principled tone, he emphasized the individual rights that were sacrificed by this law:

This argument with respect to volume of traffic seems to us to be without merit. It makes the constitutional right depend upon the number of persons who may be discriminated against, whereas the essence of the constitutional right is that it is a personal one. Whether or not particular facilities shall be provided may doubtless be conditioned upon there being a reasonable demand therefor, but, if facilities are provided, substantial equality of treatment of persons traveling under like conditions cannot be refused. It is the individual who is entitled to the equal protection of the laws, and if he is denied by a common carrier, acting in the matter under the authority of a state law, a facility or convenience in the course of his journey which under substantially the same circumstances is furnished to another traveler, he may properly complain that his constitutional privilege has been invaded.[150]

Again, the significance of *McCabe* was that it marked the first time that the Court gave weight to the equality half of the separate but equal standard.[151] Schmidt thus views this case as "a challenge to the entire structure of Jim Crow law built up since the 1880's" and "the beginnings

---
[147] Id.
[148] Id. at 160–61.
[149] Id. at 162–64.
[150] Id. at 161–62.
[151] Schmidt, "Heyday," 492–93.

of corrosion in the constitutional mandate for racial separation."[152] This is likely an overstatement, which Schmidt himself acknowledges as a possibility.[153] Notwithstanding *McCabe*'s support for racial equality, Jim Crow lived on for another four decades. Schmidt might have thought it inevitable that the Court's acceptance of racial equality in this case would eventually necessitate a frontal assault on Jim Crow at some later date, but given the extended life of Jim Crow after this ruling, it seems clear that legal and political orders need not be so principled and conceptually coherent. Contrary to Schmidt's interpretation, *McCabe*'s validation of the separate but equal principle likely had the opposite effect: with this ruling and with the newly established potential of the separate but equal standard to accommodate racially egalitarian impulses, the Court now enjoyed another analytical tool with which to manage boundary tensions within the Jim Crow system, should egalitarian values become resurgent within certain social contexts. If the Court wished to give weight to egalitarian values within a given context, but without repudiating Jim Crow, it need only read the "equality" component of the separate but equal compromise more robustly (or do the opposite if it were not so inclined). Egalitarian values did eventually enjoy such a resurgence beginning in the New Deal era, and the tension-managing potential of the separate but equal standard was subsequently demonstrated.

The Resurgence of Racial Egalitarianism

By the later New Deal era, signs of progress toward racial equality were present. Although there was no fundamental turn against Jim Crow at this time, the symbolic inclusion of African Americans within the New Deal coalition – reflected both in their formal inclusion in New Deal programs and in the prominence afforded to supporters of African American rights, including Harold Ickes and Eleanor Roosevelt – helped create a more open and hospitable environment for such goals. In 1940, an important victory for African American rights occurred with Roosevelt's creation of the Fair Employment Practices Commission, which undertook remedial action against racial discrimination in employment in the defense industries. Related to these shifts was the growing strategic value of African American votes as swing votes in the North because of the Great Migration from the South. African American interests seemingly enjoyed a

---

[152] Ibid., 492.
[153] Ibid., 494.

The Entrenchment and Maintenance of the Jim Crow Order 231

more sympathetic reception from certain sectors of elite opinion, including Supreme Court justices.[154]

But even larger changes were afoot in the post–World War II era. First, the dynamics pushing in favor of African American rights in the late 1930s were also present in the late 1940s and early 1950s, although they were even more significant during these later years. Continued African American migration to the North – because of the war – only added to their growing importance as a swing-voting constituency. Civil rights were accordingly a significant concern for both Democrats and Republicans in the 1948 election, and Truman moved to desegregate the military by executive order that year.[155] Sympathy for African American rights among elites, already present to some extent in the late 1930s, continued to grow.[156] In addition, the cause of African American rights was aided by an entirely new circumstance: the Cold War. U.S. foreign policy considerations in countering Soviet propaganda – regarding American racism – in Third World Nations made it crucial for federal governmental actors to address southern racial practices.[157] This foreign policy interest was particularly evident in the Truman Justice Department's amicus brief for two cases: *McLaurin v. Oklahoma State Regents*[158] and *Sweatt v. Painter*.[159] The Justice Department's involvement here marked the first time it intervened in a school segregation case, and its brief pushed in favor of desegregation by urging the Court to consider the negative foreign policy implications of segregation.[160]

***Gaines* and *Sweatt* as Tension Management.** With egalitarian values resurgent in the broader polity, the Jim Crow legal order would not endure by standing still. For a judiciary inclined to stabilize and maintain

---

[154] Klarman, *Jim Crow*, 100–01, 110–15, 151, 179; Alan Brinkley, *The End of Reform: New Deal Liberalism in Recession and War* (New York: Vintage Books, 1996), 167; David M. Kennedy, *Freedom from Fear: The American People in Depression and War, 1929–1945* (New York: Oxford University Press, 1999), 767–68.

[155] Klarman, *Jim Crow*, 178–81; Michael Barone, *Our Country: The Shaping of America from Roosevelt to Reagan* (New York: Free Press, 1990), 215; James T. Patterson, *Grand Expectations: The United States, 1945–1974* (New York: Oxford University Press, 1996), 150–51.

[156] Klarman, *Jim Crow*, 210–11.

[157] Mary L. Dudziak, *Cold War Civil Rights: Race and the Image of American Democracy* (Princeton, NJ: Princeton University Press, 2000), 100, 104–07; Klarman, *Jim Crow*, 182–84.

[158] 339 U.S. 637 (1950).

[159] 339 U.S. 629 (1950).

[160] Dudziak, *Cold War*, 94–96; Klarman, *Jim Crow*, 210.

governing boundaries, it would have to find ways to bend that order while reaffirming those core boundaries. Thus, in *Missouri ex rel. Gaines v. Canada*,[161] segregation in education suffered a defeat in 1938. Lloyd Gaines was an African American citizen of Missouri who had graduated from Lincoln University, that state's principal undergraduate institution for African Americans. Gaines subsequently applied to and was denied admission to the University of Missouri's law school. His rejection was due to the state's policy of segregated education, even at the graduate level, as provided for in state court interpretations of state constitutional and statutory law.[162] However, Section 9622 of the Revised Statutes of Missouri provided for its African American citizens to attend out-of-state, integrated universities for coursework not provided at Lincoln, at Missouri's expense.[163] Gaines was encouraged to seek aid under this provision, given the existence of state law schools in Kansas, Nebraska, Iowa, and Illinois that had admitted nonresident African Americans. Instead, Gaines pursued judicial action to be admitted to the University of Missouri's law school.[164]

The state court had stressed items related to the quality of education an African American could receive at an out-of-state law school. It noted that the quality of education at such schools was comparable to that at the University of Missouri, and further, that the substance of the curriculum was largely the same across all of these law schools.[165] However, Hughes, who wrote for a 6–2 majority, thought this line of inquiry was beside the point. Emphasizing the issue in a more abstract manner – in a tone similar to the one he took in his *McCabe* ruling – the crucial point was whether there was substantial equality in the privileges conferred by the state. Thus, the issue was not about the relative quality of different law schools; it was about the comparability of privileges conferred by Missouri itself across the two races. In this regard, Missouri clearly failed to provide substantial equality.[166]

The Court further emphasized that this obligation for racial equality, emanating from the Equal Protection Clause, rested on the state of Missouri alone. It could not be met by another state. Finally, citing *McCabe*,

---

[161] 305 U.S. 337 (1938).
[162] Id. at 342–45.
[163] Id. at 342–43; Klarman, *Jim Crow*, 148.
[164] 305 U.S. at 342, 343.
[165] Id. at 348–49.
[166] Id. at 349–50.

The Entrenchment and Maintenance of the Jim Crow Order 233

Hughes emphasized that the limited demand for legal education among African Americans could not excuse the state from its obligation to provide equal privileges for them in this context.[167] Gaines was accordingly admitted to Missouri's law school in the absence of any separate state law school for African Americans,[168] over the dissents of Justices McReynolds and Butler.[169]

Although the resurgence of racial egalitarianism at the close of the 1930s clearly aligned with the concession to racial integration in *Gaines*, this was still an accommodation, rather than a direct challenge, within the Jim Crow order. After all, the subject here was segregation in higher education, not segregation in elementary and secondary education – the latter of which lay closer to the heart of the Jim Crow order. Furthermore, this ruling did not contain a requirement for integration. Integration was called for in this case only because of Missouri's lack of any separate African American law school.[170]

Finally, and more important, the Court achieved this conflicted result through the tension-managing flexibility of the separate but equal standard; in this context, the Court simply chose to interpret the equality component of the standard in a manner robust enough to support its specific ruling. Beyond this particular focus, however, the separate but equal standard was left with considerable flexibility – and future tension-managing potential – in the aftermath of *Gaines*. Indeed, the Court endorsed a not-exceedingly clear requirement of "substantially equal."[171] Although it is easy to see how an absolute deprivation in this case (i.e., no African American law school) could run afoul of this standard, it also remained a very open question as to what sorts of in-state, separate but equal schemes could pass constitutional muster.

In the subsequent case of *Sweatt v. Painter*,[172] the state of Texas took a stab at fulfilling the separate but equal requirement with its creation of a separate state law school. In this case, an African American man applied to and was rejected from the University of Texas (UT) law school solely

---

[167] Id. at 350–51.
[168] Id. at 352.
[169] Id. at 353–54 (McReynolds, J., dissenting).
[170] Id. at 352 ("We are of the opinion that the ruling was error, and that petitioner was entitled to be admitted to the law school of the State University in the absence of other and proper provision for his legal training within the State."). See also id. at 344.
[171] Id. at 351.
[172] 339 U.S. 629 (1950).

because of his race. At the time of his application, there was no separate state law school for African Americans.[173] He subsequently brought suit in the state courts, and although the state trial court agreed with him that there was a Fourteenth Amendment violation, it did not grant his request to enroll at the UT law school because the state was then in the process of establishing a new, separate African American law school.[174]

Vinson, writing for a unanimous Supreme Court, disagreed. Despite the efforts of the state in attempting to open the new law school for African Americans, and despite the opening of an additional law school for African Americans at the Texas State University for Negroes, it was apparent to the Court that neither of these institutions was capable of providing educational and professional benefits comparable to the UT law school in terms of faculty, curriculum, academic resources, student activities, and providing student interaction with the wider legal world.[175] In addition, more abstractly, the Court noted another inequality:

> What is more important, the University of Texas Law School possesses to a far greater degree those qualities which are incapable of objective measurement but which make for greatness in a law school. Such qualities, to name but a few, include reputation of the faculty, experience of the administration, position and influence of the alumni, standing in the community, traditions and prestige. It is difficult to believe that one who had a free choice between these law schools would consider the question close.[176]

The Court concluded that the plaintiff, being entitled to a legal education equivalent to that offered to whites in Texas, should be admitted to the UT law school.[177]

The Court's analysis in *Sweatt* of the comparability of the two African American law schools to the UT law school seemingly ratcheted up the "equality" component of the separate but equal standard from its status in *Gaines*. This should not have been surprising: the case arose in 1950 in the midst of relatively greater social and political support for racial egalitarianism. As noted earlier, the resurgence in racial egalitarian values was even more significant by this later point relative to the 1930s. In the aftermath of *Sweatt*, the Court left serious doubt that any racially separate

---

[173] Id. at 631.
[174] Id. at 631–32.
[175] Id. at 632–34.
[176] Id. at 634.
[177] Id. at 635–36.

The Entrenchment and Maintenance of the Jim Crow Order 235

law school could ever pass constitutional muster under the Fourteenth Amendment.[178]

Yet *Sweatt*'s endorsement of the separate but equal standard and its self-conscious limitation to the context of higher education points to a tension-management concern here. As the Court stated in its second-to-last paragraph:

> In accordance with these cases [the Court cited several precedents, including *Gaines*], petitioner may claim his full constitutional right: legal education equivalent to that offered by the State to students of other races. Such education is not available to him in a separate law school as offered by the State. We cannot, therefore, agree with respondents that the doctrine of *Plessy* v. *Ferguson*, requires affirmance of the judgment below. Nor need we reach petitioner's contention that *Plessy* v. *Ferguson* should be reexamined in the light of contemporary knowledge respecting the purposes of the Fourteenth Amendment and the effects of racial segregation.[179]

There was no frontal assault on Jim Crow in this case and no clear suggestion that elementary or secondary education would be next, or had to be next, for racial integration.[180] Indeed, given that so much of the Court's analysis was specific to the study of law – in discussing the importance of the intangible attributes of the UT law school, for example – much analytical room remained for distinguishing the context of higher education, or the context of legal education, from other educational contexts. The push for equality in *Sweatt* could easily have been categorically limited to this context.[181] Even as the era of Jim Crow was winding down, the potential remained after *Sweatt* for future flexibility in adjudicating racial equality demands within the Jim Crow legal framework.[182] Despite the social and political forces pressing for greater legal equality, the Court at this point exhibited a continuing interest in maintaining that larger framework.

---

[178] See Klarman, *Jim Crow*, 206.
[179] 339 U.S. at 635–36 (citations omitted).
[180] Relevant to this point, the Court also included comments endorsing judicial modesty. Id. at 631.
[181] Klarman, *Jim Crow*, 211–12.
[182] Handed down on the same day as *Sweatt* was *McLaurin v. Oklahoma State Regents*, 339 U.S. 637 (1950). In this case, the Court confronted Oklahoma's scheme for segregation in higher education. The state had admitted an African American man to a white Ph.D. program in education at the University of Oklahoma after receiving an adverse ruling from a federal district court. Id. at 639. However, Oklahoma's admission came with a twist: the African American man was segregated *within* the University of Oklahoma. Id. at 639–40. The Supreme Court quickly concluded that this was a violation of the Fourteenth Amendment's Equal Protection Clause. Id. at 642.

CONCLUSION

The transformation in race relations from the 1860s to the 1890s was truly a remarkable period of political development. This period witnessed the permanent dismantling of slavery, an institution at the heart of the antebellum era, and the drawn-out, conflicted, and eventual rise of a new status quo in race relations: Jim Crow. It should not be surprising that the processes of recalibration required such an extended amount of time: with the uprooting of slavery and the massive disruption this posed to the political system, an extended period of subsequent readjustment and recalibration was required to construct out of all of the puzzle pieces a new durable system of governance.

Once this new order emerged in the 1890s – with clearly defined allocations of governing authority and clearly defined individual rights and responsibilities for the newly emancipated – it was evident that Jim Crow embodied both consequential departures and continuities with its predecessor, slavery. Stated otherwise, Jim Crow secured some of Reconstruction's core gains but also embodied severe disappointments for racial egalitarians. Evaluating the historical period from a developmental perspective, however, there is a sense in which such a compromise and its allowance for widespread racial subordination in the South was, to some extent, foreordained. Reform ambitions were always strongest – and enjoyed the greatest consensus within the reform coalition – when it came to formal guarantees of racial equality and ending slavery. In contrast, related but distinct goals to dismantle federalism and reshape the South by projecting federal authority into the region enjoyed only mixed support within this reform coalition. Given where popular support lay, Jim Crow itself may not have been inevitable – as the first half of this chapter argues – but some form of widespread racial subordination in the South was likely unavoidable.

8

The Entrenchment and Maintenance of Industrial Pluralism

The Wagner Act dismantled a system of labor relations based on master-servant common law doctrines, but two uncertainties arose in its wake. The first uncertainty, as discussed in Chapter 4, concerned the scope of the act and its ambiguous implications for resilient governing authorities and rights at the outer edges of reform. In the late 1930s, however, the Supreme Court eventually codified key limits on reform. It preserved employer prerogatives not directly bearing on the right to unionize, and in doing so, legally clarified that the Wagner Act did not legitimize and countenance more aggressive union practices.

Thus, in *NLRB v. Mackay Radio & Telegraph Co.*,[1] the Court defended ownership rights by denying economic strikers a general right of reinstatement; in *NLRB v. Sands Manufacturing Co.*,[2] the Court defended the employer's right to stand on the original collective bargaining agreement by denying the protections of the Wagner Act to workers who were striking over a contract modification; and in *NLRB v. Fansteel Metallurgical Corporation*,[3] it denied the protections of the Wagner Act to employees who had engaged in a sit-down strike in response to the employer's unfair labor practices. Given these delimiting settlements, the conservative nature of the emerging post-Wagner system of labor relations could be gleaned by the late 1930s. If nothing else, the Court's treatment of economic strikers and sit-down strikers in these cases

---

[1] 304 U.S. 333 (1938).
[2] 306 U.S. 332 (1939).
[3] 306 U.S. 240 (1939).

encompassed strong support for more regularized forms of labor-management conflict resolution.

Yet even with the legal clarity these rulings provided, a significant uncertainty remained: How would competing authorities and rights be formally delineated within or internal to the domain of reform? Notwithstanding the permanence of the Wagner Act and the resilience of certain key employer prerogatives at the outer edges of its authority, how exactly would labor-employer industrial conflict be managed? What legal structures would resolve industrial conflicts, and what role would the state play in these processes of conflict resolution? These questions had to be resolved before any new system of governance could emerge.

These lingering uncertainties were put to rest with the National War Labor Board's promotion of voluntary arbitration in the early 1940s and the Supreme Court's endorsement of voluntary arbitration as the preferred method of resolving industrial conflict in 1960. A recalibration of authorities and rights internal to reform, that was also built on the earlier delimiting settlement, resulted in a new order in labor relations known as "industrial pluralism."[4]

In using the term, I largely follow Katherine Stone's description of industrial pluralism as a discrete set of legal and political views on labor relations articulated by prolabor liberals.[5] These views, which enjoyed widespread prominence in the post–World War II era, both (1) prioritized union interests over individual employee interests, and (2) viewed a series of steps of formal grievance procedures, with binding arbitration usually as the final step, as the preferred means for managing industrial conflict between employer and union.[6] As such, industrial pluralism can be understood as a synthesis of both reform and delimiting

---

[4] Throughout, I will use "industrial pluralism" and "voluntary arbitration" interchangeably.

[5] Katherine Van Wezel Stone, "The Post-War Paradigm in American Labor Law," *Yale Law Journal* 90, no. 7 (June 1981): 1516, 1516n29; Staughton Lynd, "Government without Rights: The Labor Law Vision of Archibald Cox," *Industrial Relations Law Journal* 4, no. 3 (1981): 487.

[6] Stone articulates the following as the main tenets of industrial pluralism: "(1) the workplace under collective bargaining can be analogized to a political democracy; (2) private arbitration is a necessary element in the workplace mini-democracy; (3) in order to foster arbitration and to ensure the functioning of the mini-democracy, the processes of the state must not intervene; (4) individual rights in collective bargaining must yield to the collective rights of the union; and (5) under the Act, labor's only rights are to bargain collectively and to arbitrate its disputes with its employer." Stone, "Post-War Paradigm," 1516. She subsequently stated that (2) and (3) "are the most central to the industrial pluralist vision" and "constitute the backbone of the paradigm." Katherine van Wezel

principles. It reflected a commitment to collective bargaining with its emphasis on mutually agreed upon grievance procedures between labor and management. At the same time, industrial pluralism reflected a principle of restraining aggressive unionism – embodied in the judicial delimiting rulings of the late 1930s – with its commitment to managing industrial conflict in a more orderly, regularized manner.

My first task in this chapter is to highlight the existence of some lingering ambiguities after the judicial delimitation of the 1930s. After canvassing some of the major political events of the 1940s that facilitated the rise of industrial pluralism, I discuss the rise of an *alternative* vision of labor relations that – counter to the industrial pluralist commitment to arbitration – would have channeled the resolution of industrial conflict into the federal courts instead. Thus, during this time, political uncertainty existed precisely because both were viable options for resolving internal uncertainties and for ordering labor relations. Admittedly, these two competing alternatives constituted only a *qualified* uncertainty. Neither the federal-judicial vision nor industrial pluralism purported to challenge the terms of the preceding delimitation.

With the Court's definitive and principled endorsement of private, voluntary arbitration in its rulings in the *Steelworker's Trilogy*[7] in 1960, even this qualified uncertainty finally gave way to a new, solidified industrial pluralist order. As with *Plessy* and *Williams* in Chapter 7, the significance of the *Steelworkers Trilogy* is twofold: first, these cases help illuminate a crucial aspect of the political processes of construction. Second, these

---

Stone, "Re-Envisioning Labor Law: A Response to Professor Finkin," *Maryland Law Review* 45, no. 4 (1986): 985.

Many others have similarly referred to either a post–World War II paradigm of industrial pluralism or a widespread post-war commitment to private, voluntary arbitration. See, e.g., Melvyn Dubofsky, *The State & Labor in Modern America* (Chapel Hill: University of North Carolina Press, 1994), 213–14; James B. Atleson, "Wartime Labor Regulation, the Industrial Pluralists, and the Law of Collective Bargaining," in *Industrial Democracy in America: The Ambiguous Promise*, eds. Nelson Lichtenstein and Howell John Harris (Cambridge: Cambridge University Press, 1993), 142–75; Matthew W. Finkin, "Revisionism in Labor Law," *Maryland Law Review* 43 (Fall 1984): 55–58; Lynd, "Government without Rights"; Clyde W. Summers, "Individual Rights in Collective Agreements and Arbitration," *New York University Law Review* 37, no. 3 (May 1962): 362–63; Christopher L. Tomlins, "The New Deal, Collective Bargaining, and the Triumph of Industrial Pluralism," *Industrial and Labor Relations Review* 39, no. 1 (October 1985): 19–34.

[7] *United Steelworkers of America v. American Manufacturing Co.*, 363 U.S. 564 (1960); *United Steelworkers of America v. Enterprise Wheel & Car Corp.* 363 U.S. 593 (1960); *United Steelworkers of America v. Warrior & Gulf Navigation Co.*, 363 U.S. 574 (1960).

TABLE 8.1 *Construction and Tension Management after the Wagner Act*

Lingering uncertainty	How to structure the resolution of employer-labor industrial conflicts
Emergence of the new system of governance	From the National War Labor Board
Entrenchment of the new system of governance	By the Supreme Court in *The Steelworkers Trilogy*
Judicial tension management	*Vaca v. Sipes*

cases also point to the distinctiveness of "order-affirming rulings" as a particular mode of adjudication. As with *Plessy* and *Williams*, the *Steelworkers Trilogy* conclusively signaled the legal codification of industrial pluralism.

Tracing the entrenchment of industrial pluralism, as summarized in part in Table 8.1, is a primary task of this chapter, but a second task is following the developmental story past construction to the subsequent era of equilibrium or normal politics. Specifically, I focus on one particularly significant conflict that arose in post–New Deal labor relations and highlight how the Court resolved tensions by acting as the manager and protector of the reigning industrial pluralist status quo. The site of the conflict I examine lies in the Court's treatment of "hybrid" Section 301/duty of fair representation claims. The significance of this body of doctrine stems not just from how the Court's adjudicative resolutions shored up the legal structure of industrial pluralism; the Court's treatment of these hybrid claims also directs attention to the manner in which it resolved these conflicts, namely through tension-managing rulings.

PART I: THE ENTRENCHMENT OF INDUSTRIAL PLURALISM

Uncertainties after Delimitation: Labor in the 1940s

The Rise of Voluntary Arbitration

The rise of voluntary arbitration was rooted primarily in the state's regulation of industrial conflict during World War II. By 1941, defense-related spending had begun, and by March of that year, Congress had passed the Lend-Lease Program, presenting an opportune time for labor to press its goals.[8] In the midst of this new and growing defense production effort

---

[8] Nelson Lichtenstein, *Labor's War at Home: The CIO in World War II* (Cambridge: Cambridge University Press, 1982), 45.

The Entrenchment and Maintenance of Industrial Pluralism 241

that gave labor a much stronger bargaining position, the CIO looked to reverse its stagnant campaigning efforts, which had persisted since the late 1930s, in the mass-production industries and to press for wage increases and unionizing new sectors of industry.[9] A wave of major strikes in 1941 resulted, which surpassed the strike waves of 1934 and 1937.[10]

The unions did enjoy significant gains from these efforts,[11] but Roosevelt's response was an equally notable consequence: he created the National Defense Mediation Board (the NDMB) by executive order in March 1941 to mediate industrial disputes (although it could not arbitrate or compel compliance).[12] The NDMB proved to be only a temporary solution: its ability to manage industrial conflicts was permanently crippled by November 1941 when the CIO's two representatives on the board resigned. These resignations were prompted by the board's refusal to allow the United Mine Workers to extend their "union shop"[13] contract to the "captive mines" of the large steel corporations.[14] The real significance of the NDMB, however, is that it set a precedent for a successor board – the National War Labor Board (NWLB). The NWLB actively encouraged voluntary arbitration in industry.

After Pearl Harbor in December 1941, Roosevelt convened a labor-management conference and made clear the necessity of both a no-strike pledge (which the unions had already voluntarily agreed to) and the peaceful resolution of industrial disputes during the war. The conference responded by recommending a new, more powerful war labor board with all-encompassing jurisdiction over labor issues.[15] Subsequently, Roosevelt created the National War Labor Board on January 12, 1942, by Executive Order 9017.[16] The board had jurisdiction over "'labor disputes

---

[9] Dubofsky, *State & Labor*, 171–72; Lichtenstein, *Labor's War*, 45.
[10] Dubofsky, *State & Labor*, 172; Lichtenstein, *Labor's War*, 46.
[11] Dubofsky, *State & Labor*, 172–73.
[12] Ibid., 178; Lichtenstein, *Labor's War*, 51.
[13] "Union shops" were workplaces that required workers to join the union within a set amount of time.
[14] Dubofsky, *State & Labor*, 179–81; Lichtenstein, *Labor's War*, 69–70; Christopher L. Tomlins, *The State and the Unions: Labor Relations, Law, and the Organized Labor Movement in America, 1880–1960* (Cambridge: Cambridge University Press, 1985), 257.
[15] Dubofsky, *State & Labor*, 182; Lichtenstein, *Labor's War*, 70–71; Robert H. Zieger, *American Workers, American Unions, 1920–1985* (Baltimore: Johns Hopkins University Press, 1986), 87–88; Robert H. Zieger, *The CIO, 1935–1955* (Chapel Hill: University of North Carolina Press, 1995), 169; Atleson, "Wartime Labor Regulation," 147.
[16] Atleson, "Wartime Labor Regulation," 147; Jesse Freidin and Francis J. Ulman, "Arbitration and the National War Labor Board," *Harvard Law Review* 58, no. 3 (February 1945): 313.

which might interrupt work which contributes to the effective prosecution of the war,' and 'to finally determine the dispute' through 'mediation, voluntary arbitration, or arbitration under rules provided by the Board.'"[17]

During the war, the NWLB's actions had compulsory elements, such as mandating settlements and keeping a firm grip on wage increases.[18] Its true legacy, however, was that it actively encouraged voluntary grievance procedures and arbitration throughout industry to manage industrial conflict. The NWLB even went so far as to order arbitration in some circumstances.[19] Because of these efforts, historians see the NWLB's actions as perhaps the most pivotal factor in setting the terms for the post–World War II labor relations system.[20]

The point should not be overstated. The post-war dominance of voluntary arbitration was not a foregone conclusion by the end of the war, as is discussed later. Still, it was the actions of the NWLB, a body created by the exigency of war and charged with the crucial wartime task of keeping production continuous, that thrust arbitration to prominence as an attractive means to order labor relations.

Anti-Labor Legislation in the 1940s

If the spread of voluntary arbitration was hemming in the scope of developmental possibilities, legislation aimed at curbing union influence was also achieving a similar effect. These legislative developments suggest that even if some uncertainty remained in the task of recalibrating labor's rights, the scope of that uncertainty grew smaller as the 1940s wore on.

In 1943, workers engaged in a series of strikes protesting the NWLB and National Wage Stabilization Board rulings that had kept their wages

---

[17] Executive Order No. 9017, 7 Code of Federal Regulations 237 (1942), quoted in Freidin and Ulman, "Arbitration," 313.
[18] Dubofsky, *State & Labor*, 185–86; Lichtenstein, *Labor's War*, 71–72.
[19] Atleson, "Wartime Labor Regulation," 146; Freidin and Ulman, "Arbitration," 344.
[20] For example, Nelson Lichtenstein argues that by promoting voluntary arbitration, the NWLB institutionalized one form of collective bargaining – a form that privileged industrial peace and continuous production – over alternative forms. These alternative forms encompassed more democratic unions, shop-floor union militancy, and ongoing conflict between labor and management, which were rejected. Nelson Lichtenstein, "Industrial Democracy, Contract Unionism, and the National War Labor Board," *Labor Law Journal* 33 (August 1982): 524–31. In a similar vein, James Atleson has also noted: "By 1960, the date of the Supreme Court's trilogy, arbitration clauses were found in over 90 percent of collective agreements. The Supreme Court may have wished to support the arbitration process, but the War Labor Board had already accomplished that result over fifteen years earlier," Atleson, "Wartime Labor Regulation," 154n41. See also ibid., 146–49; Tomlins, *The State*, 257.

artificially low during wartime in order to prevent inflation and to ensure high production. The most conspicuous of the strikers were the United Mine Workers, led by John Lewis.[21] Similar to the aftermath of the 1941 strike wave, labor enjoyed some economic gains in 1943, but in the process it again riled up antagonistic public opinion. After the 1941 strikes, antilabor sentiment failed to prompt any new antilabor legislation, but the second time around resulted in the Smith-Connally Act. The act, also known as the War Labor Disputes Act, was enacted over FDR's veto in 1943.[22] Among other things, it made the NWLB's decisions final and binding, it authorized the president to seize industries threatened by strikes, it created criminal liability for strikers on government-controlled property, and it curbed strikes by requiring NLRB-supervised prestrike votes and mandatory prestrike cooling off periods.[23]

A similar sequence of events occurred in 1946 with a wave of 4,630 strikes involving 5 million workers. The strikes were motivated by labor's desire to secure and build on their gains during the war years and to ensure that it could bargain toward new peacetime arrangements from a position of strength.[24] The antilabor consequences of this effort, however, were significant. In 1946, the Case Bill aimed to weaken both labor's right to strike and the powers of the NLRB. Only Truman's veto stopped the bill.[25] This was only the start; in the 1946 elections, Republicans captured majorities in both houses of Congress for the first time since 1930, aided significantly by public antipathy toward labor. This Congress enacted the Taft-Hartley Act.[26]

The Taft-Hartley Act did not constitute a repudiation of the Wagner Act; the institution of collective bargaining remained well intact after 1947.[27] But the act imposed consequential new limitations on union

---

[21] Dubofsky, *State & Labor*, 185, 188; Alan Brinkley, *The End of Reform: New Deal Liberalism in Recession and War* (New York: Vintage Books, 1996), 215–16.
[22] Dubofsky, *State & Labor*, 173–75, 190–91; Brinkley, *End of Reform*, 216.
[23] Dubofsky, *State & Labor*, 190; Lichtenstein, *Labor's War*, 167–68; Zieger, *American Workers*, 109.
[24] Dubofsky, *State & Labor*, 192–95.
[25] Ibid., 194; James A. Gross, *Broken Promise: The Subversion of U.S. Labor Relations Policy, 1947–1994* (Philadelphia: Temple University Press, 1995), 5; Zieger, *American Workers*, 109.
[26] Gross, *Broken Promise*, 5; Bruce J. Schulman, *From Cotton Belt to Sunbelt: Federal Policy, Economic Development, and the Transformation of the South, 1938–1980* (New York: Oxford University Press, 1991, 1994), 81; Tomlins, *The State*, 288; Zieger, *American Workers*, 109.
[27] For views that Taft-Hartley constituted a continuation and *not* a repudiation of the New Deal, and NLRB and court rulings prior to 1947, see Tomlins, *The State*, 251,

activism that foreclosed opportunities for labor to expand its reach in the post–World War II era. One crucial change was the prohibition of secondary boycotts as an unfair labor practice, provided for in Section 8(b)(4)(A) – later amended to Section 8(b)(4)(B) – of the Taft-Hartley Amendments to the National Labor Relations Act (NLRA). Secondary boycotts – or the use of economic pressure by unions on businesses with which it had no direct relationship – took away an invaluable means by which "allied unions [could take action] in support of their striking brethren."[28] Most significantly, this provision prevented established unions in the North from projecting their collective influence into the South to aid local unions there.[29] Similarly, "closed shops" – union security agreements that required workers to be union members at the time of hiring – were banned by Section 8(a)(3) of the Taft-Hartley Amendments to the NLRA.[30] Furthermore, Section 14(b) of the Taft-Hartley Amendments authorized states to pass "right to work" laws that could prohibit "union shops" – workplaces that required workers to join the union within a set amount of time. As with the prohibition on secondary boycotts, these changes essentially confined unionism to areas in the North where it had already been established and closed off the South as a new potential territory for organizing in the future.[31]

Incomplete Construction

Seemingly any lingering developmental uncertainties after delimitation had been put to rest by 1947. The Taft-Hartley revisions to the National

---

282–316; Dubofsky, *State & Labor*, 206; David Plotke, *Building a Democratic Political Order* (Cambridge: Cambridge University Press, 1996), 256–61; James T. Patterson, *Grand Expectations: The United States, 1945–1974* (New York: Oxford University Press, 1996), 52.

[28] Schulman, *Sunbelt*, 81.

[29] Lichtenstein, *Labor's War*, 239; Tomlins, *The State*, 251.

[30] Dubofsky, *State & Labor*, 204; Patterson, *Grand Expectations*, 51; Tomlins, *The State*, 297.

[31] Dubofsky, *State & Labor*, 204; Patterson, *Grand Expectations*, 51; Schulman, *Sunbelt*, 81; Tomlins, *The State*, 297–98. See also Katznelson and Farhang, who see the increasingly hostile posture of southern Democrats toward unions and labor interests during the 1940s as crucial in ultimately dictating the terms of post–World War II political development. Ira Katznelson and Sean Farhang, "The Southern Imposition: Congress and Labor in the New Deal and Fair Deal," *Studies in American Political Development* 19 (Spring 2005): 6–7. Section 14(b) states: "Nothing in this Act shall be construed as authorizing the execution or application of agreements requiring membership in a labor organization as a condition of employment in any State or Territory in which such execution or application is prohibited by State or Territorial law." Labor Management Relations Act, 1947, Pub. L. 101, § 14(b), 61 Stat. 136, 151 (1947).

Labor Relations Act effectively closed off any possibility of major changes to the balance of power between labor and management – particularly through new union organizing efforts in the South. Thus, the judicial delimitation of the 1930s was the start of a trend in which unions seemed outmatched in fighting the tide of growing governmental constraints placed on their collective activities. The onset of World War II and other events merely fed the growing belief that aggressive unionism had to be kept in check, and union action during the 1940s to either expand their influence or fight for greater gains were met with little else but a growing political antipathy.

Meanwhile, voluntary arbitration had become entrenched in industry because of the NWLB's efforts. Indeed, the state's support of voluntary arbitration had even been codified in the text of Taft-Hartley's Title II, which stated: "Final adjustment by a method agreed upon by the parties is hereby declared to be the desirable method for settlement of grievance disputes arising over the application or interpretation of an existing collective-bargaining agreement."[32]

Even if developmental uncertainties were seemingly giving way to a new voluntary arbitration order, however, the processes of construction remained incomplete. Courts could undermine the dominance of voluntary arbitration in industry through a significant opening in the Taft-Hartley Act. Congress had been concerned that the variation in state laws on contract and procedure would make it too difficult to enforce collective bargaining agreements in state judicial forums, so it attempted to address this issue by enacting Section 301 of the Taft-Hartley Act.[33] Section 301(a) of the act provided:

Suits for violation of contracts between an employer and a labor organization representing employees in an industry affecting commerce as defined in this Act, or between any such labor organizations, may be brought in any district court of the United States having jurisdiction of the parties, without respect to the amount in controversy or without regard to the citizenship of the parties.[34]

The threat to voluntary arbitration was clear: prolabor defenders of industrial pluralism saw the potential for Section 301 to funnel industrial conflicts into the courts rather than into private voluntary grievance procedures, including arbitration. Thus, as early as the late 1940s, academics

---

[32] § 203(d), 61 Stat. at 154.
[33] Robert A. Gorman and Matthew W. Finkin, *Basic Text on Labor Law*, 2d. ed. (St. Paul, MN: Thomson West, 2004), 736.
[34] § 301, 61 Stat. at 156.

strongly cautioned against this type of judicial involvement because it could create a dramatically different role for the state in managing industrial conflict relative to a system of voluntary arbitration.[35] Industrial conflicts that were adjudicated rather than arbitrated would be subject to different rules of procedure, a wider array of legal remedies, and, very notably, a degree of public accountability.[36]

Voluntary arbitration would not become firmly entrenched until after the Court had dealt with this loophole, rejected the federal-judicial vision of labor relations, and given its blessing to the former. Once it gave its sweeping, principled affirmation to industrial pluralism (through a somewhat circuitous route), however, a post–Wagner Act system of labor relations was codified and legally entrenched.

Judicial Affirmation of the New Order: The Supreme Court's Legitimization of Industrial Pluralism

In *Association of Westinghouse Salaried Employees v. Westinghouse Electric Corp.*,[37] a labor organization sued an employer under Section 301 of the Taft-Hartley Act over a wage dispute concerning some 4,000 employees. Five members of the Court concluded that the provision did not confer jurisdiction to the federal courts for this type of suit, thereby, in effect, containing the aforementioned threat of Section 301 to industrial pluralism (although the Court's opinion commanded only three votes).

Frankfurter, writing for the Court, arrived at this conclusion by casting doubts on any potential interpretation of Section 301 that could escape fundamental challenges on either constitutional or statutory grounds. First, Frankfurter noted, one might assume that Section 301 was merely a procedural provision that would allow the federal courts to serve as a forum for labor disputes but would not mandate that federal law

---

[35] Stone, "Post-War Paradigm," 1525–26. Notable examples of critical commentary on this point include Harry Shulman, "Reason, Contract, and Law in Labor Relations," *Harvard Law Review* 68, no. 6 (1955): 999–1024; Alexander M. Bickel and Harry H. Wellington, "Legislative Purpose and the Judicial Process: The Lincoln Mills Case," *Harvard Law Review* 71, no. 1 (November 1957): 1–39.

[36] Katherine Van Wezel Stone, "The Legacy of Industrial Pluralism: The Tension between Individual Employment Rights and the New Deal Collective Bargaining System," *University of Chicago Law Review* 59, no. 2 (Spring 1992): 629–30. And indeed, these were differences that might have made for a more favorable allocation of rights for labor than under a regime of voluntary arbitration. Ibid.

[37] 348 U.S. 437 (1955).

resolve these disputes. Presumably state law would be applied instead.[38] If that were the case, the constitutional grounds allowing federal jurisdiction would be unclear. Article III requires that federal jurisdiction be based on either diversity of state citizenship in the dispute or on the fact that the disputes themselves are "Cases, in Law and Equity, arising under this Constitution, the Laws of the United States, and Treatises made, or which shall be made, under their Authority."[39] If, however, Section 301 were merely procedural and called for the application of state law in the federal courts, nondiverse labor disputes heard in the federal courts (under the authority of Section 301) would not fall within either of these two jurisdictional grants to the federal courts.[40]

To avoid this constitutional difficulty, one might assume instead that Section 301 was both procedural and substantive, and that it called for the federal courts to apply a body of federal common law to labor disputes arising under it.[41] This would resolve the constitutional concern, as nondiverse labor disputes would now implicate a matter of federal law. Yet, among other things, Frankfurter argued that such an interpretation would run afoul of a legislative history that did not support such a significant undertaking by the federal courts.[42] Further, this interpretation of Section 301 would put federal and state laws on a collision course with respect to the adjudication of collective bargaining agreements, with the former potentially uprooting the latter.[43] Given these various constitutional and statutory difficulties, Frankfurter narrowed the scope of this "doubtful legislation";[44] he ultimately concluded Congress did not intend to allow suits of this sort to be heard in the federal courts under Section 301, given that the employees in this particular case could readily seek to vindicate their individual wage claims in the state courts as individuals.[45]

At the end of *Westinghouse*, then, the threat to industrial pluralism contained in Section 301 had seemingly been neutralized. By emphasizing the constitutional and statutory difficulties attendant on allowing the

---

[38] Id. at 443–44.
[39] Article III, § 2.
[40] *Westinghouse*, 348 U.S. at 449–52. Frankfurter's skepticism that a procedural view of Section 301 could be justified under a federal question jurisdictional rationale was supported with reference to the doctrine on federally incorporated organizations and trustees in bankruptcy. Id. at 450–52.
[41] Id. at 452–53.
[42] Id. at 444–49.
[43] Id. at 455.
[44] Id. at 459.
[45] Id. at 460–61.

federal courts to step in with primary oversight over such industrial grievances, the Court shied away from major judicial involvement in industrial disputes.

Only Douglas, dissenting for both himself and Black, asserted that Section 301 did confer federal jurisdiction over this suit. He contended that the provision was substantive in calling for the application of federal law – thereby addressing the constitutional difficulty over federal jurisdiction identified by Frankfurter. Douglas concluded that the union should have standing to bring this case.[46]

Two years later in *Textile Workers Union of America v. Lincoln Mills of Alabama*,[47] Douglas and his substantive views of Section 301 spoke for a majority of the Court. In this case, a union and an employer had a collective bargaining agreement that provided for no strikes and for a detailed grievance procedure that culminated in arbitration. When disputes arose concerning workloads and work assignments, these disputes progressed through the grievance procedures until arbitration was reached. At this point, however, the employer refused to arbitrate. The union sought to compel arbitration.[48]

Again, the key question concerned the reach of Section 301. Not surprisingly, Douglas concluded that the federal courts had jurisdiction over the case and were empowered to fashion a body of federal common law to enforce collective bargaining agreements – including, where appropriate, compelling arbitration. First, Douglas asserted that Section 301(a) must be read more substantively than just a bare grant of federal jurisdiction. More than this, it embodied a federal policy to promote industrial peace; its promotion of the enforceability of collective bargaining agreements would, he seemingly indicated, undercut the incidence of strikes.[49] Second, Douglas claimed that the federal courts should approach arbitration agreements with certain predispositions: since agreements to arbitrate in collective bargaining agreements should be understood as the employer's quid pro quo for no employee strikes, the federal policy to encourage industrial peace, or nonstriking, was best served by federal jurisdiction of Section 301 claims to enforce agreements to arbitrate.[50]

Recall that in *Westinghouse,* Frankfurter raised both constitutional and statutory concerns about nondiverse labor disputes in the federal

---

[46] Id. at 465–67 (Douglas, J., dissenting).
[47] 353 U.S. 448 (1957).
[48] Id. at 449.
[49] Id. at 453–55.
[50] Id. at 455–56.

courts. In *Lincoln Mills*, Douglas quickly dismissed these anxieties by directing the federal courts to fashion a federal common law to apply to suits arising under Section 301(a), thus eliminating the federal jurisdiction problem.[51] Finally, Douglas asserted that the limitations on injunctions in the Norris-LaGuardia Act did not undercut the judiciary's authority to compel specific performance of agreements to arbitrate under Section 301(a).[52]

Even though the Court asserted its authority to compel specific performance of arbitration in *Lincoln Mills*, thereby leading to an arbitration-friendly ruling, the ruling clearly posed a threat to the dominance of arbitration. In *Lincoln Mills*, Douglas asserted the Court's authority to adjudicate the merits of disputes over collective bargaining agreements, thereby at least opening the door to granting the judiciary primary oversight to manage industrial conflict. Frankfurter, in his dissent, vigorously opposed this bold move. He stated:

> A union, like any other combatant engaged in a particular fight, is ready to make an ally of an old enemy, and so we also find unions resorting to the otherwise much excoriated labor injunction. Such intermittent yielding to expediency does not change the fact that judicial intervention is ill-suited to the special characteristics of the arbitration process in labor disputes; nor are the conditions for its effective functioning thereby altered.[53]

Further:

> Arbitration agreements are for specific terms, generally much shorter than the time required for adjudication of a contested lawsuit through the available stages of trial and appeal. Renegotiation of agreements cannot await the outcome of such litigation; nor can the parties' continuing relation await it. Cases under § 301 will probably present unusual rather than representative situations. A "rule" derived from them is more likely to discombobulate than to compose. A "uniform corpus" cannot be expected to evolve, certainly not within a time to serve its assumed function.[54]

In noting judicial incapability for dealing with industrial disputes, Frankfurter echoed comments from Harry Schulman (dean of the Yale Law School and labor arbitrator) two years before[55] – which Frankfurter

---

[51] Id. at 456–57.
[52] Id. at 457–59.
[53] Id. at 462–63 (Frankfurter, J., dissenting).
[54] Id. at 463–64. (Frankfurter, J., dissenting).
[55] "But the courts cannot, by occasional sporadic decision, restore the parties' [to a collective bargaining agreement] continuing relationship; and their intervention in such cases may seriously affect the going systems of self-government. When their autonomous

cited in his dissent.[56] Alexander Bickel and Harry Wellington later seconded these sentiments after the *Lincoln Mills* ruling.[57]

The threat of judicial intervention in *Lincoln Mills* ultimately led nowhere, however. The *Steelworkers Trilogy* – a set of three rulings all written by Douglas – provided the jurisprudential foundations for industrial pluralism and brought this period of construction to a close. These cases clarified that Douglas's assertion of judicial authority in *Lincoln Mills* would promote voluntary arbitration rather than undermine it in favor of adjudication in the courts, and they enjoyed broad support on the Court: in each of the *Trilogy* cases, Douglas's opinions for the Court carried six votes. These votes, when combined with Frankfurter's concurrences in each case, meant that seven out of the eight justices who participated in the *Trilogy* supported industrial pluralist principles.

In the first *Trilogy* case, *United Steelworkers of America v. American Manufacturing Co.*,[58] an employee left his job and settled a claim for compensation benefits due to his assertion that he was permanently disabled. The employee then attempted to return to his job based on a seniority provision in the collective bargaining agreement. A dispute subsequently arose between the union (acting for the employee) and the employer. Because the collective bargaining agreement required arbitration of all grievances arising from the agreement, the union demanded arbitration over the employee's demand to return. The employer refused arbitration on several grounds, however: the employee had previously been compensated for his disability claim, and the employer claimed that this type of dispute was not subject to arbitration under the collective bargaining agreement.[59]

Douglas's opinion for the Court was straightforward: the only judicial inquiry was determining whether the collective bargaining agreement's

---

system breaks down, might not the parties better be left to the usual methods for adjustment of labor disputes rather than to court actions on the contract or on the arbitration award?" Shulman, "Reason," 1024.

[56] *Lincoln Mills*, 353 U.S. at 463 (Frankfurter, J., dissenting).

[57] "What section 301 really demands of the federal courts, therefore, is not the application but the creation in case after case, with the scant assistance of bits and pieces of statutory commands, of a law of labor contracts the chief source of which is to be the common law of commercial contracts. The plain fact is that the courts are enormously unequal to the task and its imposition on them is therefore capable of damaging their usefulness for the essential duties that they are suited to perform." Bickel and Wellington, "Legislative Purpose," 22–23 (citations omitted).

[58] 363 U.S. 564 (1960).

[59] Id. at 564–66.

provision to arbitrate was applicable to this dispute. If arbitration were warranted, the merits of the claim itself should be left for the arbitrator. To quote Douglas:

The collective agreement calls for the submission of grievances in the categories which it describes, irrespective of whether a court may deem them to be meritorious. In our role of developing a meaningful body of law to govern the interpretation and enforcement of collective bargaining agreements, we think special heed should be given to the context in which collective bargaining agreements are negotiated and the purpose which they are intended to serve. The function of the court is very limited when the parties have agreed to submit all questions of contract interpretation to the arbitrator. It is confined to ascertaining whether the party seeking arbitration is making a claim which on its face is governed by the contract. Whether the moving party is right or wrong is a question of contract interpretation for the arbitrator. In these circumstances the moving party should not be deprived of the arbitrator's judgment, when it was his judgment and all that it connotes that was bargained for.[60]

Sounding industrial pluralist themes that recur in the other two *Trilogy* cases, Douglas strongly endorsed judicial self-restraint and registered approval for letting the private, voluntary agreement of the parties govern the dispute. Since this was clearly a dispute over the terms of the collective bargaining agreement, arbitration in this case was appropriate.[61]

Similarly, in *United Steelworkers of America v. Enterprise Wheel & Car Corp.*,[62] eleven employees left their jobs in protest when a fellow employee was discharged. Upon returning to work the next day, the employer informed the eleven that they too were effectively discharged. Thereafter, a dispute arose between the union and employer over the status of these eleven workers. The collective bargaining agreement did provide for arbitration, which occurred on the orders of the federal district court after the employer initially refused to arbitrate. The arbitrator ordered the reinstatement of the eleven with back pay. The decision presented ancillary complexities, however, given that the collective bargaining agreement had expired between the time of discharge and the time of the arbitrator's award. The employer refused to comply with the award, and the case continued to the Supreme Court.[63]

In his ruling in this case, Justice Douglas's opinion for six votes once again defended industrial pluralist values by asserting judicial deference

[60] Id. at 567–68 (citations omitted).
[61] Id. at 569.
[62] 363 U.S. 593 (1960).
[63] Id. at 594–96.

toward arbitration awards in order to preserve the integrity and the finality of arbitration.[64] So long as the arbitrator was properly passing judgment on matters within his authority under the contract, Douglas asserted, courts should not evaluate the merits of the underlying grievance itself.[65]

Finally, in *United Steelworkers of America v. Warrior & Gulf Navigation Co.*,[66] the third and most complex case of the *Trilogy*, a labor dispute arose when the employer contracted out work that had formerly been done by its own employees. The employer made this change even while its former employees, who previously maintained the employer's barges (the type of work in question), were being laid off. The union accused the employer of bringing about a partial lockout. The collective bargaining agreement contained a provision for arbitration as the final step in a series of grievance procedures, but the agreement also excepted from arbitration "matters which are strictly a function of management."[67] The question was whether the Court would compel arbitration, given that the employer's decision to contract out work was arguably a matter that was "strictly a function of management," and thus possibly outside the arbitration clause of the agreement.[68]

Writing for six votes again, Douglas held that the dispute was subject to arbitration, touching on several previously mentioned themes. First, despite the potential for vigorous state intervention contemplated in *Lincoln Mills*, Douglas made it clear that no such result would follow here. To the contrary, Douglas clarified that he viewed Section 301 as a tool for promoting voluntary arbitration between labor and employers.[69] In underscoring arbitration's appeal, Douglas sounded industrial pluralist themes that, in fact, were prominent in the Frankfurter dissent in *Lincoln Mills*:

The grievance machinery under a collective bargaining agreement is at the very heart of the system of industrial self-government. Arbitration is the means of solving the unforeseeable by molding a system of private law for all the problems which may arise and to provide for their solution in a way which will generally accord with the variant needs and desires of the parties. The processing of disputes

---

[64] Id. at 596, 599. However, Douglas also ordered a minor adjustment on a back-pay issue. Id. at 599.
[65] Id. at 598–99.
[66] 363 U.S. 574 (1960).
[67] Id. at 576.
[68] Id. at 575–78.
[69] Id. at 577–81.

through the grievance machinery is actually a vehicle by which meaning and content are given to the collective bargaining agreement.[70]

Furthermore, arbitration allowed the arbitrator, with greater expertise compared to a judge, to resolve grievances. Such a task required performance of "functions which are not normal to the courts."[71]

Second, to preserve the integrity of arbitration, Douglas asserted that judicial oversight should generally be limited to determining whether a given dispute was arbitrable.[72] Further, given congressional preferences toward promoting arbitration, there should be a judicial predisposition against a finding of nonarbitration in labor disputes.[73] As Douglas stated: "An order to arbitrate the particular grievance should not be denied unless it may be said with positive assurance that the arbitration clause is not susceptible of an interpretation that covers the asserted dispute. Doubts should be resolved in favor of coverage."[74]

In the present case, it was *not* so clear to the Court that the employer's decision to contract out the work was excludable from arbitration as a matter that was "strictly a function of management."[75] Because there was no explicit provision in the collective bargaining agreement that excluded from the arbitration provision any management decisions to contract out work, Douglas concluded that the dispute should go to arbitration.[76]

With the Court's decisive, principled affirmation of industrial pluralism in the *Steelworkers Trilogy*, the formal processes of governance construction in labor relations were finally closed twenty-five years after they were initiated with the Wagner Act. Voluntary arbitration may have been widespread in industry prior to 1960, but no lasting political equilibrium could have been established without the Supreme Court's approval. Had the Court taken a different turn after *Lincoln Mills*, industrial conflict resolution could have centered on adjudication rather than arbitration.

Taking stock of the developments occurring within this twenty-five year period, no single fork-in-the-road moment separated the old order of master-servant common law–based labor relations from the new regime of collective bargaining and voluntary arbitration. Rather, there were several critical periods during which crucial developments – the Wagner

---

[70] Id. at 581.
[71] Id.
[72] Id. at 582–83.
[73] Id. at 582.
[74] Id. at 582–83 (citations omitted).
[75] Id. at 583.
[76] Id. at 584–85.

Act's dismantling of the old order, the judicial delimitation of the Wagner Act, the restraints on unionism in the 1940s, the threat of Section 301 to arbitration in the 1950s – eventually narrowed the range of political alternatives until finally, in 1960, a new system of governance legally solidified.

PART II: THE MAINTENANCE OF INDUSTRIAL PLURALISM

In studying recalibration, we have seen the Court assume two distinct roles. Following the initial dismantling reform, the Court assumed the role of delimiter in demarcating the outer boundaries of reform. Subsequent to delimitation, the Court assumed the role of affirmer in legally legitimating the new institutional order – as indicated by the *Steelworkers Trilogy*. However, as labor relations settled into the industrial pluralist framework legitimated in 1960, the Court assumed a new role: that of manager in negotiating tensions arising within this order. The remainder of this chapter illustrates this third, distinctive role of the Court.

Judicial Tension-Management: Section 301 and the Duty of Fair Representation

Between the finality of arbitration and the prioritization of union interests over employee rights – both constituting core industrial pluralist commitments – only the former has been discussed up to this point. The latter was nevertheless a key commitment as well, and prioritizing rights *within* labor was considered essential to maximizing union strength in the collective bargaining process.[77] By the late 1960s, both the commitment to arbitration and the priority of union rights over individual employee rights remained intact. Yet a heightened judicial interest in protecting individual rights in labor disputes began to challenge both of these principles. This challenge emerged most evidently in a series of "hybrid" Section 301 (of the Taft-Hartley Act) and duty of fair representation (DFR) cases in the 1960s, and they directly pitted the interests of employees against both employers *and* their union representatives.

Growing Incongruities

The judicial commitment to individual employee rights that surfaced in the 1960s had roots in doctrine established in prior decades; specifically,

[77] See, e.g., *J. I. Case Co. v. NLRB*, 321 U.S. 332 (1944).

the employee– and individual rights–centered duty of fair representation, which regulates unions in their treatment of the employees they are representing, was initially established in 1944. *Steele v. Louisville & Nashville Railroad Co.*[78] first articulated this concept, in which the Court confronted racially discriminatory acts by the Brotherhood of Locomotive Firemen and Engineers against black railroad workers – workers the Brotherhood was supposed to be representing in its collective bargaining dealings with the Nashville Railroad Company. The union was instead restricting employment opportunities for African American workers.[79]

In a unanimous opinion, the Court reasoned that the Railway Labor Act conferred certain privileges on the Brotherhood – such as the authority to be the exclusive bargaining representative for the railroad workers. But the Railway Labor Act also imposed a corresponding duty on the Brotherhood to exercise that authority with fairness, and certainly without hostility, toward all employees. To quote the Court:

> We hold that the language of the Act to which we have referred, read in the light of the purposes of the Act, expresses the aim of Congress to impose on the bargaining representative of a craft or class of employees the duty to exercise fairly the power conferred upon it in behalf of all those for whom it acts, without hostile discrimination against them.[80]

The Court left the contours of this duty somewhat vague but articulated an equal protection–sounding standard and cited equal protection cases in support of it:

> Without attempting to mark the allowable limits of differences in the terms of contracts based on differences of conditions to which they apply, it is enough for present purposes to say that the statutory power to represent a craft and to make contracts as to wages, hours and working conditions does not include the authority to make among members of the craft discriminations not based on such relevant differences. Here the discriminations based on race alone are obviously irrelevant and invidious. Congress plainly did not undertake to authorize the bargaining representative to make such discriminations. Cf. *Yick Wo v. Hopkins*, 118 U.S. 356; *Yu Cong Eng v. Trinidad*, 271 U.S. 500; *Missouri ex rel. Gaines v. Canada*, 305 U.S. 337; *Hill v. Texas*, 316 U.S. 400.[81]

---

[78] 323 U.S. 192 (1944).
[79] Id. at 193–97.
[80] Id. at 202–03.
[81] Id. at 203.

In the subsequent cases of *Ford Motor Co. v. Huffman*[82] and *Syres v. Oil Workers International Union*,[83] the Court extended the duty of fair representation to unions empowered as exclusive bargaining agents under the National Labor Relations Act. Despite these developments, however, no significant incongruity opened up in these earlier years between the individual rights–oriented DFR and group rights–oriented commitments of industrial pluralism. This is likely because of the fact that, as Schiller notes, the DFR did not possess much vitality in nonracial cases in the 1940s and 1950s. Although judges energetically applied the duty in racially discriminatory labor cases, the federal and state courts had a strong track record of not finding any union violations of the duty – no matter how severe the action by the union – in nonracial cases. Because of its limited application, then, the individual rights aspect of the DFR posed little challenge to industrial pluralism through the 1950s.[84]

The terrain shifted in the late 1950s and 1960s, however, as the intellectual and political climate moved toward a preoccupation with individual rights over group pluralism.[85] Scholarship emphasized the importance of protecting the individual rights of employees when the interests of the union and employee diverged.[86] With these changes, the incongruity between protecting individual employee rights and the tenets of industrial pluralism became clearer, and a significant amount of academic scholarship was produced in response to these tensions.[87]

Two rulings in the 1960s, only a few years after the *Steelworkers Trilogy*, added to this tension by bolstering the legitimacy of individual employee rights. First, in *Humphrey v. Moore*,[88] the Court applied the duty of fair representation beyond the context of contract negotiation – the context in *Steele* – to the context of union enforcement or

---

[82] 345 U.S. 330, 337–39 (1953).
[83] 350 U.S. 892 (1955).
[84] Reuel E. Schiller, "From Group Rights to Individual Liberties: Post-War Labor Law, Liberalism, and the Waning of Union Strength," *Berkeley Journal of Employment & Labor Law* 20, no. 1 (1999): 27–28.
[85] Ibid., 57–58, 62.
[86] See, e.g., Summers, "Individual Rights;" Harry H. Wellington, "Union Democracy and Fair Representation: Federal Responsibility in a Federal System," *Yale Law Journal* 67, no. 8 (July 1958): 1327–62. Neither of these articles limited their concern to racial discriminatory cases. For a discussion on the changing nature of labor law scholarship at this time, see Schiller, "Group Rights," 62n360.
[87] In addition to Summers, "Individual Rights" and Wellington, "Union Democracy," see David E. Feller, "A General Theory of the Collective Bargaining Agreement," *California Law Review* 61, no. 3 (May 1973): 664–65n5, for a listing of relevant articles.
[88] 375 U.S. 335 (1964).

administration of the collective bargaining agreement. The Court articulated a new standard for the duty, signaling its interest in nonracial DFR claims[89] (although in this particular case, it found the union did not breach the duty):

> As far as this record shows, the union took its position *honestly, in good faith and without hostility or arbitrary discrimination*.... By choosing to integrate seniority lists based upon length of service at either company, the union *acted upon wholly relevant considerations, not upon capricious or arbitrary factors*. The evidence shows no breach by the union of its duty of fair representation.[90]

Second, in *Smith v. Evening News Association*,[91] the Court ruled that federal courts had jurisdiction under Section 301 of the Taft-Hartley Act to hear breach of contract claims brought by individual employees against their employer, in order for the employees to vindicate their individual rights under the collective bargaining agreement.[92]

A vigorous application of the DFR principle threatened industrial pluralist commitments because it challenged placing union group interests above the interests of the individual employee. The DFR was, by definition, individual oriented. But the *Smith* ruling seemed to open slightly the possibility for another tenet of industrial pluralism to be directly challenged, namely the finality of voluntary arbitration. If individual employee suits on breaches of the collective bargaining agreement could now be heard in the courts, a new potential path was opened for individual employees – who had disputes with their employers – to do an end run around voluntary grievance procedures. If employees could now seek redress for industrial disputes not just through voluntary grievance procedures but also through adjudication, this would threaten the vitality of voluntary arbitration as the principal means for managing industrial disputes.[93]

To be sure, the *Smith* case itself did not pose this type of direct threat to arbitration. In that case, the Court had noted that "there was no grievance arbitration procedure in this contract which had to be exhausted before

---

[89] Schiller, "Group Rights," 62–63.
[90] 375 U.S. at 350 (emphasis added).
[91] 371 U.S. 195 (1962).
[92] The matter in question here – the employer's antiunion discriminatory acts – was an unfair labor practice arguably within the NLRB's exclusive jurisdiction. However, the Court ruled in *Smith* that it also had jurisdiction over the matter via Section 301 because the discrimination posed a violation by the employer of a clause in the collective bargaining agreement. Id. at 197–98.
[93] Stone, "Post-War Paradigm," 1535–38.

recourse could be had to the courts."⁹⁴ Only three years later, *Republic Steel Corp. v. Maddox*⁹⁵ made clear that an employee seeking to recover severance pay from his employer first had to at least attempt to use the grievance procedures set out in the collective bargaining agreement *before* trying to recover via litigation. In *Maddox*, the Court reaffirmed its commitment to industrial pluralist values:

> As a general rule in cases to which federal law applies, federal labor policy requires that individual employees wishing to assert contract grievances must *attempt* use of the contract grievance procedure agreed upon by employer and union as the mode of redress.... But unless the contract provides otherwise, there can be no doubt that the employee must afford the union the opportunity to act on his behalf. Congress has expressly approved contract grievance procedures as a preferred method for settling disputes and stabilizing the "common law" of the plant.⁹⁶

The limited scope of the *Smith* and *Republic Steel Corp.* decisions seemingly left a narrow space for individual employee Section 301 claims to seriously challenge the finality of arbitration – at least up to this point.

Eventually, however, "hybrid" Section 301 (employee vs. employer)/ DFR (employee vs. union) suits that combined elements of both the DFR and *Smith* suits came to pose the most interesting challenge to industrial pluralism: How should the courts respond when union officials, potentially in violation of their DFR, failed to utilize grievance procedures to press an employee's complaint *against the employer*? In such situations, the employee's grievance could no longer continue to arbitration, as voluntary grievance procedures in most collective bargaining agreements reserved the discretion for proceeding to arbitration only to the union and the employer – and not the employee.

Courts seemingly had two options with these hybrid cases, the first being to turn an unsympathetic eye to the employee's interest and not allow litigation to address employee complaints. Doing so would obviously bear a cost for that employee, but it would also allow industrial self-government to continue without interference from the courts, while preserving the autonomy of unions and arbitration processes. Conversely, courts might open their doors to these breach-of-contract claims brought

---

⁹⁴ 371 U.S. at 196n1 (citations omitted). Although as Feller notes, the collective bargaining agreement at issue in *Smith* did contain provisions for arbitration. These provisions simply failed to appear in the complaint that reached the Court. Feller, "General Theory," 692n155.
⁹⁵ 379 U.S. 650 (1965).
⁹⁶ Id. at 652–53 (citations omitted).

by individual employees against their employers. Doing so, however, would heighten the role of the courts in resolving industrial disputes and bear obvious costs to industrial pluralism. These specific circumstances demanded judicial tension management, and in *Vaca v. Sipes*,[97] the Court crafted an interesting compromise.[98]

Vaca v. Sipes *as Tension Management*
The complex facts of *Vaca* were as follows: the dispute centered on an employee with a long history of high blood pressure. Upon becoming ill, the employee took an extended leave from his work. However, after a break, his condition improved, and he received approval from his family physician to return to work. A doctor for the employer also examined the employee, however, and reached a different conclusion. This doctor did not allow the employee to be reinstated. At this point, the employee obtained approval to return to work from a second, outside doctor. The employee briefly returned to work, but the employer soon discharged him permanently (once the employer's doctor learned of his return).[99]

Faced with these obstacles, the employee then turned to the union for help so he could be reinstated. The collective bargaining agreement between the union and the employer provided grievance procedures, and these procedures progressed up to the fourth stage with no resolution (arbitration constituted the fifth and final stage of the grievance process). However, before going on to arbitration, the union decided to send the employee to another doctor, at the union's expense, since the key issue was whether the employee's health problems justified the discharge. The fourth doctor's examination suggested that the employee's health really was poor, and the union's executive board voted against taking the employee's grievance to arbitration.[100] Thus, with the grievance procedure permanently stuck at the fourth stage, the employee brought

---

[97] 386 U.S. 171 (1967).
[98] The depth of scholarship devoted to addressing these issues after *Vaca* indicates the severity of the tension prompted by Section 301/DFR suits. See, e.g., Benjamin Aaron, "The Duty of Fair Representation: An Overview," in *The Duty of Fair Representation*, ed. Jean T. McKelvey (Ithaca, NY: Cornell University Press, 1977), 8–24; Feller, "General Theory;" Thomas P. Lewis, "Fair Representation in Grievance Administration: Vaca v. Sipes," *Supreme Court Review* (1967): 81–126; Lea S. VanderVelde, "A Fair Process Model for the Union's Fair Representation Duty," *Minnesota Law Review* 67, no. 6 (July 1983): 1093–96; Stone, "Post-War Paradigm," 1535–38, 1541–42.
[99] 386 U.S. at 174–75.
[100] Id. at 175.

suit against the union for "'arbitrarily, capriciously and without just or reasonable reason or cause'"[101] refusing to take his grievance to arbitration with the employer. The employee brought a separate suit against the employer for breach of the collective bargaining agreement for his unjustified discharge.[102]

Assuming the employee had a legitimate grievance, the sequence of events demonstrated how employee individual rights could be squeezed between the interlocking processes of adjudication and arbitration. If the employee brought suit against the employer for breach of contract under Section 301, the employer could defend itself on the grounds that the collective bargaining agreement's grievance procedures had not been exhausted. On the other hand, at least in this case, those procedures had not been exhausted because they were at the discretion of the employee's union representatives – who had decided not to press the employee's claims.[103] Respecting the dictates of industrial pluralism and union autonomy, and thereby deferring to the union's decision, would leave the employee with no redress. Doing the opposite and allowing the employee easy access to the courts would threaten to undermine the union's authority and the efficacy of grievance procedures.

The Court first asserted its jurisdiction to hear the employee's claim against the union. Past precedents suggested that union breaches of the DFR were an unfair labor practice under the NLRA and should thus fall within the NLRB's exclusive jurisdiction.[104] The Court rejected this view, however, on statutory grounds as well as on precedent. The DFR was originally a judicial innovation in *Steele*, the Court noted, and had remained a judicial concern long afterward. This, among other things, led the Court to question whether the NLRB might really have a comparative expertise on the types of issues presented in DFR cases.[105]

More notable were the pragmatic considerations that moved the Court to assume jurisdiction over this case. In particular, its first major conclusion was to strike the balance between individual rights and industrial pluralism by finding that an employee could bring a Section 301 suit against an employer in the courts, *even if* grievance procedures had not been exhausted, so long as the employee could show that the union had violated its DFR in its choice not to initiate arbitration.

[101] Id. at 173.
[102] Id. at 176, 176n4.
[103] Id. at 184–85.
[104] Id. at 176–79.
[105] Id. at 179–81.

Given this rule, courts would need to have jurisdiction over DFR claims; Section 301 claims brought by an employee against an employer in court were unquestionably appropriate for the courts (under *Smith*), and given the Court's newly announced rule, exercising jurisdiction over and adjudicating Section 301 claims might necessarily encompass the DFR question.[106]

Aside from the jurisdictional argument, however, the Court's aforementioned conclusion on how to strike the balance between individual rights and industrial pluralism constituted an important first step toward resolving the main substantive issue in *Vaca*. Indeed, the fact that the Court focused on the DFR as a means to accommodate these conflicting authorities illustrates the tension-managing nature of the *Vaca* ruling. Once it could be shown that the union violated this duty, industrial pluralism values would give way to the rights of the individual employee. Otherwise, industrial pluralism and voluntary arbitration outcomes would remain the default.

Still, this was not a conclusive settlement of the issue since another key question remained: How high was the threshold to prove a DFR violation? The Court's answer embodied the competing values inherent in the hybrid Section 301/DFR claims.

On the one hand, the Court expressed concern for the individual rights of the employee throughout the opinion and firmly stated that the union should not arbitrarily undercut those rights. Indeed, such concerns had initially given rise to the DFR itself.[107] On the other hand, the Court rejected the notion that employees necessarily possessed an absolute right to have their grievances arbitrated. If a union's mere decision to not take a grievance to arbitration violated the DFR, such a circumstance would, in effect, overly privilege individual rights. This circumstance would also create a number of negative consequences for the autonomy of collective bargaining from state control and union autonomy from its individual employee members.[108]

---

[106] Id. at 184, 185–88. The Court offered two additional, related pragmatic justifications. First, given that the NLRB's General Counsel had "unreviewable discretion to refuse to initiate an unfair labor practice complaint," if the courts were deprived of jurisdiction to hear DFR cases, employees might lack any forum for review of their complaints against the union. Id. at 181–83. Second, there was the issue of remedy: having one forum that could entertain both Section 301 and DFR claims would make fashioning a remedy in response to the actions of both union and employer easier. Id. at 187–88, 188n12.

[107] Id. at 190–91.

[108] Id. at 192.

Specifically, a low threshold for showing a DFR violation would reduce union discretion in matters for which it wanted to settle grievances short of arbitration because they would be motivated to arbitrate every complaint to avoid liability. A low threshold would also intrude into union decision making and undermine the union's authority to collectively bargain or credibly strike deals with management on issues such as grievance procedures. More generally, a low threshold for proving DFR violations would make it easy for employees to get breach of contract claims against their employers into the courts under Section 301, thus undermining arbitration as the primary means of managing labor-management conflicts.[109]

The balance struck in *Vaca*, and the doctrinal innovation that would be crucial as a tension-management device, emerged in the standard for establishing a DFR violation for unprocessed grievances: "*arbitrary or bad-faith conduct* on the part of the Union in processing [a] grievance."[110] If an employee met this standard, they could opt to adjudicate their Section 301 claims. If an employee did not meet this standard, they would be stuck with the outcome of voluntary grievance procedures. The standard was cognizant of individual employee rights, yet difficult enough to meet that it posed real constraints on individual employees for joint Section 301/DFR claims in the courts. Given the union's efforts on behalf of the employee in *Vaca*, the Court ruled that the employee had not met the standard for showing a DFR violation.[111]

As a technical doctrinal test formulated in abstract terms, and nestled within competing doctrinal commitments, this standard displayed another common characteristic of tension-managing doctrinal devices: although it was consequential, it was also formulated in vague and abstract enough terms so that it would remain flexible for future applications. Thus, Justice Black – who generally criticized the Court's ruling for going too far in undercutting employees' individual rights – noted the following point in his dissent concerning the vagueness of the Court's standard:

Henceforth, in almost every § 301 breach-of-contract suit by an employee against an employer, the employee will have the additional burden of proving that the union acted arbitrarily or in bad faith. The Court never explains what is meant by this vague phrase or how trial judges are intelligently to translate it to a jury. Must the employee prove that the union in fact acted arbitrarily, or will it be sufficient

---

[109] Id. at 191–92; Stone, "Post-War Paradigm," 1537–38.
[110] 386 U.S. at 193 (emphasis added).
[111] Id. at 194–95.

to show that the employee's grievance was so meritorious that a reasonable union would not have refused to carry it to arbitration?[112]

Nevertheless, while Justice Black criticized the standard's vagueness, he implicitly recognized its flexibility – a characteristic that commended it as a useful doctrinal device for managing conflicting judicial values.

Finally, these tension-managing features of the ruling also point to an interpretation that diverges, to some extent, from Katherine Stone's view of *Vaca*. I should first note that much of the preceding analysis tracks Stone's views on the incongruity posed by the *Vaca* ruling for the reigning industrial pluralist order in the post–World War II era. That said, in 1981, Stone interpreted *Vaca*'s incongruity as signaling the then-impending collapse of the industrial pluralist structure because the ruling moved toward accommodating individual employee rights.[113] By recognizing an exception to the priority of union interests over employee interests, and by opening the door a little wider for Section 301 claims to enter the courts, the Court's ruling in *Vaca* could reasonably have been seen at the time as the initial crack in the dam leading to the collapse of the entire industrial pluralist structure. However, examining *Vaca* through the lens of recalibration and tension management underscores that conflicting commitments in this area of policy are to be expected; thus, the Court's attempt to accommodate individual rights within the industrial pluralist structure was not necessarily a sign of the system's collapse – it was a sign of that system's vitality. Later doctrinal developments support the validity of this latter interpretation.

After Vaca

In *Hines v. Anchor Motor Freight*,[114] a subsequent hybrid Section 301/DFR case, the Court extended the tension-management device of the DFR standard beyond the context presented in *Vaca*. In *Vaca*, the union refused to take a matter to arbitration; in *Hines*, the standard regulated how unions handled grievances during arbitration. In *Hines*, an employer accused several employees of profiting from travel reimbursements, and the employer subsequently discharged the employees for cause.[115] The employees suspected that their employer's evidence against them was faulty, and they urged the union to investigate this matter before

---

[112] Id. at 210 (Black, J., dissenting).
[113] Stone, "Post-War Paradigm," 1541–42.
[114] 424 U.S. 554 (1976).
[115] Id. at 556–58.

their upcoming arbitration hearing. The union failed to do so, however, and presented no evidence to contradict the employer's evidence at the hearing.[116] The ruling at the hearing went against the employees, and they were discharged.[117] Later investigation revealed that the employer's evidence against the employees was indeed faulty.[118] As a result, the employees brought suit against the union for violating its DFR by "arbitrarily and in bad faith depriving petitioners of their employment and permitting their discharge without sufficient proof."[119] They also brought suit against the employer for breach of the contract under Section 301, given their claim that there was no just cause for the discharge.[120]

The sole issue before the Court was whether the lower courts' summary judgment for the employer was appropriate. The Court began its analysis on this issue with an overview of the pull between the industrial pluralism commitments and the demands of employee individual rights. On the former, it stated:

[Courts] should not undertake to review the merits of arbitration awards but should defer to the tribunal chosen by the parties finally to settle their disputes. Otherwise "plenary review by a court of the merits would make meaningless the provisions that the arbitrator's decision is final, for in reality it would almost never be final." *Steelworkers v. Enterprise Corp.*, 363 U.S. 593, 599 (1960).[121]

At the same time, commitment to the finality of arbitration had to be tempered by concerns for the individual employee. Hence, the Court also canvassed the DFR precedents and included an extended discussion of *Vaca*.[122] Given, however, that the grievance had gone to arbitration in the present case, the question here was distinct from that posed in *Vaca*. In this case, the issue turned on whether the Court felt the need to strike a balance between individual rights and industrial pluralism in regulating how unions handle grievances in arbitration. To this, the Court ruled that an employee could receive adjudicative relief against the employer (and union) if they proved a violation of the union's DFR during the arbitration process:

Even though under *Vaca* the employer may not insist on exhaustion of grievance procedures when the union has breached its representation duty, it is urged that

[116] Id. at 557.
[117] Id. at 557–58.
[118] Id. at 559.
[119] Id. at 558.
[120] Id.
[121] Id. at 563.
[122] Id. at 563–67.

when the procedures have been followed and a decision favorable to the employer announced, the employer must be protected from relitigation by the express contractual provision declaring a decision to be final and binding. We disagree. The union's breach of duty relieves the employee of an express or implied requirement that disputes be settled through contractual grievance procedures; if it seriously undermines the integrity of the arbitral process the union's breach also removes the bar of the finality provisions of the contract.[123]

The Court argued that to do otherwise would lead to highly perverse consequences. The Court of Appeals suggested that an employee could only receive judicial relief if the employer were itself guilty of misconduct in the arbitration process. If this were the standard, however, a DFR violation by the union during arbitration would not be enough for an employee to gain entry into the courts for a Section 301 claim against the employer; indeed, the employee would have no remedy against the employer no matter how egregious the union's abuse of its duty was.[124] According to the Court, surely this could not have been Congress' intent.[125]

Rehnquist's dissent criticized the majority for significantly extending the reach of employee Section 301 claims against their employers and undermining the fundamental principles of the industrial pluralist system.[126] But the majority hardly saw itself involved in the task of repudiation. This was tension management, and so long as a moderately consequential barrier existed for employees trying to show a DFR violation, this would prevent some employee Section 301 claims from being adjudicated in the courts. Thus, this barrier could preserve a significant degree of integrity for the industrial pluralist system. As the majority stated:

It is urged that the reversal of the Court of Appeals will undermine not only the finality rule but the entire collective-bargaining process. Employers, it is said, will be far less willing to give up their untrammeled right to discharge without cause and to agree to private settlement procedures. But the burden on employees will remain a substantial one, far too heavy in the opinion of some. To prevail against either the company or the Union, petitioners must not only show that their discharge was contrary to the contract but must also carry the burden of demonstrating breach of duty by the Union. As the District Court indicated, this involves more than demonstrating mere errors in judgment.[127]

The *Hines* ruling might seem to support Stone's assertion that the Court's initial willingness to expand the leeway for employee Section 301 claims

[123] Id. at 567.
[124] Id. at 570.
[125] Id.
[126] Id. at 574 (Rehnquist, J., dissenting)
[127] Id. at 570–71 (citations omitted).

against their employers in *Vaca* spelled the beginning of the end of the industrial pluralist system. Indeed, she interpreted the *Hines* ruling as indicative and supportive of this trend.[128] But the Court's subsequent ruling in *Air Line Pilots Association v. O'Neill*[129] (a ruling handed down seven years after Stone wrote her article) suggests that *Vaca* and *Hines* should more appropriately be interpreted as tension-managing opinions aimed at maintaining the industrial pluralist system. *O'Neill* involved employee dissatisfaction when a union agreed to settle an ongoing strike with the employer. Some of the affected employees brought suit against the union, claiming it had breached its DFR by negotiating and accepting the settlement.[130]

Although this was a straightforward DFR case rather than a hybrid Section 301/DFR case, the Court's elaboration on the DFR standard is noteworthy in two respects. First, the Court ruled that the duty attaches to the union, not just in contract administration and enforcement, but in contract negotiation as well.[131] Second, and more important, the Court corrected the Court of Appeals' application of the DFR-*Vaca* standard as requiring the absence of "arbitrary, discriminatory, or in bad faith" actions. It agreed that the Court of Appeals correctly applied the *Vaca* standard to a union engaged in negotiating activity.[132] But it criticized the Court of Appeals' application of that standard for interpreting the "arbitrary" component of the standard too expansively. The appellate court had held:

We think a decision to be non-arbitrary must be (1) based upon relevant, permissible union factors which excludes the possibility of it being based upon motivations such as personal animosity or political favoritism; (2) *a rational result of the consideration of these factors*; and (3) inclusive of a fair and impartial consideration of the interests of all employees.[133]

But this standard, the Court wrote, set too low a threshold to prompt judicial oversight of union activity: "We are persuaded, however, that the Court of Appeals' further refinement of the arbitrariness component of the standard authorizes more judicial review of the substance of negotiated agreements than is consistent with national labor policy."[134] In response,

[128] Stone, "Post-War Paradigm," 1541.
[129] 499 U.S. 65 (1991).
[130] Id. at 68–71.
[131] Id. at 77.
[132] Id. at 71, 77.
[133] Quoted in id. at 72 (citations omitted) (emphasis added by the Court of Appeals).
[134] Id. at 77.

the Court defined the arbitrariness component of the DFR standard as follows: "The final product of the bargaining process may constitute evidence of a breach of duty only if it can be fairly characterized as so far outside a 'wide range of reasonableness,' that it is wholly 'irrational' or 'arbitrary.'"[135] In other words, the Court demonstrated a preference – unanimously in this case – for maintaining a more deferential standard toward union autonomy than the Court of Appeals had adopted.

It is questionable just how much clarity this elaboration on the "arbitrary" component of the DFR standard brought as the words themselves appear to have provided for a continued judicial flexibility. What was clear, though, was that the Court wanted to ratchet up the threshold for showing a DFR violation. Furthermore, and related, the Court indicated that *Vaca* had *not* signaled an impending implosion of either the industrial pluralist system or the judiciary's commitment to industrial pluralist values. Rather, twenty-four years after *Vaca*, the Court was endeavoring to put additional teeth into the tension-management barrier between individual employee rights and industrial pluralism in order to maintain the integrity of the latter. As the Court stated:

> As we acknowledged above, Congress did not intend judicial review of a union's performance to permit the court to substitute its own view of the proper bargain for that reached by the union. Rather, Congress envisioned the relationship between the courts and labor unions as similar to that between the courts and the legislature. Any substantive examination of a union's performance, therefore, must be highly deferential, recognizing the wide latitude that negotiators need for the effective performance of their bargaining responsibilities.[136]

O'Neill clarified that the *Vaca* ruling was a sign of industrial pluralism's continuing resilience; the boundary tensions posed by a growing judicial and intellectual commitment to individual employee rights at that time were contained within the larger legal structure. And presently, the *Steelworkers Trilogy* remains central in American labor law.[137]

---

[135] Id. at 78 (citations omitted).
[136] Id. (citations omitted).
[137] "Throughout the nearly half century that has elapsed since *Steelworkers*, the Court has continually reaffirmed the centrality of arbitration to the resolution of labor disputes, and indeed has expanded the favor for arbitration into other contexts." Richard A. Bales, "The Arbitrability of Side and Settlement Agreements in the Collective Bargaining Context," *West Virginia Law Review* 105, no. 3 (Spring 2003): 576; ibid., 585–86; William B. Gould IV, "Keynote Address: *Steelworkers Trilogy* after a Half Century" (paper presented at the annual meeting of the National Academy of Arbitrators, Philadelphia, PA, May 27, 2010), 3 ("*Steelworkers Trilogy* gave birth to a labor arbitration law jurisprudence which has been with us for a half century and which, in

Ironically, however, even if Stone's prediction was incorrect, subsequent trends in labor relations have also suggested how her general prediction about industrial pluralism's growing weaknesses proved to be correct. As events unfolded, the primary danger to industrial pluralism was not the internal threat of implosion – with union autonomy and arbitration incapable of reaching a stable balance with employee rights. The primary danger, rather, was an external threat posed by the entire structure's increasing irrelevance to employment relations. The centrality of unions in the industrial pluralist scheme, and the decline of unions since the 1960s, fed that irrelevance. This decline – which has been especially pronounced since the 1980s – has made the governing principles of industrial pluralism increasingly inapplicable to more and more employees and has thus made the acute conflict between individual and union rights that was present in *Vaca* a moot point of controversy for all but the small minority of those who are unionized.[138] Even though the industrial pluralist structure remains intact and even hegemonic where it remains applicable, labor relations in America have increasingly bypassed it – along with the institution of collective bargaining – in favor of federal and state employment laws and state judicial developments that focus on individual employee guarantees.[139] The real challenge to industrial pluralism has turned out to emanate not from any decisions reached in *Vaca* but rather from problems in the health and vitality of the unions themselves.

CONCLUSION

Following the transformation in labor relations from dismantling reform, to delimitation, to construction, and finally to regime maintenance

---

my view, will likely be with us when our successors are here a half century from now – though, if ironies squared over the first half century can be any guide to the future, with significant shifts both in substance and perhaps even statutory form.").

[138] On the decline of unions, see R. Bales, "A New Direction for American Labor Law: Individual Autonomy and the Compulsory Arbitration of Individual Employment Rights," *Houston Law Review* 30, no. 5 (Spring 1994): 1871; Richard A. Bales, "The Discord between Collective Bargaining and Individual Employment Rights: Theoretical Origins and a Proposed Solution," *Boston University Law Review* 77, no. 4 (October 1997): 693–701; Stone, "Legacy," 578–79.

[139] Bales, "New Direction," 1864–81; Bales, "Discord," 688–89; William R. Corbett, "Waiting for the Labor Law of the Twenty-First Century: Everything Old Is New Again," *Berkley Journal of Employment & Labor Law* 23, no. 2 (2002): 269–73; Gary Minda, "Arbitration in the Post-Cold-War Era – Justice Kennedy's View of Postexpiration Arbitrability in *Litton Financial Printing Division v. NLRB*," *Stetson Law Review* 22, no. 1 (Fall 1992): 113; Stone, "Legacy," 591–93, 636.

demonstrates the broader point that achieving major political change in American politics is an extremely protracted affair. From the passage of the Wagner Act in 1935 to the Supreme Court's affirmation of arbitration in 1960, this historical narrative on labor relations spanned twenty-five years.

Taking the long view of the transformation in labor relations allows us to take stock of an additional and related point: the story of the transformation in labor rights is clearly not that of a straightforward narrative directly leading from the original intent of the Wagner Act to industrial pluralism. Rather, this is a narrative with a number of twists and turns, with developmental alternatives presented at several crucial turning points in the mid-twentieth century – even as these alternatives grew increasingly limited over time.

9

The Entrenchment and Maintenance of the Anticlassification Order

After *Brown v. Board of Education*[1] in 1954, the Civil Rights Act of 1964, and the Voting Rights Act of 1965, the foundations of Jim Crow were irreversibly dismantled. Elements of racial subordination persisted in the South and elsewhere, but the logic of racial subordination in the post–civil rights era was something both functionally and formally distinct from what had existed before. To the extent that racial segregation in public schooling or infringements on minority voting would persist, they would not enjoy explicit legal support.

However, as with the preceding case studies, this political change prompted particular uncertainties. Chapter 5 discusses how reforms in constitutional equal protection prompted crucial questions of just *how far* this reform effort would reach into – and reshape – other governmental operations. The Supreme Court crystallized and elaborated on emergent political developments as it established an "anticlassification" interpretation of constitutional equal protection in *Milliken v. Bradley*[2] and *Washington v. Davis*.[3] As a result, alternative developmental paths – such as an antisubordination view of constitutional equal protection – were legally bypassed after the mid-1970s.

Thus, with respect to constitutional equal protection matters under the Fourteenth Amendment and under the Due Process Clause of the Fifth Amendment, the scope of judicial intervention and judicial oversight of local, state, and federal governmental actions was limited to only those

[1] 347 U.S. 483 (1954).
[2] 418 U.S. 717 (1974).
[3] 426 U.S. 229 (1976).

actions that exhibited either explicit or implicit racial classifications (i.e., those laws that were motivated by a racially discriminatory purpose). At the same time, the judiciary would not be nearly as attentive, demanding, or skeptical with respect to those laws that were facially neutral with respect to race or exhibited no racially discriminatory purpose – but that happened to have a disproportionate burdensome *effect* on racial minorities. Judicial delimitation had clarified that the assault on racial inequality, under the banner of constitutional equal protection, would not subsequently morph into an analogous legal assault on socioeconomic inequality as well.

As with the prior historical cases, this delimitation in the 1970s carried lasting consequences for the emerging postreform system of governance. With the antisubordination view of equal protection taken off the table in the mid-1970s, it was all but guaranteed that a wide range of governmental actions would lie beyond the reach of legal challenges by minority citizens or the skeptical oversight of the judiciary (assuming it was even inclined to be skeptical). Such insulated governmental actions included, for example, the use of certain civil service exams[4] or the application of local zoning laws,[5] where the actions may have had a disparate negative impact on minorities but where there was no evidence of a clear, racially discriminatory purpose. (And the absence of any such discriminatory intent might be due to either the cleverness of state actors or to the selective indifference[6] of state actors toward minorities.) The post–civil rights era, at least in the context of constitutional equal protection, mirrors the prior historical cases in underscoring the limits of transforming governance. Although the discarding of the old order may be permanent, delimitation clarifies that the principles of reform will be narrowly construed.

Yet even if judicial delimitation clarified one set of uncertainties at the outer edges of reform, another postreform uncertainty remained regarding the formal allocation of authority and rights internal to the domain of reform. Long after *Milliken* and *Davis* were decided, uncertainties persisted regarding the constitutional legitimacy of "benign" state-sponsored racial preferences or affirmative action. Whether the state could or could not employ such policies would have very significant

---

[4] See, e.g., id.
[5] See, *Village of Arlington Heights v. Metropolitan Housing Development Corp.*, 429 U.S. 252 (1977).
[6] See, e.g., Paul Brest, "Foreword: In Defense of the Antidiscrimination Principle," *Harvard Law Review* 90, no. 1 (November 1976): 7–8.

implications for the rights of minorities – both in relation to the state and in relation to the nonminority groups disadvantaged by such policies.

Assessing the legal viability of affirmative action could not be gleaned by simply examining prior political developments. Both a commitment to racial preferences *and* hostility to racial preferences could be made consistent with the prior commitments of reform and judicial delimitation. That is, neither a pro- nor anti-affirmative action stance necessarily sat in tension with the prior dismantling of Jim Crow. And neither stance necessarily implied tension with the prior delimiting settlement limiting minority challenges to state actions. Affirmative action policies, of course, speak only to voluntary governmental actions.

Determining how affirmative action would fit within the emerging post–Jim Crow system of governance on race relations was a question of great magnitude – even if the transformative stakes may have been less than they were in the mid-1970s. It was nearly twenty years after *Davis* before the Court decisively answered this question. Notably, this was roughly the same amount of time for the periods of construction in both the post-Reconstruction and the post–New Deal eras. The more technical legal question that occupied the Court during these two decades was whether governmental affirmative action programs challenged on constitutional grounds should or should not be subject to "strict scrutiny" under the Court's equal protection analysis.[7]

The answer to this question would essentially determine the viability of affirmative action as a policy option. If the Court determined that racial preferences should be treated identically to other racial classifications and thus be subject to strict scrutiny, supporters of affirmative action in the 1970s, 1980s, and 1990s could have reasonably interpreted this to mean a de facto prohibition on affirmative action given past trends in constitutional history (until 2003, arguably no challenged law subject to strict scrutiny analysis under the Equal Protection Clause had ever been

---

[7] The default, and lowest level of scrutiny is "rationality review." Applicable to general economic and social legislation, a challenged state action must be "rationally related" to a "legitimate governmental purpose" to be upheld. See, e.g., *Williamson v. Lee Optical Co.*, 348 U.S. 483 (1955). "Intermediate scrutiny" demands that challenged state actions be "substantially related" to an "important governmental purpose" in order to be upheld (applicable to gender classifications, for example). See, e.g., *Craig v. Boren*, 429 U.S. 190 (1976). And finally for "strict scrutiny," challenged state actions must be shown to be "narrowly tailored," or even "necessary," to a "compelling governmental purpose" to be upheld. The paradigmatic type of classification triggering strict scrutiny is a racial classification. See, e.g., *Korematsu v. United States*, 323 U.S. 214 (1944).

TABLE 9.1 *Construction and Tension Management after the Transformation in Constitutional Equal Protection*

Lingering uncertainty	The place of voluntary affirmative action within the anticlassification order
Emergence of the new system of governance	From the Supreme Court
Entrenchment of the new system of governance	By the Supreme Court in *City of Richmond v. Croson, Adarand v. Pena*
Judicial tension management	(1) In higher education affirmative action: *Grutter v. Bollinger* (2) In voting rights: *Shaw v. Reno, Miller v. Johnson*

upheld by the Court).[8] Strict scrutiny was said to be "strict" only in theory, as it often turned out to be "fatal in fact."[9]

In this chapter, the first task is to illustrate the continuing and lingering uncertainties after delimitation. To that end, the chapter will very briefly trace the Court's treatment of government-sponsored affirmative action programs beginning in the late 1970s to the mid-1990s. This narrative is hardly straightforward, and it appropriately reflects the existence of viable developmental alternatives during this time. Uncertainties, however, were finally settled in the 1995 case of *Adarand Constructors, Inc. v. Pena*, where a sharply divided Court conclusively established strict scrutiny as the appropriate standard of review for both federal and state governmental affirmative action programs.[10]

The significance of *Adarand* for the present argument lies in both illuminating the political processes of construction and in demonstrating the recurrence of an order-affirming mode of adjudication. With this order-affirming decision, minority rights in the aftermath of Jim Crow had been definitively recalibrated. The principled, judicial affirmation of an anticlassification system of race relations ensured that it would be legally entrenched as the new status quo in constitutional race relations, as noted in part by Table 9.1.

---

[8] Richard A. Primus, "Equal Protection and Disparate Impact: Round Three," *Harvard Law Review* 117, no. 2 (December 2003): 501.
[9] Gerald Gunther, "Foreword: In Search of Evolving Doctrine on a Changing Court: A Model for a Newer Equal Protection," *Harvard Law Review* 86, no. 1 (November 1972): 8. See also, *Fullilove v. Klutznick*, 448 U.S. 448, 507 (1980) (Powell, J., concurring).
[10] 515 U.S. 200 (1995).

As with Chapters 7 and 8, tracing the entrenchment of the new status quo is only half of the historical narrative. Part II of this chapter focuses on how the new anticlassification regime has interacted with and accommodated both resurgent values and new policy circumstances that have supported the use of race-conscious policies to aid racial minorities. Exploring the Court's role in managing boundary tensions with its rulings in higher education affirmative action and minority vote dilution – the former a policy context wholly contained within constitutional equal protection and the latter a policy context partly within it – only further demonstrates the resilience of the legal and political principles that were established with judicial delimitation and with *Adarand*. Indeed, the post-*Adarand* era in constitutional equal protection is truly one of normal politics and political equilibrium because this governing order has accommodated conflicting political and institutional forces within its core principles. Although the exploration of the anticlassification order will focus only on judicial-centered case studies of tension management, these cases will shed further light on the contours of the current status quo, illuminate some recent trends in the Court's jurisprudence on race, and underscore the Court's commitment to stability in the midst of a political equilibrium. Finally, these case studies also underscore tension management as a distinctive mode of adjudication for periods of political equilibrium.

PART I: THE ENTRENCHMENT OF THE ANTICLASSIFICATION ORDER

Uncertainties after Delimitation: The Constitutional Legitimacy of Affirmative Action

From the late 1970s to the mid-1990s, the Supreme Court's affirmative action decisions were highly divided. This divisiveness is the most striking indicator of the developmental uncertainties lingering after the delimitation of reform in the 1970s. Indeed, it is not difficult to imagine alternative paths in the development of constitutional equal protection occurring as late as 1989 or even in the mid-1990s. The Court plausibly could have settled on a more deferential stance toward government-sponsored affirmative action. Alternative paths were bypassed, however, in favor of the consolidation of anticlassification principles in 1995. As a result, the Court is likely to apply strict scrutiny to all racial classifications evaluated under constitutional equal protection in the foreseeable future.

The present case study of construction is notably more of a judicial story than the case studies in Chapters 7 and 8. In the first case study, the Supreme Court's affirmation of Jim Crow was in response to changing dynamics at the federal government level and the appearance of legislation put forth by the southern state governments. Similarly, the Court's later affirmation of industrial pluralism took place only after voluntary arbitration had first been promoted by the National War Labor Board during the early 1940s and then widely adopted in industry.

In contrast, the present story of construction is about the judicial affirmation of anticlassification principles with relatively less extrajudicial stimulus. The Court's entrenchment of the anticlassification principle was a function of the judiciary's own active opposition to legislative efforts at the state and federal levels to establish affirmative action programs. The principal engine for construction in the present case study was the Court itself.

This was an ironic development given that judicial delimitation in the mid-1970s saw the Court delimiting reform in the cases of *Milliken v. Bradley*[11] and *Washington v. Davis*[12] at least partially in the name of *defending* legislative prerogatives. As the Court appeared to suggest in those cases, it was a virtue of the anticlassification principle that it kept local, state, and federal legislative organs free of too much judicial meddling in the context of school desegregation or employment discrimination. In later years, however, judicial meddling in the service of undercutting government-sponsored racial preferences proved to be more acceptable to the Court.

The doctrinal story for affirmative action and constitutional equal protection begins with *Bakke*, where a narrow majority validated the idea of race consciousness in higher education admissions.[13] The admissions policy at the University of California–Davis's medical school reserved 16 slots, within each entering class of 100, for disadvantaged students who were also racial minorities. A rejected white applicant challenged the program. He claimed that the admissions policy violated, among other things, the Equal Protection Clause of the Fourteenth Amendment and Title VI of the Civil Rights Act of 1964.[14]

---

[11] 418 U.S. 717 (1974).
[12] 426 U.S. 229 (1976).
[13] 438 U.S. 265 (1978).
[14] Id. at 272–79. The Title VI issues were, however, ignored by the parties themselves in their arguments before the Supreme Court. Id. at 281.

Stevens, writing for Burger, Stewart, and Rehnquist, avoided the constitutional issue entirely.[15] He instead concluded to not uphold the Davis program because it violated Title VI of the Civil Rights Act.[16] A four-person bloc, encompassing Brennan, White, Marshall, and Blackmun, asserted instead that intermediate scrutiny was the proper standard for evaluating the Davis admissions policy and concluded that the program should be upheld.[17]

Situated between these two voting blocs was Justice Powell, whose opinion for the Court commanded two different voting majorities for each of its two principal conclusions. Powell asserted that strict scrutiny was the appropriate standard for this affirmative action program.[18] He also concluded that the Davis program failed strict scrutiny because it failed the "means" component of the strict scrutiny test; the program was not narrowly tailored or necessary to achieve the school's goal of student diversity.[19] His vote, added to the Stevens bloc, was the majority for striking down the Davis program. Yet Powell also explicitly endorsed the Harvard College admissions policy, which did not employ racial quotas – akin to the Davis set-aside – but instead evaluated the race of their potential students as merely a "plus" factor.[20] This assertion, combined with the Brennan bloc, totaled five votes for the conclusion that universities could consider race when making admission decisions.[21] Finally, of most relevance here, Powell's opinion for the Court left no clarity on what level of scrutiny would be applied to affirmative action programs going forward. The Stevens bloc's focus on the statutory issue, combined with Powell's focus on the constitutionality of the program, ensured that no majority of the Court converged to conclude that strict scrutiny was the appropriate standard of review for affirmative action.

Things took a decidedly less favorable turn for affirmative action proponents nine years later in the case of *City of Richmond v. J. A. Croson Company*.[22] There, the focus was on a Richmond, Virginia, municipal

---

[15] Id. at 411–12 (Stevens, J., concurring in part and dissenting in part).
[16] Id. at 412–18.
[17] Id. at 357–59, 362, 373–74 (Brennan, J., concurring in part and dissenting in part). See also id. at 396–402 (Marshall, J., concurring in part and dissenting in part).
[18] Id. at 289–305.
[19] Id. at 305–16.
[20] Id. at 316–20, 321–24 (Appendix to Opinion of Powell, J., outlining the Harvard College Admissions Program).
[21] Id. at 326.
[22] 488 U.S. 469 (1989).

set-aside program favoring minority-owned subcontractors.[23] The set-aside plan was subsequently challenged on equal protection grounds under the Fourteenth Amendment.[24] The case brought affirmative action before a Court that now included three Reagan appointments: O'Connor, Scalia, and Kennedy. These three had, in turn, replaced an affirmative action supporter in Powell, an opponent in Stewart, and a swing vote in Chief Justice Burger. The Court's composition alone did not favor a positive outcome for the set-aside, and the expected result ensued.

Although the Court's earlier ruling in *Fullilove v. Klutznick* had upheld a federal affirmative action program with six votes (and with no majority coalescing on the scrutiny question),[25] O'Connor's opinion for the Court in *Croson* first asserted that *Fullilove* was not applicable to this case.[26] Crucial to reaching this conclusion was the greater leeway she afforded to Congress, relative to the states, in instituting an affirmative action program.[27] Second, O'Connor asserted that the proper standard of review was strict scrutiny, and that this level of review was appropriate for all racial classifications – at least at the state level – regardless of whether the racial classification burdened or benefited racial minorities.[28] Given this standard of review, O'Connor concluded that the program failed on both the purpose and the means components of the test.[29]

On the key assertion that strict scrutiny was appropriate for this affirmative action program, O'Connor's opinion carried five votes: her own vote and those of Rehnquist, White, Kennedy,[30] and Scalia.[31] This was a bare majority, and although the ruling was perhaps limited to only local and state governmental actions given the *Fullilove* precedent, it also marked the first time that a clear majority of the Court had agreed on strict scrutiny as the standard of review for affirmative action – a point noted by Justice Marshall in his dissent.[32] Strict scrutiny had seemingly gained a strong foothold.

A year later in *Metro Broadcasting, Inc. v. FCC*, the Court upheld a federal affirmative action program with five votes and did so using

[23] Id. at 477–78.
[24] Id. at 483.
[25] 448 U.S. 448, 490, 517–22 (1980).
[26] 488 U.S. at 486–91.
[27] Id. at 490.
[28] Id. at 494.
[29] Id. at 499–508.
[30] Id. at 476 (noting votes for Part III-A).
[31] Id. at 520 (Scalia, J., concurring).
[32] Id. at 551 (Marshall, J., dissenting).

an intermediate scrutiny standard.[33] *Metro Broadcasting* proved to be a short-lived detour, however. Five years later, in *Adarand Constructors, Inc. v. Pena*,[34] the Court's focus was drawn to "subcontractor compensation clauses" that were included in most contracts awarded by federal governmental agencies. These clauses provided for extra compensation to prime contractors who hired racial minority subcontractors.[35]

Major changes had occurred to the Court's composition since *Metro Broadcasting* five years earlier. It had lost its core liberal bloc of supporters for affirmative action in Brennan, Marshall, and Blackmun, and had lost the generally supportive White as well. In return, it had gained three consistent affirmative action supporters in Souter, Ginsburg, and Breyer, and one opponent in Thomas. Thomas's vote, combined with the conservative bloc of O'Connor, Scalia, Kennedy, and Rehnquist, subsequently composed the five-person majority that O'Connor wrote for in *Adarand*.

O'Connor's opinion set forth the conceptual foundation of the ruling by first asserting three key propositions about affirmative action that could be gleaned, she argued, from the Court's past doctrine through *Croson*: "First, skepticism: 'Any preference based on racial or ethnic criteria must necessarily receive a most searching examination.' Second, consistency: 'The standard of review under the Equal Protection Clause is not dependent on the race of those burdened or benefited by a particular classification.' . . . And third, congruence: 'Equal protection analysis in the Fifth Amendment area is the same as that under the Fourteenth Amendment.'"[36] Thus, this ruling enjoyed five votes establishing strict scrutiny as the proper standard for reviewing governmental affirmative action across the board, regardless of whether the program was federal or state in origin.[37] O'Connor went on to overrule *Metro Broadcasting* and *Fullilove* to the extent that they conflicted with the ruling in *Croson*.[38]

---

[33] 497 U.S. 547, 563–79 (1990).
[34] 515 U.S. 200 (1995).
[35] Id. at 204–10.
[36] Id. at 223–24 (citations omitted).
[37] Id. at 224. At the time, one could have conceivably discerned a small silver lining in *Adarand* for affirmative action supporters, however. O'Connor's dissent in *Metro Broadcasting* had suggested her willingness to grant a broader judicial deference to congressional affirmative action programs that were enacted pursuant to Congress's Section 5 authority under the Fourteenth Amendment. 497 U.S. 547, 605–09 (1990) (O'Connor, J., dissenting). The *Adarand* ruling did not specifically signal her rejection of that view, since the challenge involved in this case did not directly implicate Congress's Section 5 authority. 515 U.S. at 230–31, 235. See also id. at 268–69 (Souter, J., dissenting).
[38] Id. at 227, 235.

The Entrenchment of the Anticlassification Order

With the *Adarand* ruling, the anticlassification principle enjoyed its final triumph with its extension into the realm of race-conscious affirmative action programs. There was now a recognizable jurisprudential order that cohered around a general, all-encompassing suspicion of governmental racial classifying whether invidious or benign in function, and whether employed by federal or state and local actors. And as with the other case studies, this new order had been entrenched in *Adarand* via a distinctive mode of adjudication: conclusive, principled judicial affirmation. From the divisiveness of the *Bakke* ruling, and through the flip-flopping between *Croson*, *Metro Broadcasting*, and *Adarand*, finally a majority of the Court – slim though it was – had achieved a jurisprudential settlement that brought this period of construction to a close.

Subsequent political developments reinforced the choices made by the Court as public opinion had grown increasingly hostile to affirmative action through the 1980s and 1990s.[39] Arguably, a larger countermovement of sorts against affirmative action began in the 1980s, encompassing a number of conservative judicial appointments to the federal courts after twelve years of Reagan and George H. W. Bush, opposition to affirmative action in the Republican 104th and 105th Congresses, and advocacy from conservative think tanks and public interest law groups.[40] Likewise, after *Adarand* in 1995, Proposition 209 in California had received national attention. Passed in 1996, and later upheld in the federal courts, Proposition 209 banned state government–sponsored affirmative action in California.[41] Also enjoying widespread notice in the post-*Adarand* period was the Fifth Circuit Court of Appeals decision in *Hopwood v. State of Texas*,[42] which questioned *Bakke*'s authority as a controlling

---

[39] Terry H. Anderson, "The Strange Career of Affirmative Action," *South Central Review* 22, no. 2 (Summer 2005): 122–25.

[40] Robert A. Rhoads, Victor Saenz, and Rozana Carducci, "Higher Education Reform as a Social Movement: The Case of Affirmative Action," *The Review of Higher Education* 28, no. 2 (Winter 2005): 204–07.

[41] Terry H. Anderson, *The Pursuit of Fairness: A History of Affirmative Action* (New York: Oxford University Press, 2004), 256–57; Carol M. Swain, "Affirmative Action: Legislative History, Judicial Interpretations, Public Consensus," in *American Becoming: Racial Trends and Their Consequences*, eds. Neil J. Smelser, William Julius Wilson, and Faith Mitchell, vol. 1 (Washington, DC: National Academy Press, 2001), 330; Rhoads et al., "Higher Education," 207–08; Peter H. Schuck, "Affirmative Action: Past, Present, and Future," *Yale Law & Policy Review* 20, no. 1 (2002): 54.

[42] 78 F.3d 932 (5th Cir. 1996).

precedent (given its fractured holding)[43] and ruled that student diversity was not a compelling purpose for the University of Texas law school's affirmative action program for admissions.[44] That decision struck down the admissions policy at issue because it violated equal protection (although the Court did conclude that racial preferences could be allowed to remedy the present effects of a state entity's own past discrimination – if such discrimination could be shown).[45] Subsequent to *Hopwood*, the Texas state attorney general issued an opinion extending that case's critical view of racial preferences to public contracting generally and to all public higher education entities.[46]

And yet, even in the midst of these victories for the anticlassification principle, race-consciousness had not been fully vanquished in the post-*Adarand* era. As legally entrenched as the new strict scrutiny regime may have been after *Adarand*, it was not nearly hegemonic enough to accomplish such a feat. Thus, how the recently consolidated strict scrutiny regime managed newly emergent boundary tensions – specifically in the form of persistent affirmative action efforts in public university admissions, and in the form of majority-minority electoral districting – is the subject of Part II of this chapter. Although these subsequent legal tensions do point to the limits of the anticlassification order, the successful management of them within and alongside the anticlassification framework also underscores the resilience of this governing structure.

PART II: THE MAINTENANCE OF THE
ANTICLASSIFICATION ORDER

Judicial Tension Management, Case 1: Affirmative Action in Higher Education, Again

In 1996, Akhil Amar and Neal Katyal wrote, "*Bakke*, it seems, now hangs by a thread."[47] They subsequently asked, "Thus, after *Adarand*,

---

[43] Id. at 944.
[44] Id. at 944–48.
[45] Id. at 948–50. See Paul Brest et al., *Processes of Constitutional Decisionmaking: Cases and Materials*, 4th ed. (New York: Aspen, 2000), 973–76.
[46] J. Edward Kellough, *Understanding Affirmative Action: Politics, Discrimination, and the Search for Justice* (Washington DC: Georgetown University Press, 2006), 115; Rhoads et al., "Higher Education," 208.
[47] Akhil Reed Amar and Neal Kumar Katyal, "*Bakke's Fate*," *UCLA Law Review* 43, no. 6 (August 1996): 1745.

a huge question remains: What happens to *Bakke*? Put another way, though *Adarand* said virtually nothing about education, did the Court somehow overrule *Bakke sub silentio*?"[48] And yet, there were strong reasons for affirmative action supporters to think that if any type of affirmative action program could survive, it would be in programs in higher education admissions. First, in *Adarand*, O'Connor herself had expressed her openness to upholding affirmative action in another context.[49] At the least, this indicated that O'Connor's vote, added to the four votes of the liberal bloc of Stevens, Souter, Ginsburg, and Breyer, could uphold an affirmative action program. More pointedly, the longer *Bakke* stayed on the books, the harder it would be to dislodge it. By the mid-1990s, the ruling had been entrenched for nearly two decades and had greatly influenced admissions programs across the nation owing to Powell's discussion and endorsement of the Harvard admissions program. Even if public opinion had grown increasingly anti-affirmative action, these programs enjoyed strong support among universities and their administrators. Growing societal reliance interests in the *Bakke* ruling – coupled with the fact that the Court's two principal swing voters at the time, Kennedy and O'Connor, happened to be philosophically predisposed to maintaining entrenched precedents – boded well for the next time affirmative action in higher education was brought before this particular Court.[50]

The case of affirmative action in higher education, and its growing conflict with prevailing anticlassification norms in the late 1990s, is thus analogous to the cases of separate but equal litigation in higher education during the Jim Crow era and hybrid Section 301/Duty of Fair Representation claims in the industrial pluralist era. What ties all of these diverse legal developments together is that the source of boundary tension within the reigning order in each case did *not* arise from new ideas or policies. Rather, the source of tension arose from the growing prominence and resurgence of established ideas, commitments, and policy options.

In *Grutter v. Bollinger*, the Court very notably managed the tensions surrounding higher education affirmative action.[51] The focus in this case was on the University of Michigan law school's admission policy. That policy had allowed the law school to consider race as part of an

---

[48] Ibid. at 1747.
[49] 515 U.S. 200, 237 (1995).
[50] Amar and Katyal, "*Bakke*," 1769–70; Jennifer L. Hochschild, "The Strange Career of Affirmative Action," *Ohio State Law Journal* 59, no. 3 (1998): 1018–19.
[51] 539 U.S. 306 (2003).

unquantified, holistic review of individual applicants, although admissions personnel had stated their explicit goal of securing a "critical mass" of minority students.[52] A rejected white applicant challenged the policy claiming that it discriminated on the basis of race and violated the Equal Protection Clause and Title VI of the Civil Rights Act of 1964.[53]

O'Connor – writing for a majority of five, including herself and the liberal bloc of Stevens, Souter, Ginsburg, and Breyer – first asserted that strict scrutiny was the appropriate standard to apply.[54] Further, in line with *Bakke*, O'Connor concluded that the law school's goal in maintaining a diverse student body was a compelling purpose.[55] It was, however, on the next question – whether this program was narrowly tailored to serve the purpose of student diversity – that O'Connor surprised. She concluded that the law school's program passed the narrow tailoring requirement of strict scrutiny.[56]

O'Connor cited *Bakke* in asserting that the racial quota epitomized the unconstitutional treatment of race for admissions purposes.[57] But in favor of the Michigan law school program was that it did not look like a quota to the Court majority.[58] Racial considerations by admissions personnel in the law school were oriented toward an individualized, flexible treatment of race as only one aspect of the applicant's whole person.[59] The Court found that even though race-neutral alternatives – such as basing admissions on a lottery system or lowering general admissions standards – may be more narrowly tailored than the racial preferences used by the law school, these were nevertheless not realistic alternatives. The alternatives were not realistic because they would require the law school to sacrifice other values such as its academic standards or its discretionary ability to provide for a broad array of diverse qualities through nuanced consideration of applicant qualities.[60] Thus, the Court concluded by upholding the law school's policy, although it also stated an apparent twenty-five year time limit on racial preferences in university admissions.[61]

As seen in Chapters 7 and 8, an absence of conceptual clarity is a hallmark of tension-managing rulings. These rulings are easy to critique on

---

[52] Id. at 306, 312–16, 318 (2003).
[53] Id. at 316–17.
[54] Id. at 326.
[55] Id. at 327–33.
[56] Id. at 333–34.
[57] Id. at 334, 341.
[58] Id. at 335–36.
[59] Id. at 337.
[60] Id. at 340.
[61] Id. at 343.

legal-conceptual grounds precisely because they accommodate various, conflicting values. This description is apt for *Grutter*. Again, according to the University of Michigan law school, racial considerations in their admissions process took place against the context of trying to assemble a "critical mass" of minority students for each class. They argued that a "critical mass" was not a racial quota and was consistent with the doctrinal prohibition on quotas.[62] However, Rehnquist, in a dissent joined by Scalia, Kennedy, and Thomas, claimed a strong relationship between the percentage of racial minority applicants to the law school and the percentage of admitted racial minority applicants to the law school: the two seemed to be closely correlated for the years between 1995 and 2000.[63] In other words, in result at least, the admissions policy actually looked a great deal like a de facto racial quota.[64] Indeed, it is not hard to reach the conclusion that if the Court had applied a more conventional form of strict scrutiny in *Grutter*, the Michigan law school program probably should have been struck down.

Yet when confronted with a social practice that clearly sat in tension with prevailing doctrine and the principles of color blindness at the heart of the anticlassification order, the Court validated this de facto quota instead of striking it down. Due in no small part to the depth of support affirmative action enjoyed in higher education and in elite sectors of American society, the tension posed by these programs was "managed" by the Court.[65] The Court majority held fast to the not terribly convincing conclusion that the Michigan law school was engaged in something qualitatively different from a racial quota. More precisely, the Court majority chose to interpret and apply strict scrutiny's narrow tailoring requirement in a manner flexible enough so that it could validate Michigan law school's de facto racial quota. *Grutter* thus demonstrates the conceptual flexibility of a typical tension-management ruling. This makes it very easy to critique on more legal-conceptual grounds for either not taking a hard enough look at the law school's program or for not applying "real" strict scrutiny.[66]

---

[62] Id. at 318.
[63] Id. at 380–86 (Rehnquist, J., dissenting).
[64] Id. at 383–86 (Rehnquist, J., dissenting).
[65] See, e.g., Neal Devins, "Explaining *Grutter v. Bollinger*," *University of Pennsylvania Law Review* 152, no. 1 (November 2003): 366–70.
[66] Another critique of *Grutter* was the differential treatment the Court majority afforded it relative to its companion case, *Gratz*, which dealt with the University of Michigan's "point system" for affirmative action in undergraduate admissions. 539 U.S. 244, 293–94 (2003) (Souter, J., dissenting). To be precise, only O'Connor and Breyer saw a difference between the two affirmative action programs.

Yet the ruling's conceptual flexibility also speaks to its value as a tension-management ruling. Looking ahead, the contours of affirmative action in public higher education remain underdetermined due in significant part to *Grutter*. It is clear that racial quotas are constitutionally prohibited, and that "point systems," such as that in *Gratz* (*Grutter*'s companion case), will likely remain prohibited as well. In terms of what *Grutter* means in an affirmative sense, however, the only definitive signpost provided by the Court in that ruling was that race can be lawfully considered for admissions decisions if it is within the context of "individualized consideration."[67] What this vague requirement entails in terms of discrete practices is not exceedingly clear, as Scalia noted in dissent.[68] "Individualized consideration" could perhaps come to be understood in a succession of future rulings by the Court as something like the Michigan law school program, or, it might not. The Court's 2013 ruling in *Fisher v. University of Texas at Austin* provided little additional clarity on this point.[69]

At the same time, the *Grutter* ruling was clear and definitive on a separate point: it demonstrated the resilience of anticlassification principles. Even if the narrow tailoring requirement was reshaped in a noteworthy way in that case, that idea, along with other core concepts at the heart of the anticlassification order, was also endorsed and applied in *Grutter*. Thus, there were clear threads of continuity between *Grutter* and earlier anticlassification precedents. For example, the Court's majority and dissenters all agreed that strict scrutiny was the applicable test; likewise, there was significant focus on the diversity rationale (having been previously validated by Powell in *Bakke*). Although certain anticlassification legal principles proved to be quite malleable in the hands of O'Connor and the *Grutter* majority, this malleability was disciplined or contained within the ideas and principles of a still-resilient legal regime.

Rather than being a direct challenge to it, subsequent appointments to the Court as well as the Court's rulings on race have only underscored both the vitality of the anticlassification legal order and *Grutter*'s status

---

[67] 539 U.S. 306, 334, 337 (2003).
[68] Id. at 348 (Scalia, J., dissenting). See David Crump, "The Narrow Tailoring Issue in the Affirmative Action Cases: Reconsidering the Supreme Court's Approval in *Gratz* and *Grutter* of Race-Based Decision-Making by Individualized Discretion," *Florida Law Review* 56, no. 3 (July 2004): 497–98, 520–22.
[69] See *Fisher v. University of Texas at Austin*, 133 S. Ct. 2411, 2421 (2013) (Justice Kennedy, for the Court, declined to revisit the question of whether the Michigan law school program was constitutionally acceptable.)

as an innovation within that order. Among the four appointments to the Court since *Grutter*, the replacement of O'Connor with Alito was arguably the most significant because it removed O'Connor's centrist swing vote that the liberal bloc had benefited from in assembling a five-person majority in *Grutter*. Whatever possibilities may have existed for a new era of affirmative action after *Grutter* – however small they may have been – were foreclosed with this switch. The impact was subsequently demonstrated by the Court's ruling in *Parents Involved in Community Schools v. Seattle School District No. 1*, where the Court struck down voluntarily adopted student assignment that took race into account in Seattle, Washington and Jefferson County, Kentucky.[70]

Roberts's opinion for the Court, citing *Grutter* and *Adarand*, confirmed the applicability of strict scrutiny to these plans.[71] According to a majority of the Court, and notwithstanding Breyer's push to apply *Grutter*'s version of an easier-strict scrutiny in this case,[72] the appropriate standard was "real" strict scrutiny.[73] In the portions of Roberts's opinion that commanded five votes, Roberts pushed at the unconstitutionality of the plans by emphasizing that they fell short of strict scrutiny's narrow tailoring requirement. More specifically, the consideration of race in both school districts was not individualized enough, the Court questioned the districts' need for considering race given its limited impact on enrollment patterns, and it faulted the school districts for failing to further explore race-neutral alternatives.[74] Five justices also distinguished *Grutter* from the present case because of the uniqueness of the higher educational context.[75]

In the subsequent case of *Fisher v. University of Texas at Austin*, the Court once again confronted affirmative action in the context of higher education and remained on the tension-management path marked out by *Grutter*. Kennedy's opinion for seven justices unambiguously endorsed *Grutter* as valid precedent,[76] and reaffirmed that educational diversity qualified as a "compelling" goal for equal protection analysis.[77]

---

[70] 551 U.S. 701 (2007).
[71] Id. at 720.
[72] Id. at 829–837 (Breyer, J., dissenting).
[73] Id. at 720, 740–45; id. at 783–84, 791 (Kennedy, J., concurring in part and concurring in judgment).
[74] Id. at 723–25, 733–35.
[75] Id. at 724–25 (citations omitted).
[76] 133 S. Ct. at 2417, 2419, 2421.
[77] Id. at 2417–18.

Kennedy's opinion also had the usual trappings of an anticlassification opinion in its emphatic endorsement of strict scrutiny as the proper standard to apply for affirmative action.[78] Furthermore, the primary upshot of the opinion was to emphasize that judicial scrutiny of affirmative action required a "stricter" form of narrow tailoring to ensure that a university's chosen means of promoting racial diversity were indeed narrowly tailored or even necessary to achieve this goal.[79] If anything, then, *Fisher* modestly ratcheted up the significance of anticlassification values in this context, although Kennedy saw his elaboration on the narrow tailoring requirement as consistent with *Grutter*.[80]

In the aftermath of *Parents Involved* and *Fisher*, it seems clear that the anticlassification regime is alive and kicking, and that *Grutter* was more the "odd" case rather than the start of a new transformation. The more relevant uncertainty at present is about the viability of higher education affirmative action rather than the future of the anticlassification order. On the one hand, higher education affirmative action seems to enjoy relatively significant institutional and elite support; this was an often-observed fact about *Gratz* and *Grutter*. For example, Neal Devins noted that a total of 102 amicus briefs were filed in these two cases, with 83 supporting the affirmative action programs.[81] Among those in support of the programs were state governments, business and labor interests, universities (of course), and military leaders.[82] Furthermore, race-conscious admissions programs are particularly entrenched in the nation's universities, as Justice O'Connor noted in *Grutter*.[83] Finally, it is noteworthy that *Grutter* was still categorically endorsed in *Fisher*. All of these considerations suggest the continued vitality of antisubordination values within this one area of social policy and the plausibility of future uncertainties and future judicial tension management here. Nevertheless, the Court will soon engage this issue again in the future,[84] and we may yet see even stronger reassertions of anticlassification values.

---

[78] Id. at 2417–19.
[79] Id. at 2419–22.
[80] Id. at 2419–20. Ginsburg, however, read *Grutter* differently. See id. at 2434, 2434n3 (Ginsburg, J., dissenting).
[81] Devins, "Explaining *Grutter*," 366.
[82] Ibid., 367–69.
[83] 539 U.S. 306, 323 (2003).
[84] *Schuette v. Coalition to Defend Affirmative Action*, 701 F.3d 466 (6th Cir. 2012), *cert. granted*, 133 S. Ct. 1633 (U.S. Mar. 25, 2013) (No. 12–682).

Judicial Tension Management, Case 2: Drawing Majority-Minority Electoral Districts

Although entrenched institutional interests and the support of elites had managed to preserve race consciousness in higher education admissions, it has also remained alive and well in the post-*Adarand* era in another crucial context: voting. Indeed, under the Court's jurisprudence stemming from the Voting Rights Act of 1965, state actors had employed race consciousness in evaluating minority vote dilution claims. Concerns about minority vote dilution had, in turn, led to the trend of state actors drawing majority-minority districts (MMDs) as a remedial measure in the 1990s. It was not difficult to see how this body of jurisprudence was on a collision course with the increasingly dominant anticlassification order in the equal protection domain.

The conflicts created by MMDs were, however, distinct from the conflicts confronted by the Court in *Grutter*. Affirmative action had been a policy concern since the early 1970s, it had maintained a consistent presence throughout three decades, and it had reached the Court as early as 1978 with the *Bakke* ruling. In contrast, MMDs were a recent policy phenomenon when they surfaced in front of the Court; they were not a major concern in the early 1980s.[85] Although the Court had confronted the MMD issue as early as 1977,[86] it only burst onto the legal and political scene with the round of electoral redistricting that began after 1990.[87] Thus, similar to residential segregation ordinances in the Jim Crow era, the boundary tensions presented by the MMD issue stemmed from the reigning institutional order's confronting of new circumstances and new policy options.[88]

The Court's Minority Vote Dilution Jurisprudence

As part of the federal effort to dismantle Jim Crow, the Voting Rights Act of 1965 sought to vindicate the guarantees of the Fifteenth Amendment by first securing basic access to the political process for African Americans.

---

[85] Richard H. Pildes, "Principled Limitations on Racial and Partisan Redistricting," *Yale Law Journal* 106, no. 8 (June 1997): 2518–25.
[86] *United Jewish Organizations of Williamsburgh, Inc. v. Carey*, 430 U.S. 144 (1977).
[87] Grant M. Hayden, "Resolving the Dilemma of Minority Representation," *California Law Review* 92, no. 6 (December 2004): 1604; Pildes, "Limitations," 2512–18.
[88] Heather Gerken notes that MMDs constituted the "fourth generation" of racial classifications that confronted the Court. Heather K. Gerken, "Understanding the Right to an Undiluted Vote," *Harvard Law Review* 114, no. 6 (April 2001): 1694–95.

Section 2 of the act stated that "no voting qualification or prerequisite to voting, or standard, practice, or procedure shall be imposed or applied by any State or political subdivision to deny or abridge the right of any citizen of the United States to vote on account of race or color."[89] Section 4 of the act also suspended the use of literacy tests, character tests, and so forth, in any state or political subdivision where less than half the voting-age population was registered to vote or where less than half the voting-age population had voted in the presidential election of 1964 (thus targeting the southern states).[90] And finally, Section 5 of the act required "covered" jurisdictions – those jurisdictions where Section 4 was applicable – to submit any proposed changes in electoral procedures to either the D.C. Federal District Court for approval or to the attorney general for "preclearance."[91] Within two years of this enactment, African American voter registration saw dramatic gains in the South.[92]

Yet if the battle for minority access to the vote was quickly won, a second battle immediately arose with respect to the use of certain electoral structures, by various jurisdictions, to "dilute" minority voting power. The most common method of accomplishing such a dilution was to take a group of minority voters – a group that might be sufficient to account for an overall majority in a single-member district – and join it with other majority-white single-member districts in order to create a single at-large or multimember voting district, where minority voting power would be submerged.[93] But key doctrinal and statutory developments from the late 1960s to the 1980s responded to this second wave of threats, and these efforts pushed the Court toward a voting rights jurisprudence that became increasingly race conscious and energetic in protecting minority voting.

First, in *Allen v. State Board of Elections*,[94] the Court was confronted with a number of changes in electoral laws from Mississippi and Virginia.

---

[89] Voting Rights Act of 1965, Pub. L. No. 89–110, § 2, 79 Stat. 437, 437 (1965).
[90] § 4, 79 Stat. at 438–39.
[91] § 5, 79 Stat. at 439.
[92] J. Morgan Kousser, *Colorblind Injustice: Minority Voting Rights and the Undoing of the Second Reconstruction* (Chapel Hill: University of North Carolina Press, 1999), 55. Notably, in the 2013 case of *Shelby County v. Holder*, the formula for determining Section 5 coverage in Section 4(b) was struck down by the Court, thus leaving Section 5 presently inoperable. 133 S. Ct. 2612, 2627, 2631 (2013).
[93] Kousser, *Injustice*, 55; Gerken, "Understanding," 1672; Hayden, "Dilemma," 1600; Samuel Issacharoff, "Polarized Voting and the Political Process: The Transformation of Voting Rights Jurisprudence," *Michigan Law Review* 90, no. 7 (June 1992): 1839–40.
[94] 393 U.S. 544 (1969).

The most significant was a Mississippi law that allowed for members of the various county boards of supervisors to be elected at large by voters within their county. Previously, board members had been elected from individual districts within each county.[95] The most interesting question posed was whether this particular amendment constituted a "voting qualification or prerequisite to voting, or standard, practice, or procedure with respect to voting," thus implicating Section 5 of the Voting Rights Act.[96] The Court answered in the affirmative and endorsed a more expansive interpretation of voting rights and of the act.[97]

Allen involved a proposed change in electoral structures in a "covered" jurisdiction, hence it was challengeable through Section 5. For those electoral changes that did not fall as easily within the orbit of Section 5, however, challenges in defense of minority voting could also be mounted through the Equal Protection Clause of the Fourteenth Amendment. In *White v. Regester*,[98] the Court held that multimember districting in two Texas counties was unconstitutional under the Equal Protection Clause for diluting the votes of African Americans in one district and diluting the votes of Mexican Americans in the other. Even though the Court's basis for finding dilution was not clear,[99] its language suggested that to some extent, electoral outcomes were relevant to the inquiry of whether the multimember districting schemes were constitutional. The standard articulated by the Court was as follows:

To sustain such claims [of minority vote dilution], it is not enough that the racial group allegedly discriminated against has not had legislative seats in proportion to its voting potential. *The plaintiffs' burden is to produce evidence to support findings that the political processes leading to nomination and election were not equally open to participation by the group in question – that its members had less opportunity than did other residents in the district to participate in the political processes and to elect legislators of their choice.*[100]

The group-oriented, effects-oriented nature of the *White* standard thus moved the Court toward embracing race consciousness in evaluating minority vote dilution. It also created a rather hospitable judicial standard

---

[95] Id. at 550.
[96] Id.
[97] Id. at 569.
[98] 412 U.S. 755 (1973).
[99] On this point, see Issacharoff, "Polarized Voting," 1844–46.
[100] 412 U.S. at 765–66 (citations and footnotes omitted) (emphasis added).

for litigant challenges to vote diluting electoral structures.[101] Challenging litigants experienced a slight hiccup seven years later, however, in *City of Mobile v. Bolden*.[102] In dealing with a vote dilution claim against an at-large electoral system (established in 1911) in Mobile, the Court asserted that demonstrating a racially discriminatory purpose in the adoption and maintenance of the at-large structure was the proper standard for showing an unconstitutional vote dilution under the Fourteenth Amendment.[103] *Bolden*, in short, sought to import the racially discriminatory purpose or anticlassification ideal from *Washington v. Davis*[104] into the voting rights context.

However, anticlassification principles had a limited effect in this context as antisubordination, race-conscious values quickly reemerged as the dominant principle. When the Voting Rights Act came up for renewal in the early 1980s, only two years after *Bolden*, Congress responded to the latter's holding by revising Section 2 of the act to read:

SEC. 2. (a) No voting qualification or prerequisite to voting or standard, practice, or procedure shall be imposed or applied by any State or political subdivision *in a manner which results* in a denial or abridgement of the right of any citizen of the United States to vote on account of race or color, or in contravention of the guarantees set forth in section 4(f)(2), as provided in subsection (b).

(b) A violation of subsection (a) is established if, based on the *totality of circumstances*, it is shown that the political processes leading to nomination or election in the State or political subdivision *are not equally open to participation by members of a class of citizens protected by subsection (a) in that its members have less opportunity than other members of the electorate to participate in the political process and to elect representatives of their choice*. The extent to which members of a protected class have been elected to office in the State or political subdivision is one circumstance which may be considered: Provided, That nothing in this section establishes a right to have members of a protected class elected in numbers equal to their proportion in the population.[105]

As indicated by the changed language in Section 2(a) (which here is italicized), and the adoption of language from the *White* ruling in a wholly new Section 2(b), Congress accomplished significant changes with these

---

[101] The group-oriented nature of the *White* ruling leads Issacharoff to see this case as analogous to *Griggs* and its establishment of disparate impact claims in employment discrimination. Issacharoff, "Polarized Voting," 1843.
[102] 446 U.S. 55 (1980).
[103] Id. at 58, 65–74.
[104] 426 U.S. 229 (1976).
[105] Voting Rights Act Amendments of 1982, Pub. L. No. 97-205, § 3, 96 Stat. 131, 134 (emphasis added).

statutory amendments to the Voting Rights Act. At least with respect to statutory claims of vote dilution, Congress had established an "effects" standard along the lines of the *White* ruling – and had codified that ruling's emphasis on group interests and race consciousness. In so acting, Congress also divorced the constitutional and statutory standards for vote dilution. The standards for a vote dilution claim under the Voting Rights Act were now distinct from the Court's constitutional equal protection standard articulated in *Bolden*. The effect of these changes was important for litigating vote dilution claims. Even though the Court had erected higher barriers for plaintiffs wishing to prevail on such claims under the Fourteenth Amendment in *Bolden*, litigants could now bypass those difficulties by grounding their attacks on vote dilution in the newly amended Section 2 of the Voting Rights Act.[106]

The Court first applied the amended Section 2 in *Thornburg v. Gingles*[107] in which it confronted a challenge to a North Carolina redistricting plan for the state legislature. The plan employed a number of multimember districts that submerged African American voters within overall white majorities.[108] Brennan's opinion for the Court aimed to simplify the mandate of the Section 2 amendments for the showing of a vote dilution claim:

> These circumstances are necessary preconditions for multimember districts to operate to impair minority voters' ability to elect representatives of their choice for the following reasons. *First*, the minority group must be able to demonstrate that it is sufficiently large and geographically compact to constitute a majority in a single-member district.... *Second*, the minority group must be able to show that it is politically cohesive.... *Third*, the minority must be able to demonstrate that the white majority votes sufficiently as a bloc to enable it – in the absence of special circumstances, such as the minority candidate running unopposed – usually to defeat the minority's preferred candidate.[109]

Brennan's list of requirements expressed fidelity to an "effects" standard in line with the spirit of the Section 2 amendments and the preceding *White* standard. And as significantly, it expressed fidelity to the group or race consciousness present in the *White* ruling.

Ultimately, it was the efficacy of Section 2 and Section 5 in protecting racial minorities from vote dilutive electoral structures that led, in part,

---

[106] Kousser, *Injustice*, 57; Gerken, "Understanding," 1674; Hayden, "Dilemma," 1602; Issacharoff, "Polarized Voting," 1846–47.
[107] 478 U.S. 30 (1986).
[108] Id. at 34–35, 38.
[109] Id. at 50–51 (citations omitted) (emphasis added).

to the creation of MMDs in the 1990s. First, *Gingles* ensured a cause of action for a plaintiff under Section 2 whenever the aforementioned conditions were present.[110] When they were, presumably an MMD could be created as a remedy given the first component of Brennan's test – that "the minority group must be able to demonstrate that it is sufficiently large and geographically compact to constitute a majority in a single-member district."[111] Either to head off litigation or in response to it, the creation of MMDs was facilitated by state governments acting in response to potential or actual liability under Section 2.[112] Second, given the expansive interpretation of Section 5 present in early cases such as *Allen*, state redistricting for covered jurisdictions fell within the scope of Section 5. Years later in the 1990s, the Department of Justice employed its preclearance authority under this portion of the Voting Rights Act to push aggressively for the creation of MMDs in covered jurisdictions.[113]

Thus on the one hand, the question prompted by the appearance of MMDs concerned the stability and integrity of the anticlassification order. If left unchecked, the rise of MMDs would pose a threat to the dominance of anticlassification principles not just with regard to issues of racial equality generally but also within the Equal Protection Clause itself (which was actually the textual basis for plaintiff challenges to MMDs). On the other hand, however, if the Court were to engage in too direct an assault on MMDs, a second tension might arise concerning the stability and integrity of an established voting rights jurisprudence generally oriented toward race consciousness.[114] The task, then, for a stability-minded Court lay in navigating between these two extremes and in finding a way to reinforce the centrality of anticlassification principles without wholly dismantling separate and distinct doctrinal frameworks that spoke to antisubordination principles. This is ultimately what narrow majorities of the Court accomplished in their treatment of MMDs in *Shaw v. Reno*[115] and *Miller v. Johnson*.[116]

---

[110] Although *Gingles* dealt with a multimember district, it was definitively extended to single-member districting schemes in *Growe v. Emison*, 507 U.S. 25, 40–42 (1993).

[111] 478 U.S. at 50 (1986).

[112] Hayden, "Dilemma," 1603–04; Pamela S. Karlan, "Easing the Spring: Strict Scrutiny and Affirmative Action after the Redistricting Cases," *William and Mary Law Review* 43, no. 4 (March 2002): 1574–75.

[113] Hayden, "Dilemma," 1603; Karlan, "Spring," 1574–75.

[114] While *Shelby* worked a dramatic change to this voting rights jurisprudence, Roberts's opinion for the Court pointedly emphasized that § 2 was not implicated in that ruling. 133 S. Ct. 2612, 2619, 2631 (2013).

[115] 509 U.S. 630 (1993).

[116] 515 U.S. 900 (1995).

Shaw v. Reno *as Tension Management*

Shaw dealt with a North Carolina reapportionment plan for its seats in the U.S. House of Representatives. The plan contained two irregularly shaped MMDs.[117] The second one had been added after an earlier reapportionment plan containing only one MMD had been denied preclearance by the attorney general under Section 5 of the Voting Rights Act.[118] The plan was challenged by residents who were registered to vote in a county that lay partly in the second MMD. These residents claimed that the plan embodied a racial gerrymander violating the Equal Protection Clause of the Fourteenth Amendment.[119] They did not allege that the plan diluted white voting strength but rather "that the deliberate segregation of voters into separate districts on the basis of race violated their constitutional right to participate in a 'color-blind' electoral process."[120]

O'Connor, writing for the same five-person majority that appeared in *Adarand* two years later, concluded that this was a cognizable claim.[121] She also left no doubt that the Court's equal protection precedents in other doctrinal areas were applicable to and controlling for MMDs: strict scrutiny standards would regulate race-conscious redistricting of the type involved here – even if done to benefit minorities.[122] Applying the standard could be difficult, however. How would the Court know whether any given redistricting plan necessarily involved racial classifications that could trigger strict scrutiny? The key indicator aiding the Court would be *shape*; when the Court was confronted with "redistricting legislation that is so bizarre on its face that it is 'unexplainable on grounds other than race,'"[123] this key circumstance would demand that the redistricting legislation receive "the same close scrutiny that we give other state laws that classify citizens by race."[124] The more bizarre the shape, the easier it would be to conclude that a racial classification deserving of the Court's strict scrutiny was at work.[125] Further, a bizarrely shaped MMD would, for all intents and purposes, function as a de facto racial classification in political representation, with all the attendant perverse consequences – such as encouraging popular notions of both intractable racial political

---

[117] 509 U.S. at 633.
[118] Id. at 633–36.
[119] Id. at 636–37.
[120] Id. at 641–42.
[121] Id. at 644, 649.
[122] Id. at 642–44, 650–51, 653, 657–58.
[123] Id. at 644.
[124] Id.
[125] Id. at 646–47.

differences between African Americans and whites and inherent commonalities of interest within each race.[126] O'Connor asserted that such a circumstance would promote a "political apartheid."[127]

Even though the Court imported anticlassification principles into the voting rights context, and even with the new geographic constraint on MMDs, it was apparent that *Shaw* aimed more at tension management rather than any kind of repudiation of Voting Rights Act–jurisprudence. Indeed, the Court's ruling ceded ground to the continued use of race in redistricting. Recall that the Court took care to limit its ruling on the use of heightened scrutiny for race and redistricting to only those plans that employed particularly irregular shapes, as in the present case.[128] Thus, when an MMD employed racial considerations but did not possess a bizarre shape, it might escape strict scrutiny. In the same way that other tension-managing doctrinal innovations mediated between competing institutional authorities and rights, shape was the mediating principle between the pull of anticlassification principles – embedded in the authority of the Court's equal protection jurisprudence – and the pull of race-conscious values – embedded in the authority of voting rights precedents.

As many scholars noted at the time, *Shaw* was indeed a compromise opinion.[129] It was a compromise made out of practicality in part. As O'Connor conceded in her opinion, racial classifying of some sort is inescapable in district line drawing by state actors;[130] there is simply no way to avoid it or stamp it out. But its compromise orientation was also likely due to the fact that any result more hostile to MMDs would require

---

[126] Id. at 647–49.
[127] Id. at 647. Such statements support Pildes and Niemi's interpretation of *Shaw* as being centrally concerned with the "expressive harms" posed by bizarrely shaped MMDs. Richard H. Pildes and Richard G. Niemi, "Expressive Harms, 'Bizarre Districts,' and Voting Rights: Evaluating Election-District Appearances after *Shaw v. Reno*," Michigan Law Review 92, no. 3 (December 1993): 506–16. Others, however, see *Shaw* as more a discriminatory intent case, with geographic shape being important as an indicator of forbidden intent. Kousser, *Injustice*, 390–92.
[128] 509 U.S. at 642, 644, 649.
[129] The ruling generated much academic commentary in the mid-1990s, and a number of scholars characterized it as a "compromise" decision in its determination that the use of race in redistricting was only limited and not wholly condemned. Parallels between this ruling and Powell's *Bakke* ruling were evident to many. T. Alexander Aleinikoff and Samuel Issacharoff, "Race and Redistricting: Drawing Constitutional Lines after *Shaw v. Reno*," Michigan Law Review 92, no. 3 (December 1993): 608–18, 643–50; Karlan, "Easing;" Pildes and Niemi, "Expressive Harms," 495–99, 503–05.
[130] 509 U.S. at 646.

a frontal assault on the Court's prior voting rights jurisprudence.[131] So long as the obligations of Sections 2 and 5 of the VRA were left intact, state actors seeking to comply with them might have to take race into account in drawing MMDs. They might have to do so in order to avoid vote dilution litigation under Section 2. And if they were subject to Section 5, states seeking to comply with the "nonretrogression principle" of Section 5 – which required that the electoral influence of racial minorities not backslide with any proposed voting changes – might accordingly have to take race into account in order to attain preclearance from the attorney general.[132] Indeed, the North Carolina plan in question in *Shaw* had added the controversial second MMD at the suggestion of the attorney general in order for the plan to attain preclearance.[133]

The Court was simply not willing to launch such an assault. In O'Connor's explicit comments on the reach of the Voting Rights Act in *Shaw*, she only reinforced the theme of compromise and tension management already implicit in her discussion on the applicability of strict scrutiny to redistricting. On the one hand, she made it clear that the act would not wholly escape the reach of the anticlassification principle. With respect to a redistricting plan that was motivated in part by the desire to comply with Section 5, she stated: "The Voting Rights Act and our case law make clear that a reapportionment plan that satisfies Section 5 still may be enjoined as unconstitutional."[134] At the same time, she left open the question of how much legal cover a state might enjoy for considering race in order to comply with Section 2 of the Voting Rights Act.[135] And as she stated in her concluding paragraph, had North Carolina drawn another more geographically compact MMD, the ruling here "express[es] no view as to whether appellants successfully could have challenged such a district under the Fourteenth Amendment."[136] Notably, in the subsequent case of *Bush v. Vera*,[137] five justices seemed to indicate that a state's attempt to comply with Section 2 of the Voting

---

[131] The *Shaw* ruling also posed a conflict with the Court's previous controlling precedent on MMDs in *United Jewish Organizations of Williamsburgh, Inc. v. Carey (UJO)*, 430 U.S. 144 (1977). O'Connor distinguished the two cases by asserting that the challenging party's complaint was different across each. 509 U.S. at 651–52. Justice White found this effort to distinguish *UJO* from *Shaw* highly questionable. Id. at 658–59, 664–74 (White, J., dissenting).
[132] O'Connor took note of such possible arguments. Id. at 654–55.
[133] Id. at 635.
[134] Id. at 654–55 (citations omitted).
[135] Id. at 656.
[136] Id. at 657.
[137] 517 U.S. 952 (1996).

Rights Act would count as a "compelling interest" for the purposes of a strict scrutiny inquiry.[138]

The same tension-management dynamic was also on display in the subsequent case of *Miller v. Johnson*, in which the Court examined a Georgia congressional redistricting plan that included three MMDs.[139] Kennedy, writing for a five-person majority identical to *Shaw*'s five-person majority, clarified that although bizarre geography was still significant as evidentiary support for the likelihood that racial considerations had been unduly influential in the drawing of district lines by state actors,[140] it was not the central legal consideration in assessing whether a redistricting plan ran afoul of the Equal Protection Clause.[141] Rather, the Court moved toward another tension-management mediating principle – a "predominant racial motivation" test: if race was shown to be the predominant motivation for a redistricting plan, it would be subject to strict scrutiny. If the plan was not so motivated, it would be able to escape strict scrutiny.[142]

Although the new *Miller* standard did have a wider potential applicability than the *Shaw* standard, it did not have greater clarity or firmness. Fundamentally, it demanded judgment calls on whether racial considerations were unconstitutionally excessive or within bounds in a given redistricting plan.[143] In this, it exhibited the very same vague and flexible characteristic of the *Shaw* geography standard and of the *Grutter* "individualized consideration" standard – both of which also allowed for race considerations but only within certain boundaries. Like them, the new standard bore the familiar characteristics of a useful tension-management device.[144]

---

[138] The five were: (1) O'Connor, id. at 990, 992 (O'Connor, J., concurring); (2) Stevens; (3) Ginsburg; and (4) Breyer, id. at 1033 (Stevens, J., dissenting) (joined by Ginsburg and Breyer); and (5) Souter, id. at 1065 (Souter, J., dissenting) (joined by Ginsburg and Breyer).

[139] 515 U.S. 900, 903, 905–10 (1995).

[140] Id. at 912–14.

[141] Id. at 915.

[142] Id. at 916, 920.

[143] For an illustration of the malleability of the "predominant racial motivation" standard, compare the Court's ruling in *Shaw v. Hunt*, 517 U.S. 899, 905–07 (1996), with Justice Stevens's dissent in that case, id. at 930–39 (Stevens, J., dissenting).

[144] The subsequent cases of *Hunt v. Cromartie*, 526 U.S. 541 (1999) and *Easley v. Cromartie*, 532 U.S. 234 (2001) clarified that the *Miller* standard was indeed a tension-management principle; the former demonstrated how racial considerations in district line drawing *could* survive judicial scrutiny.

CONCLUSION

As with the construction of governance after Reconstruction, and after the Wagner Act, no new equilibrium or normal politics in the domain of constitutional equal protection seamlessly arose after the dismantling of Jim Crow. Certain items were decisively settled early on. Formalized school segregation was permanently discarded, and by the mid-1970s, it was clear that no constitutional equal protection revolution in socioeconomic inequality would be in the cards. But with respect to the precise contours of equal protection principles, as they related to race in the post–Jim Crow era, full clarity was not attained until the anticlassification principle was extended to affirmative action in the mid-1990s.

A second lesson is also illustrated by examining the anticlassification regime. Not only did constructing the new order require an extended amount of time to occur; once that new order was in place it almost immediately had to bend, accommodate, and compromise in order to manage boundary tensions – first in the domain of voting rights in the 1990s and then later in the domain of affirmative action less than a decade after *Adarand*. These two case studies of judicial tension management demonstrate that even after it has been decisively entrenched, construction of the new governance is subject to continuing political contestation and institutional conflict. Nevertheless, the governing order's resilience was also demonstrated by its ability to accommodate this conflict and tension.

10

Explaining Order-Affirming and Tension-Managing Judicial Behavior

Chapters 7, 8, and 9 highlight a number of judicial rulings that functioned either to codify and legally entrench emerging systems of governance or to manage conflicts within an established legal order. Collectively, these rulings might suggest two conclusions. First, the consistent appearance of certain types or modes of adjudication across the case studies indicates a broader political process that regularly arises in the aftermath of certain kinds of open-ended reforms. A second conclusion, which concerns the central role of the Supreme Court within these recurrent political processes, is the focus of the present chapter. The judiciary itself appears to be consistently motivated to promote stability during periods of transformative recalibration, by creating and then maintaining durable governing arrangements in the aftermath of reform.

My claim is not that the judicial interest in stability wholly accounts for all judicial actions in these transformed areas of policy. Rather, a judicial-institutional interest in stability operates in tandem with external forces – such as appointments pressures and political-cultural forces – in dictating judicial outcomes. The judicial interest in stability dictates judicial behavior *within* the constraints imposed by external forces. In the context of delimitation, where the influence of appointments and political-cultural forces was more subdued, I have argued that the stability interest could account for the Supreme Court's actions to a greater extent. However, in the context of order-affirming and tension-managing rulings, my claim necessarily becomes more modest given that, by the time such rulings surface, these external forces have become more prominent. As the polity moves farther away from the initial moment of reform, political life inevitably becomes more regularized and normal. In this latter context,

TABLE 10.1 *A Summary of Order-Affirming Rulings*

Order-Affirming Rulings	
The post-Reconstruction era	*Plessy v. Ferguson*
	Williams v. Mississippi
	Giles v. Harris
The post–New Deal era	*United Steelworkers of America v. American Manufacturing Co.*
	United Steelworkers of America v. Enterprise Wheel & Car Corp.
	United Steelworkers of America v. Warrior & Gulf Navigation Co.
The post–civil rights era	*City of Richmond v. J. A. Croson Co.*
	Adarand Constructors, Inc. v. Pena

the Supreme Court is much more likely to have some appointments and political-cultural pressures bearing down on its members relevant to the issues of recalibration. As the constraints imposed by external forces become sharper during construction and political equilibrium, the range of judicial actions that can be explained by the judicial interest in stability accordingly shrinks.

Still, a theory of judicial-institutional interest in stability does nevertheless offer one very important benefit for understanding judicial action during these later periods. Even if this interest may not be capable of accounting for as broad a range of judicial actions, it is capable of explaining and accounting for the Court's use of particular modes of adjudication.

JUDICIAL BEHAVIOR AND CONSTRUCTION

The analysis in Chapters 7, 8, and 9 demonstrates that when the Court is confronted with questions concerning how to organize governing authorities and rights during periods of construction, it will uphold legal structures in a broader, more definitive, and more principled manner. An "order-affirming" mode of adjudication recurs because the judiciary possesses an institutional interest in entrenching new, durable forms of governance in order to promote basic legality values. A summary of order-affirming rulings is provided in Table 10.1.

For example, it seems very plausible in the case of the post-Reconstruction era that without definitive *judicial* resolution on the issues of southern segregation and disfranchisement offered in *Plessy* and *Williams*, a durable system of governance in southern race relations would not have emerged at that time. The polity's continuing lack of clarity on foundational legal questions would have ensured at least some continued legal contestation on first principles.

Similarly, the Court decisively and conclusively affirmed another recalibration of authority and rights with the *Steelworkers Trilogy* – this time, for labor relations. Here as well it is easy to imagine that, absent a conclusive resolution on "internal" uncertainties, a significant degree of political unsettlement and legal confusion would have continued. Recall that some proponents of industrial pluralism greeted Douglas's opinion in *Lincoln Mills* with considerable anxiety about the potential intrusiveness of the federal courts in managing industrial disputes.[1] The fears of the industrial pluralists at this time point to alternative possibilities in a world without the resolution offered by the *Steelworkers Trilogy*. Finally, the period of construction in the post–civil rights era was brought to a close by the Supreme Court's eventual settlement of the legal uncertainties surrounding affirmative action in *Croson* and *Adarand*. Prior Supreme Court rulings on affirmative action from *Bakke* to *Adarand* illustrate what could have ensued had the Court not eventually reached a definitive conclusion. Its willingness in each of these three historical eras to minimize uncertainties, as well as to set new systems of social relations on sturdy legal foundations, suggests that a recurrent judicial-institutional interest lay toward facilitating the entrenchment of legal order and legal settlement.

By comparison, consider the explanatory benefits that an appointments thesis or a political-cultural thesis might offer for this same set of order-affirming rulings. An appointments thesis could certainly illuminate the outcomes of the affirmative action cases. One would be very hard pressed, however, to make an appointments-related claim to explain the rulings in *Plessy*, *Williams v. Mississippi*, or the *Steelworkers Trilogy*. It is difficult to imagine that the central issues in those cases played a crucial role in the appointments of anything like a majority of any of those Courts.

A more powerful externalist argument would most likely emphasize the more general influence of social, political, and cultural forces on judicial behavior in these cases. Indeed, none of these rulings contradict the externalist view that judicial outcomes tend to align with prevailing political and social forces. For example, a number of scholars have

---

[1] See Chapter 8.

noted that *Plessy* and *Williams* were very much in line with prevailing public sentiment.[2] On post–New Deal labor relations, James Atleson has similarly noted that the *Steelworkers Trilogy* was merely following social and economic trends that had long been in place. As he states: "By 1960, the date of the Supreme Court's trilogy, arbitration clauses were found in over 90 percent of collective agreements. The Supreme Court may have wished to support the arbitration process, but the War Labor Board had already accomplished that result over fifteen years earlier."[3] With regard to the affirmative action rulings, not only were Republican judicial appointments a major factor in the Court's skepticism toward these programs; these rulings were probably in line with emerging public sentiment through the 1980s and 1990s as well.[4] Similarly, a focus on externalist influences on the Court would be capable of explaining the highly divisive nature of its votes on affirmative action rulings up through *Adarand*.

Still, while externalist forces clearly aligned with the judicial outcomes in these cases, how much do those forces explain? One could start with the claims in the preceding paragraph and proceed to the bolder claim that social and political forces not only supported these judicial outcomes but also determined them *and* their modes of resolution. However, this latter assertion runs into difficulties and ultimately demonstrates the limits of both the appointments and political-cultural accounts of order-affirming rulings.

Although an externalist would hardly be surprised by the Court's hostile attitude toward racial preferences in *Adarand* in 1995, or its sympathetic posture toward arbitration in the *Steelworkers Trilogy* in 1960, other viable options were nevertheless available to the Court at these times. Such alternatives would have been congruent with prevailing public sentiment and would have been plausible courses of judicial action. For example, in *United Steelworkers of America v. Warrior & Gulf*

---

[2] Edward L. Ayers, *The Promise of the New South: Life after Reconstruction* (New York: Oxford University Press, 1992), 327; Michael J. Klarman, *From Jim Crow to Civil Rights: The Supreme Court and the Struggle for Racial Equality* (New York: Oxford University Press, 2004), 21–23, 38–39; Benno C. Schmidt, Jr., "Principle and Prejudice: The Supreme Court and Race in the Progressive Era, Part 1: The Heyday of Jim Crow," *Columbia Law Review* 82, no. 3 (April 1982): 469.

[3] James B. Atleson, "Wartime Labor Regulation, the Industrial Pluralists, and the Law of Collective Bargaining," in *Industrial Democracy in America: The Ambiguous Promise*, eds. Nelson Lichtenstein and Howell John Harris (Cambridge: Cambridge University Press, 1993), 154n41 (citations omitted).

[4] Anderson, "Affirmative Action," 122–25.

Navigation Co.,[5] one of the *Steelworkers Trilogy*, the Court might easily have ruled that arbitration was appropriate for the specific dispute. It did not need to also assert the more sweeping, principled point that "an order to arbitrate the particular grievance should not be denied unless it may be said with positive assurance that the arbitration clause is not susceptible of an interpretation that covers the asserted dispute. Doubts should be resolved in favor of coverage."[6] A narrower, more fact-specific ruling would have hardly looked countermajoritarian.

In *Adarand* as well, public sentiment against affirmative action was probably not so monolithic in 1995 as to demand a judicial conclusion that all racial classifications be subject to strict scrutiny. The Court could have simply declared a rule of strict scrutiny for racial preferences in federal governmental contracting – which was the context of the dispute in *Adarand*. Alternatively, the Court might have stated a general rule of strict scrutiny for federal governmental racial preferences, while also explicitly carving out an exception for more deferential judicial review of racial preferences enacted under Congress' Section 5 authority.[7] Had such alternative judicial outcomes been reached in *Adarand*, an externalist theorist of judicial behavior would have had little difficulty in making the argument that such outcomes were aligned with prevailing political and social sentiment.

The same point carries over to the Jim Crow cases, particularly with respect to the Court's ruling in *Williams v. Mississippi*. Although it is hard to imagine an alternative outcome and mode of settlement for *Plessy*, given the nature of that ruling and given where political and social forces lay on the segregation in public accommodations issue, other options were available to the *Williams* Court. For example, suppose that in an alternative ruling the Court chose to uphold Mississippi's registration, residency, and poll tax requirements but decided to strike down Mississippi's "understanding" test as too obvious a tool of black disfranchisement, in violation of either the Equal Protection Clause or the Fifteenth Amendment.[8] There is no doubt that someone focused on external judicial influences could plausibly argue that this more liberal hypothetical

---

[5] 363 U.S. 574 (1960).
[6] Id. at 582–83.
[7] See Chapter 9, note 37.
[8] Again, this test required voters to either read or "understand" provisions of the Mississippi state constitution. Ayers, *Promise*, 148–49. Mississippi's disfranchisement scheme is discussed in ibid., 146–49.

ruling would be largely consistent with prevailing public opinion as well. This hypothetical ruling would have hardly stemmed the tide of black disfranchisement in the South, given the ruling's approval for all other remaining aspects of the Mississippi disfranchisement scheme, including the poll tax – which proved to be the most effective disfranchising tool in many southern states.[9] Precedent would have offered support for striking down the understanding test,[10] and although this hypothetical ruling would have likely sparked more southern complaints about federal intervention, it is doubtful that those states would have been that outraged: most did not even have understanding clause provisions in their tool kit of disfranchising laws.[11]

In sum, although public opinion and social forces undoubtedly imposed boundaries on feasible judicial action in each of the three historical periods, the judiciary retained a number of plausible options *within* those boundaries on how to actually decide these cases. Externalist accounts of judicial behavior, however, offer relatively little to help explain why the Court chose one plausible alternative over another.

Considering these cases through the lens of a judicial interest in stability, we can speculate on why one can find strands of argument indicating decisive – even sweeping – affirmative legal resolutions in them. The benefit of resolving cases in this manner is precisely that it minimizes legal uncertainties to the greatest extent. Furthermore, such rulings, and their articulation of foundational legal standards, serve as the most attractive means of entrenching new forms of governance for judicial actors who are inclined to do so.

This still leaves the highly divisive nature of the *Croson* and *Adarand* rulings, which might, at first glance, undercut an institutional explanation for those cases. Yet the explanatory burden is not to demonstrate that an institutional interest in stability wholly explains that outcome; rather, it is to show the existence of a judicial-institutional interest in the midst of other increasingly significant external influences on the Court. In this regard, the judicial concern with stability can be gleaned from these rulings, notwithstanding the vote counts. In *Croson*, although five votes

---

[9] Michael Perman, *Struggle for Mastery: Disfranchisement in the South, 1888–1908* (Chapel Hill: University of North Carolina Press, 2001), 313–14.
[10] See the discussion of Yick Wo v. Hopkins, 118 U.S. 356 (1886), in Chapter 7, pp. 214–15.
[11] Only four southern states employed an "understanding" test. J. Morgan Kousser, *The Shaping of Southern Politics: Suffrage Restriction and the Establishment of the One-Party South, 1880–1910* (New Haven, CT: Yale University Press, 1974), 239.

did come together for the establishment of strict scrutiny for nonfederal affirmative action programs, Marshall's dissenting opinion – which spoke for three votes – asserted that intermediate scrutiny was the appropriate standard to apply.[12] Certainly the Court was divided as to how it might promote stability in race relations, but the fact that at least eight justices sought to articulate a foundational legal standard for this internal uncertainty suggests the presence of a judicial-institutional interest in stability.

Adarand is admittedly a more difficult case to explain. The three dissenting opinions in *Adarand* – offered by Stevens,[13] Souter,[14] and Ginsburg[15] – did not focus on articulating, in broad categorical terms, an alternative legal standard for adjudicating affirmative action programs. One might interpret this omission as perhaps conceding, to an extent, their agreement with the Court's articulation of a "strict-er" scrutiny standard (thus suggesting that the main point of disagreement for the dissenters was the Court's actual application of the standard). More realistically, this omission was likely a function of the dissenters recognizing the inevitability of some form of the strict scrutiny standard – owing in part, no doubt, to the *Croson* ruling itself – and wishing to carve out some wiggle room for future disputes. Thus, the significant stability-promoting effect of the earlier ruling in *Croson* likely reduced the need for judicial convergence on a more definitive, order-affirming result in *Adarand*.

The vote totals in the other order-affirming rulings are also noteworthy in suggesting a structural, judicial-institutional motive: *Plessy* was a 7–1 ruling; *Williams v. Mississippi* was unanimous; and the *Steelworkers Trilogy*, with Black absent for all three cases and with a couple of voting complications, still evidenced a seemingly consistent seven-vote majority in favor of core industrial pluralist principles. Notwithstanding these vote tallies, however, the best evidence for a recurrent judicial-institutional interest in stability across the cases emanates from the recurrence of order-affirming legal arguments and decisions across three quite diverse historical contexts.

---

[12] Marshall was joined by Brennan and Blackmun in dissent. 488 U.S. 469, 535–36 (1989) (Marshall, J., dissenting). Marshall, Brennan, and Blackmun had similarly advocated for an intermediate scrutiny standard for affirmative action in *Bakke* (where they were joined by White), 438 U.S. 265, 359 (1978) (Brennan, J., concurring in part and dissenting in part), and in *Fullilove v. Klutznick*, 448 U.S. 448, 517–22 (1980) (Marshall, J., concurring).
[13] 515 U.S. 200, 242 (1995). (Stevens, J., dissenting).
[14] Id. at 264 (Souter, J., dissenting).
[15] Id. at 271 (Ginsburg, J., dissenting).

TABLE 10.2 *A Summary of Tension-Management Rulings*

Tension-Management Rulings	
The post-Reconstruction era	*Buchanan v. Warley*
	Missouri ex rel. Gaines v. Canada
	Sweatt v. Painter
The post–New Deal era	*Vaca v. Sipes*
The post–civil rights era	*Grutter v. Bollinger*
	Shaw v. Reno
	Miller v. Johnson

JUDICIAL BEHAVIOR AND JUDICIAL TENSION MANAGEMENT

Finally, consider these various theories of judicial behavior in light of the judicial tension-management rulings, summarized in Table 10.2.

An appointments thesis has mixed results when applied to the tension-management cases. An appointments thesis may have some relevance in *Grutter, Shaw, Miller*, and perhaps *Sweatt*, but it has no apparent relevance for *Gaines, Buchanan*, or *Vaca*. Further, it would be difficult to make the more exacting historical claim that the particular tension-management principles articulated in these various cases were directly related to the appointment of a majority of the justices on these various Courts. However, an externalist approach to judicial behavior that focused on broader social, political, and cultural forces would be more promising. Indeed, a political-cultural theory of judicial behavior could undoubtedly illuminate many important aspects of these rulings. Scholars have argued, for example, that the Court's qualified endorsement of racial preferences in *Grutter* – especially when combined with the Court's simultaneous disapproval of the Michigan undergraduate affirmative action program in *Gratz* – accurately reflected the broader public ambivalence about both affirmative action and color blindness.[16] As with the Court's earlier affirmative action cases, a focus on externalist influences on the Court would also align quite well with the repeated appearance of 5–4 majority votes in the various post–civil rights era tension-managing cases I discuss. One could also probably tell a similar historical narrative about hybrid Section 301/DFR suits, in which broader societal forces

---

[16] Neal Devins, "Explaining *Grutter v. Bollinger*," *University of Pennsylvania Law Review* 152, no. 1 (November 2003): 347–48.

probably demanded some recognition of individual employee rights, but not necessarily to the extent of dismantling industrial pluralism.

One possible problem for a proponent of externalist theories might be *Buchanan*: the impetus for protecting African American property rights was apparently more of a judicial commitment than a commitment rooted in broader society. Indeed, to the extent that any broader public sentiment might be discerned, it cut in the opposite direction against African American rights, given that the residential segregation ordinances were generally recently enacted laws at the time of *Buchanan*'s ruling.[17] This ruling actually seemed, to an extent, to reflect judicial independence from broader society. Yet even if an externalist account does not offer us much help in understanding the egalitarian pull of *Buchanan*, it does offer an explanation as to why this ruling did not initiate a broader assault on Jim Crow: broader public sentiment in 1917 clearly would not have supported such a change.[18]

Although externalist accounts may be sufficient to explain why "compromise" rulings resulted from the tension-management legal controversies, jurisprudential compromises can be achieved in any number of ways. It is in explaining modes of legal resolution that an institutional approach to judicial behavior is helpful. In the case of *Grutter*, the Court's key analytical move was to establish an "individualized consideration" requirement for determining whether a given affirmative action plan was sufficiently narrowly tailored to satisfy strict scrutiny. Again, this individualized consideration requirement was the substance of the jurisprudential compromise in *Grutter*.[19] Yet, as noted earlier, this was a very vague compromise standard. Scalia stated the following in his *Grutter* dissent:

Unlike a clear constitutional holding that racial preferences in state educational institutions are impermissible, or even a clear anticonstitutional holding that racial preferences in state educational institutions are OK, today's *Grutter-Gratz* split double header seems perversely designed to prolong the controversy and the litigation. Some future lawsuits will presumably focus on whether the discriminatory scheme in question contains enough evaluation of the applicant "as an individual," and sufficiently avoids "separate admissions tracks" to fall under

---

[17] Klarman, *Jim Crow*, 79.
[18] It is for these reasons that Klarman's interpretation of *Buchanan* largely sees this case as being driven by judicial values. External forces factor into his analysis only as constraints that tolerated *Buchanan* because that ruling did not seriously challenge residential segregation in practice. Ibid., 83, 90–93, 142–43.
[19] See Chapter 9.

Grutter rather than *Gratz*. Some will focus on whether a university has gone beyond the bounds of a "'good-faith effort'" and has so zealously pursued its "critical mass" as to make it an unconstitutional *de facto* quota system, rather than merely "'a permissible goal.'" Other lawsuits may focus on whether, in the particular setting at issue, any educational benefits flow from racial diversity.... I do not look forward to any of these cases.[20]

A similar vagueness characterized the method of compromise achieved in *Vaca*. Recall that the dividing line between employee rights and industrial pluralism established in that case was the standard the Court set forth for defining a violation of the duty of fair representation, namely: *"arbitrary or bad-faith conduct* on the part of the Union in processing [a] grievance."[21] As already noted in Chapter 8, Justice Black's dissent – which generally criticized the Court's ruling for going too far in undercutting employees' individual rights – noted the following point concerning the vagueness of the Court's standard:

Henceforth, in almost every § 301 breach-of-contract suit by an employee against an employer, the employee will have the additional burden of proving that the union acted arbitrarily or in bad faith. The Court never explains what is meant by this vague phrase or how trial judges are intelligently to translate it to a jury. Must the employee prove that the union in fact acted arbitrarily, or will it be sufficient to show that the employee's grievance was so meritorious that a reasonable union would not have refused to carry it to arbitration?[22]

One can, of course, imagine alternative ways that broader societal ambivalence about racial preferences or employee rights might have been reflected in these cases. One can easily imagine alternative, but still compromise-oriented rulings in which the Court set out more definitive statements on what "individualized consideration" entailed or what the duty of fair representation entailed, or provided detailed discussion of the kinds of admissions programs or types of union conduct that would fall on either side of these two requirements.

The Court's choice to articulate vague standards of jurisprudential compromise in these two cases, however, indicates that additional considerations were at play beyond externalist constraints. One such consideration is an institutional interest in stability and in preserving the integrity of established boundaries and doctrinal principles. The Court's inclination to resolve tensions by articulating vague legal rules in these

---

[20] 539 U.S. 306, 348–49 (2003) (citations omitted) (Scalia, J., dissenting).
[21] *Vaca v. Sipes*, 386 U.S. 171, 193 (1967) (emphasis added).
[22] Id. at 210 (Black, J., dissenting).

cases is indicative of this interest in stability. Unlike jurisprudential compromises built on specific terms and conditions that might prevent a Court from integrating future exceptions and future tensions *within* the reigning order, vague standards are valuable for their opposite effect: they aid the resiliency of the status quo–governing order by preserving flexibility to the Court in dealing with future controversies.

Not surprisingly, we find similarly vague standards articulated in other tension-management cases, such as *Gaines*'s endorsement of the flexible "substantially equal" requirement for the latter half of the "separate but equal" standard[23] and *Shaw v. Reno*'s and *Miller v. Johnson*'s standards for determining when the application of strict scrutiny to redistricting plans was appropriate.

In the case of *Buchanan*, the Court's approach to tension management was somewhat different. Here, recall that the Court categorized residential segregation ordinances as an item that touched on civil rights. In doing so, it was able to manage tensions by striking down those segregation laws without fundamentally challenging the institution of Jim Crow. Superficially at least, the *Buchanan* ruling stands out as tension management of a different kind.

The tension-managing ruling of *Buchanan* likely reflected a convenient means of preserving the reigning Jim Crow order, given the particular conditions surrounding that case. The situation in *Buchanan* was not one for which broader societal forces were ambivalent about residential segregation in the same way that they were ambivalent about color blindness in *Grutter* or perhaps even industrial pluralism in *Vaca*. In *Buchanan*, the push for greater liberalism came from forces inside the Court.

That is, the Court itself was pressing against societal preferences. As such, the stability-related problem it confronted was to ensure that its own judicial innovations did not undermine the integrity of the still-dominant Jim Crow order. Hence the Court's approach to upholding African American rights while managing tensions was not to articulate a vague, open-ended standard of compromise. Nor, of course, did the Court defend African American rights through a candid, substantive discussion on the nature and demands of racial equality. Rather, a racially egalitarian outcome was achieved on the basis of a seemingly technical legal matter that was firmly rooted in the prevailing doctrinal categories. The *Buchanan* compromise, in short, stemmed from a technical, conceptual argument – all the better to mask the judicially driven innovation that it contained.

[23] *Missouri ex rel. Gaines v. Canada*, 305 U.S. 337, 351 (1938).

Given the ruling's lack of critique or explicit anxiety about the Jim Crow framework, it was also a ruling that aimed to aid the resiliency of the Jim Crow order. Analyzing judicial-institutional interests thus illuminates the subtleties of Justice Day's argument, which may not be as apparent from a more political-cultural perspective on judicial behavior.

A quick glance at the large majorities in the vote counts for several of the tension-managing rulings also suggests an institutional motive at work. For example, *Buchanan* and *Sweatt* were unanimous decisions, *Gaines* enjoyed a 6–2 majority, and the majority opinion in *Vaca v. Sipes* enjoyed five votes. Further, three additional votes in *Vaca* concurred with the result and were arguably even more sympathetic to preserving industrial pluralism values than Justice White's opinion for the Court.[24]

Finally, an institutional concern with stability is consistent with, and largely supported by, the post–civil rights era case studies, such as *Grutter*, *Shaw*, and *Miller* – despite the fact that all three were closely divided 5–4 decisions. In all three of these cases, the vote splits did not reflect a divergence of opinion on whether to preserve status quo governing arrangements. Rather, in each of these three cases, the Court consistently split into two factions: One group recognized boundary tensions within the reigning order and sought to accommodate those tensions. The other group simply did not recognize any such tensions, and offered a full-throated endorsement of the status quo. In other words, every vote in each of these three cases is consistent with a stability-promoting judicial goal. Although I would not claim that a judicial-institutional interest in stability could wholly explain all of the opinions in these cases (or in any of the other tension-managing cases), I would claim that the judicial

---

[24] Fortas's concurrence, which was joined by Warren and Harlan, expressed a strong disinclination toward having the Court regulate union-employee relations. In Fortas's opinion, the National Labor Relations Board was the more appropriate venue for these matters. 386 U.S. 171, 198 (Fortas J., concurring). As such, Fortas's divergence from the majority could be seen as somewhat analogous to the closely divided cases of *Shaw*, *Miller*, and *Grutter*: Fortas, Harlan, and Warren were simply not as sympathetic as the Court majority to the notion of employees pressing their rights in the judicial forum. For these three at least, their disagreement with the tension-managing ruling of the majority resided less in any preference *against* maintaining the prevailing status quo. Rather, their divergence from the majority likely stemmed more from the fact that they simply did not believe any great tension existed that required managing. The one justice who pressed a somewhat antistability, anti-tension-managing sentiment was Black; relative to the majority opinion, Black's dissent pressed for a more robust employee right to utilize the courts and sue employers for breaches of the collective bargaining agreement. His opinion evidenced the least allegiance to industrial pluralism principles among the three opinions in this case. 386 U.S. at 203–10 (Black J., dissenting).

concern with stability is consistent with the reasoning in these cases and perhaps explains some of the most interesting aspects of these opinions.

For example, a justice in *Grutter* who was only concerned with stability would seek to uphold the legal principles of the reigning anticlassification order and would endorse strict scrutiny as the appropriate regulative principle for affirmative action. For the four dissenters in that case at least, their conservative political ideology easily aligned with a judicial interest in stability. The real evidence of a tension-management dynamic at work in this case, however, lay with the Court majority – who faced the much more difficult task of integrating its sympathy for race consciousness in higher education *within* a reigning anticlassification political order that would call for strict scrutiny to be applied to the Michigan law school program. A Court so inclined toward race consciousness, but unconcerned with stability concerns, might have upheld the Michigan program by simply declaring that intermediate scrutiny was the appropriate standard of review for benign racial classifications. Yet the Court majority in *Grutter* reached the same result by stating its fidelity to strict scrutiny – and thus stating its fidelity to the reigning anticlassification order – while also bending that order to accommodate the Michigan program. More strikingly than the four dissenters then, the five justices in the latter group – O'Connor, Stevens, Souter, Ginsburg, and Breyer – exhibited their commitment to stability and maintaining entrenched legal principles with their endorsement and reshaping of strict scrutiny's narrow tailoring requirement. They in particular offer the best evidence of a continuing commitment to stability in this case.

Likewise, a similar story might be told about the closely divided votes in *Shaw* and *Miller*. The four liberal dissenters in those cases simply viewed the intrusion of anticlassification principles into the domain of voting rights as a mistake. It was unnecessary for them to endorse the majority's tension-managing device because for the dissenters, there was no tension to manage. For them, the objective that best aligned with their political and legal preferences – while also promoting a more qualified form of stability for the anticlassification order – was leaving the voting rights doctrine free from such an intrusion by anticlassification principles.

The truly relevant site of tension management in these cases, and the best evidence of an institutional motive at work in these rulings, lay in the actions of the conservative majority. This five-person conservative bloc was most sympathetic to anticlassification values and was willing to disrupt established doctrine to preserve the integrity of that emergent order. At the same time, stability considerations dictated that this sympathy had to have limits; the conservative bloc sought to extend the logic of anticlassification principles into voting rights in order to preserve the integrity of that governing structure, but they did so without wholly dismantling an established Voting Rights Act jurisprudence. The end result was that these five justices converged on a form of compromise that expanded the reach of anticlassification principles and codified their centrality in the voting rights context, while also maintaining the legitimacy of some preexisting voting rights doctrines and leaving room for future compromises. This was certainly more stability promoting than the alternative of pressing anticlassification principles toward a wholesale assault on race consciousness in the voting context. It was the actions of the conservative majority and their unwillingness to discard and prohibit all forms of race consciousness in voting rights, notwithstanding their commitment to the anticlassification principle, that are the strongest support for an underlying judicial-institutional interest in stability and maintenance in these cases.

Notwithstanding the aforementioned, the best evidence of the institutional nature of the judicial commitment to stability is that tension-managing strands of argument and legal reasoning recur in contexts as diverse as residential segregation ordinances in the early twentieth century, individual employee rights in the 1960s, and affirmative action in 2003. Indeed, the recurrence of this mode of adjudication itself offers the best evidence of a structural dynamic underlying Supreme Court behavior during periods of political equilibrium in the aftermath of transformative reform.

11

Conclusion

In the Introduction, I note that while comparative historical scholars have studied in depth the initial, disruptive aspects of the major reforms in American history, the absence of sustained, systematic attention to processes of postreform recalibration has led to a noteworthy underemphasis on the *repeated* disjunction between initial, more radical principles of reform and the new, decidedly less radical governing arrangements that arise in the aftermath of reform. To be sure, legal and historical scholars who specialize in particular historical eras may be quite familiar with specific periods in which incongruities arose between initial acts of reform and the subsequent systems of governance. But in-depth explorations of single case studies inevitably leaves one less equipped to offer more generalizable claims about why periods of "Thermidor," "retrenchment," or "backlash" repeatedly appear in crucial periods of American political history. Perhaps for this reason, the conservative results of postreform recalibration are, with some exceptions, often treated as merely surprising, unexpected twists in the course of legal and political development. The preceding chapters attempt to correct this oversight in the literature.

This book illuminates several key points. The first is a claim about political development and the construction of governance in American politics. I argue that a process of recalibration is likely to arise in the aftermath of many political reforms that involve lasting rearrangements of governing authority and individual rights (Claim 1). Recalibration processes are the means by which indeterminate reform principles are fashioned and shaped into new governing arrangements and new systems of social relations.

In the three preceding case studies, I examine recalibration in the context of particularly "dense" areas of policy. These are contexts in which the prereform system of governance was defined by deeply entrenched governing authorities and individual rights, including federalism, various employer prerogatives not directly bearing on the right to unionize, and the prerogatives of nonjudicial institutions. I claim in Chapter 1 that when open-ended reforms occur in such dense contexts, the ensuing recalibration effects are pronounced (Claim 1.1). My case studies bear this out. In each historical period, there was an extended, formal process of recalibration encompassing more than two decades, from the moment of initial legal reform to the legal entrenchment of new governing arrangements. Further, in terms of end results, the product of each recalibration was the legal codification of a new system of governance that proved to be highly durable and central to the overall governing structure of the polity in subsequent years. Indeed, two of these systems of governance – industrial pluralism and the anticlassification order – continue on as central and defining features of modern labor law and modern constitutional equal protection, respectively.

In addition, as I claim in Chapter 1, when recalibration effects are pronounced, they result in legal outcomes that *delimit* rather than complicate or expand on the original reform ambitions (Claim 1.2). A comparison of each set of initial reforms against the end result of recalibration processes bears this out as well. The Court's affirmation of the Jim Crow order was a particularly dramatic delimitation of Reconstruction era principles of formal legal equality, the Court's endorsement of industrial pluralism was a delimitation of the Wagner Act's more open-ended commitment to collective bargaining, and the Court's codification of the anticlassification order was a delimitation of the broader possibilities suggested by the judicial transformation of constitutional equal protection in the civil rights era.

Finally, I have also sought to demonstrate in my three case studies that when particularly open-ended reforms prompt "transformative recalibrations" in the aftermath of reform, a distinct political process emerges: (1) formal legal enactment → (2) delimitation (legislative stalemate followed by *judicial* delimitation) → (3) construction (articulation of new governing arrangements followed by conclusive entrenchment by the Court) → (4) a legal reconstruction of governance. Again, the phenomenon of a "transformative recalibration" is a label that I have attached to the political processes and dynamics encompassed within delimitation and construction (Claim 2).

The view of political change that emerges from the case studies is one for which formal processes of change are prolonged, and where postreform recalibration is driven by crucial uncertainties over the redrawing of boundaries, both external and internal to the domain of reform. Thus, in one sense, political contingency hardly disappears with the initial enactment of reform because *foundational* legal and political questions remain for the polity to confront for decades after the repudiation of the old order. In another sense, however, one of the running themes of the case studies has also been that the developmental uncertainties within these processes of recalibration is neither limitless nor constant. Rather, the range of alternative outcomes for the new system of governance gradually narrows over time. Thus, during delimitation, the crucial work of clarifying the outer reach of reforms culminates in definitive legal settlements that, in turn, constrain but do not wholly determine the alternative governing arrangements that emerge during construction.

Situating the historical case studies within this analytical framework, I summarize the substantive arguments of the preceding chapters in Table 11.1.

Illuminating the processes of recalibration sheds light on the conservative elements of the creation of governance. Yet, although my focus has been on the containment and delimitation of reform principles, there is a corresponding political dynamic that I allude to in the preceding chapters that is also worth emphasizing: the *resilience* of those reform principles (Claim 1.4). That is, postreform recalibration processes may have legally delimited more expansive notions of racial equality in the 1870s and 1970s and more aggressive forms of unionism in the late 1930s. But in the aftermath of post-Reconstruction recalibration, the abolition of slavery and the constitutional enshrinement of a formal legal commitment to racial equality persisted. As previously discussed, the commitment to a formal racial equality in the post-Reconstruction era was still substantive enough to permit more liberal judicial outcomes in cases such as *Buchanan*, and *Sweatt* many years later. Likewise, the federal governmental commitment to collective bargaining endured; the resilience of the Wagner Act's foundational commitment is indicated, of course, by the fact that collective bargaining principles lay at the very core of the industrial pluralist order. And the resilience of reform principles from the civil rights era is indicated not just by the seemingly consensual agreement on antidiscrimination norms in present-day constitutional equal protection doctrine; it is also indicated by the persistence of benign race consciousness in certain policy contexts – such as higher education affirmative

TABLE 11.1 *Summary of Recalibration and Political Development*

	Legal Reform	Delimiting Political Outcome	Construction Political Outcome
The Reconstruction era	The Reconstruction Amendments	The federal governmental protection of African American rights is delimited by the Supreme Court with reference to the demands of federalism or state governmental autonomy.	The Jim Crow order
The New Deal era	The Wagner Act	The federal governmental protection of labor rights is delimited by the Supreme Court with reference to employer prerogatives not directly tied to the right of employees to unionize, and with reference to the demands of industrial peace.	The industrial pluralist order
The civil rights era	*Brown v. Board of Education* and the civil rights legislation of the 1960s	The scope of constitutional equal protection for racial minorities is delimited by the Supreme Court with reference to the demands of preserving traditional nonjudicial prerogatives.	The anticlassification order

action, employment discrimination, voting rights, and in the prevalence of "equal opportunity" programs among private employers as well.[1]

Emphasizing the resilience of reform puts forth perhaps a more optimistic spin on the possibilities for political change. These historical examples indicate that real political development did indeed occur during each of these historical eras – where certain governing authorities were permanently discarded and replaced by something new, and where new ideas became deeply entrenched among political elites and within civil society.

The third principal claim of the book is a theory of judicial behavior during episodes of transformative recalibration. In examining the case studies, a prominent, recurring pattern may be found in the Court's adoption of several distinct roles, in a precise sequence, during each period of recalibration. It is possible to see within these cases the Court acting first as a *delimiter*; then as an *affirmer* of the emerging system of governance; and then finally, during eras of political equilibrium, it assumes the role of *manager* in maintaining or preserving the reigning system of governance.

The Court's adoption of these various roles has been indicated by the distinct modes of adjudication or arguments that it uses in each particular stage of recalibration and political development. The various cases discussed are thus presented in Table 11.2.

I do not claim that the judiciary self-consciously acts with these roles in mind nor that these rulings can only be interpreted in the manner in which I read them. But the recurrence of certain strands of argument against the backdrop of recurrent and particular legal and political uncertainties strongly suggests that a set of ideas and a set of judicial actions are deeply intertwined with the peculiarities of postreform dynamics. Specifically, I claim in Chapter 1, and elaborate in Chapters 6 and 10, that these rulings can be understood as the result of a judicial-institutional interest within the Supreme Court to promote stability – as that stability interest interacts with a changing background of social and political constraints (Claims 3 and 3.1). The judiciary promotes stability in its rulings when it clarifies and maintains the boundaries between competing authorities and rights, both internal and external to the primary domain of reform. It is the Court's inclination to accomplish such tasks, against a background of varying social and political constraints, that presses it to offer statements that delimit the reach of reform; entrench an emerging system

---

[1] On equal opportunity programs, see, e.g., Frank Dobbin, *Inventing Equal Opportunity* (Princeton, NJ: Princeton University Press, 2009).

TABLE 11.2 *Summary of Modes of Adjudication*

	Delimiting Judicial Rulings	Order-Affirming Judicial Rulings	Tension-Managing Judicial Rulings
The Reconstruction era	*Blyew v. United States* *Slaughter-House Cases* *United States v. Cruikshank* *United States v. Reese* *Virginia v. Rives* *The Civil Rights Cases*	*Plessy v. Ferguson* *Williams v. Mississippi* *Giles v. Harris*	*Buchanan v. Warley* *Missouri ex rel. Gaines v. Canada* *Sweatt v. Painter*
The New Deal era	*NLRB v. Mackay Radio and Telegraph Co.* *NLRB v. Sands Manufacturing Co.* *NLRB v. Fansteel Metallurgical Corp.*	*United Steelworkers of America v. American Manufacturing Co.* *United Steelworkers of America v. Enterprise Wheel & Car Corp.* *United Steelworkers of America v. Warrior & Gulf Navigation Co.*	*Vaca v. Sipes*
The civil rights era	*Milliken v. Bradley* *Washington v. Davis*	*City of Richmond v. J. A. Croson Co.* *Adarand Constructors, Inc. v. Pena*	*Grutter v. Bollinger* *Shaw v. Reno* *Miller v. Johnson*

317

of governance during construction in a definitive, sweeping manner; and maintain an entrenched system of governance with vague, sometimes incoherent judicial rulings during times of equilibrium. In offering this institutional interest theory of judicial behavior, my goal has been, in part, to shed light on a set of judicial motives that remain underemphasized in the larger literature. Of at least equal importance, my historical case studies also aim to demonstrate the centrality of the Supreme Court in the codification and maintenance of fundamental legal orders. Although transformative recalibration is not caused by the Court, transformative recalibration is the result of the Court crystallizing and codifying broader, emergent political developments (Claim 4).

Having rearticulated the primary claims of this book, let me conclude by addressing one final point regarding broader implications of the theory. I believe that the primary claims outlined here carry relevance for contemporary politics. First, with respect to the general claims regarding recalibration, recognition of the dynamics of formal governance construction in American politics provides one key lesson for would-be reformers in the present and future: that one should not become too content with the passage of a momentous piece of reform legislation or even – if one were extraordinarily fortunate – the enactment of a new constitutional amendment. As we have seen, new, abstract principles of reform do not easily translate into fully fleshed out governing arrangements. If reformers are seeking to secure a particular reform goal, what they need is not only the legal enshrinement of new reform principles; rather, just as crucially, they also need favorable judicial rulings that recalibrate competing governing authorities and individual rights in a manner sympathetic to their policy goals.[2] Yet the flip side of this point offers a lesson for opponents of reform in contemporary American politics as well. In light of the lessons gleaned from the rise of the Jim Crow order, the industrial pluralist order, and the anticlassification order, one can still maintain significant optimism even after seeing major reforms legally enacted against one's political preferences. The scope of contestation over reform and governance construction remains substantial for decades after the initial acts of dismantling, and those who are opposed to reform enjoy tremendous opportunities to shape the terms of the new order in the aftermath of the initial political defeat.

---

[2] On this point, see also Richard M. Valelly, *The Two Reconstructions: The Struggle for Black Enfranchisement* (Chicago: University of Chicago Press, 2004), 19.

The contemporary relevance of my claim about judicial behavior is perhaps easier to recognize. A sequential pattern in Supreme Court modes of adjudication offers insight into what kinds of arguments might be expected from future Courts in particular circumstances. Consider the Court's tension-management rulings in the civil rights era–case study discussed in Chapter 9, which implicated legal and political dynamics still very much alive in the present time. The theory offered here suggests that in implicated doctrinal areas, we are likely to see either full-throated judicial reassertions of anticlassification values – as seen in *Parents Involved* – or tension-management rulings within that order – as seen in *Grutter* and, to a degree, *Fisher* – in the near future. These descriptions apply to other recent rulings on race by the Court as well: the measured and qualified reassertion of anticlassification values in the context of Title VII by the Court in *Ricci v. DeStefano*;[3] the not-so-subtle avoidance by the Court of a definitive, principled, and broad legal resolution in *Northwest Austin Municipal Utility District No. One v. Holder*;[4] and then later the dramatic reassertion of anticlassification (and federalism) values in the context of the Voting Rights Act in *Shelby County v. Holder*.[5]

Barring serious disruption to this system of governance in the near future – whether from outside the Court or within it – lawyers seeking changes that undermine the anticlassification order in constitutional equal protection should bear this point in mind in gauging their reform aspirations. Relatedly, supporters of the anticlassification order can, perhaps, rest relatively easier in the near future and comfortably limit their concerns to only those doctrinal contexts in which antisubordination commitments remain particularly strong – and in which tension-management rulings are more plausible. As things stand, the scope of the possible in the domain of constitutional law and race seems relatively narrow. We remain quite clearly within an era of normal politics, at least within this policy domain.

Beyond these contemporary points of relevance, however, my aspiration is that some inherent intellectual or historical value might also be gleaned from recognizing how several crucial aspects of the evolving American polity – such as post-Reconstruction race relations, the federal

---

[3] 557 U.S. 557 (2009).
[4] 557 U.S. 193 (2009); Richard L. Hasen, "Constitutional Avoidance and Anti-Avoidance by the Roberts Court," *Supreme Court Review*, no. 1 (2009): 181, 182, 213.
[5] 133 S. Ct. 2612 (2013).

governmental commitment to unions, and the entrenched constitutional norm of color blindness – actually evolved. The story offered here is not one of an unbridled optimism and wonder at the genius of American reform efforts. But I also hope that this book has not offered reasons for contemporary reformers to be wholly skeptical or cynical about the possibilities for political transformation in America.

Bibliography

Statutes and Executive Orders

Civil Rights Act of 1866, ch. 31, § 1, 14 Statutes at Large 27 (1866).
Civil Rights Act of 1875, ch. 114, § 1, 18 Statutes at Large 335 (1875).
Civil Rights Act of 1964, Pub. L. No. 88–352, 78 Statutes at Large 241 (1964).
Education Amendments of 1972, Pub. L. No. 92–318, § 802(a), 86 Statutes at Large 235 (1972).
Education Amendments of 1972, Pub. L. No. 92–318, § 803, 86 Statutes at Large 372 (1972).
Education Amendments of 1974, Pub. L. No. 93–380, § 215(b), 88 Statutes at Large 484 (1974).
Elementary and Secondary Education Act, Pub. L. No. 89-10, 79 Statutes at Large 27 (1965).
Enforcement Act of May 31, 1870, ch. 114, § 6, 16 Statutes at Large 140, 141 (1870).
Executive Order No. 9017, 7 Code of Federal Regulations 237 (1942).
Labor Management Relations (Taft-Hartley) Act, § 203(d), Pub. L. No. 80-101, 61 Statutes at Large 154, 29 U. S. C. § 173(d) (1947).
Social Security Act, Pub. L. No. 271, 49 Statutes at Large 620 (1935).
Voting Rights Act of 1965, Pub. L. No. 89–110, § 2, 79 Statutes at Large 437 (1965).
Voting Rights Act Amendments of 1982, Pub. L. No. 97–205, § 3, 96 Statutes at Large 131 (1982).
Wagner Act, Pub. L. No. 74–198, 49 Statutes at Large 449 (1935).

Briefs and Oral Arguments

Allen, Charles. Brief of Charles Allen. Slaughter-House Cases, 83 U.S. 36 (1873).
Becker, Benjamin V., Max Swiren, Don M. Peebles, Ben W. Heineman, Sidney H. Block. Brief for Fansteel Metallurgical Corporation. National Labor Relations Board v. Fansteel Metallurgical Corporation, 306 U.S. 240 (1939).

Black, J. S. Argument for the State of Kentucky. Blyew v. United States, 80 U.S. 581 (1872).
Bork, Robert H., and J. Stanley Pottinger. Memorandum for the United States as Amicus Curiae. Milliken v. Bradley, 418 U.S. 717 (1974).
Bose, Lewis C., and William M. Evans. Brief and Appendix Amicus Curiae in Support of Petitioners, Submitted by Amici Curiae, Metropolitan School Districts of Lawrence, Warren and Wayne Townships, Marion County, Indiana. Milliken v. Bradley, 418 U.S. 717 (1974).
Brown, Richard L., and Richard D. Wagner. Brief of the School Town of Speedway, Indiana and the School City of Beech Grove, Indiana, Amici Curiae. Milliken v. Bradley, 418 U.S. 717 (1974).
Bryon, David S. Brief for Defendants. U.S. v. Cruikshank, 92 U.S. 542 (1876). In *Landmark Briefs and Arguments of the Supreme Court of the United States: Constitutional Law*, edited by Phillip B. Kurland and Gerhard Casper, 315–45. Arlington, VA: University Publications of America, 1975.
Caldwell, Isaac. Brief against the Constitutionality of the Civil Rights Act of April, 1866. Blyew v. United States, 80 U.S. 581 (1872).
Campbell, John A. Brief for Defendants. U.S. v. Cruikshank, 92 U.S. 542 (1876). In *Landmark Briefs and Arguments of the Supreme Court of the United States: Constitutional Law*, edited by Phillip B. Kurland and Gerhard Casper, 381–409. Arlington, VA: University Publications of America, 1975.
Campbell, John A. Plaintiffs Brief. Slaughter-House Cases, 83 U.S. 36 (1873).
Campbell, John A. Plaintiffs Brief upon Re-argument. Slaughter-House Cases, 83 U.S. 36 (1873).
Durant, Thomas J. Brief of Counsel of Defendant in Error. Slaughter-House Cases, 83 U.S. 36 (1873).
Durant, Thomas J. Brief of Counsel of State of Louisiana, and of Crescent City Live Stock Landing and Slaughter House Company, Defendants in Error. Slaughter-House Cases, 83 U.S. 36 (1873).
Fellows, J. A. Q. History, Object, Aim and Intent of the 13th, 14th, and 15th Amendments, and of the Contemporaneous Legislation. Slaughter-House Cases, 83 U.S. 36 (1873).
Field, David D. Argument of Mr. David Dudley Field On behalf of the Defendants. U.S. v. Cruikshank, 92 U.S. 542 (1876). In *Landmark Briefs and Arguments of the Supreme Court of the United States: Constitutional Law*, edited by Phillip B. Kurland and Gerhard Casper, 419–54. Arlington, VA: University Publications of America, 1975.
Field, David D. Brief for the Defendants. U.S. v. Cruikshank, 92 U.S. 542 (1876). In *Landmark Briefs and Arguments of the Supreme Court of the United States: Constitutional Law*, edited by Phillip B. Kurland and Gerhard Casper, 411–17. Arlington, VA: University Publications of America, 1975.
Field, James G., and WM. J. Robertson. Brief for the Petitioner. Virginia v. Rives, 100 U.S. 313 (1880).
Fuhrman, Harold H. Motion for Leave to File Brief Amicus Curiae and Brief for National Suburban League as Amicus Curiae. Milliken v. Bradley, 418 U.S. 717 (1974).

Jackson, Robert H., Charles A. Horsky, Charles Fahy, Robert B. Watts, Laurence A. Knapp, Mortimer B. Wolf, and Samuel Edes. Brief for the National Labor Relations Board. National Labor Relations Board v. The Sands Manufacturing Company, 306 U.S. 332 (1939).

Jackson, Robert H., Charles A. Horsky, Charles Fahy, Robert B. Watts, Laurence A. Knapp, Mortimer B. Wolf, and Ruth Weyand. Brief for the National Labor Relations Board. National Labor Relations Board v. Fansteel Metallurgical Corporation, 306 U.S. 240 (1939).

Jackson, Robert H., Charles A. Horsky, Charles Fahy, Robert B. Watts, Laurence A. Knapp, Mortimer B. Wolf, and Ruth Weyand. Reply Brief for the National Labor Relations Board. National Labor Relations Board v. Fansteel Metallurgical Corporation, 306 U.S. 240 (1939).

Jackson, Robert H., Robert L. Stern, Henry M. Hart, Jr., Charles Fahy, Robert B. Watts, Laurence A. Knapp, and Mortimer B. Wolf. Brief for the National Labor Relations Board. NLRB v. Mackay Radio & Telegraph Co., 304 U.S. 333 (1938).

Jackson, Robert H., Robert L. Stern, Henry M. Hart, Jr., Charles Fahy, Robert B. Watts, Laurence A. Knapp, and Mortimer B. Wolf. Reply Brief for the National Labor Relations Board. NLRB v. Mackay Radio & Telegraph Co., 304 U.S. 333 (1938).

Kelley, Frank J. et al., Reply Brief of Petitioners. Milliken v. Bradley, 418 U.S. 717 (1974).

Marr, R. H. Brief for Defendants. U.S. v. Cruikshank, 92 U.S. 542 (1876). In *Landmark Briefs and Arguments of the Supreme Court of the United States: Constitutional Law*, edited by Phillip B. Kurland and Gerhard Casper, 347–79. Arlington, VA: University Publications of America, 1975.

Myers, Louis W., Howard L. Kern, and Homer I. Mitchell. Brief for Respondent. NLRB v. Mackay Radio & Telegraph Co., 304 U.S. 333 (1938).

Sendak, Theodore L., Donald P. Bogard, and William F. Harvey. Brief on the Merits in Support of Petitioners Submitted Amicus Curiae by the State of Indiana. Milliken v. Bradley, 418 U.S. 717 (1974).

Smoyer, Harry E., and Welles K. Stanley. Respondent's Brief. National Labor Relations Board v. The Sands Manufacturing Company, 306 U.S. 332 (1939).

White, Robert. Brief for the Defendant in Error. Strauder v. West Virginia, 100 U.S. 303 (1880).

Cases

Adarand Constructors, Inc. v. Pena, 515 U.S. 200 (1995).
Air Line Pilots Association v. O'Neill, 499 U.S. 65 (1991).
Alexander v. Holmes County Board of Education, 396 U.S. 19 (1969).
Allen v. State Board of Elections, 393 U.S. 544 (1969).
Association of Westinghouse Salaried Employees v. Westinghouse Electric Corp., 348 U.S. 437 (1955).
Berea College v. Kentucky, 211 U.S. 45 (1908).
Blyew v. United States, 80 U.S. 581 (1872).

Brown v. Board of Education, 347 U.S. 483 (1954).
Buchanan v. Warley, 245 U.S. 60 (1917).
Bunting v. Oregon, 243 U.S. 426 (1917).
Bush v. Vera, 517 U.S. 952 (1996).
Carey v. City of Atlanta, 84 S.E. 456 (Ga. 1915).
City of Mobile v. Bolden, 446 U.S. 55 (1980).
City of Richmond v. J. A. Croson Co., 488 U.S. 469 (1989).
Civil Rights Cases, 109 U.S. 3 (1883).
Corrigan v. Buckley, 271 U.S. 323 (1926).
Craig v. Boren, 429 U.S. 190 (1976).
Drummond v. Acree, 409 U.S. 1228 (1972).
Easley v. Cromartie, 532 U.S. 234 (2001).
Ex parte McCardle, 74 U.S. 506 (1869).
Ex parte Milligan, 71 U.S. 2 (1866).
Ex parte Siebold, 100 U.S. 371 (1879).
Ex parte Virginia, 100 U.S. 339 (1880).
Ex parte Yarbrough, 110 U.S. 651 (1884).
Fisher v. University of Texas at Austin, 133 S. Ct. 2411 (2013).
Ford Motor Co. v. Huffman, 345 U.S. 330 (1953).
Fullilove v. Klutznick, 448 U.S. 448 (1980).
Giles v. Harris, 189 U.S. 475 (1903).
Giles v. Teasley, 193 U.S. 146 (1904).
Globe Machinery and Stamping Company, 3 N.L.R.B. 294 (1937).
Gratz v. Bollinger, 539 U.S. 244 (2003).
Green v. County School Board, 391 U.S. 430 (1968).
Griggs v. Duke Power Co., 401 U.S. 424 (1971).
Growe v. Emison, 507 U.S. 25 (1993).
Grutter v. Bollinger, 539 U.S. 306 (2003).
Hines v. Anchor Motor Freight, Inc., 424 U.S. 554 (1976).
Hopwood v. State of Texas, 78 F.3d 932 (5th Cir. 1996).
Humphrey v. Moore, 375 U.S. 335 (1964).
Hunt v. Cromartie, 526 U.S. 541 (1999).
James v. Bowman, 190 U.S. 127 (1903).
J. I. Case Co. v. National Labor Relations Board, 321 U.S. 332 (1944).
Keyes v. School District No. 1, 413 U.S. 189 (1973).
Korematsu v. United States, 323 U.S. 214 (1944).
Lochner v. New York, 198 U.S. 45 (1905).
McCabe v. Atchison, Topeka, & Santa Fe Railway Company, 235 U.S. 151 (1914).
McLaurin v. Oklahoma State Regents, 339 U.S. 637 (1950).
Metro Broadcasting, Inc. v. Federal Communications Commission, 497 U.S. 547 (1990).
Miller v. Johnson, 515 U.S. 900 (1995).
Milliken v. Bradley, 418 U.S. 717 (1974).
Missouri ex rel. Gaines v. Canada, 305 U.S. 337 (1938).
Muller v. Oregon, 208 U.S. 412 (1908).

National Labor Relations Board v. Fansteel Metallurgical Corp., 306 U.S. 240 (1939).
National Labor Relations Board v. Jones & Laughlin Steel Corp., 301 U.S. 1 (1937).
National Labor Relations Board v. Mackay Radio & Telegraph Co., 304 U.S. 333 (1938).
National Labor Relations Board v. Pennsylvania Greyhound Lines, Inc., 303 U.S. 261 (1938).
National Labor Relations Board v. Sands Manufacturing Co., 306 U.S. 332 (1939).
Neal v. Delaware, 103 U.S. 370 (1880).
Northwest Austin Municipal Utility District No. One v. Holder, 557 U.S. 193 (2009).
Parents Involved in Community Schools v. Seattle School District No. 1, 551 U.S. 701 (2006).
Personnel Administrator of Massachusetts v. Feeney, 442 U.S. 256 (1979).
Plessy v. Ferguson, 163 U.S. 537 (1896).
Regents of the University of California v. Bakke, 438 U.S. 265 (1978).
Republic Steel Corp. v. Maddox, 379 U.S. 650 (1965).
Ricci v. DeStefano, 557 U.S. 557 (2009).
San Antonio v. Rodriguez, 411 U.S. 1 (1973).
Schuette v. Coalition to Defend Affirmative Action, 701 F.3d 466 (6th Cir. 2012), cert. granted, 133 S. Ct. 1633 (U.S. Mar. 25, 2013) (No. 12–682).
Shaw v. Hunt, 517 U.S. 899 (1996).
Shaw v. Reno, 509 U.S. 630 (1993).
Shelby County v. Holder, 133 S. Ct. 2612 (2013).
Slaughter-House Cases, 83 U.S. 36 (1873).
Smith v. Evening News Association, 371 U.S. 195 (1962).
Steele v. Louisville & Nashville Railroad Co., 323 U.S. 192 (1944).
Strauder v. West Virginia, 100 U.S. 303 (1880).
Swann v. Charlotte-Mecklenberg Board of Education, 402 U.S. 1 (1971).
Sweatt v. Painter, 339 U.S. 629 (1950).
Syres v. Oil Workers International Union, 350 U.S. 892 (1955).
Textile Workers Union of America v. Lincoln Mills of Alabama, 353 U.S. 448 (1957).
Thornburg v. Gingles, 478 U.S. 30 (1986).
United Jewish Organizations of Williamsburgh, Inc. v. Carey, 430 U.S. 144 (1977).
United States v. Cruikshank, 92 U.S. 542 (1876).
United States v. Darby, 312 U.S. 100 (1941).
United States v. Harris, 106 U.S. 629 (1883).
United States v. Lopez, 514 U.S. 549 (1995).
United States v. Ortega, 24 U.S. 467 (1826).
United States v. Reese, 92 U.S. 214 (1876).
United Steelworkers of America v. American Manufacturing Co., 363 U.S. 564 (1960).

United Steelworkers of America v. Enterprise Wheel & Car Corp., 363 U.S. 593 (1960).
United Steelworkers of America v. Warrior & Gulf Navigation Co., 363 U.S. 574 (1960).
Vaca v. Sipes, 386 U.S. 171 (1967).
Village of Arlington Heights v. Metropolitan Housing Development Corp., 429 U.S. 252 (1977).
Virginia v. Rives, 100 U.S. 313 (1880).
Washington v. Davis, 426 U.S. 229 (1976).
White v. Regester, 412 U.S. 755 (1973).
Wickard v. Filburn, 317 U.S. 111 (1942).
Williams v. Mississippi, 170 U.S. 213 (1898).
Williamson v. Lee Optical Co., 348 U.S. 483 (1955).
Yick Wo v. Hopkins, 118 U.S. 356 (1886).

Books, Articles, Book Chapters, Papers, and Speeches

Aaron, Benjamin. "The Duty of Fair Representation: An Overview." In *The Duty of Fair Representation*, edited by Jean T. McKelvey, 8–24. Ithaca, NY: Cornell University Press, 1977.
Abraham, Henry J. *Justices, Presidents, and Senators: A History of the U.S. Supreme Court Appointments from Washington to Clinton*. rev. ed. Lanham, MD: Rowman & Littlefield, 1999.
Ackerman, Bruce A. *Foundations*. Vol. 1 of *We the People*. Cambridge, MA: Harvard University Press, 1991.
Ackerman, Bruce A. "Revolution on a Human Scale." *Yale Law Journal* 108, no. 8 (June 1999): 2279–2349.
Ackerman, Bruce A. *Transformations*. Vol. 2 of *We the People*. Cambridge, MA: Harvard University Press, 1998.
Ackerman, Bruce A. "Transformative Appointments." *Harvard Law Review* 101, no. 6 (April 1988): 1164–84.
"A Doubtful Law." *Harper's Weekly*, February 27, 1875.
Aleinikoff, T. Alexander, and Samuel Issacharoff. "Race and Redistricting: Drawing Constitutional Lines after *Shaw v. Reno*." *Michigan Law Review* 92, no. 3 (December 1993): 588–651.
Alexander, Larry, and Frederick Schauer. "On Extrajudicial Constitutional Interpretation." *Harvard Law Review* 110, no. 7 (May 1997): 1359–87.
Aman, Alfred C., Jr., and William T. Mayton. *Administrative Law*, 2nd ed. St. Paul, MN: West, 2001.
Amar, Akhil Reed. *Bill of Rights: Creation and Reconstruction*. New Haven, CT: Yale University Press, 1998.
Amar, Akhil Reed, and Neal Kumar Katyal. "*Bakke*'s Fate." *UCLA Law Review* 43, no. 6 (August 1996): 1745–80.
Amar, Vikram D. "Jury Service as Political Participation Akin to Voting." *Cornell Law Review* 80, no. 2 (1995): 203–59.
Anderson, Terry H. *The Pursuit of Fairness: A History of Affirmative Action*. New York: Oxford University Press, 2004.

Anderson, Terry H. "The Strange Career of Affirmative Action." *South Central Review* 22, no. 2 (Summer 2005): 110–29.
Atleson, James B. *Values and Assumptions in American Labor Law.* Amherst: University of Massachusetts Press, 1983.
Atleson, James B. "Wartime Labor Regulation, the Industrial Pluralists, and the Law of Collective Bargaining." In *Industrial Democracy in America: The Ambiguous Promise,* edited by Nelson Lichtenstein and Howell John Harris, 142–75. Cambridge: Cambridge University Press, 1993.
Avins, Alfred. "Social Equality and the Fourteenth Amendment: The Original Understanding." *Houston Law Review* 4, no. 4 (Spring 1967): 640–56.
Ayers, Edward L. *The Promise of the New South: Life after Reconstruction.* New York: Oxford University Press, 1992.
Aynes, Richard L. "Constricting the Law of Freedom: Justice Miller, the Fourteenth Amendment, and the *Slaughter-House Cases.*" *Chicago-Kent Law Review* 70, no. 2 (1994): 627–88.
Bales, Richard A. "The Arbitrability of Side and Settlement Agreements in the Collective Bargaining Context." *West Virginia Law Review* 105, no. 3 (Spring 2003): 575–600.
Bales, Richard A. "The Discord between Collective Bargaining and Individual Employment Rights: Theoretical Origins and a Proposed Reconciliation." *Boston University Law Review* 77, no. 4 (October 1997): 687–760.
Bales, R. "A New Direction for American Labor Law: Individual Autonomy and the Compulsory Arbitration of Individual Employment Rights." *Houston Law Review* 30, no. 5 (Spring 1994): 1863–1913.
Balkin, Jack M., and Sanford Levinson. "The Processes of Constitutional Change: From Partisan Entrenchment to the National Surveillance State." *Fordham Law Review* 75, no. 2 (November 2006): 489–535.
Balkin, Jack M., and Sanford Levinson. "Understanding the Constitutional Revolution." *Virginia Law Review* 87, no. 6 (October 2001): 1045–1104.
Balkin, Jack M., and Reva B. Siegel. "The American Civil Rights Tradition: Anticlassification or Antisubordination?" *University of Miami Law Review* 58, no. 1 (October 2003): 9–33.
Barone, Michael. *Our Country: The Shaping of America from Roosevelt to Reagan.* New York: Free Press, 1990.
Barron, Paul. "A Theory of Protected Employer Rights: A Revisionist Analysis of the Supreme Court's Interpretation of the National Labor Relations Act." *Texas Law Review* 59, no. 3 (March 1981): 421–75.
Baugh, Joyce A. *The Detroit School Busing Case:* Milliken v. Bradley *and the Controversy over Desegregation.* Lawrence: University Press of Kansas, 2011.
Benedict, Michael Les. *A Compromise of Principle: Congressional Republicans and Reconstruction, 1863–1869.* New York: W. W. Norton, 1974.
Benedict, Michael Les. "Preserving Federalism: Reconstruction and the Waite Court." *Supreme Court Review* (1979): 39–79.
Bernstein, David E. "Philip Sober Controlling Philip Drunk: *Buchanan v. Warley* in Historical Perspective." *Vanderbilt Law Review* 51, no. 4 (May 1998): 797–879.

Bernstein, Irving. *Turbulent Years: A History of the American Worker, 1933–1941*. Boston: Houghton Mifflin, 1970.

Bickel, Alexander M., and Harry H. Wellington. "Legislative Purpose and the Judicial Process: The Lincoln Mills Case." *Harvard Law Review* 71, no. 1 (November 1957): 1–39.

Brandwein, Pamela. "The Civil Rights Cases and the Lost Language of State Neglect." In *The Supreme Court & American Political Development*," edited by Ronald Kahn and Ken I. Kersch, 275–325. Lawrence: University Press of Kansas, 2006.

Brest, Paul. "Foreword: In Defense of the Antidiscrimination Principle." *Harvard Law Review* 90, no. 1 (November 1976): 1–54.

Brest, Paul, Sanford Levinson, Jack M. Balkin, and Akhil Reed Amar. *Processes of Constitutional Decisionmaking: Cases and Materials*, 4th ed. New York: Aspen Publishers, 2000.

Brigham, John. "The Constitution of the Supreme Court." In *The Supreme Court in American Politics*, edited by Cornell W. Clayton and Howard Gillman, 15–27. Lawrence: University Press of Kansas, 1999.

Brinkley, Alan. *The End of Reform: New Deal Liberalism in Recession and War*. New York: Vintage Books, 1996.

Brinton, Crane. *The Anatomy of Revolution*, revised and expanded edition. New York: Vintage, 1965.

Brown, Michael K. "State Capacity and Political Choice: Interpreting the Failure of the Third New Deal." *Studies in American Political Development* 9 (Spring 1995): 167–212.

Burnham, Walter D. "Constitutional Moments and Punctuated Equilibria: A Political Scientist Confronts Bruce Ackerman's *We the People*." *Yale Law Journal* 108, no. 8 (June 1999): 2237–77.

Burnham, Walter D. *Critical Elections and the Mainsprings of American Politics*. New York: W. W. Norton & Company, Inc., 1970.

Calabresi, Guido. *A Common Law for the Age of Statutes*. Cambridge, MA: Harvard University Press, 1982.

Carter, Dan T. *When the War Was Over: The Failure of Self-Reconstruction in the South, 1865–1867*. Baton Rouge: Louisiana State University Press, 1985.

Casebeer, Kenneth M. "Holder of the Pen: An Interview with Leon Keyserling on Drafting the Wagner Act." *University of Miami Law Review* 42, no. 2 (November 1987): 285–363.

Cell, John W. *The Highest Stage of White Supremacy: The Origins of Segregation in South Africa and the American South*. New York: Cambridge University Press, 1982.

Clayton, Cornell W., and Howard Gillman, eds. *Supreme Court Decision-Making: New Institutionalist Approaches*. Chicago: University of Chicago Press, 1999.

Clayton, Cornell W., and Howard Gillman, eds. *The Supreme Court in American Politics: New Institutionalist Interpretations*. Lawrence: University Press of Kansas, 1999.

Comment: "The Radical Potential of the Wagner Act: The Duty to Bargain Collectively." *University of Pennsylvania Law Review* 129, no. 6 (June 1981): 1392–1426.

Corbett, William R. "Waiting for the Labor Law of the Twenty-First Century: Everything Old Is New Again." *Berkeley Journal of Employment & Labor Law* 23, no. 2 (2002): 259–306.

Cox Richardson, Heather. *The Death of Reconstruction: Race, Labor, and Politics in the Post–Civil War North, 1865–1901.* Cambridge, MA: Harvard University Press, 2001.

Crump, David. "The Narrow Tailoring Issue in the Affirmative Action Cases: Reconsidering the Supreme Court's Approval in *Gratz* and *Grutter* of Race-Based Decision-Making by Individualized Discretion." *Florida Law Review* 56, no. 3 (July 2004): 483–539.

Dahl, Robert A. "Decision-Making in a Democracy: The Supreme Court as a National Policy-Maker," *Journal of Public Law* 6, no. 2 (Fall 1957): 279–95.

Derber, Milton. "The New Deal and Labor." In *The New Deal: The National Level*, edited by John Braeman, Robert H. Bremner, and David Brody, 110–32. Columbus: Ohio State University Press, 1975.

DeSantis, Vincent P. *Republicans Face the Southern Question: The New Departure Years, 1877–1897.* Baltimore: Johns Hopkins University Press, 1959.

DeSantis, Vincent P. "Rutherford B. Hayes and the Removal of the Troops and the End of Reconstruction." In *Region, Race, and Reconstruction: Essays in Honor of C. Vann Woodward*, edited by J. Morgan Kousser and James M. McPherson, 417–47. New York: Oxford University Press, 1982.

De Tocqueville, Alexis. *Democracy in America*, edited by J. P. Mayer, translated by George Lawrence. New York: Harper Perennial, 1988.

Devins, Neal. "Explaining *Grutter v. Bollinger*." *University of Pennsylvania Law Review* 152, no. 1 (November 2003): 347–83.

Dobbin, Frank. *Inventing Equal Opportunity*. Princeton, NJ: Princeton University Press, 2009.

Dubofsky, Melvyn. *The State & Labor in Modern America*. Chapel Hill: University of North Carolina Press, 1994.

Dudziak, Mary L. *Cold War Civil Rights: Race and the Image of American Democracy*. Princeton, NJ: Princeton University Press, 2000.

Ely, James W., Jr. "Reflections on *Buchanan v. Warley*, Property Rights, and Race." *Vanderbilt Law Review* 51, no. 4 (May 1998): 953–73.

Epstein, Lee, and Jack Knight. *The Choices Justices Make*. Washington, DC: C. Q. Press, 1998.

Eskridge, William N., Jr., and John Ferejohn. "The Article I, Section 7 Game." *Georgetown Law Journal* 80, no. 3 (February 1992): 523–64.

Eskridge, William N., Jr., and Philip P. Frickey. "Foreword: Law as Equilibrium." *Harvard Law Review* 108, no. 1 (November 1994): 26–108.

Eskridge, William N., Jr., Philip P. Frickey, and Elizabeth Garrett. *Cases and Materials on Legislation*, 4th ed. St. Paul, MN: Thomson West, 2007.

Feller, David E. "A General Theory of the Collective Bargaining Agreement." *California Law Review* 61, no. 3 (May 1973): 663–856.

Ferejohn, John. "Judicializing Politics, Politicizing Law." *Law & Contemporary Problems* 65, no. 3 (Summer 2002): 41–68.
Finkin, Matthew W. "Revisionism in Labor Law." *Maryland Law Review* 43 (Fall 1984): 23–92.
Fiss, Owen M. "Groups and the Equal Protection Clause." *Philosophy and Public Affairs* 5, no. 2 (Winter 1976): 107–77.
Flamm, Michael W. *Law and Order: Street Crime, Civil Unrest, and the Crisis of Liberalism in the 1960s.* New York: Columbia University Press, 2005.
Foner, Eric. *Reconstruction: America's Unfinished Revolution, 1863–1877.* New York: Perennial, 1989. First published 1988 by Harper & Row.
Forbath, William F. "The New Deal Constitution in Exile." *Duke Law Journal* 51, no. 1 (October 2001): 165–222.
Franklin, John H. "The Enforcement of the Civil Rights Act of 1875." *Prologue: Journal of the National Archives* 6 (Winter 1974): 225–35.
Freidin, Jesse, and Francis J. Ulman. "Arbitration and the National War Labor Board." *Harvard Law Review* 58, no. 3 (February 1945): 309–60.
Friedman, Barry. "The Politics of Judicial Review." *Texas Law Review* 84, no. 2 (December 2005): 257–337.
Gerken, Heather K. "Understanding the Right to an Undiluted Vote." *Harvard Law Review* 114, no. 6 (April 2001): 1663–1743.
Getman, Julius G., and Thomas C. Kohler. "The Story of *NLRB v. Mackay Radio & Telegraph Co.*" In *Labor Law Stories*, edited by Laura J. Cooper and Catherine L. Fisk, 13–54. New York: Foundation Press, 2005.
Gillette, William. *Retreat from Reconstruction, 1869–1879.* Baton Rouge: Louisiana State University Press, 1979.
Gillman, Howard. "The Court as an Idea, Not a Building (or a Game): Interpretative Institutionalism and the Analysis of Supreme Court Decision-Making." In *Supreme Court Decision-Making*, edited by Cornell W. Clayton and Howard Gillman, 65–87. Chicago: University of Chicago Press, 1999.
Goldman, Robert M. *A Free Ballot and a Fair Count: The Department of Justice and the Enforcement of Voting Rights in the South, 1877–1893.* New York: Garland, 1990, 2001.
Goldman, Robert M. *Reconstruction & Black Suffrage: Losing the Right to Vote in Reese and Cruikshank.* Lawrence: University Press of Kansas, 2001.
Goldstein, Robert D. "*Blyew*: Variations on a Jurisdictional Theme." *Stanford Law Review* 41, no. 3 (February 1989): 469–566.
Goodman, Frank I. "De Facto School Segregation: A Constitutional and Empirical Analysis." *California Law Review* 60, no. 2 (March 1972): 275–437.
Gorman, Robert A., and Matthew W. Finkin. *Basic Text on Labor Law*, 2d. ed. St. Paul, MN: Thomson West, 2004.
Gould, William B., IV. "Keynote Address: *Steelworkers Trilogy* after a Half Century." Paper presented at the Annual Meeting of the National Academy of Arbitrators, Philadelphia, PA, May 27, 2010.
Graber, Mark A. "The Nonmajoritarian Difficulty: Legislative Deference to the Judiciary." *Studies in American Political Development* 7 (Spring 1993): 35–73.
Graham, Hugh D. *The Civil Rights Era: Origins and Development of National Policy, 1960–1972.* New York: Oxford University Press, 1990.

Gross, James A. *Broken Promise: The Subversion of U.S. Labor Relations Policy, 1947–1994*. Philadelphia: Temple University Press, 1995.
Gross, James A. *The Reshaping of the National Labor Relations Board: National Labor Policy in Transition, 1937–1947*. Albany: State University of New York Press, 1981.
Gunther, Gerald. "Foreword: In Search of Evolving Doctrine on a Changing Court: A Model for a Newer Equal Protection." *Harvard Law Review* 86, no. 1 (November 1972): 1–48.
Gutfreund, Owen D. *Twentieth-Century Sprawl: Highways and the Reshaping of the American Landscape*. New York: Oxford University Press, 2004.
Harris, William C. "Mississippi: Republican Factionalism and Mismanagement." In *Reconstruction and Redemption in the South*, edited by Otto H. Olsen, 78–112. Baton Rouge: Louisiana State University Press, 1980.
Hasen, Richard L. "Constitutional Avoidance and Anti-Avoidance by the Roberts Court." *Supreme Court Review* 2009, no. 1 (2009): 181–223.
Hayden, Grant M. "Resolving the Dilemma of Minority Representation." *California Law Review* 92, no. 6 (December 2004): 1589–1637.
Hirshson, Stanley P. *Farewell to the Bloody Shirt: Northern Republicans & the Southern Negro, 1877–1893*. Chicago: Quadrangle Books, 1962, 1968.
Hochschild, Jennifer L. "The Strange Career of Affirmative Action." *Ohio State Law Journal* 59, no. 3 (1998): 997–1037.
Hyman, Harold M., and William M. Wiecek. *Equal Justice Under Law*. New York: Harper & Row, 1982.
Issacharoff, Samuel. "Polarized Voting and the Political Process: The Transformation of Voting Rights Jurisprudence." *Michigan Law Review* 90, no. 7 (June 1992): 1833–91.
Jeffries, John W. "The 'New' New Deal: FDR and American Liberalism, 1937–1945." *Political Science Quarterly* 105, no. 3 (Autumn 1990): 397–418.
Jeffries, John W. "A 'Third New Deal'? Liberal Policy and the American State, 1937–1945." *Journal of Policy History* 8, no. 4 (October 1996): 387–409.
Johnson, Lyndon. "Remarks on the Signing of the Voting Rights Act." (Speech, Washington, DC, August 6, 1965).
Kaczorowski, Robert J. *The Politics of Judicial Interpretation: The Federal Courts, Department of Justice, and Civil Rights, 1866–1876*. New York: Fordham University Press, 1985, 2005.
Kagan, Robert A. *Adversarial Legalism: The American Way of Law*. Cambridge, MA: Harvard University Press, 2001.
Karlan, Pamela S. "Easing the Spring: Strict Scrutiny and Affirmative Action after the Redistricting Cases." *William and Mary Law Review* 43, no. 4 (March 2002): 1569–1603.
Katznelson, Ira, and Sean Farhang. "The Southern Imposition: Congress and Labor in the New Deal and Fair Deal." *Studies in American Political Development* 19 (Spring 2005): 1–30.
Katznelson, Ira, and Bruce Pietrykowski. "Rebuilding the American State: Evidence from the 1940s." *Studies in American Political Development* 5 (Fall 1991): 301–39.

Keller, Morton. *Affairs of State: Public Life in Late Nineteenth Century America.* Cambridge, MA: Harvard University Press, 1977.

Kellough, J. Edward. *Understanding Affirmative Action: Politics, Discrimination, and the Search for Justice.* Washington, DC: Georgetown University Press, 2006.

Kersch, Ken I. "The New Deal Triumph as the End of History? The Judicial Negotiation of Labor Rights and Civil Rights." In *The Supreme Court & American Political Development,* edited by Ronald Kahn and Ken I. Kersch, 169–226. Lawrence: University Press of Kansas, 2006.

Kennedy, David M. *Freedom from Fear: The American People in Depression and War, 1929–1945.* New York: Oxford University Press, 1999.

Kessler-Harris, Alice. *In Pursuit of Equity: Women, Men, and the Quest for Economic Citizenship in 20th-Century America.* New York: Oxford University Press, 2001.

King, Desmond S., and Rogers M. Smith. *Still a House Divided: Race and Politics in Obama's America.* Princeton, NJ: Princeton University Press, 2011.

Klare, Karl E. "Judicial Deradicalization of the Wagner Act and the Origins of Modern Legal Consciousness, 1937–1941." *Minnesota Law Review* 62, no. 3 (March 1978): 265–339.

Klarman, Michael J. *From Jim Crow to Civil Rights: The Supreme Court and the Struggle for Racial Equality.* New York: Oxford University Press, 2004.

Klarman, Michael J. "Race and the Court in the Progressive Era." *Vanderbilt Law Review* 51, no. 4 (May 1998): 881–952.

Kotlowski, Dean J. *Nixon's Civil Rights: Politics, Principle, and Policy.* Cambridge, MA: Harvard University Press, 2001.

Kousser, J. Morgan. *Colorblind Injustice: Minority Voting Rights and the Undoing of the Second Reconstruction.* Chapel Hill: University of North Carolina Press, 1999.

Kousser, J. Morgan. *The Shaping of Southern Politics: Suffrage Restriction and the Establishment of the One-Party South, 1880–1910.* New Haven, CT: Yale University Press, 1974.

Labbé, Ronald M., and Jonathan Lurie. *The Slaughterhouse Cases: Regulation, Reconstruction, and the Fourteenth Amendment.* Lawrence: University Press of Kansas, 2003.

Lash, Kurt T. "The Origins of the Privileges or Immunities Clause, Part II: John Bingham and the Second Draft of the Fourteenth Amendment." *Georgetown Law Journal* 99, no. 2 (January 2011): 329–433.

Lassiter, Matthew D. *The Silent Majority: Suburban Politics in the Sunbelt South.* Princeton, NJ: Princeton University Press, 2006.

Lemann, Nicholas. *Redemption: The Last Battle of the Civil War.* New York: Farrar, Straus, and Giroux, 2006.

Leuchtenburg, William E. *Franklin D. Roosevelt and the New Deal 1932–1940.* New York: Harper & Row, 1963.

Lewis, Thomas P. "Fair Representation in Grievance Administration: *Vaca v. Sipes.*" *Supreme Court Review* (1967): 81–126.

Lichtenstein, Nelson. "Industrial Democracy, Contract Unionism, and the National War Labor Board." *Labor Law Journal* 33 (August 1982): 524–31.

Lichtenstein, Nelson. *Labor's War at Home: The CIO in World War II.* Cambridge: Cambridge University Press, 1982.
Lieberman, Robert C. *Shifting the Color Line: Race and the American Welfare State.* Cambridge, MA: Harvard University Press, 1998.
Lovell, George I. *Legislative Deferrals: Statutory Ambiguity, Judicial Power, and American Democracy.* New York: Cambridge University Press, 2003.
Lynd, Staughton. "Government without Rights: The Labor Vision of Archibald Cox." *Industrial Relations Law Journal* 4, no. 3 (1981): 483–95.
Mason, Robert. *Richard Nixon and the Quest for a New Majority.* Chapel Hill: University of North Carolina Press, 2004.
Matusow, Allen J. *The Unraveling of America: A History of Liberalism in the 1960s.* New York: Harper & Row, 1984.
May, Dean L. *From New Deal to New Economics: The American Liberal Response to the Recession of 1937.* New York: Garland Press, 1981.
Mayhew, David R. "Wars and American Politics." *Perspectives on Politics* 3, no. 3 (September 2005): 473–93.
McConnell, Michael W. "The Forgotten Constitutional Moment." *Constitutional Commentary* 11, no. 1 (Winter 1994): 115–44.
McConnell, Michael W. "Originalism and the Desegregation Decisions." *Virginia Law Review* 81, no. 4 (May 1995): 947–1140.
McFeely, William S. *Grant: A Biography.* New York: W. W. Norton, 1981.
McPherson, James M. "Abolitionists and the Civil Rights Act of 1875." *Journal of American History* 52, no. 3 (December 1965): 493–510.
Millis, Harry A., and Emily Clark Brown. *From the Wagner Act to Taft-Hartley: A Study of National Labor Policy and Labor Relations.* 1950; repr., Chicago: University of Chicago Press, 1957.
Minda, Gary. "Arbitration in the Post-Cold-War Era – Justice Kennedy's View of Postexpiration Arbitrability in *Litton Financial Printing Division v. NLRB.*" *Stetson Law Review* 22, no. 1 (Fall 1992): 83–114.
Morone, James A. *The Democratic Wish: Popular Participation and the Limits of American Government.* New Haven, CT: Yale University Press, 1990, 1998.
Note, "The Strange Career of 'State Action' under the Fifteenth Amendment." *Yale Law Journal* 74, no. 8 (July 1965): 1448–61.
Obama, Barack. "Remarks on House of Representatives Passage of Health Care Reform Act." (Speech, Washington, DC, March 21, 2010).
Orfield, Gary. "Congress, the President, and Anti-Busing Legislation, 1966–1974." *Journal of Law and Education* 4, no. 1 (January 1975): 81–139.
Orfield, Gary. "The Southern Dilemma: Losing *Brown*, Fearing *Plessy*." In *School Resegregation: Must the South Turn Back?*, edited by John Charles Boger and Gary Orfield, 1–25. Chapel Hill: University of North Carolina Press, 2005.
Orren, Karen. *Belated Feudalism: Labor, The Law, and Liberal Development in the United States.* New York: Cambridge University Press, 1999.
Orren, Karen, and Stephen Skowronek. *The Search for American Political Development.* Cambridge: Cambridge University Press, 2004.
Ortiz, Daniel R. "The Myth of Intent in Equal Protection." *Stanford Law Review* 41, no. 5 (May 1989): 1105–51.
Patashnik, Eric. *Reforms at Risk.* Princeton, NJ: Princeton University Press, 2008.

Patterson, James T. *Congressional Conservatism and the New Deal: The Growth of the Conservative Coalition in Congress, 1933–1939*. Lexington: University of Kentucky Press, 1967.

Patterson, James T. *Grand Expectations: The United States, 1945–1974*. New York: Oxford University Press, 1996.

Perman, Michael. "Counter Reconstruction: The Role of Violence in Southern Redemption." In *The Facts of Reconstruction: Essays in Honor of John Hope Franklin*, edited by Eric Anderson and Alfred A. Moss, Jr., 121–140. Baton Rouge: Louisiana State University Press, 1991.

Perman, Michael. *The Road to Redemption: Southern Politics, 1869–1879*. Chapel Hill: University of North Carolina Press, 1984.

Perman, Michael. *Struggle for Mastery: Disfranchisement in the South, 1888–1908*. Chapel Hill: University of North Carolina Press, 2001.

Pierson, Paul. *Politics in Time: History, Institutions, and Social Analysis*. Princeton, NJ: Princeton University Press, 2004.

Pildes, Richard H. "Principled Limitations on Racial and Partisan Redistricting." *Yale Law Journal* 106, no. 8 (June 1997): 2505–61.

Pildes, Richard H., and Richard G. Niemi. "Expressive Harms, 'Bizarre Districts,' and Voting Rights: Evaluating Election-District Appearances After *Shaw v. Reno*." *Michigan Law Review* 92, no. 3 (December 1993): 483–587.

Plotke, David. *Building a Democratic Political Order*. Cambridge: Cambridge University Press, 1996.

Polenberg, Richard. "The Decline of the New Deal, 1937–1940." In *The New Deal: The National Level*, edited by John Braeman, Robert H. Bremner, and David Brody, vol. 1, 246–66. Columbus: Ohio State University Press, 1975.

Pope, Jim. "Worker Lawmaking, Sit-Down Strikes, and the Shaping of American Industrial Relations." *Law and History Review* 24, no. 1 (Spring 2006): 45–113.

Powe, Lucas A., Jr. *The Warren Court and American Politics*. Cambridge, MA: Harvard University Press, 2000.

Primus, Richard A. "Equal Protection and Disparate Impact: Round Three." *Harvard Law Review* 117, no. 2 (December 2003): 494–587.

Rabinowitz, Howard N. "More Than the Woodward Thesis: Assessing the Strange Career of Jim Crow." *Journal of American History* 75, no. 3 (December 1988): 842–56.

Rable, George C. *But There Was No Peace: The Role of Violence in the Politics of Reconstruction*. Athens: University of Georgia Press, 1984.

Redding, Kent, and David R. James. "Estimating Levels and Modeling Determinants of Black and White Voter Turnout in the South, 1880 to 1912." *Historical Methods* 34, no. 4 (Fall 2001): 141–58.

Rhoads, Robert A., Victor Saenz, and Rozana Carducci. "Higher Education Reform as a Social Movement: The Case of Affirmative Action." *The Review of Higher Education* 28, no. 2 (Winter 2005): 191–220.

Rose, Mark H. *Interstate: Express Highway Politics, 1939–1989*, revised edition. Knoxville: University of Tennessee Press, 1990.

Rosenberg, Gerald N. *The Hollow Hope*. Chicago: University of Chicago Press, 1991.

Schiller, Reuel E. "From Group Rights to Individual Liberties: Post-War Labor Law, Liberalism, and the Waning of Union Strength." *Berkeley Journal of Employment & Labor Law* 20, no. 1 (1999): 1–73.
Schmidt, Benno C., Jr. "Juries, Jurisdiction, and Race Discrimination: The Lost Promise of *Strauder v. West Virginia*." *Texas Law Review* 61, no. 8 (May 1983): 1401–99.
Schmidt, Benno C., Jr. "Principle and Prejudice: The Supreme Court and Race in the Progressive Era, Part 1: The Heyday of Jim Crow." *Columbia Law Review* 82, no. 3 (April 1982): 444–524.
Schmidt, Benno C., Jr. "Principle and Prejudice: The Supreme Court and Race in the Progressive Era, Part 3: Black Disfranchisement from the KKK to the Grandfather Clause." *Columbia Law Review* 82, no. 5 (June 1982): 835–905.
Schuck, Peter H. "Affirmative Action: Past, Present, and Future." *Yale Law & Policy Review* 20, no. 1 (2002): 1–96.
Schulman, Bruce J. *From Cotton Belt to Sunbelt: Federal Policy, Economic Development, and the Transformation of the South, 1938–1980*. New York: Oxford University Press, 1994.
Shulman, Harry. "Reason, Contract, and Law in Labor Relations." *Harvard Law Review* 68, no. 6 (April 1955): 999–1024.
Siegel, Reva B. "Constitutional Culture, Social Movement Conflict and Constitutional Change: The Case of the de facto ERA." *California Law Review* 94, no. 5 (2006): 1323–1419.
Siegel, Reva B. "Why Equal Protection No Longer Protects: The Evolving Forms of Status-Enforcing State Action." *Stanford Law Review* 49, no. 5 (May 1997): 1111–48.
Simpson, Brooks D. *The Reconstruction Presidents*. Lawrence: University Press of Kansas, 1998.
Skrentny, John D. *The Ironies of Affirmative Action: Politics, Culture, and Justice in America*. Chicago: University of Chicago Press, 1996.
Smith, Rogers M. *Civic Ideals: Conflicting Visions of Citizenship in U.S. History*. New Haven, CT: Yale University Press, 1997.
Smith, Rogers M. "Political Jurisprudence, the 'New Institutionalism,' and the Future of Public Law." *American Political Science Review* 82, no. 1 (March 1988): 89–108.
Staszak, Sarah. "Institutions, Rulemaking, and the Politics of Judicial Retrenchment." *Studies in American Political Development* 24 (October 2010): 168–89.
Stone, Geoffrey R., Robert H. Seidman, Cass R. Sunstein, Mark Tushnet, Pamela Karlan, Rebecca Tushnet, and Laura Tushnet. *Constitutional Law*, 5th ed. New York: Aspen, 2005.
Strauss, David A. "Discriminatory Intent and the Taming of *Brown*." *University of Chicago Law Review* 56, no. 3 (Summer 1989): 935–1015.
Sullivan, Kathleen M., and Gerald Gunther. *Constitutional Law*, 14th ed. Westbury, NY: Foundation Press, 2001.
Summers, Clyde W. "Individual Rights in Collective Agreements and Arbitration." *New York University Law Review* 37, no. 3 (May 1962): 362–410.
Summers, Mark W. *Rum, Romanism, & Rebellion: The Making of a President, 1884*. Chapel Hill: University of North Carolina Press, 2000.

Swain, Carol M. "Affirmative Action: Legislative History, Judicial Interpretations, Public Consensus." In *American Becoming: Racial Trends and Their Consequences*, edited by Neil J. Smelser, William Julius Wilson, and Faith Mitchell, vol. 1, 319–47. Washington, DC: National Academy Press, 2001.

Swinney, Everette. *Suppressing the Ku Klux Klan: The Enforcement of the Reconstruction Amendments, 1870–1877*. New York: Garland, 1987.

Teles, Stephen M. *The Rise of the Conservative Legal Movement*. Princeton, NJ: Princeton University Press, 2008.

Tomlins, Christopher L. "The New Deal, Collective Bargaining, and the Triumph of Industrial Pluralism." *Industrial and Labor Relations Review* 39, no. 1 (October 1985): 19–34.

Tomlins, Christopher L. *The State and the Unions: Labor Relations, Law, and the Organized Labor Movement in America, 1880–1960*. Cambridge: Cambridge University Press, 1985.

Tunnell, Ted. *Crucible of Reconstruction: War, Radicalism, and Race in Louisiana, 1862–1877*. Baton Rouge: Louisiana State University Press, 1984.

Tushnet, Mark. "The Politics of Equality in Constitutional Law: The Equal Protection Clause, Dr. Du Bois, and Charles Hamilton Houston." *Journal of American History* 74, no. 3 (December 1987): 884–903.

Tushnet, Mark. "Progressive Era Race Relations Cases in Their 'Traditional' Context." *Vanderbilt Law Review* 51, no. 4 (May 1998): 993–1002.

Tushnet, Mark. "The Supreme Court and the National Political Order." In *The Supreme Court & American Political Development*, edited by Ronald Kahn and Ken I. Kersch, 117–37. Lawrence: University Press of Kansas, 2006.

Unger, Irwin, and Debi Unger. *Turning Point: 1968*. New York: Scribner, 1988.

U.S. Congress. *Congressional Record*. 43rd Cong., 2d sess., 1853.

Valelly, Richard M. "Partisan Entrepreneurship and Policy Windows: George Frisbie Hoar and the 1890 Federal Elections Bill." In *Formative Acts: American Politics in the Making*, edited by Stephen Skowronek and Matthew Glassman, 126–49. Philadelphia: University of Pennsylvania Press, 2007.

Valelly, Richard M. *The Two Reconstructions: The Struggle for Black Enfranchisement*. Chicago: University of Chicago Press, 2004.

VanderVelde, Lea S. "A Fair Process Model for the Union's Fair Representation Duty." *Minnesota Law Review* 67, no. 6 (July 1983): 1079–1164.

Van Wezel Stone, Katherine. "The Legacy of Industrial Pluralism: The Tension between Individual Employment Rights and the New Deal Collective Bargaining System." *University of Chicago Law Review* 59, no. 2 (Spring 1992): 575–644.

Van Wezel Stone, Katherine. "The Post-War Paradigm in American Labor Law." *Yale Law Journal* 90, no. 7 (June 1981): 1509–80.

Van Wezel Stone, Katherine. "Re-Envisioning Labor Law: A Response to Professor Finkin." *Maryland Law Review* 45, no. 4 (1986): 978–1013.

Wang, Xi. *The Trial of Democracy: Black Suffrage and Northern Republicans, 1860–1910*. Athens: University of Georgia Press, 1997.

Weaver, Vesla A. "Frontlash: Race and the Development of Punitive Crime Policy." *Studies in American Political Development* 21 (Fall 2007): 230–65.

Weiler, Paul. "Striking a New Balance: Freedom of Contract and the Prospects for Union Representation." *Harvard Law Review* 98, no. 2 (December 1984): 351–420.
Weisbrot, Robert. *Freedom Bound: A History of America's Civil Rights Movement.* New York: Norton, 1990.
Wellington, Harry H. "Union Democracy and Fair Representation: Federal Responsibility in a Federal System." *Yale Law Journal* 67, no. 8 (July 1958): 1327–62.
Whittington, Keith E. "'Interpose Your Friendly Hand': Political Supports for the Exercise of Judicial Review by the United States Supreme Court." *American Political Science Review* 99, no. 4 (November 2005): 583–96.
Whittington, Keith E. "Once More Unto the Breach: PostBehavioralist Approaches to Judicial Politics." *Law & Social Inquiry* 25, no. 2 (Spring 2000): 601–34.
Whittington, Keith E. *Political Foundations of Judicial Supremacy: The Presidency, the Supreme Court, and Constitutional Leadership in U.S. History.* Princeton, NJ: Princeton University Press, 2007.
Wildenthal, Brian H. "The Lost Compromise: Reassessing the Early Understanding in Court and Congress on Incorporation of the Bill of Rights in the Fourteenth Amendment." *Ohio State Law Journal* 61, no. 3 (2000): 1051–1173.
Williams, Lou F. *The Great South Carolina Ku Klux Klan Trials, 1871–1872.* Athens: University of Georgia Press, 1996.
Williamson, Joel. *The Crucible of Race: Black-White Relations in the American South since Emancipation.* New York: Oxford University Press, 1984.
Wilson, Theodore Brantner. *The Black Codes of the South.* Tuscaloosa: University of Alabama Press, 1965.
Wood, Gordon S. *The Creation of the American Republic, 1776–1787.* New York: W. W. Norton, 1969.
Wood, Gordon S. *The Radicalism of the American Revolution.* New York: Vintage Books, 1991.
Woodward, C. Vann. "Strange Career Critics: Long May They Persevere." *Journal of American History* 75, no. 3 (December 1988): 857–68.
Woodward, C. Vann. *The Strange Career of Jim Crow.* New York: Oxford University Press, 1955, 2002.
Wyatt-Brown, Bertram. "The Civil Rights Act of 1875." *The Western Political Quarterly* 18, no. 4 (December 1965): 763–75.
Zieger, Robert H. *American Workers, American Unions, 1920–1985.* Baltimore: Johns Hopkins University Press, 1986.
Zieger, Robert H. *The CIO, 1935–1955.* Chapel Hill: University of North Carolina Press, 1995.

Index

Ackerman, Bruce, 7–9
Adarand Constructors, Inc. v. Pena, 273, 278
Air Line Pilots Association v. O'Neill, 266
Alexander v. Holmes County Board of Education, 163
Allen, Charles, 87
Allen v. State Board of Elections, 288–289
American Federation of Labor (AFL), 147–148
American Revolution, 19–20
anticlassification order, 274–278
  affirmative action constitutional legitimacy, 274–278
  entrenchment of, 279–280
  judicial tension management, affirmative action in education and, 280–286
  judicial tension management, majority-minority districts (MMDs) and, 287–296
  maintenance of, 280–296
  Miller v. Johnson as tension management, 296
  minority vote dilution jurisprudence, 287–292
  Proposition 209 and, 279
  Shaw v. Reno as tension management, 293–296
Arthur, Chester, 200
Association of Westinghouse Salaried Employees v. Westinghouse Electric Corporation, 246–248

Bakke, 275–276
Black Codes, 30–31, 68
Black, Hugo, 262–263, 307
Black, Jeremiah, 81–83
Blyew v. United States, 67, 80–85, 193
Bradley, Joseph, 104–105
Berea College v. Kentucky, 224
Brennan, William, 164–166, 291
Brown, Henry Billings, 213
Brown v. Board of Education, 3, 186
Buchanan v. Warley, 52, 221–227
Bunting v. Oregon, 222
Burger, Warren, 165, 168–169, 172
Burnham, Walter Dean, 7–9
Bush v. Vera, 295–296
Byrnes, James, 116–117
Byron, David, 93–94

Caldwell, Issac, 81–83
Campbell, John, 86, 92
Carey v. City of Atlanta, 224
Case Bill, 243
City of Mobile v. Bolden, 290–291
City of Richmond v. J.A. Croson Company, 276–277
Civil Rights Act of 1866, 80–85, 100, 193
Civil Rights Act of 1875, 77, 104
Civil Rights Act of 1964, 20–22
Civil Rights Act of 1964, Title VI, 155–156
Civil Rights Act of 1964, Title VII, 173
Civil Rights Cases, 67, 77, 104–107, 193
Colfax Massacre, 71

Commerce Clause, 22
constitutional equal protection, civil rights era, delimitation
  anticlassification order, 152–153
  construction, tension management and, 273, 315
  governing crisis, urban race riots, 157–159
  governing crisis, Vietnam War and Tet Offensive, 159–160
  judicial delimitation, 166–167
  legislative stalemate, 160–163
  post reform uncertainties, 152–153
  recalibration, transformation in, 155
  school desegregation and, 156

Day, William, 222–224
Douglas, William, 171–172, 248–249, 250–254
Durant, Thomas, 87, 88
Duty of Fair Representation (DFR), 254–268

Education Amendments of 1972, 161
Education Amendments of 1974, 161
Elementary and Secondary School Education Act, 155–156
Emancipation, the Reconstruction Era, delimitation
  Black Codes, 30–31, 68
  governing crisis, Panic of 1873, 75–76
  governing crisis, southern civil disorder in 1870s, 69–75
  judicial delimitation of Reconstruction, 78–80
  judicial reform and, 163–166
  legislative stalemate, 76–78
  post-Reconstruction, recalibration, 66–67
Enforcement Acts, 92, 195
  federal prosecution under, 201–204
Ex parte Virginia, 97–104
Ex parte Yarbrough, 107, 204–206

Fair Employment Practices Commission, 230
Fair Labor Standards Act of 1938, 120
Fansteel Metallurgical Corporation. See *NLRB v. Fansteel Metallurgical Corporation*
Field, David, 92

Fisher v. University of Texas at Austin, 285–286
Ford Motor Company v. Huffman, 256
Frankfurter, Felix, 246–248, 252–253
Fullilove v. Klutznick, 277

Garfield, James, 199–200
General Motors (GM), 114–116
Giles v. Harris, 215–216
Globe Machine & Stamping Company, 147
governance, 12–14, 271, 312–313
Grant, Ulysses S., 69–72
Green v. County School Board, 164–165
Green, William, 147–148
Griggs v. Duke Power Company, 173
Grutter v. Bollinger, 52, 281–282
Guffey Coal Bill, 116–117

Halleck, Charles, 149
Harper's Weekly, 73–74
Harrison, Benjamin, 200–201
Hawley, Joseph, 73, 74
Hayes, Rutherford, 198–199, 201
Hines v. Anchor Motor Freight, 263–266
Holmes, Oliver Wendell Jr., 216
Hopwood v. State of Texas, 279–280
Hughes, Charles, 143, 229, 232–233
Humphrey v. Moore, 256–257

individual rights, 13–14
industrial pluralism
  anti-labor legislation in the 1940s, 242–246
  defined, 238–239
  incomplete construction and, 244–246
  judicial tension management, Section 301, Duty of Fair Representation (DFR) and, 254–268
  labor in the 1940s, rise of voluntary arbitration, 240–242
  Supreme Court legitimization of, 246–254
institutional actors, 14
institutional authority, 13–14

Jim Crow laws
  Buchanan as tension management, 225–227
  construction, tension management post-Reconstruction, 195–197

Index

delimitation uncertainties, Republican coalition-building, enforcement efforts, 197–201
dismantling of, 270
federal prosecutions in South under Enforcement Acts, 201–204
Gaines, Sweatt as judicial tension-management, 231–235
judicial affirmation of, 212–216
judicial tension management, 195–197, 217–227, 235
Mississippi Plan and, 211
racial egalitarianism resurgence and, 230–235
residential segregation, judicial tension management and, 218–227
rise of, 106
segregation statutes and, 211–212
separate but equal standard, judicial tension management and, 228–235
Southern disenfranchisement and, 209–211
tension-management principles, 217–218
tripartite categorization of rights and, 218–227
Johnson, Lyndon, 160
Johnson, Reverdy, 92
judicial delimiting rulings
appointments thesis and, 179–185, 189, 300, 305
judicial-institutional theory and, 187–190
political-cultural thesis and, 182–187
summary, 179
Supreme Court justices, *Brown*, post-civil rights era rulings, 186
Supreme Court justices, New Deal era, 183
Supreme Court justices, post-Reconstruction, 179–181
judicial preference for stability, 298–299
judicial behavior, construction, 299–304
judicial behavior, tension management, 305–311
order-affirming rulings, summary, 299
public opinion and, 302–303
tension-management rulings, summary, 305

Kellog, William Pitt, 71
Kennedy, Anthony, 285–286, 296
Keyes v. School District No. 1, 165–166

labor rights, New Deal era, Wagner Act, delimitation
governing crisis, Court-Packing Plan and Executive Reorganization, 117–119
governing crisis, Recession of 1937, 119
governing crisis, sit-down strikes, 114–117
judicial delimitation, 121–122
legislative stalemate, 120–121, 145–150
recalibration and, 113
Wagner Act passage and, 110–111
Land-Lease Program, 240
Leiserson, William, 148
Lodge Bill, 195, 206–208

Mackay Radio. See *NLRB v. Mackay Radio & Telegraph Company*
Madden, J. Warren, 150
Mahone, William, 201
Marr, R. H., 94–95
Marshall, Thurgood, 167, 171–172
McCabe v. Atchison, Topeka, & Santa Fe Railway Company, 228–230
McEnery, John, 71
McLaurin v. Oklahoma State Regents, 231
Metro Broadcasting, Inc. v. FCC, 277–278
Miller, Samuel, 88–90, 175, 204–206
Miller v. Johnson, 296
Milliken v. Bradley, 154–155, 167–172, 270, 275
Millis, Harry, 150
Mississippi Plan, 211
modes of adjudication. See transformative recalibration, Supreme Court, modes of adjudication
Muller v. Oregon, 222
Murphy, Frank, 114

National Advisory Commission on Civil Disorders (Kerner Commission), 157
National Defense Mediation Board (NDMB), 241
National Labor Relations Act (NLRA), 143, 243–244
National Resources Planning Board, 118
National War Labor Board (NWLB), 241–243, 275

Neal v. Delaware, 103
Nixon, Richard, 154, 162–163
NLRB v. Fansteel Metallurgical Corporation, 139–145, 237–238
NLRB v. Jones & Laughlin Steel Corporation, 112, 124
NLRB v. Mackay Radio & Telegraph Company, 123–132, 237–238
NLRB v. Sands Manufacturing Company, 132–139, 237–238
Northwest Austin Municipal Utility District No. One v. Holder, 319

O'Connor, Sandra Day, 277–278, 281–282, 293, 294–295
order-affirming rulings. *See* transformative recalibration, Supreme Court, modes of adjudication

Parents Involved in Community Schools v. Seattle School District No. 1, 176–177, 284–285
Philadelphia Plan, 162–163
Pierson, Paul, 7–11
Plessy v. Ferguson, 194–195, 212–214
political change, scholarly work, 6–12
Powell, Lewis F. Jr., 276
Proposition 209, California, 279

Railway Labor Act, 255
Reagan, Ronald, 158
recalibration, 12–14. *See also* transformative recalibration
  conditions for, 17–19, 26
  defined, 16–17
  general theory of, 17–27
  historical, notable examples of, 17–19, 24
  labor rights, New Deal era, delimitation and, 113
  major to moderate effects continuum, 19
  political process of construction and, 36
  post-Reconstruction, 66–67
  scope in context of post-Reconstruction, post-New Deal, Post-civil rights era, 28
Reconstruction Enforcement Acts, 78
Reed, Stanley, 145
Regents of the University of California v. Bakke, 275–276

Rehnquist, William, 265
Republic Steel Corporation v. Maddox, 258
Ricci v. DeStefano, 319
Rives, Alexander, 99
Roberts, John, 284–285
Roberts, Owen, 129, 134–135
Robinson, Joseph, 116–117
Roosevelt, Franklin D., 113–114, 117, 120, 149–150, 241
Routzohn, Harry, 149

San Antonio School District v. Rodriguez, 169
Sands Manufacturing. *See NLRB v. Sands Manufacturing Company*
Scalia, Antonin, 306–307
Schultz, George, 162
Section 301, Taft-Hartley Act, 243–244, 254–268
Shaw v. Reno, 293–296
Shelby County v. Holder, 319
Slaughter-House Cases, 85–91, 175, 193
Smith, Donald Wakefield, 148
Smith, Howard, 148–149
Smith v. Evening News Association, 257–258
Smith-Connally Act, 146, 242–243
Social Security Act of 1935, 22–23
Stanbery, Henry, 96–97
Steele v. Louisville & Nashville Railroad Company, 255
Steelworker's Trilogy, 239–240, 250–254
Stevens, John Paul, 276
Stone, Katherine, 263
Strauder v. West Virginia, 97–104, 156, 164
Strong, William, 81–83, 98–100, 102–103
Supreme Court. *See also* transformative recalibration, Supreme Court, modes of adjudication
Swann v. Charlotte-Mecklenburg Board of Education, 165
Sweatt v. Painter, 231
Syres v. Oil Workers International Union, 256

Taft-Hartley Act, 243–244
tension-management rulings. *See* transformative recalibration, Supreme Court, modes of adjudication

Textile Workers Union of America v. Lincoln Mills of Alabama, 248–250, 252–253
Thomas, Elbert, 150
Thornburg v. Gingles, 291
Title VI, Civil Rights Act of 1964, 155–156
Title VII, Civil Rights Act of 1964, 20–22, 173
transformative recalibration, political process, 27–29, 313–314
  construction, institutional arrangements, judicial affirmation and, 34–37
  construction, internal uncertainties, 39
  contemporary politics and, 318
  delimitation, 29–30
  delimitation, external uncertainties, 38
  judicial delimitation, 33–34
  legal enactment of reform, 29
  open-ended reform, uncertain internal/external boundaries, 38
  process overview, 37–39
  reconstruction of governance and, 28–29
  reform and legislative stalemate, political responses, 30–33
  stable political order, prior to reform, 37
transformative recalibration, Supreme Court and political system
  constraints on judiciary, 57–58
  judicial efficiency and, 53–57
transformative recalibration, Supreme Court, modes of adjudication, 319
  delimiting judicial rulings, 48–49
  judicial preference for stability and, 40–43
  judicial-institutional interests, influences on judicial behavior, 43–48
  order-affirming rulings, 49–51
  order-maintenance, tension-management judicial rulings, 51–53
  summary, 317

United States v. Cruikshank, 91–96, 193
United States v. Reese, 96–97
United Steelworkers of America v. American Manufacturing Company, 250–251
United Steelworkers of America v. Enterprise Wheel & Car Corporation, 251–252
United Steelworkers of America v. Warrior & Gulf Navigation Company, 252

Vaca v. Sipes, 52, 258–263
Valelly, Richard, 11–12
Virginia v. Rives, 97–104, 193
Voting Rights Act of 1965, 20–22, 287–291, 294–296

Wagner Act, 4, 110–111, 237, 240
  See also labor rights, New Deal era, Wagner Act, delimitation
Wagner-Steagall National Housing Act, 120
Waite, Morrison, 95–97
Washington v. Davis, 154–155, 172–176, 270, 275
Wheeler, William, 72
White, Byron, 173–176
White v. Regester, 289–290
Williams v. Mississippi, 194–195, 211, 214–215

Yick Wo v. Hopkins, 214–215

CPSIA information can be obtained
at www.ICGtesting.com
Printed in the USA
BVOW04s1921120317
478414BV00001B/49/P